VOICES FROM AN EMPIRE

Volume 8
MINNESOTA MONOGRAPHS IN THE HUMANITIES
Gerhard Weiss, founding editor
Leonard Unger, editor

University of Minnesota Press, Minneapolis

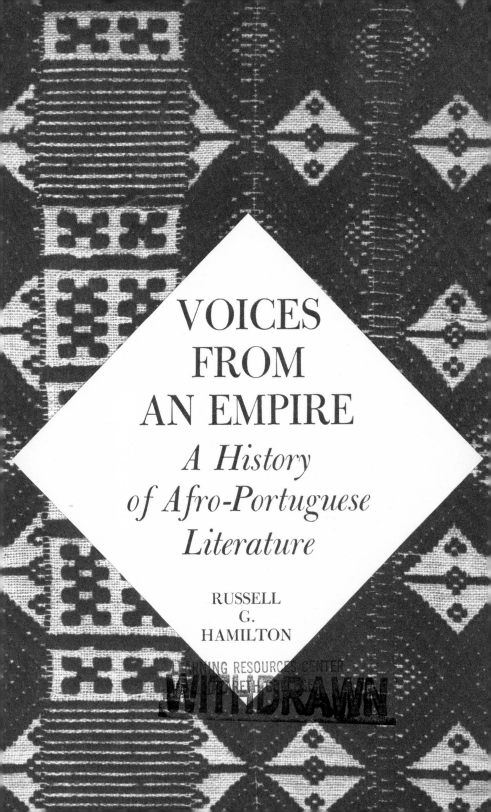

VOICES
FROM
AN EMPIRE

*A History
of Afro-Portuguese
Literature*

RUSSELL
G.
HAMILTON

Library of Congress Catalog Card Number 74-24416

ISBN 0-8166-0745-1

To my parents, Lucinda and Russell, Sr., and
to Carlos Vieira Dias and José Craveirinha,
companions on my excursions through the musseques
of Luanda and Lourenço Marques' Xipamanine

Preface

Since the completion of the body of this study there have been some startling changes in Portugal and Portuguese Africa. The first significant occurrence came on 25 April 1974 with the unexpected overthrow of the right-wing dictatorship that had ruled Portugal for nearly fifty years. General António de Spínola, a seasoned campaigner of the African wars, assumed leadership as interim president of a regime that included political moderates, socialists, and communists. In February of 1974 General Spínola had published *Portugal e o futuro* (Portugal and the Future), a book conceded to have inspired young army officers to revolt.

The focal point of Spínola's book was Portugal's future as it concerned her African provinces and the thirteen-year-old guerrilla wars being waged there. Paradoxically, Spínola, a member of the rightist military establishment, helped fan the flames of long-standing discontent over untenable economic conditions at home and he rallied an overwhelming majority of the Portuguese people around the conviction that they must extricate themselves from the costly and futile African wars.

In September of 1974 President Spínola resigned under pressure from leftist army officers, but he had already begun to honor his promise to grant freedom to the African territories. And indeed Portugal recognized the new nation of Guinea-Bissau, formerly Portuguese Guinea, and a provisional, black liberation government took over rule in Mozambique preparatory to full independence in June 1975.

My title, *Voices from an Empire*, was conceived as a poetic and ironic label for a sui generis Lusophone literature produced in the shadow of what many had come to consider an absurd nationalistic mythology. Given the historic transformations that have already come to pass and with those that are likely to occur, I hope that my title's intended irony will become even more meaningful as a symbolic expression of the social environment in which Afro-Portuguese writers have lifted their voices.

I give English translations of all titles, lines of poetry, and prose passages, both primary and secondary, used in this study. In the case of poetry I also supply the original, and unless otherwise indicated all translations are mine.

~~~~~~

For permission to use poems or lines of poetry in this study acknowledgment is made to the following. M. António: "A sombra branca," "Avó negra," "O tocador de dicanza," "Poesia de amor," "Simples poema de amor," and "Viagem à terra natal" from *100 poemas*, "Para depois" from *Rosto de Europa*, "O leão morreu, o campo ficou livre!" and "Transplantado coração" from *Coração transplantado*, to the author; José Craveirinha: "Escape" and "Lustre à cidade" from *Caliban*, 1, to Rui Knopfli; Tomás Vieira da Cruz: "Bailundos," "Cana doce," "Colono," and "Febre lenta" from *Quissange*, to Tomás Jorge; Carlos Estermann: "Morte de um guerreiro" from *Etnografia do sudoeste de Angola*, v. 1, to the Junta de Investigacões do Ultramar, Lisbon; Tomás Jorge: "Manguinha" and "Welvitchia Mirabilis" from *Areal*, to the author; Rui Knopfli: "A descoberta da rosa," "Ars poética," and "Hackensack" from *Mangas verdes com sal*, "Mulato" and "Winds of Change" from *Reino submarino*, to the author; Rui

Nogar: "Do himeneu vocábulo" from *Caliban*, 1, to Rui Knopfli; Jorge de Sena: "Noções de linguística" from *Caliban*, 3/4, to Rui Knopfli; Noémia de Sousa: "Sangue negro," "Se me quiseres conhecer" from *Présence Africaine: Nouvelle somme de poésie du monde noir*, No. 57, to *Présence Africaine*, Paris; Malangatana Gowenha Valente: "O mineiro sobrevivente" from *Présence Africaine: Nouvelle somme de poésie du monde noir*, No. 57, to *Présence Africaine*, Paris; Geraldo Bessa Victor: "Bemvinda, bemvinda," "Mística do Império," and "O homem negro e o carvão" from *Ao som das marimbas*, "Canção de um negro com alma de branco" and "O feitiço do batuque" from *Cubata abandonada*, "Amor" and "O menino negro não entrou na roda" from *Mucanda*, to the author.

Every effort was made to trace all copyright holders and authors whose poetry is quoted in this book.

In carrying out research for a study of this nature one confronts the problem of the scarcity of primary and secondary materials. With these difficulties in mind I acknowledge here the assistance and generosity of a number of people. The names cited represent only those whose exclusion would be tantamount to gross ingratitude on my part. Many people aided me, either directly or indirectly, but it is with great appreciation that I mention the following. Gerald Moser, himself a pioneering scholar in Afro-Portuguese literature, was kind enough to direct me, in Lisbon, to the Portuguese writer and critic Manuel Ferreira, whose private library became my domain for many months and whose friendship I value. Among the many who helped me during my stay in Portugal and in parts of Portuguese Africa I must thank the Cape Verdeans Arnaldo França, Jaime de Figueiredo, Félix Monteiro, Baltasar Lopes da Silva, Oswaldo Osório, and António Aurélio Gonçalves, the Angolans Aires d'Almeida Santos, Domingos Van-Dúnem, Arnaldo Santos, and Linda Graça. Also in Luanda, Carlos Vieira Dias and José Maria combined to make my stay there pleasant and culturally rewarding. During my months in Portugal the Angolan poets Mário António and Tomás

Jorge and the Angolan painter-sculptor Teresa Gama were generous with their help as was my friend Luis Bernardo Honwana who, a Mozambican himself, saw me off from Lisbon with letters of introduction that opened important doors for me in Lourenço Marques. In the capital of Mozambique I was graciously received by Rui Knopfli, Eugénio Lisboa, and José Craveirinha. The latter, my cicerone through that European city of nonwhite suburbs, introduced me to the cultural and culinary delights of a black and *mestiço* Mozambique as well as to an African perspective of the literary life there.

The ideas and opinions expressed in this book do not necessarily represent those of the many who helped me, and, indeed, some of my attitudes are undoubtedly contrary to the ideas, theories, and perceptions of people whom I respect and admire. It goes without saying that any mistakes or misstatements are solely my responsibility.

In completing these acknowledgments, I extend my appreciation to the University of Minnesota for my sabbatical leave and to the Fulbright and Gulbenkian foundations as well as to the Graduate School of the University of Minnesota for awarding me research grants. My special thanks to my colleagues Constance A. Sullivan and Peter Lock for their close reading of the manuscript and for their thoughtful suggestions. Finally, Cherie Y. Hamilton's help with the bibliography was indispensable and her encouragement was inspirational.

The pattern used on the jacket and title page is that of a traditional shawl or sash worn by women of the Cape Verde Islands. During the slave trade these *panos d'obra*, woven from island-grown cotton on crude looms, were used as articles of barter on the nearby West African coast.

R. G. H.

Minneapolis
October 1974

Contents

VOICES FROM AN EMPIRE

Introduction

When Gomes Eanes de Zurara, official chronicler of the Portuguese court, wrote his panegyric *Feitos da Guiné* (Exploits in Guinea, 1453) he did more than set down the deeds of the first Europeans to penetrate sub-Saharan Africa. Zurara, who himself never went beyond Morocco, helped form some of Europe's first impressions of black Africa. And along with their unique role as revealers of Africa to Europe, the Portuguese, over five centuries, have continually added to a mythology of their sacred mission on the so-called dark continent. They have held firmly to their attitudes even when other European nations openly denounced Portuguese colonial policies as inept and eventually, during the nineteenth-century "scramble for Africa," wrested large tracts of territory from Portuguese dominion. In the twentieth century, with its anticolonialism and Third World self-determination, the Portuguese have held to their sense of civilizing mission as tenaciously as they have held on to their remaining African territories.

Despite their early and continuous existence the Portuguese regions of Africa have received relatively little attention. While English- and French-speaking Africa attracts worldwide attention, Portuguese Africa seems to arouse only sporadic interest, usually in conjunction with the policies and strife of white-controlled southern Africa.

Our purpose in the course of this study will be to elucidate the modern cultural history of Portuguese Africa, relate it to important social and political factors, and, in so doing, form a basis for a comprehensive and analytical picture of the creative writing produced in the five Lusophone regions.

Some students of modern African literature have acknowledged the existence of Afro-Portuguese writing, and, in truth, this acknowledgment has increased steadily since the early 1960s. The assiduous and innovative German Africanist Janheinz Jahn included only twenty-six Afro-Portuguese items in his *Bibliography of Neo-African Literature* (1965), but by 1971 he had documented over one hundred titles in his *Bibliography of Creative African Writing*, compiled in conjunction with Claus Peter Dressler. This increase more meaningfully reflects the extent and nature of the writing that has been produced in Cape Verde, Portuguese Guinea, the islands of São Tomé and Príncipe, Angola, and Mozambique. Most anthologies of modern African literature written in European languages include a sampling of poetry and prose fiction from Portuguese Africa, but very few critical studies have been devoted to Lusophone writing.

At a time when African literature in English and French has attracted wide critical attention, even to the point of becoming a vogue, Afro-Portuguese writing warrants more than just cataloguing, anthologizing, and a passing critical comment. This does not mean to say that there has been no serious interest on the part of scholars; and perhaps the lack of an even greater interest can be laid to the following factors. First, Portuguese as a literary vehicle does not enjoy the prestige or projection of French and English, which means that traditionally the literature produced in that language has not always received the attention it deserves, and this is true whether the work in question comes from Portugal, Brazil, or Portuguese Africa. Secondly, the fact that the five Lusophone areas of Africa continue under Portuguese governance means an often negative effect on the literature produced there. The territories' political status has sometimes curtailed the free and continued development of a mature literary expression, and this has doubtlessly discouraged Africanists and others from pursuing the study of writing which, except for a small corpus of militant poems and stories, may be perceived by many as bearing the stamp of colonialism. More importantly, the small editions (some in mimeograph form) and the relatively limited distribution of Afro-Portuguese works not only reduce the general readership but also limit the opportunities for critical evaluation. Many foreign critics must depend on anthologized material, usually in French and English translation, and even those who read Portuguese find the inaccessibility of works a major problem.

In English translation Ezequiel Mphahlele's *African Writing Today* (1967) contains four poems and one prose selection from Portuguese Africa, and Gerald Moore and Ulli Beier's *Modern Poetry from Africa* (revised edition, 1968) includes nine Afro-Portuguese poems. The Angolan Mário de Andrade compiled *La poésie africaine d'expression portugaise* (African Poetry of Portuguese Expression, 1969), an anthology of Afro-Portuguese poetry in French translation. Translations in several European languages, including Swedish, Russian, and Czechoslovakian, but mainly French and English, have appeared in other anthologies and in journals or reviews such as *Black Orpheus* and *Présence africaine* (African Presence).[1] The latter review issued an anthology, *Nouvelle somme de poesie du monde noir* (New Sum of Poetry from the Black World, 1966), in which the editors reprinted all selections, including thirty-seven from Portuguese Africa, in their original language of composition. And Andrade, besides his French-language anthology, edited or collaborated on the editing of three Afro-Portuguese anthologies of poetry and prose in the original. Andrade's most recent effort, the two-volume (one volume of poetry, the other of prose) *Literatura africana de expressão portuguesa* (African Literature of Portuguese Expression, 1967, 1968), was originally published in Algeria in an extremely limited edition which was reissued in 1970 by Kraus Reprint of Liechtenstein.[2]

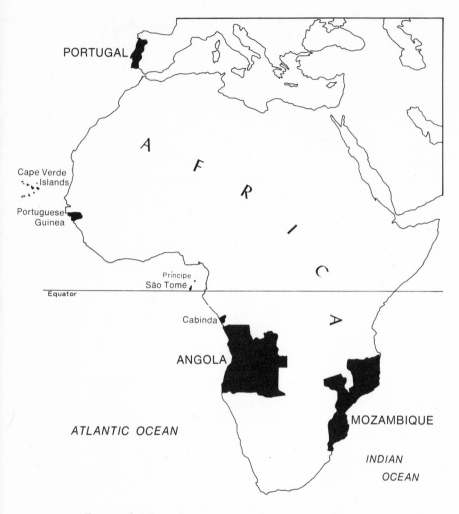

PORTUGAL

AFRICA

Cape Verde
Islands

Portuguese
Guinea

Príncipe
São Tomé

Equator

Cabinda

ANGOLA

MOZAMBIQUE

ATLANTIC OCEAN

INDIAN
OCEAN

Except for introductory remarks in the anthologies and a few articles in journals, scant critical material has appeared in Europe on the literature of Portuguese Africa. Even in Portugal that which comes from the African provinces receives only perfunctory attention, and this generally by critics who reflect the official Portuguese line on their overseas territories. This type of critic usually limits himself to propagandistic and impressionistic appraisals of the literature; or, if he does apply a serious methodology, he must exercise a caution that hampers the full treatment of a subject that has frequent political implications. Since the rise of independence sentiment in Portuguese Africa during the late 1950s, and especially since the outbreak of armed conflict in Angola in 1961, the very few serious critics, both in the provinces and in Portugal proper, have had to work under the onus of censorship and the threat of official reprimand. Because most of the present criticism of Afro-Portuguese literature comes from more or less "official" commentators, liberals and even some leftist-leaning intellectuals of Portugal display a kind of disdain for many of the works and much of the critical writing which, justly or unjustly, bear the mark of government approbation. But there also exists the problem of Eurocentric snobbery, on the part of some of these same liberals, toward a generally immature literature produced in the overseas provinces and sometimes dressed in the trappings of a non-Western tradition. Conversely, some of the Afro-Portuguese elite who participated in the initial literary and cultural movements but who now live in exile often write on the subject from the standpoint of an African literature purely at the service of a nationalist cause. Granted that this is an important consideration, it is not the only one to be used in appraising the historical development of Afro-Portuguese literature.

Despite all the factors outlined above—the neglect, the disdain, and the distortions—Afro-Portuguese literature has begun to come into its own with the beginnings of a serious critical following, particularly among Luso-Brazilianists in the United States. In 1962 the American university professor Gerald Moser published a revelatory article entitled "African Literature in the Portuguese Language" and in 1967 appeared his "African Literature in Portuguese: The First Written, the Last Discovered." The title of the second article suggests the relative, historical neglect of Afro-Portuguese letters.[3] Moser has since brought these articles together along with several new ones in the volume *Essays on Portuguese-African Literature* (1969). In the course of this study I shall have occasion to refer to the existing criticism. Meanwhile, some attention must be devoted to a definition of what has been referred to as Afro-Portuguese literature.

Terms and Definitions

No little controversy has arisen over what to call African literature written in European languages. The somewhat cumbersome
term African literature of Portuguese (or English or French)
expression has some obvious drawbacks. Thus far we have used
African literature of Portuguese expression interchangeably with
Afro-Portuguese, and in citing the titles of Moser's essays we
have employed the terms Portuguese-African and African literature in Portuguese.

Janheinz Jahn prefers yet another designation for the modern
writing of Africa—neo-African literature, which he defines as
"the heir of two traditions: traditional African literature and
Western literature. A work which shows no European influences,
including not being written down, belongs to traditional African
literature, not neo-African. The boundary between the two is easy
to draw: it is the boundary between oral and written literature.
Conversely, a work which reveals no African stylistic features or
patterns of expression belongs to Western, not neo-African literature, even if written by an African."[4] Jahn himself recognizes the
shortcomings of the distinctions he makes when he confesses that
owing to scholarly neglect we do not know the full nature of
African traditions. It might also be said that Jahn's definition is
so simple that it is difficult to apply, particularly to the literature
of Portuguese Africa, as I shall demonstrate shortly.

Without reviewing all the intricacies of the debate that still
rages over terms, definitions, and even the question of how legitimate it is to accept a European language as the vehicle of an
authentic African literature, it does behoove us to attempt to
situate Afro-Portuguese writing within the total context of what
Jahn calls neo-African literature. At least one critic, Simon
Mpondo, has questioned the term neo-African as being less logical, within Jahn's own system, than, for example, Afro-European.[5] Afro-European describes the literature as a mixture of
African and European elements, and just plain African literature,
which Mpondo prefers, avoids the issue by also encompassing

oral expression. Jahn's phrase conveys the sense of a new phenomenon and labels a unique order of literary expression with a term that seems less synthetic and less temporary than Afro-European. Having said this, I hasten to defend my use of the equally contrived and transitory, but more specific and delimiting Afro-Portuguese. For my purposes Afro-Portuguese literature falls within the general category of this new order and at the same time, as a distinctive Lusophone phenomenon, it embraces the African stylistic features and patterns of expression which Jahn speaks of as characteristic of neo-African literature. Because the literature of Portuguese Africa is still in its formative stage, we should perhaps postpone the application of a more authoritative term and definition.

In defining the literature of Africa one is faced with the problem of who should be considered a neo-African writer. The most obvious criterion would seem to be the color of the writer's skin, and in Anglophone and Francophone Africa this standard can be easily applied. Such is not the case in Cape Verde, Guinea, São Tomé and Príncipe, Angola, and Mozambique where exclusiveness based on race or color presents problems for a number of historical, cultural, and social reasons, which will be treated in the body of this study. In fact at the opposite extreme of the "black only" requisite one finds, especially in the writings of "official" critics, the inclusion of many white authors, some in metropolitan Portugal, others born there but living in the African provinces. We shall have to deal with the matter of the African-born and/or -raised white writer whose work may, but often does not, display discernible African themes and stylistic features yet whose presence cannot rightfully be ignored in any appraisal of creative writing in Portuguese Africa. This presence has particular significance in Mozambique, but both in that territory and in Angola are found white writers who do participate, whether genuinely or not, in what might be called a regionalist or African perspective, which is, of course, the principal focus of this study. It should be noted at this point that while accepting the fact that the word *African* can be applied to all racial types the term will be employed throughout, unless otherwise specified, to designate those individuals of a black African ethnic heritage.

At this time the term Afro-Portuguese literature offers a latitude in which to assess the modern cultural and literary factors that have been at work in the five areas of Portuguese Africa. When Angolan, Mozambican, or Cape Verdean literature is used to describe the distinctive regional movements, it is done so with the designation Afro-Portuguese in mind. Again, at this time in history the recognition of a mature, autochthonous literature in any of the Afro-Portuguese regions may be too early. Some members of the individual regionalist movements would probably disagree with this hesitation, but for the time being it is necessary to take this attitude in tracing the development of a cultural and literary phenomenon that shows certain points of unity in its broad confines and which, while included in the context of a neo-African awakening, differs markedly from the situation in the Francophone and Anglophone areas.[6]

A definition implies a method, and a valid approach would appear to be an evaluative process that sees Afro-Portuguese literature as a cultural awakening modified in several regional settings. I shall have more to say on the subject of method in the final section of this introduction. First, however, the nature of the general phenomenon and what makes Afro-Portuguese writing unique among the literatures of modern Africa will be discussed.

Lusotropicology and Négritude

The Portuguese have officially referred to their African territories as overseas provinces, but for all practical purposes they are colonies in an age when political colonialism has all but disappeared from Africa. This in itself explains some of the striking differences between Portuguese Africa's literature and that of the black independent nations.

Mário de Andrade sees African literature of Portuguese expression as writing at the service of a cause, and to the extent that this is true there exists an obvious unity between all Afro-Portuguese regions, as Andrade observes in the introduction to one of his anthologies: "the methods of Portuguese colonization and the present terms by which the oppressed express themselves create an identity dilemma for the writer whether he comes from Cape Verde or Angola."[7] The roots of the dilemma go deep into historical factors that have determined the peculiar brand of self-awareness in regions of Portuguese Africa.

Assimilação (assimilation), since 1921 until fairly recently an official policy which permitted the "civilized" African to achieve social and political equality with his European counterpart, resembles the French African *assimilation* in its implications for the black and *mestiço*[8] elites of Portuguese Africa. For although a proportionately insignificant number of Africans became Portuguese citizens under the policy, those who did composed a privileged group influenced by a set of values, attitudes, and myths that the Portuguese have fashioned around their centuries' long presence in nonwhite areas of the world. Lusotropicology has come to be the scientific expression of these values, attitudes, and myths.

Most commonly associated with the theories of its best-known exponent, the Brazilian sociologist Gilberto Freyre, Lusotropicology describes the Portuguese's supposed ability to adapt to life in tropical regions and to adopt the ways and customs of the indigenous inhabitants. Out of this idea of amiable contact with nonwhite peoples has come a cult of miscegenation and a uniquely acculturated but dominantly Lusitanian society. Brazil stands as an example of the success of Lusotropicology, but even in that multiracial society harmony and the acceptance of Indian and African cultural heritages do not quite correspond to social and economic realities as they affect the so-called "man of color." Whatever the truths behind the myths of Brazil's racial tolerance and acculturation and its cult of miscegenation, they all have to be seen in the light of that nation's colonization, historical development, and one hundred and fifty years of political sovereignty within the Portuguese-speaking world of tropical and subtropical regions. The Portuguese African territories, precisely because of varying factors of colonization and historical development, present differing modes of Lusotropicalist acculturation.

In the Cape Verde islands, where a population largely mixed along racial or at least cultural lines has long had nominal or symbolic control over its destiny, assimilation never existed as official policy. Later it will be seen how creolization[9] and Lusotropicology have had an effect on literary expression in Cape Verde as well as in the Guinea Gulf islands of São Tomé and Príncipe. By contrast, the large continental territories of Angola and Mozambique, where while some intensive but limited creolization, and even Africanization of Europeans, did occur, can, because of their numerically small African elites, give only token credibility to the claim of acculturation. In Angola and Mozambique most of the black population continues to exist as wards of the Lisbon government and to live under the domination of the local white minority despite some recent modifications in the official indigenous code. Along with other abuses this code has meant the recruitment of thousands of "natives" for contract work on plantations, or just simply a pattern of forced labor for the unassimilated African.[10] Still, in spite of past oppression and continuing repression, the myths and realities of Lusotropicology have had an often mitigating effect on the attitudes of the creole and African elites toward their regional self-awareness and, more importantly, the manner in which they have reacted to such black philosophical, cultural, and literary movements as négritude.

Before considering how négritude fits into the general pattern of Afro-Portuguese literary expression we should take a rapid look at that cultural, philosophical, spiritual, and literary movement of French African and French Caribbean origin. According to most sources, the Senegalese president-poet Léopold Senghor and the Martinican poet Aimé Césaire coined the word *négritude* between 1933 and 1935 when they were students in Paris.[11] Since that time négritude's meaning and validity have aroused as much controversy as the question of what to call African literature of European expression.

Senghor offers this succinct definition: "Négritude is the cultural patrimony, the values, and above all the spirit of black African civilization."[12] But négritude is multifaceted, and it is Janheinz Jahn who brings a measure of synthesis to the definitions by listing shades of meaning extracted from what Senghor, Césaire, and Jean-Paul Sartre have written on the subject. Basically, then, négritude is an "instrument" (for liberation), a "style," an "attitude," a "way of being," the "black man's being-in-the-world," and finally the "sum of black Africa's cultural values."[13] Some of these meanings are rather vague and esoteric although expressive of négritude's essence; and here we might reiterate that négritude is also a movement of black literary expression.

Négritude has had its detractors, one of the most famous being the Martinican psychiatrist and anticolonialist writer Frantz Fanon who objected to the emotionalism and exoticism inherent in the black movement of cultural and spiritual rebirth.[14] Criticism has also come from some important Anglophone writers such as South African Ezequiel Mphahlele and the Nigerian Wole Soyinka. Soyinka made the now famous pronouncement that the tiger does not go about proclaiming his "tigritude," but that you know some "tigritude" has been emanated when you come across the remains of a duiker.[15] Jahn has defended négritude with the claim that the Anglophone writers, particularly the Nigerians, are the legitimate heirs to négritude (*Neo-African Literature*, p. 226) And indeed négritude does, in one or more of its several facets, continue to exert an influence on neo-African literature even though as a movement it has become less important as a method for literary expression and racial identity.

For some, however, négritude has become a convenient catch-phrase for any and all manifestations of blackness in the writing of Africans or anyone else descended from Africans whether in the Caribbean, Latin America, or the United States. In this respect, Richard A. Preto-Rodas, in his monograph entitled *Negritude as a Theme in the Poetry of the Portuguese-Speaking World* (1970), applies négritude in a broad fashion to include the writing of black and *mestiço* authors from the eighteenth century to the present in Brazil and Portuguese Africa. This application perhaps extends négritude somewhat out of its historical limits and makes it unwieldy as a specific literary and pan-Africanist movement, particularly when we talk of the literature of the Portuguese-speaking world.

We can rightfully speak of négritude themes and we might reasonably expect that Portuguese Africa, given its development along lines similar to those of Francophone areas, would be fertile ground for such a movement. After all, négritude does involve a conscious reaction to the processes of assimilation and acculturation that theoretically turn Africans into black Europeans. But the French-speaking areas did not have the equivalent of Lusotropicology, which in combination with the circumstances of Portuguese patterns of colonization created a cultural and psychological climate that modified the treatment of négritude in Portuguese Africa. When the individual regions of Portuguese Africa, where négritude did gain some adherents, are dealt with in greater detail, it will be seen how Lusotropicology, creolization, and the presence of white intellectuals exerted an influence on the cultural and literary movements.

Basically, the precepts of négritude run counter to official Portuguese policies and attitudes on Africa, and in some respects négritude, especially as a political pan-Africanist movement, represents a form of subversion. In very recent years, however, some "official" Portuguese commentators have made attempts to adjust négritude to national policies on Africa. By way of example, and there are several, the Portuguese novelist Maria da Graça Freire wrote a three-part article, "Portugueses e a negritude," for a Lisbon newspaper. She talks about a symbiosis of Lusitanian and African values, which suggests that she either misunderstands or deliberately distorts the fundamental philosophy of négritude. Freire employs the term *espaço português* (Portuguese space) to designate the geographical extent and spiritual unity of the Lusitanian family of territories; and her thesis involves a softening of the usually stated policy of integration and acculturation when she writes that "in the Portuguese space, as elsewhere in the world, we hold that each race has its own characteristics and that there are no privileged races, and that there should be neither white racism nor black racism: all groups should have their place in the family of peoples for the well-being of all mankind."[16] If we accept Sartre's assessment of négritude as containing "anti-racist racism," then Freire does indeed conceive of a sui generis form of Portuguese négritude.

Freire proceeds to borrow some of the more glamorous pronouncements on négritude to make her point of the integration of the black man in the Portuguese space. In *Diário de Notícias* she writes, "The black Portuguese need not be detribalized if he does not wish to be: man-movement-rhythm, a universal force that is never isolated because it is one with nature, 'he lives traditionally of the land and one with the land, in and with the cosmos' (Senghor) and all in him is music, force, joy of living." Although Freire makes certain conciliatory gestures toward négritude's separatist aspects when she accepts the idea of the African unaffected by Western values, she tempers this acceptance by referring to the "uncivilized native" as a black Portuguese. And even though she quotes Senghor, there remains the nagging suggestion that it is not too difficult for the European to align négritude's exoticism with colonialist attitudes of paternalism toward the carefree child of nature.

Further on in her article Freire illustrates her view of Portuguese négritude with the following lines from the São Tomé poet Francisco José Tenreiro's "Canção do mestiço" (*Mestiço's Song*):

> a minha gargalhada livre
> que encheu o branco de calor! . . .
>
> Mestiço!
>
> Quando amo a branca
> sou branco . . .

> Quando amo a negra
> sou negro.
> Pois é . . .[17]

(My free and open laugh/that filled the white man with rage!
. . .//*Mestiço*!//When I love the white woman/I am white . . ./
When I love the black woman/I am black./That's right . . .)

Although many have called Tenreiro the first Afro-Portuguese
négritude poet, this example of his work can best be described
as a case of *mulattitude*.

This same Tenreiro wrote an article, "Acerca da literatura
negra" (Concerning Black Literature), which discusses the subject of black writing in Cuba, Brazil, and the United States; it
then goes on to characterize négritude as a movement that had
sought to establish a frank, humanistic, and fraternal dialogue
between Africa and Europe.[18] A dialogue between Africa and
Europe may be putting it too mildly; but perhaps the fact that
Tenreiro was writing for a Portuguese magazine accounts for the
toning down of what he himself, as a négritude poet (at least in
several of his major poems), actually saw as a defiant confrontation with Europe.

A few other Afro-Portuguese spokesmen have attempted to see
négritude in its relationship to the cultural and literary movements of their regions. The Cape Verdeans, caught up in a sense
of their creole uniqueness, have often insisted on Cape Verdeanness as opposed to négritude. Two of the most cogent
supporters of this attitude are Manuel Duarte, who wrote "Caboverdianidade e africanidade" (Cape Verdeanness and Africanness), and Gabriel Mariano, author of "Negritude e caboverdianidade" (Négritude and Cape Verdeanness).[19] On the other hand,
the Angolan Andrade summed up what he saw as the impact of
a black ideology on Afro-Portuguese literature when he commented that "one finds no document comparable to the manifesto of 'Legitime Défense' which put forth an ideology of revolt
and formulated an orientation for black writers of French ex-

pression."[20] Nevertheless, négritude, particularly in its aesthetics, magico-incantation, and ancestralism, has left its mark on the poetry of some of the best Afro-Portuguese writers.

The Role of Portugal and Brazil in Afro-Portuguese Literature

The links between metropolitan Portugal and the African provinces naturally extend to the realm of literary influences on the regional movements. Except for Cape Verde, Portuguese modernism of the 1920s had little influence on the phenomenon of Afro-Portuguese literature. In Cape Verde, however, the precepts of cosmopolitanism and a new aesthetic ideal espoused by the founders of the Coimbra-based review *Presença* (Presence, 1927–40) served as a catalyst for a sense of modernity among some members of the elite.

More extensive and profound in its influence was Portuguese neorealism, a literary current that reached its peak in the 1940s and that can best be described as a kind of new naturalism with elements of humanism and stylized reportage. Young neorealist writers of prose fiction produced for the collective conscience; they exposed and conceptualized the plight of the masses in social-realist works. The growing regionalist awareness in the African provinces had an affinity for Portuguese neorealism, and some of the Afro-Portuguese writers followed the lead of their counterparts in Portugal. A number of the most representative writers from the African provinces began their literary careers under the direct influence of neorealism while students in Lisbon and Coimbra.

Significantly, the spirit of Portuguese neorealism was in no small way nurtured by what had occurred in Brazil during the first decades of this century. More specifically, the movement known as *modernismo* erupted as a defiant call for Brazil's cultural, literary, and linguistic independence in 1922, the one-hundredth anniversary of that nation's political autonomy.[21] In February 1922, in São Paulo, painters, writers, and intellectuals organized the now symbolic *Semana de Arte Moderna* (Week of

Modern Art). These young iconoclasts—as they were looked upon by many members of the literary and intellectual establishment—took advantage of the artistic event to declare their sense of Brazilianness. The rebellious spirit of *modernismo* spread to other parts of the country and in the Northeast coincided with a social regionalism that, in the 1930s, would give rise to a vigorous, new Brazilian novel.

Because the intellectual elite of Portuguese Africa could see its own tropical regions mirrored in Brazilian socioeconomic realities, particularly those of the Northeast, they readily seized on the techniques, style, and most of all the spirit of *modernismo* and Northeast regionalism. And there exist several important similarities between Portuguese Africa and Brazil: ethnic, social, and even climatic (Cape Verde and some of the Northeast states of Brazil are plagued by extended, periodic drought). Afro-Portuguese intellectuals aligned themselves with the large and potentially powerful Lusophone tropical nation that had emerged from a colonial state and was well on its way to a mature cultural and literary expression. The romanticism and lyricism that often tempered the harshness of Brazilian social realism appealed to the committed generations of Afro-Portuguese as they struggled to come to grips with the myths and realities of Lusotropicology in conflict with their own regionalist sentiments and their growing consciousness of Africa.

As Afro-Portuguese literary movements and currents continued to develop from their first exuberant moments, Brazil and the influence of other outside models would diminish in importance. But Brazilian *modernismo* and Northeast regionalism have aided these writers in search of identity to absorb the essence of a black consciousness inherent in négritude, Caribbean negrism, and even the racial and cultural self-affirmation of black America, and to move toward an understanding of their own reality.

A Theory of Afro-Portuguese Literature

The values expressed in Afro-Portuguese literature are fundamentally Western or acculturated even when the works themselves deal with African subjects. Some members of the elite have attempted to cast their European language in an African mold; their conscious efforts to reshape language and present a black system of values have varied from region to region and from writer to writer in accordance with a number of sociological, cultural, and individual factors.

In the Cape Verde islands African themes or subject matter appear with less frequency or are more externalized than they are in other regions of Portuguese Africa. As a result of creolization and an emphasis, by many members of the *mestiço* elite, on the islands' European heritage and their ethos, most of the major Cape Verdean works lack the African aesthetic patterns and linguistic tensions found in the poetry and narrative prose of Anglophone and Francophone Africa. What is meant here by tension is the juxtaposing of the African with the European, not only in language but also in social and cultural attitudes, and the reflection of this confrontation in the aesthetic and internal structures of a given work. The values of traditional African societies account for the incantatory tone and ritualistic patterns most commonly associated with négritude. Cape Verdean literature only occasionally and perfunctorily presents these African elements. When, on the other hand, a Cape Verdean poem or story makes use of creole language and themes it may indirectly approach African aesthetic elements through the elaboration of authentic island social dimensions.

Generally speaking, however, Cape Verdean neorealist or sociologically oriented prose fiction explicitly superimposes a European system of values on the pyramidal stratification of island society: a small upper class at the apex and a large peasant and urban lower class at the base. Climatic and economic conditions determine the principal themes of Cape Verdean literature, both in poetry and in prose: drought, famine, mass emigration, the coming of the rains. Cape Verdean novelists and short story writers expose and reflect on the conditions of the suffering masses in works that often combine realist-naturalist portrayal with rhapsodic expressions of Cape Verdeanness. When the theme of Africa appears in the poetry and prose of Cape Verde, rather than the magical and ritualistic elements of négritude the subject is treated, more often than not, in the realm of the arcane or the decorative. Those few committed writers who emphasize the islands' African heritage also adopt patterns that contain a creole dynamic and foster a sense of Cape Verdean ethos. Africanness is often more a case of these writers' recognition of ethnic roots and of their implicitly anti-Western rhetoric than it is the cultivation of African cultural and aesthetic structures.

Creolization as a factor in literary expression has occurred to an extent in São Tomé and Príncipe, but these islands have not supported a significant, organized intellectual elite imbued with the sense of a regionalist ethos. While this lack of a unified cultural-literary movement has meant a correspondingly small number of writers, it has permitted a few black and *mestiço* poets to take a socially committed stance and, in one notable case, to adopt aspects of négritude. A tension between Africa and Europe has been depicted in the works of a few island writers as a result of psychological conflicts rising out of personal confrontations with Europe. Thus, the São Tomé writer in Europe, without the benefit of a substantive regional or African identity, has frequently fashioned a poetic persona or fictional protagonist whose psychic patterns mirror social conflicts. These conflicts have led, in some São Tomé and Príncipe poetry, to audacious anti-Western rhetoric or even to pan-African sentiments. Moreover, the presence on the plantation islands of semi-assimilated Africans, owing to the influx until quite recently of contract workers from Angola and Mozambique, has created a sensitivity among intellectuals toward the question of Africa.

Naturally, in the large sub-Saharan provinces of Angola and Mozambique the tensions produced by a historical confrontation between Africans and Europeans have given rise to ambivalences and identity crises among intellectuals. In Angola and Mozambique a mainly urban intelligentsia has had to seek a mode of literary expression that would translate their newfound, and sometimes ambiguous, sense of regionalist and African identity. For these reasons, the writing of those areas varies from the purely European art form and the social reportage story to the functional aesthetic of a simulated African oral tradition, to say nothing of the militant literature that accompanies the liberation movements in Angola and Mozambique.

The literature of Mozambique has been influenced by two related factors: first, the modern cultural-literary movement there has been more fragmented than the concomitant movement in Angola or the earlier search for regionalist identity in Cape Verde; secondly, the pronounced nature of racial animosities has had a significant effect on the thematic, social, and aesthetic structures of works by black, white, and *mestiço* writers. And at least one Mozambican poet has cultivated a surrealistic, négritude art, possibly as a result of the conditions just described, and surely as a manifestation of patterns of social and psychic conflicts. The section on Mozambique delves into a debate on the question of a regionalist and African literature versus universalist writing or literature qua literature (see pp. 171–175). The nature of this debate applies to all Afro-Portuguese literature.

In the study of a literary phenomenon such as that of Portuguese Africa the social and cultural conditions, from which art everywhere springs, naturally carry supreme importance. With this in mind I approach my subject, as I stated earlier, from the point of view of the modern social and cultural history of Portuguese Africa in order to gain a perspective on the literature produced there. This means that although my emphasis rests on an African thematic element and on African stylistic features I am also guided by the realities of the total picture to consider that which may be somewhat peripheral, but not incidental, to a neo-African literature. I shall deal, then, with Afro-Portuguese literature in its social, cultural, and aesthetic context.

A few words should be said on the structure of this study. I begin with Angola and offer a rather extensive appraisal of its modern cultural history and literary development because I see the regionalist movement in that colony as the most significant in terms of a neo-African orientation. I next turn my attention to the East African province of Mozambique which, while it has had a less concerted cultural and literary movement than Angola, and thus receives fewer pages devoted to background, does offer another compelling view of the Afro-Portuguese phenomenon born under the sign of a neo-African awareness. Cape Verde, on the other hand, while much less important as a case of African-oriented development, merits a long discussion because of the singular aspect and relatively early appearance of its regionalist literary and cultural movement. Portuguese Guinea, which I cover in a brief chapter in the third part of this study, has been generally ignored by commentators on Afro-Portuguese litera-ture. I, however, assess what little there exists in the way of an Afro-Portuguese literary expression in Guinea in order to give as complete a picture as possible of the total phenomenon. Similar words might be said about the islands of São Tomé and Prín-cipe; although no coordinated regional movement manifested itself there, at least one highly significant São Tomé writer emerged to give impetus to the whole of Afro-Portuguese literature.

Finally, despite their obvious interrelationships, the four parts of this study can be read independently of each other with no loss of coherence. But it should be made clear that the arrange-ment of the book does observe a historical, if not chronological, development of Afro-Portuguese literature.

PART ONE

ANGOLA

CHAPTER 1

Social
and Cultural
Background
of the Modern Era

Portugal's largest overseas province (three times as large as Texas and nearly fourteen times as large as Portugal itself) derives its name from the word *Ngola*, dynastic title of the sixteenth-century Mbundu kingdom, the Mbundu being one of the major ethnic groups of the Kimbundu people. Bounded on the north and northeast by Zaire (Congo Kinshasa), on the south by Southwest Africa, on the east by Zambia, and on the west by the South Atlantic, Angola has had a singularly tragic and, in some ways, glorious past.

The Portuguese arrived north of the Angola region, at the mouth of the Congo River, in 1493 under the command of Diogo Cão who made contact with the powerful Congo kingdom. This original encounter initiated a brief period of relatively good relations and mutual respect between the Portuguese court and the African ruler, the Manikongo. An ever-increasing interest in the acquisition of slaves and armed conflict with other peoples in the region contributed to a progressive deterioration of this good relationship between European and African. By the start of the sixteenth century the Portuguese had pushed south to the region of present-day Angola, and they subsequently established a colony

25

there in 1575 with the founding of the city of Luanda and the naming of the territorial governor Pedro Dias de Novaes.

Except for a small number of Hottentots and Bushmen in the extreme southwest, most of Angola's present African population is of Bantu stock, consisting of six ethnolinguistic groups. These groups or nations can be further broken down into over one hundred tribal or smaller ethnic groups. The most populous ethnolinguistic group, the Umbundu-speaking Ovimbundu, account for some one and a half million of Angola's total population of 5,200,000 and they inhabit the south-central highlands. Numbering just over one million, the Kimbundu, the second largest group, occupies the region around the coastal city of Luanda and north-central interior to the area around the city of Malange.

Alternating clashes and alliances with the Ngola, under the specter of the slave trade, finally ushered in a series of wars that has lasted, off and on, down to the present liberation struggle. In spite of the continuing hostilities, the larger ethnic groups, and particularly certain of their small units, have had an important role in the history of Angola, and this role depends to a large degree on the extent to which they have maintained contact with the Europeans. In this respect, the Kimbundu, because of their location around the city of Luanda, have had early and continuous dealings with the Portuguese. This contact afforded them the opportunity to avail themselves of certain aspects of Western culture which they could turn to their advantage under the Portuguese policy of civilization and assimilation.

The Emergence and Decadence of a Creole Society

Although the Portuguese made their presence very much felt as a disruptive force in Angola, as far as African political organization, culture, and values are concerned, they were never there in any great numbers, particularly in the interior regions. Estimates put the present European population at approximately 170,000 out of the total; this represents a 400 percent increase since 1940. On the other hand, Portuguese settlers, in touch with local populations in the urban and semi-urban areas of Luanda,

Dondo, and Malange, meant the beginnings of a creole society, and out of this semi-acculturated society emerged a black and *mestiço* elite. The white Angolan essayist Carlos Ervedosa characterized the period between 1926 and 1940 as a time during which Luanda's 39,000 blacks, 6000 whites, and 5500 *mestiços* lived side by side. Children played together and shared a belief in many magico-religious aspects of the African heritage. Carnival celebrations, dances, foods, and modes of dress were influenced or dominated by the African.[1]

Another Angolan of Ervedosa's generation, the *mestiço* poet Mário António, wrote a study on Angolan society entitled *Luanda "ilha" crioula* (Luanda, Creole "Island," 1968). He maintains that the cultural, if not biological, *mestiço* dominated Luanda society from the seventeenth to the nineteenth centuries.[2] But referring to an essay by Gabriel Mariano on the upward social mobility of the Cape Verdean mulatto (see page 234 for a discussion of Mariano's article), Mário António observes that while the *mestiço* in the archipelago rose from the shack to the mansion, his counterpart in Luanda went up from the increasingly more European lower city (Baixa) to the hillside black slums (*musseques*). In effect, the Luanda *mestiço* realized upward physical mobility on a downward social and economic trajectory. Still, the African elite, made up of blacks and *mestiços*, known as *filhos da terra* (sons of the land), flourished from about the middle of the nineteenth century to the beginning of the twentieth. And this elite left a legacy that would find expression in the contemporary literature of Angolan intellectuals.

Cordeiro da Matta and an African Elite

The seventeenth-century Portuguese António de Oliveira Cadornega, who wrote *História geral das guerras angolanas* (General History of the Angolan Wars, published in its entirety in 1942), qualifies as one of the first writers on Angola. It was not until the appearance of the so-called 1880 group, however, that anything resembling a literary movement with native son writers came about. With few exceptions the blacks and *mestiços* of this group found cultural and political expression through an incipient African press.

Júlio de Castro Lopo's *Jornalismo de Angola: Subsídios para a sua história* (Journalism of Angola: A Historical Outline, 1964) documents *O Echo de Angola* (The Echo of Angola), founded in Luanda on November 12, 1881, as the beginning of African intervention in the white-controlled press. By the turn of the century Africans published several newspapers that were characterized by republican idealism and an often regionalist-nationalist spirit. Some of these newspapers issued bilingual (Portuguese-Kimbundu) editions, thus giving proof of an acculturated elite's interest in preserving part of its African heritage.

At least one outstanding African intellectual emerged from this 1880 group. The self-taught Joaquim Dias Cordeiro da Matta was, as Mário António emphasizes, not only a teacher, but also a journalist, historian, philologist, folklorist, poet, and unpublished novelist.[3] Mário António prefers 1890 rather than 1880 as a convenient year to designate the first important generation of *filhos da terra*, and in 1891 Cordeiro da Matta did publish his noteworthy work, a collection of Kimbundu proverbs and riddles. In the introductory remarks to this *Philosophia popular em provérbios angolanos* (Popular Philosophy in Angolan Proverbs) Cordeiro da Matta speaks in favor of an autochthonous Angolan literature. It was the Swiss Protestant missionary Héli Chatelain who encouraged Cordeiro da Matta and other African intellectuals to proceed with their plans to cultivate an Angolan literature. And Cordeiro da Matta did himself write poetry, collected in a volume entitled *Delírios* (Delirium, 1887), but this, except for a few fragments, has been lost. As might be expected of poetry written at that time, the fragments display the mark of European romanticism, even though penned by an African who was conscious of his heritage. Cordeiro da Matta formulated his literary skills within a Western framework, and two of the poems salvaged from his collection, "Negra" and "A uma Quissama" (To a Kissama), resemble in their technique the São Tomé poet Costa Alegre's defensive juxtaposition of black and white as symbols of evil and purity (see page 378). Chatelain has contended, however, that at a given moment in his literary career Cordeiro da Matta exchanged the European muse for an African one.[4] Unfortunately, the poetry that may have resulted from this inspiration has been lost to us.

Cordeiro da Matta followed his collection of proverbs with a Kimbundu grammar and a Kimbundu-Portuguese dictionary in 1892 and 1893 respectively. Concerning the dictionary, Chatelain wrote in 1894 that it was the best Kimbundu word list to date.[5] Along with his efforts to preserve a Kimbundu heritage through folkloric and philological works, Cordeiro da Matta also attempted to record the glories of the past. Mário António reports having been told, by a nephew of Cordeiro da Matta, of a lost manuscript entitled *A verdadeira história da rainha Jinga* (The True Story of Queen Jinga). Jinga (Ginga, Nzinga), the powerful and shrewd ruler of the Mbundus, resisted Portuguese domination in the seventeenth century and has since become a compelling and glorified figure in the history of Angola. We can only guess at Cordeiro da Matta's approach in telling the story of the legendary queen, but the word *verdadeira* (true) in the title would seem to indicate his wish to correct popular misconceptions about one of Angola's African heroes.

Chatelain, himself the author of important linguistic and ethnographic works on Angola, served as mentor to the founders of a new Kimbundu awareness. He and Cordeiro da Matta combined talents on several projects dealing with language and folklore, and it was the Swiss ethnologist who guided the African intellectual's steps in matters of technique and academic discipline. Chatelain's *Kimbundu Grammar* (1888–89) and his *Folk-Tales of Angola* (1894), both written in English, the latter with original Kimbundu texts, still stand as monuments of scholarship.

Assis Júnior, a Chronicler of Creole Society

Besides Cordeiro da Matta's small literary production and the novel *Scenas d'África* (Scenes of Africa, 1892) by Pedro Machado, very little in the way of creative writing came from the 1880 and

1897 groups, as Carlos Ervedosa terms the two generations of African intellectuals.

Although not of the 1897 group, António Assis Júnior warrants attention as Angola's first important black or *mestiço* writer of prose fiction. Published in 1934, his novel *O segredo da morta* (The Dead Woman's Secret) revolves around events that occurred in the 1890s. Briefly, the story concerns a woman, Ximinha Belchior, who contracts sleeping sickness. While she is on her deathbed her pupil and namesake Ximinha Kalanga-langa, with the help of another protégé, Eduardo, steals the rings from her fingers. Ximinha Belchior reveals the identity of the wrongdoers from beyond the grave. As a work of art *O segredo da morta* can bear little critical scrutiny. But as the novel's sub-title, *Romance de costumes angolanos* (Novel of Angolan Customs), tells us, the author had more in mind than the melodramatic story of the events leading up to the heroine's death. He demonstrated a greater interest in painting a picture of Angolan creole society at the turn of the century than he did in developing the unifying but weak plot.

Attempting a literary style modeled on the novels of Victor Hugo and Anatole France, both of whom he admired, Assis Júnior offers a mixture of true events and detailed references to folklore, religious beliefs, and local customs in the area of Luanda, Sengue, and Dondo. He describes, for example, a popular celebration during which the two races mingle harmoniously and dance to both European and African music. Insisting on this cultural duality, Assis Júnior, in one of his many discursive asides, chides those Angolans who refuse to admit to their taste for such typical African foods as *funge* and palm oil. Cultural integration as a motif in Assis Júnior's novel allows for the European's dominant social position but emphasizes that even the whites in this creole milieu come by their African comportment naturally rather than by a conscious adoption. One of the principal characters, Elmira, also goes by the Kimbundu name of Kapaxi, and this duality extends to religious syncretism. Elmira, or Kapaxi, though a practicing Catholic, enjoys the protection of the African god of the Cuanza River. The life style and cultural patterns of European trader families such as Elmira's were determined by a historical expediency that saw whites cut off from "civilization" in their semirural ambient. Assis Júnior interpolates into the story the anecdotal incident of a trip that Elmira makes into the bush country to trade with generally hostile "natives." She succeeds in gaining their confidence by convincing them that despite her white skin she descends from the famous Queen Ginga.

Understandably, Assis Júnior treats the subject of Africans living in a purely "tribal" state with the same exoticism and condescension shown by white colonialists. The important distinction is that Assis Júnior makes use of various aspects of a purely African oral tradition in describing creole society; he integrates Kimbundu proverbs, transcribed in the original language, into his story. And in regard to his narrative style, Mário António points out his inept use of the Portuguese language and the novel's technical flaws, which António attributes to Assis Júnior's superficial erudition.[6] There exists little doubt that Assis Júnior's pretentious efforts to emulate European models resulted in many ingenuous and pedantic passages in O segredo da morta. We must, nevertheless, reserve final judgment on what seem to be merely technical weaknesses, by Western standards, until a critical approach more in line with African stylistic features has been devised. The novel's digressions, narrative rambling, and plethora of seemingly insignificant details may somehow fit into the story-telling rhythm of an African oral tradition. This seems particularly feasible in view of Assis Júnior's liberal use of Kimbundu phrases, coupled with the fact that his handling of the Portuguese language may suggest that his thought patterns followed the syntax and rhythm of his native tongue and thus projected an African point of view.

The real value of writers such as Cordeiro da Matta and Assis Júnior lies in their contribution to an incipient tradition that in modified form has reemerged in the cultural and literary movements of contemporary Angola.

CHAPTER 2

Colonialists,
Independents,
and Precursors

A considerable body of literature, mainly prose fiction, and almost exclusively cultivated by Europeans about Africa, appeared in the 1930s and the 1940s, although there were scattered antecedents as early as the late nineteenth century. The authors of these works often labeled them "colonial novels," an apt term in view of their inherent Western ethnocentrism. Of all the Portuguese colonies Angola has served most as the setting for these novels, primarily because more settlers and colonialists descended on that territory than on any other.

Most colonial novels have little literary value, some having been written by colonels and other military campaigners. A few titles will attest to their prevailing exoticism and sensationalism: *África selvagem* (Savage Africa, 1935) by Maria Archer; *Feitiços* (Sorceries, 1935) by Guilhermina de Azeredo; *Terras do nu e do batuque* (Lands of the Naked and the *Batuque*, 1933) by António de Aragão Paiva. The subtitle of Luís Figueira's *Princesa negra* (Black Princess, 1932) reads *O preço da civilização em África* (The Price of Civilization in Africa), and in his prologue he says of his story that "the protagonists of the drama are pioneers of a martyred and nomadic life throughout the unknown

backlands; those audacious and fearless settlers who first pene-
trated with their caravans into the bellicose lands of the African
mid-continent and contributed most to the pacification of savage
peoples."[1] This kind of literature has outlived, in spirit, old-time
colonialism in Africa. Recently it has taken the form of chauvinis-
tic, propagandistic, or simply more sophisticated exotic stories
and poetry. The armed revolt that erupted in 1961 has produced
a spate of war stories bearing such titles as *Angola heróica—120
dias com os nossos soldados* (Heroic Angola—120 Days with Our
Soldiers, 1964) by Artur Maciel and *Soldado que vais à guerra*
(Soldier, You Who Go to War, 1963), a collection of poems by
Reis Ventura. Some of this writing forces the issue of Portugal's
claim to its African territories, and other books glorify the settler,
proud of his pioneer legacy and feeling more Angolan than Portuguese. The settler does not often feel so Angolan, however, that
he forgets his dominance over the black population.

Henrique Galvão, a former high official in the Portuguese
government, is perhaps better known for his 1948 report condemning forced labor practices in the colonies and for his 1962
hijacking of a passenger liner than for his efforts as a novelist.
The Portuguese-born Galvão did author five novels set in Angola,
and although he sharply criticized his countrymen for their mis-
treatment of the black Angolan, he viewed the African from a
considerable cultural and philosophical distance and he longed
for the day when the "native" would be led by the sympathetic
white to a utopian New World in the Tropics.

In his article "Africa as a Theme in Portuguese Literature"
Gerald Moser sums up the meaning of the colonial novel when
he says of a work, *Nova largada* (New Departure, 1929), that the
author, Augusto Casimiro, "exalts a new brand of young, altruistic civil servant, who will consult with the Negro villagers, lighten
their burden, and guide them like a father to a fuller life, while
making them more useful to the Portuguese, who will develop—
and take away—their best lands."[2] In later colonial novels a spirit
of nationalism would grow stronger, but at the same time so

would a sense of the basic conflict between African and European, which is the conflict between the colonizer and the colonized.

Castro Soromenho, an Enlightened Colonial Writer

Born of European parents in Mozambique, but raised in Angola, Fernando Monteiro de Castro Soromenho (1910–1968) has received acclaim as a talented writer of narrative prose and as a white man who understood the black man's soul. And, indeed, as a writer Soromenho did ply his craft far better than his colonial predecessors and contemporaries. But his highly praised ability to understand the African has to be seen in the context of a humanism that allowed him to comprehend universal flaws and failings, whether the people involved were black or white.

First of all, it is necessary to point out that Soromenho's several novels and collections of stories fall into two distinct phases. The first phase contains stories dealing with traditional African societies. *Nhári: O drama da gente negra* (Nhári: The Drama of Black Folks, 1938) in its dramatization of African legends has the total effect of establishing the black man's existence as fatalistically tragic. In comparison with those writers who presumptuously revealed an exotic Africa to the perverse curiosity of Europe, Soromenho went further by more authentically externalizing an African psychology; we might say that he indulged in ethnographic "brain-picking" by attempting to expose the black psyche in re-created African legends. So insistently did Soromenho fashion a "lo, the poor black man" view that we may read stories such as "Gando, o feiticeiro" (Gando, the Sorcerer) with the feeling that African societies existed from hand to mouth under the biblical curse of Ham. The first paragraph of "Gando" sets the tragic mood prevalent in many of Soromenho's early stories: "At the door of a native hut, a miserable lean-to lashed by the poverty of the savage, a small black child crawled about and played on a straw mat."[3] In these stories Soromenho asks his reader to pity the black man, the illogical but nonetheless human victim of his own ignorance and barbarism. Gratuitous affirmations such as "night strikes horror to the heart of the black man"[4] give proof of Soromenho's acceptance of a common European belief in the image of the African's fear-ridden and prelogical world.

But even in this first phase of more blatant exoticism Soromenho tempers his ethnocentrism with his more than superficial knowledge of African customs in the eastern part of Angola and with his capacity to express a feeling of sympathy for the African. For instance, the young heroine of the story "Nhári" symbolizes the African's secular suffering, but in the following description the narrator combines the idea of the destiny of a race with the emotional portrait of a child victimized by the beliefs and practices of her people: "Nhári, delicate child with pretty black eyes full of suffering, staring blankly into infinity. Tiny slave girl, perhaps unaware of your own bondage. You are the symbol of the women of your race" (p. 109).

What most distinguishes Soromenho from other colonial writers is his use of African legends and sayings, and his familiarity with some of the languages of Angola. "A lagoa maldita" (The Accursed Lake) takes place in the eastern area of Moxico and offers a variation on the legend of the flood. A weak and aged leper comes upon a village at the height of a celebration; when she asks for water the villagers drive her away. The old woman then happens on a solitary hut on the outskirts of the village; there the elderly occupants give her food, water, and a place to sleep. The next morning, as the leper prepares to continue her journey, she repays the couple for their kindness by advising them to abandon their home because a great catastrophe will befall the village and the surrounding land. Because the couple respect the voice of the aged they leave their hut. That night it begins to rain, and in a short time the whole area, including the village, becomes one large lake on which swim as many black ducks as there were people in the inundated village. For eternity the ducks must swim the waters of the accursed lake. This tale derives from one of the many legends and myths Soromenho collected during his visits to African settlements in eastern Angola. In retelling the legend, however, Soromenho destroys the African dynamic of a simple, but poetically didactic story, predicated on the universal themes of charity and reward, by overburdening his narration with exotic description: adjectives such as "savage," "barbaric," "mysterious," and "fantastic" abound along with nouns like "delirium" and "sensuality" in the depiction of the wild "native" dancing. Soromenho obviously wanted to re-create an atmosphere of Sodom-like debauchery as dramatic preparation for the deluge. But in seeking to cater to his European audience he also catered to their taste for exoticism by externalizing an African reality through comparisons with certain mythic elements of the Judeo-Christian tradition. He found it expedient, for example, to compare the aged leper to a phantom who seemed to emerge like a nightmare from Dante's "Inferno."

When Soromenho abandoned his attempts to fashion stories about an Africa untouched by Europe, he embarked on a more successful phase of his literary career. In part, this success can be attributed to a change in style and technique. Gerald Moser has noted the changes that Soromenho made in the 1960 edition of *Homens sem caminho* (Men without Direction), originally published in 1942. The author purged his novel of such words as savage and simian in characterizing the African. Moser has observed that Soromenho replaced subjective terms with objective words like tribe and fetish. These two words, in particular, may represent an improvement in Soromenho's ethnocentric vocabulary, but today some Africanists avoid tribe, in favor of people or ethnic group, and certainly fetish (from the Portuguese *feitiço*, meaning charm or sorcery) suggests nothing more than European ignorance of and prejudice toward African religious beliefs.

Asked in an interview why his 1957 novel *Viragem* (Turnabout) showed marked differences over earlier works, Soromenho replied that "since in my novels new social realities arose and presented themselves to me in their contradictions, it was naturally incumbent upon me to adopt a new technique and a new literary style."[5] Mário António, in reviewing *Viragem*, dismissed the significance of the author's deletion of racist terminology and declared that the novel projected the same colonialist attitudes of Soromenho's first phase.[6]

Indeed, Soromenho never ceased to write within the colonial tradition, but he did so in a more enlightened manner when he concentrated on social transitions brought about by the confrontation of cultures. In 1949 he published his novel *Terra morta* (Dead Land), and the fact that the Portuguese authorities banned the book perhaps gives some indication of what the author meant when he spoke in his interview of "social realities" and "contradictions." More so in *Viragem* than in *Terra morta*, however, does Soromenho achieve artistic balance in treating the theme of cultural clash and society in transition; and he accomplishes this even though the novel's setting and situation resemble a class "B" movie, complete with scenes of a hot, steaming jungle, tropical tedium, and inflamed passions.

In this novel the principal characters are minor government functionaries carrying out their administrative duties in the Angolan interior. Frustrated by their inability to improve measurably their economic and social lot, they possess only the knowledge of their intrinsic superiority over the black population to sustain themselves psychologically. Soromenho pictures the Africans as beset by fears and superstitions; but in an atmosphere of tensions, mutual distrust, and insecurity the white man also has fears which, in their expression, parallel those of the black man. The fear of not being able to survive at home has driven the European to embark on his adventure in Africa; once there, the fear of death is aggravated in an ambient of the indomitable forces of nature. Paulina, the companion of the absent Portuguese district çhief, and her peasantlike grandmother scream in terror during a severe tropical storm. The superstitious grandmother invokes Saint Barbara, in the tradition of folk Catholicism, while the Africans invoke supernatural forces. The two European women harbor a fear of the unknown no less irrational than that which they attribute to the ignorant "natives."

Joana, the grandmother, plays in fact an important role in Soromenho's development of the problem of reciprocal decadence in the debasement of the Africans and the dehumanization of the Europeans. Both are victims of a set of circumstances that robs them of their personal dignity. Joana symbolizes this loss of personal dignity as she degenerates physically and morally. And this image of the worthless old woman has added significance because both in traditional African societies and in the peasant cultures of Europe the elderly are respected and often venerated members of the nuclear family. But Joana, uprooted and disoriented in an alien world, represents more of a burden than a source of counsel.

The situation of a handful of white administrators controlling the destinies and actions of thousands of Africans offers Soromenho the opportunity to assess human values in the framework of dramatic episodes. One episode recounted by the narrator tells of the Lunda chief Calendende who, after twelve years of war against the Portuguese, flees, or better, disappears into the nearby Belgian Congo, where for his people he becomes a last tenuous link with their lost grandeur and dignity as an autonomous people. At the end of the campaign against Calendende's forces, Tipóia, the black soldier, hoists the Portuguese flag over the last piece of land to be conquered from the Lunda people. Tipóia's lieutenant calls him a brave Portuguese soldier, which causes the puzzled African to ask how a black man can be Portuguese. Impatiently, the officer explains that the white Portuguese give the orders and the black Portuguese obey them.

Soromenho uses such incidents of burlesque irony to illustrate the basic tragedy of the clash of cultures and the resulting transitions. His characters illustrate this transition, and their lives stand as tragic testimonials to the clash of cultures. The author employs a series of illustrative events and objects to dramatize the story of Tipóia, the faithful black Portuguese. So thoroughly has Tipóia's sense of values been perverted that he substitutes for his loss of cultural identity a blind devotion to the government. After the wars he dons the uniform of a *cipaio* ("native" policeman), and after sixteen years of service in that capacity he finds himself tracking a fugitive. On the outskirts of a village where he suspects the man to be hiding, Tipóia falls victim to an ambush and as a result loses his rifle. The firearm, which represents, in more than a symbolic way, Europe's technological dominance over Africa, also represents Tipóia's measure of white-conceded authority. His last thread of self-respect breaks when upon returning to the compound his commanding officer has him placed under arrest for having failed in his mission and for having lost his rifle. Stripped of his uniform and banished to the bush, Tipóia is a useless object, a *thing*. In this regard, Alfredo Margarido has observed, in a critical essay, that the European had the habit of renaming the "semicivilized" African after an object.[7] In this particular case of "thingification," the Portuguese word *tipóia* describes a litter for transporting people; when the implement is no longer serviceable, the owner casts it aside. Tipóia literally becomes a thing when he stumbles off into the bush mumbling dementedly about his thirty years of service, as soldier and policeman, to the government. The African, then, came from the bush, or from his culture, to the European compound where he acquired the outer trappings that converted him into a black Portuguese. When Tipóia returns to the bush, symbolically as naked as he came, he is neither African nor Portuguese.

The Europeans in the story blame their unhappiness on the oppressive heat, on the mosquitoes, and especially on the "savages." The African is there as a constant reminder of their own human frailties. In his later novels Soromenho develops the technique of a series of similar incidents which, by their very repetitiveness, achieve the total effect of dramatizing the basic idea that in civilizing the African, the European dehumanizes him, and that in dehumanizing the African he dehumanizes himself. Paulina solemnly declares the Africans "don't have feelings like we do"; and the assistant administrator Alves claims that "we have to civilize them," as he orders a suspected thief put to the whip. But even as the European struggles to elevate his dominance over the African to a plane of moral or even physical superiority, the visceral humanity of both intercedes as a frustrating equalizer. *Catinga*, the sweaty smell of African laborers, mingles in the European's nostrils with his own acrid odor; and Joana, despite her frustration, confesses that conditions in her Portuguese village of impoverished peasants were worse than what she has encountered in Africa.

In the oppressive atmosphere the European characters find themselves directing their fears toward the unknown. Alves, thwarted in his efforts to form an amorous liaison with the neurasthenic Paulina, closes himself in his office where his feverish depression turns a Kwokwe death mask on the wall into a silent goad to all his fears and sense of personal failure. The mask seems to come alive when a small rodent scurries over it, and ashamed of his superstitious fear, the enraged European destroys the African emblem of death.

The dramatic clashes culminate when Maurício, a mulatto truck driver, explains to the administrator, whom he is bringing back to his jungle post, that he prefers black women because *mestiço* girls have had their heads filled with civilization by their white fathers. And in this novel of cultural and psychological clash between African and European the mixed offspring appears as a socially marginal man, symbolic of the painful transitions.

As an enlightened colonialist Castro Soromenho has contributed to later, more socially aware writers by leaving behind a model of the regionalist story of psychological depth.

Tomaz Vieira da Cruz, the Colonial Poet of the Mulatto Muse

Not unlike Castro Soromenho, Tomaz Vieira da Cruz confronted Africa with sympathy and compassion. Unlike Soromenho, Vieira da Cruz expressed himself in flights of intimist lyricism that both enhance and detract from his poetry.

Born in 1900 in Portugal's Ribatejo region, Vieira da Cruz left for Africa at the age of twenty-four imbued with an unshakable pride in Portugal's imperial greatness. He settled in the then colonial village of Novo Redondo where he worked as an assistant pharmacist and raised a family with his mulatto wife. His first volume of verse, *Quissange—Saudade negra* (Finger Piano—Black Yearning, 1932), offers a dedicatory sonnet entitled "Pátria

minha" (My Homeland) in which the poet evokes the sixteenth-
century Portuguese king Sebastião and the history of the Lusitanian race. The revival of Sebastianism, which during Portugal's
"Babylonian captivity" from 1580 to 1640 gave rise to a nationalistic cult predicated on the belief that the king, killed fighting the
Moors in North Africa, would return to redeem the nation's
political autonomy from Spain, characterized the symbolist *saudosismo* of Teixeira de Pascoais, the movement's founder. It was
principally through the free verse of António Boto, whom Vieira
da Cruz knew personally both in Portugal and in Angola, that
the Angolan lyricist derived inspiration for his *saudosista* patriotism and transformations of the Africa he perceived.

By the time he had written his second book of poetry on
African themes, *Tatuagem* (Tattoo, 1941), his ideological motivation had become fully apparent. On the book's title page
appears the following dedication: "Praise to the Portuguese of
Angola who march off in search of love and fortune, and who, in
these African lands, lose themselves in the anxiety of conquering
that which they deem easy to attain—but they fall and remain in
the land of the forgotten." Vieira da Cruz cultivated a pioneer
spirit replete with the melancholy of exile and overlaid with a
sentimentalized exoticism.

In *Cazumbi* (Spirits, 1950), his third collection of African
verse, he celebrates the settler who conquered the land which in
turn conquered him. The self-made, self-reliant pioneer built a
life on the untamed frontier, and in spite of his crudeness and
illiteracy he possessed the qualities of filial love, religious devotion, and artistic sensitivity. The poem "Colono" (Settler) syn-
thesizes his frontier mythology and puts forth a romanticized
thesis of two races coming together for their mutual benefit. After
glorifying the settler's physical vigor and simple intelligence,
Vieira da Cruz introduces one of his favorite themes, that of the
African woman as faithful companion to the European pioneer:

> E a primeira mulher que amou e quis
> foi sua inteiramente . . .

E era negra e bela, tal o seu destino!
E ela o acompanhou
como a mais funda raiz
acompanha a flor de altura
que perfuma as mãos cruéis
de quem a arrancou.[8]

(And the first woman he loved and wanted/was his completely
. . ./And she was black and beautiful, like her fate!/And she
accompanied him/as the deepest root/accompanies the flower to
the point/where it perfumes the cruel hands/of he who has
plucked it.)

The idea of the combined destinies of the African and the
European receives, in the metaphor of the plucked flower, the
added element of the *saudosista*'s lost illusions.

A sense of melancholy exile, Lusotropicalist *saudosismo*, and
sweet illusions are apparent in the dedication of Vieira da Cruz's
first book of poetry: "to the African people and the African
world: to that Empire of dream and marvels that was, in my
green youth and at the time of the awakening of pleasant illusions, the lovely exile of my soul . . ." An alliance, as it were, of
the two melancholy peoples gives Vieira da Cruz's exotic imagery
an ethereal touch, so that the Africa he reconstructs in his poetry,
even in allusions to its legacy of slavery and suffering, has an
unreal, romantic quality about it. And he accepts his role as
errant exoticist when he asks in the poem "Febre lenta" (Slow
Fever), "exotismo vagabundo,/onde me levas, agora?"[9] (vagabond exoticism,/where do you lead me now?) Then, under the
spell of his own airy exoticism he invokes the black or mulatto
muse in such poems as the ultraromantic sonnet "Lira" (Lyre).

Vieira da Cruz's poetry is peripheral to neo-African literature
and outdated for contemporary Euro-American tastes. In a
demystification of Vieira da Cruz's poetry, the Portuguese-born
critic Jorge de Sena alludes to those who dance with mulatto girls
to the strains of Parnassian marimbas.[10] But Mário António
comes to the defense of Vieira da Cruz by declaring that those

critics who accuse him of sensualist deformations fail to see his verse as simple love poetry.[11] Jorge de Sena's dismissal of Vieira da Cruz has validity if the poet is removed from his place, marginal though it may be, in the total historical phenomenon of Afro-Portuguese literature and is rated with his contemporaries in Europe. But, even if his poetry is judged solely on its artistic merit—and his poetry should be evaluated as poetry—it is found, as I shall attempt to demonstrate shortly, that his work is not completely without artistic value. To see Vieira da Cruz's poetry as simply love lyrics, as Mário António suggests we should, also fails to do justice to either his historical or his artistic importance as precursor to the contemporary, more socially aware generation of Angolan writers. We cannot merely slough off Vieira da Cruz's poetry as an exotic reflection of a decadent European form, nor can we defend him as just another talented and sensitive writer of love verses. Not only does his poetry have to be seen in the panorama of twentieth-century Afro-Portuguese literature—a literature conditioned by cultural and social contingencies—but it also has to be examined in the light of his reworking of the European poetic conventions and conceits of the period. The critic has to start with the understanding that the Alentejo pharmacist, with his European lyre and sonnet form, prepared the way for a successive generation of Angola poets with his intimist transformations of an African mystique.

Once Vieira da Cruz's incorrigibly European point of view is understood, such themes as the black Venus as a glorified bibelot in the hands of the aggrandized Portuguese settler gain aesthetic dimension as an artistically meaningful variable in the poet's bittersweet world of exile. Vieira da Cruz's poetic persona never comprehends the African in his own context, but the African, even while exteriorized, becomes enveloped in the poet's rarefied context of exoticism, eroticism, and humanism. He glorifies the mulatto woman as the mystery of two races; her defects are her graces, he sings, and in doing so he innocently subverts his own aesthetic acceptance of the feminine ideal.

Vieira da Cruz sees the dark Venus as sensual but also enigmatic in her mystery, and in this respect he unwittingly approximates the poetic renditions of black female charms found in some négritude poetry. But his poetic view of the black woman is often wistful and tinged with the fatalism of her people. In "Cana doce" (Sweet Cane), for example, he tells of

> Aquela preta, aquela, veio do Nâno
> e ficou na cidade a permutar
> cana de açúcar muito menos doce
> do que a luz triste do seu triste olhar.
>
> (*Tatuagem*, p. 33)

(That black woman, that one, came from Nâno/and remained in the city to barter/with sugar cane much less sweet/than the sad light of her sad gaze.)

The paradoxical blend of sad and sweet develops a subtle image, and in another poem, "Bailundos," Vieira da Cruz uses the same sense of quiet pathos for a representation of intimist expression. Employing the image of a file of Bailundo people traveling silently through the night, he concocts a metaphor of fatalism and mystery captured most strikingly in the poem's last stanzas:

> . . . Ó mensageiros tristes da saudade
> que trago dentro de mim!
> êsse caminho é eterno
> e a minha Dôr não tem fim.
>
> Haveis de caminhar,
> que nunca terá fim o vosso inferno.
>
> —Não existe humanidade,
> e o mundo foi sempre assim.
>
> (*Tatuagem*, p. 18)

(Oh, sad messengers of the yearning/I bring within me!/That road is eternal/and my Sorrow has no end.//You will have to travel on,/because your inferno has no end.//—There exists no humanity,/and the world has always been thus.)

The personalization of the image of the night-shrouded file of Bailundos into messengers of the poet's own disillusionment transcends the exotic and conjures up intimist identity within the artistic context of bittersweet melancholy.

Tomaz Vieira da Cruz, despite the simplistic and ingenuous nature of much of his poetry conceived under the onus of chauvinism, forms an important link with the generation of poets that emerged during the 1950s in Angola.

Óscar Ribas, an Apologist for Waning Traditions

Born in Luanda in 1909 to an African mother and a Portuguese father, Óscar Bento Ribas has established himself as a popular folklorist and an official spokesman for native Angolan traditions. His books and articles on the culture of Angola at the turn of the twentieth century and of the life of the African *musseques* that ring Luanda cover a range from religious rites to culinary arts. As a writer of prose fiction Ribas has concentrated on adaptations of Kimbundu stories and legends, and this in a way makes his works similar to those of Castro Soromenho's first phase. Soromenho subtitled his collection *Nhári a Drama of Black Folks*, and Ribas's *Ecos da minha terra* (Echoes of my Land, 1952) bears the subtitle *Dramas angolanos* (Angolan Dramas). Ribas, in his folkloric stories, has made the African and creole cultures of Angola accessible and acceptable to a broad spectrum of people. Despite the fact that he has been blind since the age of twenty-one, he has long been a genuine recorder of Angolan traditions. Without being an actual participant, Ribas grew up in contact with the traditions that he captures in his writings. He documents traditions in a state of disintegration. A sort of collector of cultural memorabilia, he has moved in the direction of preserving certain African modes of life in Angola; but he has done this more with the mentality of a museum curator than as a jealous guardian of the dynamics of a tradition. Paradoxically, Ribas's gentle concern for Angolan traditions earned him the 1952 Margaret Wrong prize from the International Committee on Christian Literature for Africa. This award, given specifically for *Ecos da minha terra*, has something to say about Ribas's interjection of Western piety into his writing. And what says even more about Ribas's situation in terms of an African awakening in Angola is that the Portuguese government conferred on him, in 1962, the degree of official of the Order of the Infante Dom Henrique.

Taking his 1967 collection of tales, *Sunguilando*—a Portuguese rendering of a Kimbundu term which means storytelling—as an example of Ribas's approach to the recording of oral tradition, we get a feel for his compassion for his subject matter. Ribas tempers his compassion, however, with an uneasy attitude of reproachfulness toward the "semicivilized" subjects of his recorded stories. He exhibits a somewhat comic fastidiousness when he comments on an informant's use of the vulgarism *cagar* (to shit): "among the lower classes this is common language corresponding to vernacular expression. As a consequence of this vulgarity, these people express themselves in a way that I vigorously condemn."[12] Yet, just as vigorously Ribas demands authenticity, so while condemning vulgarity with bourgeois indignation, he faithfully records. In a display of intellectual anger Ribas repudiated authorship of his book *Sunguilando* because an anonymous editor tampered with orthography and punctuation. In the introduction to his novel *Uanga* (Enchantment, 1969) he declares that his intellectual probity prevents him from claiming authorship to *Sunguilando*. This honesty, commendable though it may be, seems a little extreme, and it brings out an important factor in Ribas's concept of a native Angolan literature and culture.

Ribas's unstated concept of an African literature and cultural expression occurs through the implicitness of his editorial declarations. In *Uanga* he tells the reader that this is not a "salon" novel, but a documentary of uncultivated black society. Having self-consciously and apologetically elicited the reader's sympathy for the cultural material put forth in the novel, Ribas goes on to exult in the importance of *feitiço* in the lives of the ignorant "natives" (not to mention some "civilized" believers). Ribas's background apparently prevented him from putting his love for things Angolan into a social perspective, and like many other Afro-Portuguese writers he fell into a kind of dialectical ambivalence. While pompously taking the ignorant "natives" to task for their non-Western crudeness, he chides the colonialist for his penchant to treat the black world as a great unknown, to wrap the African in a mantle of mystery, and, in ignorance, to distort his world.

The events Ribas recounts in *Uanga* took place in 1882 when Luanda still had the look of a village. Wilderness encroached on the streets where at night forest creatures prowled. Urbanization and progress changed the face of Luanda, Ribas says resignedly, and he sadly recalls the bygone era and laments the cutting down of the city's trees which "robs us of the benefits the tree offers against the broiling sun, and takes away the romantic beauty that the tree gives to the scenic panorama. How lyrical the city would be if it could continue to be lulled by winged troubadors! While in other places arborization, the protection of birds, constitutes a cult, here, in this essentially tropical city, it inspires aversion."[13] As curious as this passage may seem, in both style and content, it is not inconsistent with the book's principal motif, the *uanga*, which besides meaning enchantment can also refer to bewitchment or the casting of a spell. Ribas exhorts Luanda to bewitch its citizenry and its visitors alike: "Do not be ashamed to bewitch: the hex is the brother of beauty. If you bewitch, you will reign like a queen. But take note: do not permit the profane treatment of your splendor. Combat slingshots and rifles [for the killing of birds] which are the rule in the great countries" (p. 21). Ribas analogizes his characters' belief in the supernatural with an innocent sense of civic pride as if to convince the city fathers that *feitiço* is a harmless aspect of Luanda's charms.

While proclaiming the authenticity of the folklore and color of the *musseques*, Ribas demonstrates a concern, in his footnotes, for defending the so-called primitive practices by comparing them with similar practices in the formative stages of Western societies. Thus, when he refers, in *Uanga*, to the African *alembamento*, which can be likened to the European dowry, he cites a similar practice among the ancient Greeks as described in the *Odyssey*. On other occasions the narrator reminds us of his Western erudition by referring to wine-drinking *musseque*-dwellers as devotees of Bacchus or describing two old African crones awakening as freeing themselves from Morpheus's grasp. In compensation for these preciosities Ribas offers a wealth of ethnographic material in *Uanga*, including Kimbundu riddles and fables presented during the traditional storytelling hours.

In many respects Óscar Ribas is a more sophisticated, better informed Assis Júnior, and a more sensitive, albeit more apologetic, Castro Soromenho. The various honors bestowed on him by government agencies give him a seal of officialdom that puts him outside of the new awareness of Angola's recent generations of writers and intellectuals. But although his delicate handling of Luanda's African heritage imparts an effeteness to a Kimbundu cultural dynamic, and even though he deals innocuously with that which was and will never be again, his documentation and renditions of native traditions have played an important role in the process of regional self-awareness among Angolan writers.

Geraldo Bessa Victor and the Cultivation of Exoticism

As a poet Bessa Victor (b. 1917) has been the object of limited praise and some negative criticism. Most critics, both metropolitan and Afro-Portuguese, have generally ignored his work. Much of the praise has come from official Portuguese sources, and as with Ribas, this adulation has been the kiss of death for the poet. Mário de Andrade has perhaps best summed up many committed Afro-Portuguese writers' attitude toward Bessa Victor when he called him a "self-exoticist."[14]

Exoticism has been something of a hallmark of Bessa Victor's poetry. After a volume of uncharacteristic verse, *Ecos dispersos* (Scattered Echoes, 1941), he published a collection of African poems, *Ao som das marimbas* (To the Strains of the Marimbas, 1943), in which he sings of the black man's dignity and his white soul. Most of the poems of this early phase are so inept in their artistic execution and so painful in their exoticism that they deserve comment merely as examples of a stage in the development of black consciousness in Angolan letters. In truth, the whole of Bessa Victor's poetic production, both the early and the later stages, represents a kind of Afro-Portuguese négritude, but distinctly unlike that of the São Tomé writer Francisco José Tenreiro. Not only does Bessa Victor's négritude lack rage and anti-racist racism, but it attempts to incorporate a Lusotropicalist patriotism. A poem entitled, appropriately, "Mística do império" (Mystique of the Empire) praises Portugal and celebrates, in the following lines, Lusitanian miscegenation:

> E a voz dos povos é quem diz, agora:
> —Deus fêz o negro e o branco.
> O português num gesto grato
> e belo e franco,
> inspirado por Deus, em boa hora,
> fêz o mulato . . .[15]

(And it is the voice of nations that cries out:/—God made the black man and the white man./The Portuguese, with a gracious,/frank, and beautiful gesture,/inspired by God,/made the mulatto . . .)

The poet's reworking of a phrase on the Portuguese's penchant for race-mixing, attributed to the nineteenth-century novelist Eça de Queirós, has to be seen as one aspect of his acceptance of a sanctimonious mythology.

In other poems from *Ao som das marimbas* Bessa Victor conjures up exotic images to defend the downtrodden race, but in "Bemvinda, bemvinda!" (Welcome, Welcome!) he exceeds the limits of poetic license when he tells the sensuous, archetypal, blackest of black women that

> Ao ver-te, o Sol,
> o eterno apaixonado vagabundo,
> suicida-se no mar,
> em dramático arrebol,

> lá ao longe, muito longe;
> e o espírito do Sol,
> feito monge,
> transforma-se no luar mais triste e mais profundo
> das noites africanas . . .
> (p. 35)

(Upon seeing you, the Sun,/that eternal impassioned vagabond,/ commits suicide in the sea/in dramatic afterglow,/there faraway, very faraway;/and the spirit of the Sun,/like a monk,/transforms itself into the saddest and most profound moonlight/of the African night . . .)

Bessa Victor's use of imagistic preciosities to adulate blackness continues in a poem that is reminiscent of one written many years before by the São Tomé poet Costa Alegre.[16] Both poets use the image of a lump of coal; the Angolan addresses the coal with the words "penso que és meu igual, meu semelhante/e chamo-te irmão" (p. 45) (I believe you are my equal, my image,/and I call you brother). He identifies with blackness in its most intense hue, and perhaps coal's compressed energy and association with the earth are supposed to represent the black man's natural humanity, but the manner in which Bessa Victor employs the metaphor has too much of the comic to attain the desired effect.

Bessa Victor has improved, both as a craftsman and as a representative Afro-Portuguese writer, in his two most recent books of poetry, *Cubata abandonada* (Abandoned Hut, 1957) and *Mucanda* (a Kimbundu word meaning letter, 1964).* He continues to cultivate exoticism, but less self-effacingly so, and with a Luso-tropicology that is more regionalistic than patriotic. Rather than seeing himself as just a black Portuguese, he insists on his Angolanness in poems such as "O feitiço do batuque" (The Enchantment of the *Batuque*):

---

* After this book had been set in galley proofs it was learned that Bessa Victor had published another poetry collection, *Monandengue* (Lisbon: Livraria Portugal, 1973).

Sinto o som do batuque nos meus ossos,
o ritmo do batuque no meu sangue.
E' a voz da marimba e do quissange,
que vibra e plange dentro de minh'alma,
—e meus sonhos, já mortos, já destroços,
ressuscitam, povoando a noite calma.[17]

(I feel the sound of the *batuque* in my bones,/the rhythm of the *batuque* in my blood./It is the voice of the marimba and of the *quissange*,/that sobs and throbs within my soul,/—and my once wrecked, once dead dreams,/come to life and fill the calm of night.)

The theme of spiritual rebirth brings the poet closer to négritude than he had ever been in his earlier poems of superficial exoticism. And his new phase of négritude brings with it the occasional note of protest, such as in the balladlike "Canção de um negro com alma de branco" (Song of a Black Man with a White Soul) in which the poor African boy from the bush goes to live in the city with his benevolent white godmother. He learns the white man's ways and his own people say that except for his black skin he is a white man. The last stanza asks two questions:

Não importa a cor da pele,
se lhe deram alma nova?
Não importa a alma nova
se é a mesma a cor da pele?
(p. 29)

(Is not the color of his skin unimportant/if they gave him a new soul?/Is not his new soul unimportant/if the color of his skin is the same?)

Bessa Victor had toned down his language by the time he got to his last two collections of poetry, and along with a simplicity of style he began to achieve irony, especially when treating themes such as color prejudice.

Often, rather than sarcasm or rage, Bessa Victor's irony contains a plea for racial harmony. One of his best-known poems,

"O menino negro não entrou na roda" (The Black Child Did Not Join in the Game), appears in the collection *Mucanda*, and despite the fact that the poet had purged his style of certain exotic images, the narrative verse has a plaintive quality that tends toward the mawkish in its implicit appeal for racial understanding. The theme of exclusion and the element of innocence, represented by the child, add sentimentality to the message:

> O menino negro não entrou na roda
> das crianças brancas. Desolado, absorto,
> ficou só, parado como olhar de cego,
> ficou só, calado como voz de morto.[18]

(The black child did not join in the game/with the white children. Desolate, absorbed,/he remained alone, still, like a blind man's gaze,/he remained alone, silent like a dead man's voice.)

The two similes, used to represent the child's exclusion from the community of other children, are an improvement over the banal images of Bessa Victor's earlier poetry, even though they do not possess the expressive subtlety of more talented poets. In other poems included in that section of *Mucanda* entitled "Menino negro" (Black Child) the poet succumbs to abject tastelessness in his efforts to sentimentalize the theme of the excluded black child. This is particularly true in "Natal do menino negro" (Black Child's Christmas) when he seizes on the image of the Christ child to illustrate his plea for racial understanding within a rather operatic framework of piety.

Finally, in *Mucanda*'s second section, "O negro e o amor" (Love and the Black Man), Bessa Victor's new racial consciousness prompts him to attach the label of négritude to one of his poems. "Amor sobre a marca da negritude" (Love over the Sign of Négritude) praises the black woman for her symbolic identity with the passion of a primitive and untrammeled Africa. Once again, however, Bessa Victor's artistic make-believe comes through in an awkward and self-conscious fashion as he invites the black woman to come to him:

Sim, vem, para mim,
isenta de complexos e programas,
porque êste amor de negro e negra
tem a missão de amar como quem ama.

(p. 37)

(Yes, come, come to me,/free of all complexes and plans,/because
this love of a black man and a black woman/has the mission of
loving as one should love.)

The idea of "mission" conveys a sense of the black man's redemp-
tive power through a love which will save humanity from its self-
destruction. In this phase of his poetry Bessa Victor tries to
exploit a non-Western exaltation which, while it gives his self-
exoticism some profundity within the philosophical precepts of
négritude, never fully frees itself from the grasp of Lusotropicalist
ideology.

Geraldo Bessa Victor precedes, and then accompanies from a
distance, the process of self-awareness in Angolan poetry. He has
etched out a place for himself, despite his exoticism and Lusotropicology, as a regionalist and an exponent of Angolanness.

As a short story writer Bessa Victor, in his volume *Sanzala sem
batuque* (Village without *Batuque*, 1967), follows Óscar Ribas's
lead in documenting social and cultural change in the urban
ghetto ambient of Luanda's *musseques*. If it were not for Bessa
Victor's reputation as a sympathizer with official government
policies and his continuing tendency to exoticize an African
reality, these stories would probably receive as much attention as
the offerings of the more nationalistic writers. Bessa Victor seems
to find an artistic vehicle for interpreting the social distortion
brought about by race and class distinctions that concentrate on
familial situations.

In the story "A filha de Ngana Chica" (Ngana Chica's Daughter), Regina, the daughter, finds herself the reluctant housekeeper and lover of an engineer recently arrived in Luanda from
Portugal. Ngana Chica eagerly agrees to the arrangement and
goes to great lengths to sabotage her daughter's romance with

Raul, a young black postal worker. Raul receives a sudden trans-
fer to another city and Regina assumes her duties in Dr. Castro's
household. After several months the doctor summons Ngana
Chica to his home in the lower city in order to inform her that
her daughter is pregnant, which, of course, makes her no longer
suitable as a companion. Besides, the engineer claims, the girl had
lost her virginity before coming to him. Fearful that the baby may
be Raul's, and therefore black, Ngana Chica tries to bring about
an abortion with herbs and potions. The attempts fail, however,
but when the baby is born Ngana Chica cries out in relief, "It's
a mulatto!"

Bessa Victor's handling of the simple plot and a theme common
to the prose fiction of Portuguese Africa convinces not only
because of its lack of preachiness but also because of its sense of
balance between humor and tragic irony. The humor and irony
make more effective the social and economic desirability of racial
"whitening" among the black slum-dwellers. The mulatto grandchild will have a better chance in life, Ngana Chica reasons, just
as she thought that her daughter would better put her third-form
education to use by entering into an amorous liaison with a rich
white man. Perhaps Bessa Victor's own political passiveness permits him to be objective—objective in that he avoids the rhetoric
of those committed writers who frequently use stories of this type
to attack social ills—when dealing with the problem of acquies-
cence to an exploitative reality. At any rate, Bessa Victor, by
virtue of his generally low-key approach to these social problems
of broad implication and also because of his familiarity with the
cultural milieu, can capture the multifaceted contradictions
inherent in the life style of urbanized Africans who aspire to cultural and biological bleaching for their heirs. Thus, Ngana Chica,
a zealous mother left to raise her child alone after the death of
her husband, becomes pathetic in her aspirations to assure
Regina's future. Her efforts to improve her offspring's lot parallel
and parody the same aspirations found in the plans of any white
bourgeois family. But the parody has overtones of frustration
insofar as it reflects a reality of self-denial. The author, however,

manages to bring out Ngana Chica's humanity through the re-creation of thought processes captured in the language of the *musseques*. When the heroine realizes that the fetus has resisted the potions, she indulges in the type of humorous soliloquy common to black American culture when self-effacing racial stereotypes serve as a form of social catharsis.[19] The irritated Ngana Chica declares: "Damn! This has got to be a black man's baby. That's why he wants so much to be born, just to be contrary. And what's more, at this time of night. Won't even let me sleep. Shoot! Seem like the evil eye or something been put on me. Lord! This is my misery. Lord have mercy!"[20] And she flavors her Portuguese speech with Kimbundu terms and interjections as she mutters deprecatory clichés.

Bessa Victor demonstrates an ear for language when interpreting social vignettes that translate juxtapositions built on color and class preferences woven into the fabric of popular attitudes. In the story "E' proibido brincar" (It Is Forbidden to Play) one black woman haughtily tells another: "My *husband* is mulatto. Yes, as you know, dear Hortense, my Julião is mulatto. There's a big difference between a *preto-fulo* [offspring of a black and a mulatto parent] who can be considered mulatto being that he's the son of a mulatto, and a coal black child of two black parents. Isn't that so? Well, my dear, mulatto is not the same as black, don't you think? Oh yes, child, make no mistake about it. The white man doesn't talk to the mulatto like he talks to the black" (p. 52). And, of course, in all her haughtiness, the woman is essentially correct. The mulatto has a better chance of being taken as "civilized" by both black and white; and in the 1930s, when this story takes place, the "uncivilized" native could be challenged at any time on whether he had paid his head tax. So when Bernardo, the husband of Hortense, and the mulatto Julião hear the command to halt they both know to whom the order is directed. When Julião arranges for Bernardo's release from jail, the former's wife spreads the news with a mixture of pride and indignation—pride because of her mulatto husband's role in the matter and indignation that Bernardo, who is no "common nigger," should have been detained in the first place. The ironies and complexities of the relationships, often within a family, between blacks and mulattoes derive from historical factors of social and economic racism fed by the cult of miscegenation. Bessa Victor effectively uses these confrontations in his story "Carnaval." The first-person narrator, a *filho da terra*, returns home to Luanda after having spent nearly twenty years in Portugal. Mário, the protagonist, would seem to be a somewhat autobiographical character, since he, like the author, studied and practiced law in Lisbon. Because the story expands and illustrates some social realities in a structure that combines dramatic interlude with nostalgic flashbacks, it deserves some commentary.

Mário arrives in Luanda on the Tuesday of Carnival, and the remembrance of past celebrations catches him up in waves of nostalgia. He walks down *musseque* streets where as a boy he took part in the African-flavored carnival. A greeting of "good afternoon, doctor" interrupts his reverie and he finds himself in the presence of the black carpenter Domingos who used to work for his family many years ago. Elated, Mário embraces the stupefied man and, surprisingly, addresses him as Uncle Domingos. During the effusiveness of his greeting the whole story of Domingos's relationship to the family passes through Mário's mind. It seems that Mário's grandmother Joana, a black woman who wore the traditional robes and who spoke Kimbundu better than she did Portuguese, had become the companion of a Portuguese settler by whom she bore a daughter. The man recognized the child as his legitimate heir and saw to it that she was properly educated and then married to a respectable mulatto by whom she had Mário. Eventually, the Portuguese returned to his native land leaving Joana free to enter into a common-law relationship with a black man by whom she had four children, one being the carpenter Domingos. Although the half-brother of Mário's mother, Domingos was treated by the family as a social inferior: "Domingos for us—for the prestige of that mulatto family, a mulatto mother, a mulatto father, mulatto children, Domingos was like any other black carpenter" (p. 113). Mário's magnanimity in symbolically accepting Domingos into the confines of the mulatto family enforces the theme of solidarity in a spirit of Angolanness. Both men, the mulatto Mário and black Domingos, lament that *their* dances, meaning African dances, no longer figure in the Luanda carnival.

Exoticism and expediency lurk in the background of Bessa Victor's works, no matter what their social significance; so while he mourns the passing of African traditions he patriotically sees change as ultimately for the good. In one of the opening paragraphs in "Carnaval" the narrator describes Luanda in a kind of hymn to progress: "Hotels and restaurants, modern residences, bathing cabanas, cars, the human ant hill the Europeanized city either constructed there or placed there, and in which elegant young men and women stand out. On the other side, the ample port, febrile with energy and dynamism, with its ships, cargoes and passengers on the docks. In the background, all the grandeur of a magnificent city" (p. 101).

At a time when the documentation of the customs and practices of the indigenous peoples in Portuguese overseas territories has found favor in official circles, Bessa Victor has contributed to a growing number of scholarly or quasi-scholarly publications. His *Quinjango no folclore angolano* (Quinjango in Angolan Folklore, 1970) deals with the legends that developed around the life of Geraldo António Victor (presumably an ancestor of Bessa Victor), a *mestiço* general who took part in the Angolan wars of pacification during the nineteenth century. And Bessa Victor's projected books include *Intelectuais angolenses do século XIX* (Angolan Intellectuals of the Nineteenth Century), *Angolismos na língua portuguesa* (Angolisms in the Portuguese Language), and a critical edition of Cordeiro da Matta's *Philosophia popular em provérbios angolenses*. It can be concluded, then, that Geraldo Bessa Victor, as poet, short story writer, essayist, and scholar, occupies a controversial but significant historical position in the panorama of Afro-Portuguese literature and in the development of a spirit of Angolanness.

In the next three chapters it will be seen how a more committed spirit of Angolan regionalism came into being and how the literary efforts of a new generation dealt with the problems and themes elaborated by precursors and independents like Castro Soromenho, Tomaz Vieira da Cruz, Óscar Ribas, and Geraldo Bessa Victor.

CHAPTER 3

"Let's Discover Angola"

Carlos Ervedosa wrote that in 1948 those *filhos da terra* who were just coming of age took stock of their situation and came forth with the slogan "Vamos descobrir Angola!" (Let's Discover Angola!)[1] Bessa Victor channeled his Angolanness into timorous expressions of nativism; intellectuals born during the twenties, thirties, and forties intoned their slogan with fervor and sometimes with anguish. Out of this new awareness came the Movimento dos Novos Intelectuais de Angola (Movement of the Young Intellectuals of Angola) and in 1950 the founding of the Associação dos Naturais de Angola (Association of the Native Sons of Angola). This new generation, men and women, black, white, and *mestiço*, came mainly from urban areas; their education in the secondary schools of Angola, and often in the universities of Portugal, while it assured them a favored status as members of the intelligentsia, also turned them into a Europeanized elite far removed from a knowledge of the history and culture of their native land.

As Luanda became increasingly "whiter," and Europeanized cities such as Nova Lisboa, Sá da Bandeira, and Lobito grew in size and importance, the *filhos da terra* began to assess the process of acculturation that was at work in Angola. There exists little evidence in the writings of the period to suggest that this first nationalist movement had overtones of independence, but no doubt cultural awareness, influenced by the stirrings of change in other regions of colonial Africa, led many of these young intellectuals to react initially with nostalgia to the gradual dilution and eventual disappearance of the popular festivals and music that had emanated from the African *musseques*. Unlike Bessa Victor and Óscar Ribas, their memorializing did not necessarily stop with nostalgia and resignation. One form of reaction to the literal banishment of African influence from the Angolan carnival, and the attending disintegration of the large dancing groups, was the organization of musical combos in the *musseques*. These groups revived African themes and created a genuinely acculturated, regional, popular music.

The instrumental and vocal group Ngola Ritmos (Angola Rhythms), founded in the fifties by Carlos Vieira Dias (better known as "Liceu"), made the first and most telling contribution to this musical, cultural revival. Original compositions based on traditional folk motifs, with lyrics in Kimbundu, combined the European guitar with African percussion instruments. One song, "Mbiri mbiri," composed by Carlos Vieira Dias, defies, in its rhythmic and melodic structure, the stereotyped *batuque* label generally applied by Europeans to African music. Significantly, the words tell a story that can be understood on both a literal level of intimist complaint and a symbolic level of social protest. The lyrics speak of a personal lament based on the Kimbundu saying "Yoso ua dimuka, u diá ngo ué lu moxi é," which, roughly translated, means "The wise person allows himself to be fooled only once." In the song's story a man is betrayed by a friend, and the refrain, "mbiri, mbiri, ngongo j'amé" (ay, ay, my suffering), underlines, on another level, the grief of the black Angolan who has adopted European ways only to find himself in a cultural void, duped by those he thought to be his friends.

Ervedosa cites Maurício Almeida Gomes's poem "Exortação" (Exhortation), which more than exhorting, asks:

Mas onde estão os filhos de Angola,
se os não oiço cantar e exaltar
tanta beleza e tanta tristeza,
tanta dor e tanta ânsia
desta terra e desta gente?[2]

(But where are Angola's sons,/if I do not hear them singing and exalting/so much beauty and so much sadness,/so much pain and so much anguish/of this land and of this people?)

This poem, with its note of urgency and its allusions to the joys and sorrows of a land and its people, suggests that the poet and many of his contemporaries wanted not only to glorify nativistically, but also to discover Angola in all its cultural and social dimensions.

The Literary-Cultural Journals

Many did respond to the exhortative question posed by Maurício Almeida Gomes's poem. The Association of the Native Sons of Angola brought out, in 1951, the first issue of a literary-cultural review called *Mensagem* (Message). This issue did little more than announce a contest for the best poetry and short stories on Angolan themes written during 1951 and the early part of 1952. Then in October 1952 the second, and last, issue (which included numbers two through four) of the projected trimestral magazine appeared. Youthful exuberance abounds in the editorial dedication to the prize winners of the literary competition sponsored by the Cultural Department of the Regional Association of the Native Sons of Angola. The judges apologetically explain that because Angola does not yet possess the spiritual maturity of the "old countries," the criteria for selecting the best works could not be too stringent. And many of those awarded prizes would soon sink into oblivion while others would form the nucleus of an active literary group.

Mário António, at the time only eighteen years old, took the first prize for poetry and the second prize for short story; he would go on to play an important role and emerge as a major figure in Angola's incipient literature. Others would likewise make their mark on the literary scene as they struggled to find a genuine Angolan expression. In the main, they, like their counterparts in Cape Verde, would follow the path of Portuguese neorealism and particularly Brazilian modernism in seeking to define their own regional identity. Unlike the Cape Verdeans, however, these Angolan intellectuals could hardly escape their Africanness and see themselves as a Romance elite. Angola has an African demographic and cultural presence that cannot be denied by any native son claiming to seek to discover the reality of his land.

The editors of *Mensagem* illustrated the second issue with drawings of typical scenes and people of Angola, thus demonstrating their desire to foster an African motif in the enhancement of native themes. Of course, vestiges of the conventionally exotic and of the colonial mentality appear in some of the literary offerings. But even under the veil of Lusotropicalist mythology strongly regionalist attitudes can be seen. The short story that captured third prize exemplifies these strong sentiments of Angolanness. "Se não fosse a Victória" (If It Weren't for Victoria), by Maria de Jesus Nunes da Silva, tells of an escaped Portuguese convict whom an African woman discovers sick and hungry in the bush. She feeds him and nurses him back to health, and he in turn takes her as his companion. After sixty years in the bush, the ex-convict, now a prototypic hardy settler, sits on his front porch with a young man recently arrived in Angola from Portugal. When he exuberantly proclaims to his visitor that Angola is whites, blacks, and *mestiços*, the young man exhibits some reluctance to accept this multiracial arrangement as he casts a suspicious and disapproving eye on Victoria, who, before his host's explanation, he believed to be a servant. With passion the old man exclaims, "If you love Angola accept her, if not, leave her!" He follows with the exalted contention that "if it were not for Victoria there would be no Angola!" The colonialist implications of the story need no comment, but at this stage of Angolan self-awareness the "love it or leave it" attitude carries not only a reactionary defensiveness, but also a desire to establish regional identity. "Se não fosse a Victória" more than confirms the judges' warning that loose criteria of artistic evaluation had been applied in the selection of prize winners. Not surprisingly, the author of the story would never be heard from again as a member of the new generation of writers. Still, her one effort reflects a general climate of nativistic fervor among the contributors to the *Mensagem* literary competition.

The second prize for poetry went to Humberto José da Silva, who would continue with his literary endeavors under the pen name Humberto da Silvan. Judges called his poem, "África," poorly written and prosaic in its beginning but excellent in its last part. In Whitmanesque tones Silvan demands a new, developed Africa. Africa needs machines to open its virgin breast, Africa needs progress, and Silvan wants to be the bard of this new order. A decidedly non-négritude poem in its exaltation of Western technology, it nevertheless conveys the spirit of enthusiasm and impatience on the part of those who want, in their regionalist idealism, to build a new Angola.

Beneath a surface of provincial, generally technically weak literary offerings, *Mensagem* contains a hint of the innovative and even the iconoclastic as a prelude to a socially and politically committed Angolan literature. Names such as Viriato da Cruz, hailed by some as the most expressively Angolan poet, lend an important standard of cultural independence to *Mensagem*. Cruz would join with Mário de Andrade and Agostinho Neto to form, some nine years later, the nucleus of a revolutionary intelligentsia. Andrade and Neto contributed, respectively, the short stories "Eme Ngana, eme muene" (Me, Sir, Me Myself) and "Náusea," both presenting slices of Luanda slum life from the black man's point of view. Mário António's story "Cipaio" (Native Policeman) won second prize as a psychological sketch about the social conditions that make the black law officer a harsh, uncompromising figure when it comes to dealing with his fellow Africans.

Several of the poetry selections in *Mensagem* possess a mild note of social protest and a strong sense of regional solidarity which transcends race and class, as would be expected in a movement imbued with idealism. António Jacinto's "Carta dum contratado" (Letter from a Contract Laborer) resembles the Cape Verdean Terêncio Anahory's "Carta para a Ilha" (Letter for the Island) in technique as well as in theme.[3] Both the Angolan and the Cape Verdean lament their brothers' travail on the São Tomé plantations, and both carry a strong message of regional peoplehood.

Alda Lara, a poet from the city of Benguela, also offers two poems of social and racial solidarity, and about her works, as well as those of several others mentioned here only in passing, more will be said in the next two chapters.

The inclusion in *Mensagem* of two poems by the Mozambican poet Noémia de Sousa, with commentary by fellow Mozambican José Craveirinha, heralds the beginning of communication between like-minded Afro-Portuguese writers in the different provinces. A note, reprinted in the Angolan journal from the Mozambican review *Itinerário* (Itinerary), praises the new Angolan poetry for being free of the conventional image of the black man as a simple, ornamental element. The editors of *Itinerário* enthusiastically proclaim the literary and cultural activities of the Movement of the Young Intellectuals of Angola who, on November 24, 1952, sponsored a well-attended poetry reading during which works by António Jacinto and Antero Abreu were recited.

In concluding this overview of the historically important journal, I should mention that articles on African culture and ethnology accompany the authentically Angolan literary pieces in *Mensagem*. Mário de Andrade, in his article "Kimbundu nas línguas de Angola" (Kimbundu among the Languages of Angola), attempts to take up where Héli Chatelain and Joaquim Cordeiro da Matta left off in their efforts on behalf of the language of the Dembos, the Jingas, and other peoples in the region of Luanda. But Andrade's purposes are more than linguistic and revelatory; his interest in the first great Kimbunduists, Chatelain and Cordeiro da Matta, is not static memorabilia, but rather a nationalistic expression of an African renaissance. And certainly the often outspokenly African voice that emerged in the two issues of *Mensagem* must have contributed to its untimely demise.

From 1945 to 1951 nineteen issues of another journal, *Cultura*, published by the Sociedade Cultural de Angola (Cultural Society of Angola), carried a wide range of articles dealing with science, literature, and the arts. *Cultura* in this early stage lacked, however, the regionalist focus of *Mensagem*: Bessa Victor, for example, submitted a European-type poem to the first issue, and the Cape Verdean Luís Romano contributed two poems, based on his experiences in Morocco, to subsequent issues. In the pages of *Cultura* appeared the occasional poems by those who would later distinguish themselves in the coordinated literary movement of young Angolan intellectuals. Humberto da Silvan, for one, as well as Agostinho Neto, published poems in the magazine's eighteenth issue. Neto's "Certeza" (Certainty) has been seen by some as the first of his radical or protest poems; if this is true, its message is very cryptically stated. Despite this poem, and others by Neto, *Cultura* maintained a diffused European provincialism up until the time it ceased publication, temporarily, in 1951.

When *Cultura* resumed publication in 1957 it had a new direction. The magazine had assumed the *Mensagem* spirit, and as if to reinforce its editorial statement of purpose organizers printed the photograph of a Luene ceremonial mask on the front cover of the opening issue. More cosmopolitan than *Mensagem*, *Cultura* included articles and reviews dealing with social and racial problems in an international context. The first issue carries such pieces as a Portuguese translation of "Race and Society" by the American sociologist Kenneth Little, reprinted from the Mozambican newspaper *O Brado Africano* (The African Roar), and a note by Augusto da Costa Dias entitled "Sobre a compreensão e defesa das culturas nacionais" (Concerning the Understanding and Defense of National Cultures). And in the second issue the editors write of how, over a twenty-year period, they have witnessed the gradual formation of an Angolan consciousness. Each issue of *Cultura*, through the twelfth, published in 1960 (a token, two-page issue appeared as the last in 1961), intensified this consciousness on the part of Angolan intellectuals.

In issue three Henrique Abranches authors "A descoberta do

movimento e sua influência na arte negra" (The Discovery of the Movement and Its Influence on Black Art), and in the following issue he returns with the article "Panorama das línguas" (Panorama of Languages) which comments on several African tongues of Angola and gives some notion of the phonology, morphology, and syntax of Umbundu. Abranches, in the spirit of Mário de Andrade's *Mensagem* article on the same subject, does not merely record, but defends the validity of African languages. On the subject of ethnomusicology Abranches offers, in *Cultura*'s eleventh issue, an illustrated essay entitled "Instrumentos e ritmo" (Instruments and Rhythm) which describes several percussion instruments played by members of ethnic groups from south of the Cuanza River. This issue also includes an article by the ethnologist Henrique Guerra defending traditional Angolan music, which, he claims, still exists in the *musseques* even though it is rarely recorded, played over the radio, or mentioned in the newspapers. Guerra takes the opportunity to call on Angolans to support and study the authentic music of Angola.

The imperative quality of *Cultura*'s message found reflection in the considerable number of poems and short stories that appeared throughout the magazine's brief existence. Some of those who had collaborated on *Mensagem*, including Mário António, Tomás Jorge, and António Cardoso, likewise contributed to *Cultura*. Several new and promising writers made their debut in the latter magazine. Notable among them are Luandino Vieira and Arnaldo Santos, both of whose works will be considered in chapters four and five.

Of particular importance in the regionalist literary movement are the beginnings of a literary criticism; the poet António Cardoso, in his review of the metropolitan Maria Bernadette's book of poems, identifies what he sees as the principal shortcomings of modern Portuguese poetry. According to the Angolan this poetry is hermetic and superficial—it lacks relevance, to use a contemporary term of American parlance. A socially committed literature suits the nationalistic temperament of Cardoso and many of his fellow writers. Cardoso's concern for the direction of Angolan poetry also led him to devote a critical article entirely to that matter in the second issue of *Cultura*. A collection by an obscure author receives the brunt of Cardoso's biting criticism of pseudo-African poetry. Even the much-praised Mário António comes under Cardoso's critical scrutiny in an article called "A poética de Mário António" (The Poetics of Mário António).

Mário António himself does not lag behind António Cardoso as an outspoken commentator on Angola's literary scene. He authored a total of seven articles and book reviews in *Cultura*, including "Considerações sobre poesia" (Some Considerations on Poetry), which broaches the subject of a theory of Angolan poetry. An editorial article in the combined ninth and tenth issues of *Cultura* echoes Cardoso's and António's desire to clarify the literary situation in Angola. The writer of the editorial declares that a critical review of all the poetry that has been and is being published is urgent so that they can arrive at some viable definition of Angolan poetry. And a broad look at black poetry by António Simões Júnior, in issue eleven, shows a concern for the general topic of African and Afro-American literature. This same issue also carries excerpts from an address, delivered by Agostinho Neto at a Lisbon symposium, on the responsibility of Angolan poets to revive the African oral tradition and incorporate it into their Lusophone poetry. In the course of his address Neto quotes Aimé Césaire at length, thus indicating that some Angolan writers were in touch with what was occurring in an important area of African literature of European expression, and later it will be seen how Neto's poetry shows definite signs of Francophone influence.

The African presence in Angola became a major concern of *Cultura*'s organizers, as evidenced in the editorial statement, in the eighth issue, which declares that no Angolan can repudiate his land's African characteristics, the vestiges of which every Angolan must work to salvage. Not a few of the short story writers heeded this advice, for despite the large number of poems and critical articles on poetry, the magazine also published many stories, at least half of which deal with traditional African society.

By turning to the African hinterland the involved writer could do his cultural probing in a less Europeanized setting than the urban slums.

Henrique Guerra provided three stories of a bucolic Africa in painful conflict with the transformations brought about by the coming of the European. João Abel, in his "O tocador de quissange" (The Finger Piano Player), presents the figure of the traditional *griot* who documents, through the retelling of legends, the history of his people. And Benúdia, pen name of Mário Guerra, brother of Henrique, uses the same storytelling figure as lyrical seer and prophet in the story "O tocador e o vento" (The Player and the Wind). Benúdia's reworking of African legends stands in marked contrast to Castro Soromenho's fatalistic depiction of tribal societies locked in their primal, static condition. Avoiding Soromenho's condescending compassion toward the unfortunate native, Benúdia, in "O menino e os caçadores" (The Boy and the Hunters), presents an image of the proud, self-reliant African. Members of the hunter clan hold sacred their obligation to the people, and the boy accepts initiation into the brotherhood with Spartan dignity. The narrator says, "Yes, the lad would be a good hunter. A hunter dedicated to hard work and sacrifice. Men struggling to sustain men. Oh, to be the people's hunter!"[4] This story, and many like it, brings the concern with an African presence to the level of myth building and socialist-realist glorification of a communal spirit.

The incipient literary movement documented in *Mensagem* and *Cultura* inspired healthy, and some not so constructive, polemic as Angolan writers progressed toward an authentic poetry and prose fiction. How this process manifested itself in Angolan creative writing is our concern in the next two chapters.

CHAPTER 4

Toward a Poetry
of Angola

At the height of its literary activity, from about 1951 to 1961, Angola's young generation struggled with the problem of poetry *in* versus poetry *of* Angola, the latter being naturally their goal as a sign of regional maturity and a readiness to take their legitimate place among other autochthonous literatures. Intellectuals such as António Cardoso inclined toward a condemnation of the Angolan's slavish imitation of European literary forms, and in his already mentioned editorial note he confronted the problem when he wrote that the situation is confused and perplexing since anyone can confer on himself the honorific title of Angolan poet or call his poems Angolan poetry.[1] Cardoso rejected the versifier who exploited African themes for the facile, exotic image. The genuinely concerned poet has often had enough difficulty in controlling his own emotionalism, which in some cases degenerates into mawkishness, without the exotic falsification of the poet-exploiter in his picturesque cover-up for a lack of talent and, perhaps more importantly, for a lack of sincerity. In both Angola and Mozambique it has been relatively easy for a person with literary pretensions to attach himself to a budding movement in the hope of gaining some small recognition. While native-born and/or raised Angolans (or Mozambicans) may be guilty of this falsification, most often it is the metropolitan Portuguese who, in rapidly seeking to establish his identity with the cultural environment, falls into the trap of picturesqueness.

Even without the intrusions of the opportunists the committed Angolan poet has a number of problems as he attempts to define his identity as an artist who writes in Portuguese while seeking to confirm his new sense of Africanness. Some of the urban poets, particularly the black and *mestiço* ones, have manifested a feeling of inadequacy resulting from either their lack or their superficial knowledge of an African language. This feeling goes hand in hand with a nagging desire to cultivate, somehow, their non-Western literary heritage in its original form. Thus, we can understand Agostinho Neto's sentiments when he laments the exclusion of traditional Angolan poetry from an anthology compiled by the Casa dos Estudantes do Império (Student Empire House).[2] These misgivings about their roles as authentic interpreters of an Angolan reality did not, however, deter poets such as Neto from their essential direction as Lusophone contributors to an African literature.

Mário António sought to dispel the dilemma by stating in his "Considerações sobre poesia" that the poetry he was referring to had nothing to do with the traditional poetry of the peoples of Angola; and he went on to describe this poetry as being socially contained and serving social ends.[3] In António's view, the new poetry of Angola uses a European technique and style to express an Angolan reality. António may do well to belabor the obvious at a time when there existed a climate of perplexity around the poetry of Angola, but his remarks also betray his own feelings of ambivalence. When, for example, he praises the thoroughly European, though Angolan-born, poet Cochat Osório, whom he calls a *poeta adulto*, he reveals a sense of intimidation of the aesthetic absolute contained in the monolith of European poetry. Osório may be a passable poet and he may even belong to what might someday be called an Angolan literature, but to label him an "adult poet" seems a gratuitous concession to the degree to which he falls outside of the mainstream of Angolan literature. As I seek to demonstrate in my analysis of Mário António's poetry, the question of poet as poet and as Angolan poet creates some curious and often pleasing thematic and stylistic effects in António's writing. Meanwhile, it can be said that the traditional poetry of the peoples of Angola cannot be revived by the young intellectuals in any other than a thematic, stylistic, and philosophical way since oral literature ceases to be such once it is written down. But to the extent that the oral tradition can be preserved in Lusophone writing, both António and Neto have succeeded in incorporating elements of this tradition into their poetry; António, in fact, has included several Kimbundu-language poems, based on traditional elements, in his most recent collection.

In Angola the intellectual elite did show an interest in collecting and documenting traditional poetry and stories. Angola was fortunate in having had early and disciplined collectors such as Cordeiro da Matta and Héli Chatelain; however, it was another missionary, Carlos Estermann, who did more than collect and record. This Catholic priest, who has spent most of his life among the peoples of southwest Angola, applied methods of literary criticism to the oral traditions he collected. He gathered samples of poetry, not just the usual fables and riddles, and subjected them to a stylistic analysis. The most striking examples of traditional Angolan poetry appear in the first of his three-volume work *Etnografia do sudoeste de Angola* (Ethnography of Southwest Angola, 1958). In his chapter on oral literature Estermann transcribes epic and lyric poetry of the Cuanhama people. About a poem called "A Song to the Rain" he says that a literal rendering would be impossible because the metaphorical allusions present difficulties for the Western mentality. He takes as an example the Cuanhama word *haisikoti*, which in the poem refers to a driving rain. Literally, the word means a road that has been trampled by cattle's beating hoofs. Then, in a translation-interpretation of the hymn to the rain he reveals the poem's structure of interlocking metaphors and personifications.

In the same study Estermann transcribes and interprets an

encomiastic poem composed in memory of Mandume, the last independent chief of the Cuanhamas. He also offers this four-line stanza announcing the death of a warrior:

(Cuanhama) Haulamba wa Nangobe alele talili,
     Simbungu alele takwena,
     Haulamba alele tawalele!
     Omukwetu umwe ineuya.[4]

(Portuguese) O bicho esfomeado de Nangove (nome poético
     da hiena) passou a noite a "chorar,"
     A hiena uivou toda a noite,
     O bicho esfomeado berrou durante a noite!
     Um companheiro nosso não regressou.

(The famished creature Nangove (poetic name for hyena) spent the night "crying,"/the hyena howled all night,/The famished creature cried out during the night!/A comrade did not return.)

The liquid sound of the Cuanhama syllables *lili* and *lele* are lost in translation, but in Portuguese as well as in English the elegy's use of subtly modified repetition in successive lines and of metonymy and a poetic name for the hyena offers an aesthetic flow that seems at once familiar and foreign to the Westerner. As in the case of the folklore of other African peoples the hyena occupies an important place in Cuanhama folklore. In fables the stupid hyena usually finds himself outwitted by the clever jackal, but in the delicately worded elegy the commonly despised scavenger's mournful howl of hunger becomes doleful crying for the lost comrade.

 The 1962 anthology *Poetas angolanos* (Angolan Poets) includes, in an appendix to the Lusophone selections, a sampling of the Cuanhama poetry as well as poems in Umbundu and Kimbundu, and consciously or unconsciously this traditional African poetry has worked its influence on a few of the members of the new generation.

An earlier anthology, the one which Neto considered uncharacteristic because it lacked traditional poetry, appeared in 1959 in mimeograph form, a limited edition of the Student Empire House in Lisbon. Even earlier, in 1950, the Cultural Department of the Association of the Native Sons of Angola issued a modest anthology, *Antologia dos novos poetas de Angola* (Anthology of Angola's New Poets), which the organizers called poor in format and appearance but rich in feeling. Carlos Ervedosa organized and Mário António prefaced the 1959 anthology published by the Student Empire House entitled *Antologia de poetas angolanos* (Anthology of Angolan Poets), while Alfredo Margarido wrote the introduction for the 1962 version of essentially the same collection. Yet another collection, *Antologia poética angolana* (Anthology of Angolan Poetry)—this one organized by Garibaldino de Andrade and Leonel Cosme of the Imbondeiro series—appeared in 1963.[5]

These anthologies heralded the coming-of-age of a contemporary Angolan literature as compilers sought the form and structure of the phenomenon by bringing together poems scattered throughout journals and newspapers. Inevitably, much overlapping occurs from anthology to anthology because of the relatively small number of poets and poems. And after 1961, the forced or voluntary exile of many of the key figures in the movement, notably Agostinho Neto, Mário de Andrade, António Jacinto, António Cardoso, and Viriato da Cruz, retarded the development of poetry of Angola.

From this period have come enough poets to warrant a consideration of the nucleus of representative writers as well as an appraisal of directions and themes. Cultural and social convergences have determined a predictably limited number of themes and stylistic approaches, but it is with these themes and the manner in which they are represented that we now concern ourselves. In adopting this thematic approach I acknowledge a similar method employed by Mário de Andrade in his poetry anthology of African literature of Portuguese expression.

Evocation and Invocation

Rare indeed is the modern Angolan poet who has not raised his or her voice to invoke the land, or Mother Africa, or even, in incantatory tones, black men of the world. Alda Lara, the white poet from the city of Benguela, depicts the image of black Mother and black Africa in "Presença africana" (African Presence), a poem in which she affirms herself as the "sister-woman" and telluric offspring of the land:

> E apesar de tudo,
> ainda sou a mesma!
> Livre e esguia,
> filha eterna de quanta rebeldia
> me sagrou.
> Mãe-África!
> Mãe forte da floresta e do deserto,
> ainda sou,
> a Irmã-Mulher
> de tudo o que em ti vibra
> puro e incerto . . .[6]

(And despite all,/I am still the same!/Free and lean,/eternal daughter of all the rebelliousness/consecrated to me./Mother-Africa!/Strong Mother of the forest and desert./I am still/the Sister-Woman/of all that, which pure and uncertain,/pulsates in you . . .)

Alda Lara continues in this rather devotional tone in lines that describe nature, cities, and then the children with swollen bellies, who represent Africa's suffering masses. So the poet encompasses all in her constancy and in her identification with the land. She employs the evocatory cry that appears so frequently in the contemporary poetry of Angola: "Minha terra . . ./Minha, eternamente . . ." (My land . . ./Mine, eternally . . .). She remains unchanged in her devotion to a land she has felt in its purely African essence, and in the poem "Noite" (Night) she uses the image of languid African nights made sad because white children have grown up to forget the stories told to them by black nursemaids.

Alda Lara's brother, Ernesto Lara Filho, in his poem "Pergunta (para meu pai)" (Question (for my Father)), also praises the land as a second-generation white Angolan. The old settler father, after many years in Benguela, has not forgotten his native Minho in Portugal. But the poet's question to his father is a pledge of filial devotion to Angola:

> Porque
> Meu Pai
> Me negas o direito simples
> de amar a minha terra
> A minha Angola[7]

(Why/My Father/Do you deny me the simple right/to love my land/My Angola?)

In many of the invocatory poems the repeated cry of "my land" or "the land is mine" underscores the subtheme of a symbolic return to the true essence of Angola. Amílcar Barca's poem, appropriately entitled "Minha terra" (My Land), ends each of its four stanzas with variations on the line "Minha terra, minha terra . . ./que a terra é tua . . ./A terra é tua, a terra é minha, a terra é nossa"[8] (My land, my land . . ./because the land is yours . . ./The land is yours, the land is mine, the land is ours). And the entire poem carries a tone of vehemence in reclaiming Angola. Accompanying the idea of a return to the land is the motif of freedom in an Angola represented by its flora and fauna. Alda Lara sings of palm trees and broad savannahs, and in his poem Barca wants to share the land with the free-flying birds.

Other poets sing of the land and contrast the idea of open space with the confinement of civilized existence. António Cardoso's "Combóio de Malange" (Malange Train) tells of his being trapped in the drudgery of his office listening to the distant train that "arfa/grande/e/livre/quando passa"[9] (panting/big/and/free/ when it passes). The train symbolizes, as it heads from Luanda toward the interior, the freedom of movement across the vast land that Cardoso invokes when he hears, in the chugging of the engine, "minha terra, minha terra, minha terra." At least two other poets employ the train's rhythmic sound and sometimes stuttering but always relentless progress. António Jacinto's "Castigo pro combóio malandro" (Punishment for the Roguish Train) pictures the old train that carries carloads of peasants from the interior villages to work in the city and hordes of contract laborers on the first leg of their long journey to the plantations of São Tomé. Jacinto portrays the mechanized contraption as an element of an imposed system, and the engine throws off sparks that burn the farmer's corn. When the train derails, the African farmer only pretends to help to put it back on the tracks:

> Comboio malandro
> você vai ver só o castigo
> vai dormir mesmo no meio do caminho.[10]

(Roguish train/you know what your punishment is goin' to be?/you will sleep right here in the middle of the line.)

The failure of the train permits the African to turn a mischievous trick on the civilized contraption, personified as a figure of social disruption, and this, in a sense, represents the depiction of a land violated. Agostinho Neto's "Combóio africano" (African Train) uses the same metaphor for similar purposes:

> Um combóio
> subindo de difícil vale africano
> chia que chia
> lento e caricato.
>
> Grita e grita
>
> quem esforçou não perdeu
> mas ainda não ganhou
>
> Muitas vidas
> ensoparam a terra
> onde assentou os rails

e se esmagam sob o peso da máquina
e no barulho da terceira classe.[11]

(A train/laboring up an African valley/hissing and hissing/slow
and grotesque//It screams and screams//he who has tried has
not lost/but neither has he won.//Many lives/have soaked the
earth/where it laid its rails/and these are crushed under the
engine's weight/and in the noise of third class.)

Jacinto's contrast of the mechanical creature and the violated
land comes out in Neto's poem, but Neto also identifies the image
of the slow, grotesque train with an implied idea of slow but constant struggle and a people's tragic but indomitable spirit in the
aphoristic lines: "he who has tried has not lost/but neither has
he won."

Inevitably, some Angolan poets glorify Africa in Whitmanesque tones with a touch of tropical sensuousness. Tomás Jorge,
the son of Tomaz Vieira da Cruz, wrote in 1949 the poem
"Manga, manguinha" (Mango, Little Mango), which has a
declamatory style about it in its celebration of Africa:

> A manga é um símbolo d'África:
> No seu sabor
> No seu aroma
> Na sua cor
> Na sua forma.
>
> A manga tem o feitio do coração!
> A África também.
> Tem um sabor forte, quente e doce!
> A África também.
> Tem um tom rubro-moreno
> Como os poentes e as queimadas
> Da minha terra apaixonada.[12]

(The mango is a symbol of Africa;/In its flavor/In its aroma/In
its color/In its form.//The mango is heart-shaped!/So is Africa./
It has a strong, hot, sweet taste!/So does Africa./It has a red-
brown hue/Like the sunsets and brush fires/Of my passionate
land.)

The poem does not so much summon as it celebrates the land, but in its celebration of Africa lies the spirit of glorification that comes as an ingredient of incantation. Tomás Jorge uses another floral emblem, this time specifically symbolic of Angola, in his 1955 poem "Welvitchia Mirabilis." As in the mango poem he depends on certain imagistic contrivances to capture the Angolan landscape on which the unique plant grows:

> Welvitchia Mirabilis
> Planta angolense
> Carnuda e verde
> Molusco exilado
> De oceanos desconhecidos
> Para o oceano sempre endurecido
> De ondas feitas por dunas.
>   (p. 68)

(Welvitchia Mirabilis/Angolan plant/Green and fleshy/Exiled mollusk/from unknown oceans/To the always hardened ocean/of waves made by dunes.)

Much of the poetry that invokes the land mystifies in images that suggest passion, heat, enigma, and antiquity. The geographic invocational-type poem receives sober incantatory treatment in Mário António's 1962 "Viagem à terra natal" (Return to the Native Land), and the title recalls Aimé Césaire's "Retour au pays natal," and, indeed, so does the spirit of the poem in its portrayal of the idea of ancestral origins:

> A terra é antiga—seu relevo o diz:
> O tempo passou com seu afago
> Sobre a lomba dos montes.[13]

(The land is ancient—her outline shows it:/Time has caressed/the rise of her hills.)

From these sensitive, topographic images António turns, in the poem's second section, to the remembrance of childhood in nostalgic and wistful communion with the ancient land which has become lost in the distance of his memories. In another of his poems António, as part of an early regionalist phase of his art, joins many of his fellow Angolan writers in the cultivated sentiment of evocative nostalgia. "Noites de luar no morro da Maianga" (Moonlit Nights on Maianga Hill) describes times of childish innocence when the familiar scenes and sounds of street vendors, courting couples, and guitars mingled with the hum of human tragedy perceived in retrospect by the adult.

Behind the evocation of bygone days lies the romantic escapism, back to childhood as the concerned elite tries to grasp realities and fantasies that have slipped away. Mário António takes a poetic excursion back into time in his "Fuga para a infância" (Flight into Childhood), and Luandino Vieira asks in his "Canção para Launda" (Song for Luanda), "Onde está Luanda?" (Where is Luanda?) In his mind Vieira reassembles fragmented images of the fisherwoman Rosa, the greengrocer Maria, and Zefa, the mulatto woman in her brightly colored African robes. This, Vieira proclaims, is the Luanda he seeks.[14]

Aires d'Almeida Santos's "Meu amor da Rua Onze" (My Eleventh Street Love) summons the past through the theme of adolescent love. For the Angolan, and particularly those from Santos's city of Benguela, the end of a childhood romance means, in a larger context, the termination of a pleasant creole existence:

> E agora
> Tudo acabou.
> Terminou
> Nosso romance.[15]

(And now/It's all over./It has ended/Our romance.)

This poem and others by the same author present the theme of the end of childhood joys, and though this smacks of nineteenth-century Romanticism, the image of the graceful, bronze girl of Eleventh Street conveys a more socially potent theme of adult disillusionment in a world of harsh confrontations. Along with this romantic escapism comes the symbolism of a ripe African or creole world, represented in another of Santos's poems by the sycamore tree. "A mulemba secou" (The Sycamore Has Withered) describes nostalgia and disillusionment as the poet savors the African word *mulemba*. Other poets would use words like *imbondeiro* (the baobab tree) to integrate their personal lyricism into the general regionalist mainstream of a literature of identity.

These poems represent only a small sampling of the evocatory and invocatory themes as they developed in this period of Angolan writing. But these same themes appear in conjunction with others that express the Angolan's need for regional identity.

Identity, Fraternity, and Alienation

Poets of the "Let's Discover Angola" generation extolled the land in their insistence on and search for identity. Like their counterparts in Mozambique, Cape Verde, and São Tomé they made ample use of the invocation of the land personified in a Mother Africa symbol; or a female relative, such as the African grandmother of a *mestiço*, may serve as a poetic point of contact with a lost identity. And this identity with an archetypal female lies at the core of African ancestralism.

One of Mário António's early poems, written when he was only sixteen or seventeen, demonstrates a feeling common among the *mestiço* writers of the distance that separates them from black Angola. His "Avó negra" (Black Grandmother) combines this sense of a vague yearning for the knowledge of ancestral origins with an equally indistinct longing for the recent past:

> Avòzinha, às vezes,
> Ouço vozes
> Que te segredam saudades
> Da tua velha sanzala
> Da cubata onde nasceste
> Das algazarras dos óbitos
> Das tentadoras mentiras do quimbanda
> Dos sonhos do alembamento
> Que supunhas merecer.

E penso que
Se pudesses
Talvez revivesses
As velhas tradições.[16]

(Little grandmother, sometimes/I hear voices/That whisper
yearningly/Of your old village/Of the hut where you were born/
Of the clamor of burial rites/Of the tempting lies of the witch
doctor/Of the dreams of the bride-price/That you knew you
deserved.//And I think/If you could/Maybe you would relive/
The old traditions.)

The poet strains to overhear voices that whisper secrets to his
grandmother, for although he identifies with an African past,
through her, he feels alienated from that reality.

The poetic persona's cautious or even detached identity in
Mário António's poem may be symptomatic of the attitude of the
mestiço, as artistically represented by the evoked images, toward
his identification with a purely African heritage, or it may be an
individual, intimist treatment of the larger question of what constitutes Angolanness. Despite inherent ambivalent attitudes toward
identity, the direct celebration of the black mother or grandmother often appears in Angolan poetry as a symbol of hope in
the future. Viriato da Cruz's "Mamã negra," subtitled "Canto da
esperança" (Song of Hope), finds all humanity represented in the
fecund, embracing warmth of the black earth-mother.

Some poets share their identity with all other members of their
generation. White Angolans, through their identification with the
land of birth or adoption, reach out to understand the African's
humanity. And again Alda Lara's spiritual humanism leads her
to bridge the racial chasm in such poems as "Presságio" (Omen),
which she dedicates to a black friend. She pledges her solidarity
to the point of martyrdom:

poderás ver-me caminhar ao longe . . .
vestida de silêncios e lírios.

com a libertação a coalhar
no fundo dos martírios . . .

E não me reconhecerás . . .[17]

(You will see me walking far off . . ./dressed in lilies and
silence,/with deliverance clotting/in the depths of martyr-
doms . . .//And you will not recognize me . . .)

The black friend will not recognize her in the purity of her new
and complete identity as a spiritual emanation of Africa. With
this spiritual and idealistic identity comes the pledge of fraternity
in Alda Lara's poem "Rumo" (Direction):

E' tempo companheiro!
Caminhemos . . .
Longe, a Terra chama por nós,
e ninguém resiste à voz
da Terra! . . .

Nela,
o mesmo sol ardente nos queimou
a mesma lua triste nos acariciou,
e se tu és negro,
e eu sou branca,
a mesma Terra nos gerou!
(p. 92)

(It is time, comrade!/Let us go together . . ./Far off, the Land
calls to us,/and no one can resist the voice/of the Land! . . .//
On Her,/the same scalding sun has burned us/the same sad moon
has caressed us/and if you are black,/and I am white,/the same
Land has engendered us!)

The poet conceives of a spiritual, abstract, and even far-off land
in her idealization of the union of identity between the black
Angolan and the white Angolan.

White Angolan poets, because of historical and social circumstances, must, in all their idealism, approach the question of
racial fraternity from a perspective different from that of the

black or *mestiço* Angolan. Attempts to bridge the gap by reverting to a time when distinctions were less prone to social and economic pressures account for the many poems that recall the carefree days of childhood when camaraderie transcended race. Ernesto Lara Filho wrote several poems that carry this camaraderie into adulthood, but almost bizarrely so in his identification with the *musseque* experience. By adopting or emulating a black life style the white poet takes on a bohemian identity. Thus Lara's 1952 poem "Sinceridade" (Sincerity), because of its racial and social juxtapositions, can be read as flamboyant exoticism, curious and naive identification, or gross insincerity:

> Sou sincero
> Eu gostava de ser negro
> Gostava de ser um Joe Louis, um Louis Armstrong,
> um Harrison Dillard, um Jess Owens,
> um Leopold Senghor, um Aimé Césaire, um Diopp
> gostava de ritmar
> de dançar como um negro.
>
> Sou sincero
> Eu gostava de ser negro
> vivendo no Harlem,
> nas plantações do Sul
> trabalhando nas minas do Rand,
> cantando ao luar da Massangarala
> ou nas favelas da Baía:
>
> Eu gostava de ser negro.
>
> E sou sincero . . .[18]

(I am sincere/I would like to be black/I would like to be a Joe Louis, a Louis Armstrong,/a Harrison Dillard, a Jess Owens,/a Leopold Senghor, an Aimé Césaire, a Diopp/I'd like to make rhythm/to dance like a black man.//I am sincere/I would like to be black/living in Harlem,/on the plantations of the South/ working in the Rand mines,/singing in the Massangarala moonlight/or in the slums of Bahia.//I would like to be black.//And I am sincere . . .)

By identifying with black American athletes and musicians, and with French-speaking proponents of négritude, and particularly through his desire to have "black" rhythm, Lara enters into an area of frivolity and stereotyped attitudes. But his insistence on his sincerity contains not only shock value and naïveté; it indicates a primal desire to participate in the glorification of a life force and a lyricism associated with the black man. The poet's wish to share the black man's arduous toil constitutes an exaltation of the degradation of the antebellum plantation and the South African gold mine, while on the other hand, he seeks to embrace the totality of the "black man's being in the world," which suggests to us, then, that the poem should be read in the context of alienation from the white world of Angola. And, indeed, Lara himself adopted a *musseque* life style, which, though it may represent vicariousness and social marginality for some, possibly reflects a more extreme psychological reaction by a white *filho da terra* to the precariousness of Angola's cultural reality.

For the black poet camaraderie comes through traditionally shared values sustained by a sense of belonging to an extended African family in which one member, notwithstanding his personal social status or level of education, carries the same stigmas and speaks in the same cadences as his less Europeanized brother. This last stanza from Agostinho Neto's "Mussunda amigo" (Mussunda Friend) illustrates a spirit of oneness:

> Os corações batem ritmos
> de noites fogueirentas
> os pés dançam sobre palcos
> de místicas tropicais
> os sons não se apagam dos ouvidos.
>
> O i-ó kalunga ua mu bangela . . .
> Nós somos![19]

(Our hearts beat rhythms/of fiery nights/our feet dance on stages/of tropical mysticism/the sounds do not die in our ears.// O i-ó kalunga ua mu bangela . . .//We are!)

The Kimbundu line has an incantatory quality and the stanza itself has a rising oratorical tone in its anaphora of *os-de-os-de* (in the English rendition, our-of-our-of). The repetition and the tropical, mystical, atavistic memories shared by the poet and his friend Mussunda surrealistically obliterate all reality that exists outside of their affirmation of solidarity and self. Most Angolan fraternity poems depict the poet facing the future with determination while remembering the good times of the past. "Mussunda amigo" begins with Neto's pledge of constancy:

> Para aqui estou eu
> Mussunda amigo
> Para aqui estou eu.
>
> Contigo.
> Com a firme vitória da tua alegria
> e da tua consciência.
>
> —o ió kalunga ua mu bangele!
> o ió kalunga ua mu bangele-le-lélé . . .

(I am here/Mussunda friend/I am here.//With you./With the firm victory of your joy/and of your conscience.//—you whom the god of death has made!/you whom the god of death has made, has made . . .)

The Kimbundu refrain, which comes from a children's game, carries both an evocation of the past and a vow of fidelity to a companion who is wrapped in a mantle of fatalistic mystery that places Mussunda on an almost abstract level of the collective conscience. And the slightly cabalistic tone of the poems adds to the mystery of Mussunda as a stabilized communal conscience, as suggested in the lines "Com a firme vitória da tua alegria/e da tua consciência." The poet in his search for identity comes back to this stable force and the Kimbundu refrain acts as a kind of code within the poem.

On the personal level the intimacy of the poet's and Mussunda's relationship comes through in their mutual social consciousness represented in images from the past:

Lembras-te?
Da tristeza daqueles tempos
em que íamos
comprar mangas
e lastimar o destino
das mulheres da Funda,
dos nossos desesperos
e das nuvens dos nossos olhos
Lembras-te?
(p. 11)

(Do you remember?/The sadness of those times/when we would go/buy mangoes/and lament the fate/of the women of Funda,/ our wailing chants,/our despair/and the haze that covered our eyes/Do you remember?)

The interrogative reminiscing frames realistic images and exhorts their mutual rage and complaint.

The social complaint relates in many Angolan poems to a feeling of alienation. Alienation from childhood means alienation from roots. António Jacinto's "Poema de alienação" (Poem of Alienation) emphasizes the frustration of cultural alienation and the duality of racial identification reflected in a search for artistic authenticity:

Não é este ainda o meu poema
o poema da minha alma e do meu sangue
não
Eu ainda não sei nem penso escrever o meu poema
o grande poema que sinto já circular em mim.[20]

(This is not yet my poem/the poem of my soul and of my blood/ no/I am not yet able nor do I know how to write my poem/the great poem I feel flowing within me.)

Then, in the poem's last stanza, which contains some of the best-known lines in Angolan poetry, Jacinto describes the white Angolan's black-white identity crisis:

Mas o meu poema não é fatalista
o meu poema é um poema que já quer
e já sabe
o meu poema sou eu-branco
montado em mim-preto
a cavalgar pela vida.
                                    (p. 44)

(But my poem is not fatalistic/my poem is a poem that already
wants/and already knows/my poem is I-white/mounted on me-
black/galloping through life.)

Even with the statement of purpose of the great poem that flows
in him the poet's declaration of identification keeps the perspective of racial alienation in order by means of the metaphor of the
white rider and black mount. This presentation of the dilemma of
cultural and racial duality graphically captures the idea of two
destinies bound to each other, even while one dominates the other.

António Cardoso's "Alienação" (Alienation) resembles Jacinto's
"Poema de alienação" in theme and style:

Estes são os versos da minha alienação
e do ódio e da razão
Que outros homens criaram
em mim.
No entanto,
no fundo seco dos meus olhos
ainda moram crianças loiras e negras
cantando uma qualquer canção de roda infantil![21]

(These are the lines of my alienation/and of the hatred and of
the reason/That other men have created/in me./But,/in the dry
depths of my eyes/still dwell black and blond children/singing
one of their childish songs!)

Cardoso's poem depicts the duality of racial animosities determined by society and of racial harmony personified in children
oblivious to each other's color.

Costa Andrade deals with the same dilemma of alienation

fostered by society in "Poema." In this love poem the black woman Chissola symbolizes an Angola separated from itself by agonizing barriers erected by unfeeling social circumstances. To poeticize this dilemma Andrade proceeds from a "geometric" image of Chissola identified with the angular line of the Huambo River. The deep blue of the water and the acacia trees in bloom help to create a vivid image of the timeless land. Timelessness is more specifically stated in the lines "longos caminhos quentes sob as acácias em flor/percorre a vida já vivida"[22] (long, hot paths under the acacias in bloom/traveled by lives already lived). The problem of racial barriers and socially unacceptable romantic liaisons emerges to this imagistic surface in the poem's next stanza:

> Que resta da ternura
> de chamar-te minha
> sem o embargo da proibição latente
> de cor? sem mil dedos de conluio
> poderoso? sem teorias longínquas
> contrariadas na prática
> incongruente?
>
> Que resta amor? da voz que te chamou:
> Amor! . . . Amor! . . .
> (p. 98)

(What remains of that tenderness/in calling you mine/without the hindrance of latent prohibitions/of color? without a thousand fingers in powerful/collusion? without distant theories/contradicted incongruously/in practice?//What remains love? of the voice that called you:/Love! . . . Love! . . .)

Andrade's use of adjectives becomes somewhat overbearing when he analyzes theories controverted by practice in his attempt to demystify the cult of miscegenation by casting it in a mold of non-erotic love. The repetition "Amor! . . . Amor! . . . Amor! . . ." suggests an echo, and the poet asks what remains of the voice of love and then goes on to make a reversal: "Eco sem voz" (Voiceless echo). The reversal fortifies the sense of mythologies that reverberate emptily:

> indecisão agriloada
> criada por condições impostas
> na sombra de mil tramas
> ancestrais.
> "A lei proíbe distinções!"
> (pp. 98–99)

(shackled indecision/created by imposed conditions/in the shadow of a thousand ancestral/plots./"The law prohibits distinctions!")

Returning to the personal level the poet faces the barriers that separate him from Chissola and assesses the dilemma of his alienation:

> Chamar-te: Amor! . . . Chissola! . . .
> Chissola! . . . e não poder fazê-lo
>   que me não crês
>   porque me julgas
>   apenas branco
> e fazê-lo
>   gritando aos brancos
>   que sou diferente, que sou Angola
> Chissola! florimos juntos sob as acácias
>
> Oh! drama do branco nascido em África!
> (p. 99)

(To call you: Love! . . . Chissola! . . ./Chissola! . . . and to be unable to do so/because you do not believe me/because you judge me/only as a white man/and to do so/shouting to the whites/that I am different, that I am Angola/Chissola! we blossomed together under the acacias//Oh! drama of the white man born in Africa!)

The complaint that he loves and not merely lusts, the defiant confirmation of his Angolanness, and the identification with the black woman in earthy oneness all convey the feeling of the alienation the Angolan poets of this generation sought to express, and overcome.

In balladlike, where are they now? reminiscences Jacinto's "O grande desafio" (The Big Match) recalls individual members of a childhood soccer team and their separate paths in adult life. As in Costa Andrade's poem, alienation reflects the artificiality of imposed conditions that define racial and socioeconomic distinctions as the team members grow up; and trite though it may be, the metaphor of the loss of teamwork does bear the message of the poet's concern.

The breakdown in real or imagined racial harmony symbolized by the rift between childhood friends has even more poignancy in those poems that express the black's or *mestiço*'s identity dilemma. Costa Andrade, using the psychological factors of his own racially mixed background, focuses on the cultural ambivalences of the *mestiço* in his poem "Mulato." Although he may derive succor from the concept of the eugenic, cosmic "man of the future," his final message calls for a leveling of distinctions:

> Nasci igual a uma mensagem
> com raízes em todos os continentes . . .
>
> Fizeram-me capaz de amar
> e de criar
> carregaram-me os ombros
> de certezas
> e deram-me a coragem de transpor
> impedimentos.
>
> Mas sou apenas Homem.
>
> Igual a ti irmão de todas as europas
> e a ti irmão que transpareces
> as áfricas futuras.[23]

(I was born equal to a message/with roots in all continents . . .// They made me capable of loving/and of creating/they burdened my shoulders/with certainties/and gave me the courage to overcome/obstacles.//But I am just a Man.//Equal to you brother of all the europes/and to you brother who reveals/future africas.)

The idea of the new human types who will overcome has meaning in direct relation to the idea of a feeling of cultural alienation that stems from the underlying belief in the *mestiço* as an individual caught between two opposing worlds.

The theme of romanticized racial mixture appears in such poems as Tomás Jorge's "Poema híbrido" (Hybrid Poem) which proclaims universality in "racial eclecticism."[24] But the realities of the *mestiço*, no matter how romanticized, contain a note of defensiveness. On the intellectual and artistic levels black, white, and *mestiço filhos da terra* display a common sense of alienation even as they struggle to crystallize their shared sense of Angolanness. The white poet sympathizes, understands, and, as we have seen, even attempts to identify with the most extreme aspects of the problem of race. From the relatively secure psychological perspective of his ambivalent situation the *mestiço* evokes and sometimes insists on his African heritage. The black poet feels the direct line of his African heritage in such a way that the road traveled from a not so distant "primitivism" to Europeanized "respectability" cannot help but arouse contradictory sentiments within him as he gropes for an Angolan expression.

Agostinho Neto uses an African ancestral technique in several of his poems to measure the distance journeyed from the *sanzala* (village) to the Western world by black children who, for the idealistic black intellectual, represent the future of the race as a result of a progress measured by their European education. Thus, there exists a basic contradiction in glorifying an African ancestralism and believing in a future predicated on the degree of a success measured unavoidably by European standards. This contradiction explains some of the artistic tension apparent in Neto's poems. In his small volume *Quatro poemas* (Four Poems, 1957) the third poem portrays the fundamental tension between "what we are" (or were) and "what we shall become":

> Minha mãe
>   (as mães negras cujos filhos
> partiram)

tu me ensinaste a esperar
como esperaste paciente nas horas difíceis

Mas em mim
a vida matou essa mística esperança

Eu não espero
sou aquele por quem se espera

A Esperança somos nós
os teus filhos
partidos para uma fé que alimenta a vida

Nós as crianças nuas das sanzalas do mato
os garotos sem-escola a jogar bola de trapos
nos areais ao meio dia
nós somos
os contratados a queimar vidas nos cafèzais
os homens negros ignorantes
que devem respeitar o branco
e temer o rico
somos os teus filhos dos bairros de pretos
além aonde não chega a luz eléctrica
os homens bêbedos a cair
abandonados ao ritmo dum batuque de morte
teus filhos
com fome
com sêde
com vergonha de te chamarmos mãe
com medo dos homens

Somos nós
a esperança em busca de vida.[25]

(My Mother/(the black mothers whose sons/have left)/you taught me to hope/as you patiently hoped during difficult hours//But in me/life has killed that mystic hope//I do not hope/I am he for whom there is hope//We are Hope/we, your children/departed toward a faith that nourishes life//We the naked babies of the forest villages/the no-school children playing with a rag ball/on the sand lots at noon/yes, we/those contracted to burn away our lives in the coffee groves/the ignorant black men/who should respect the white man/and fear the rich man/ we are your children from the black quarters/beyond where no electric lights reach/drunken men falling/given up to the *batuque* of death/your children/in hunger/in thirst/in the shame of calling you mother/in fear of crossing the street/in fear of men//We are/ hope in search of life.)

Neto assuages his realistic images of protest with a poetic technique of rapid association that takes the child from the village to the degradations of the black adult's existence to the abstract expression of fear, specifically of the black man's disorientation among men brought about, of course, by deculturation and oppression. The poet achieves a tension of language in the last stanza, "a esperanca em busca de vida," which succinctly and poetically states the crux of the dilemma: alienation from self and the search for direction. The Portuguese verb *esperar* can mean both "to hope" and "to wait," and Neto effectively plays on this double designation to convey the attitude of the African waiting at the brink of hope. Conversely, the poet does not hope or wait ("Eu não espero/sou aquele por quem se espera"); he embodies hope and personifies the African in his patient wait. But now, without the mysticism of his mother, he embraces a defiant hope that has superseded waiting.

In a similar poem, "Um aniversário" (A Birthday), Neto uses a backdrop of a troubled world to capture an African family's pride when one of their children graduates as a medical doctor. The last stanza offers the tension of contrast between a pungent African nostalgia and the cultural mulatto's European confinement:

> Este um dia do meu aniversário
> um dos nossos dias
> sabendo a tamarindo
> em que nada dizemos nada fazemos nada sofremos
> como tributo à nossa escravidão.
> (*Quatro poemas*, p. 8)

(On this my birthday/one of our days/tasting of tamarind/when we say nothing do nothing suffer nothing/as a tribute to our bondage.)

An aesthetic tension emanates from the positive use of the idea of a heritage of bondage on a day of communal oneness when all partake of the pungent taste of shared success. The silent, motionless, painless communion subverts the alienation of a people through the strength of shared experience. In this form Neto and other Angolan poets of his generation succeeded in combining identity, fraternity, and alienation on an artistic and philosophical plane that gives aesthetic appeal to their social, committed poetry. And many of these poets, in an awareness of the total function of their art, applied, along with their counterparts elsewhere, new and often iconoclastic techniques to the Portuguese language in order to effect a neo-African poetry.

The Sounds, Rhythm, and Spirit of Angola

Gerald Moser wrote that in Afro-Portuguese literature, "both in verse and prose, linguistic identification with the territorial environment is consciously pursued by the repeated evocation of certain familiar trees, foods, animals, or even climatic peculiarities, as well as a way of life, be it life in the slums of Luanda or life as seen in the villages, or life as it used to be lived back in one's childhood."[26] Intoning exotic-sounding words may indeed be the poet's or novelist's way of affirming his identification with the land, and those who depend on this technique may do so as catharsis or as a facile means of converting the European language of their regionalist work into something more authentically African. Bessa Victor, for example, employs words such as *ngoma* and *zabumba* (both being types of African drums) for exotic effect. The younger poets use similar words, but more judiciously and in a more integrated manner within the unity of a poem that eschews picturesque window dressing in its serious attempts at creating a new style.

Viriato da Cruz's ballad "Makèzu" (Kola Nut) uses Kimbundu

street cries—"Kuakie! . . . Makèzu, Makèzu"—and black Portuguese phrases in a dialogue between two ancient street vendors as they lament the passing of the old days when people believed in the magical force of the kola nut. But it is in another of Cruz's narrative poems, "Sô Santo" (Mr. Santo), that we see the fruition of his efforts to combine story with rhythm for an authentic Angolan expression. The poem tells the story of Sô Santo who has come on hard times after being a swain, the godfather of many children, and a respected landowner in one of the *musseques*. When he walks down the street a small boy asks his grandmother why everybody greets Sô Santo with such respect; and the poet uses a musical rhythm and irregular rhyme, both at the end of lines and internally, to connect the jaunty stroll to the flow of the grandmother's story:

> —Sô Santo teve riqueza . . .
> Dono de musseques e mais musseques . . .
> Padrinho de moleques e mais moleques . . .
> Macho de amantes e mais amantes,
> Beça-nganas bonitas
> Que cantam pelas rebitas:

> > "Muari-ngana Santo
> > dim-dom
> > Ual'o banda ó calaçala
> > dim-dom
> > chaluto mu muzumbo
> > dim-dom . . .²⁷

(Mr. Santo had wealth . . ./Owner of *musseques* and more *musseques* . . ./Godfather of *moleques* and more *moleques*/A man of lovers and more lovers./Pretty women/Who sing in their *rebitas*://Sô Santo/dim-dom/there he goes up the street/dim-dom/with a cigar between his lips/dim-dom.)

Moleque, a Kimbundu word, means "child," and its repetition in "moleques e mais moleques" is an augmentative technique often used in oral literature to emphasize quantity or extension by other than the less poetic "muitos muleques," for example. The entire poem derives its rhythmic structure from the *rebita*, a popular Angolan dance form. The use of Kimbundu in the *rebita* refrain sung by the *beça-nganas* fits into the spirit of an African world wherein Sô Santo's downfall may be the result of his having been abandoned by Sandu, a Kimbundu spiritual being. And Cruz goes on to suggest that Sô Santo, in this respect, represents the destiny of a people. The question of the African's lot, embellished by folk tradition and the rhythm of popular music, has obviously more importance than the exotic evoking of place names. In the final lines of the poem the conjecture about Sô Santo's fate follows him as he walks, significantly, *down* the street he used to walk *up*: "Ele é o símbolo da Raça/ou vingança de Sandu . . ." (He is the symbol of the Race/or the vengeance of Sandu . . .).

António Jacinto adorns his "Poema de alienação," already referred to a few pages back, with vendor's cries, sometimes prolonging a vowel to simulate a trailing off in sound: for example, "ma limonje ma limonjééé" and "ji ferrera ji ferrerééé . . ." (p. 42). Jacinto's preoccupation with sound results in the use of onomatopoeic words such as these from a stevedore's work song: "tué tué tué trr/arrimbuim puim puim" (p. 43). And in the same poem he issues forth the socially loaded word, with its last phoneme drawn out for effect, "monamgambééé." A form of *monamgamba*, the word means, in the context of the poem, a contract worker, and it serves as the title for another poem by Jacinto. "Poema de alienação" asks questions about who toils without fair recompense and under harsh conditions. The questions are directed abstractly to the birds, the winding stream, and the prairie wind; and the birds, the stream, and the wind answer back "monamgambééé," as the poet savors the word in its social and individual context.

In this same vein of African sounds Agostinho Neto's poetry reveals a high degree of sensitivity toward musical rhythm patterns. In a poem consisting of six tercets the syllabic rhythm varies only slightly in the third line of the second stanza; and the

syllable count in each strophe is 5-5-4, except for the second stanza
with its 5-5-3:

> Caminho do mato
> caminho da gente
> gente cansada
> Óóó-oh!
>
> Caminho do mato
> caminho do soba
> soba grande
> Óóó-oh![28]

(The forest path/the people's path/tired people/Óóó-oh!//The
forest path/the chief's path/the great chief/Óóó-oh!)

The regular beat ($-'-'/-'-'/'-'$) and the short lines quicken the
pace to simulate movement along the forest path. But the rhythm
and the lines also suggest a rapid drum beat broken regularly by
the refrain "Óóó-oh," which, in effect, serves as a drum roll.

With regard to beat, Lilyan Kesteloot has analyzed Léopold
Senghor's poetic style and its dependence on African and American jazz rhythms.[29] Janheinz Jahn added to Kesteloot's study of
Senghor's dance-step rhythm by using numbers to denote phonemic repetitions in several poems.[30] Agostinho Neto, as well as
other Afro-Portuguese poets, have read and were influenced by
Senghor, Damas, and Césaire in their attempts to effect an African stylistic technique. In Neto's poem "Caminho do mato," cited
above, the repetition of the syllable *ca* and the predominance of
certain sounds reinforce the steady beat, while in their variations
they give the effect of shifting drum patterns.

Neto uses anaphora, alliteration, and simple repetition of
word, phrase, and image, as well as lines of varying length in his
poem "Fogo e ritmo" (Fire and Rhythm); the title itself connotes
the fervor and feel of movement by means of the synesthetic
combination of heat and rhythm:

> Sons de grilhetas nas estradas
> cantos de pássaros

sob a verdura húmida das florestas
frescura na sinfonia adocicada
dos coqueirais
fogo
fogo no capim
fogo sobre o quente das chapas do Cayette.

Caminhos longos
cheios de gente cheios de gente
cheios de gente
em êxodo de toda a parte
caminhos largos para os horizontes fechados
mas caminhos
caminhos abertos para cima
da impossibilidade dos braços.

Fogueiras
     dança
       tantam
         ritmo

Ritmo na luz
ritmo na cor
ritmo no som
ritmo no movimento
ritmo nas gretas sangrentas dos pés descalços
ritmo nas unhas descarnadas
mas ritmo
ritmo.

Ó vozes dolorosas de África![31]

(Sounds of shackles on the roads/songs of birds/under the humid
green of the forests/freshness in the sweetened symphony/of the
coconut palm/fire/fire in the grass/fire over the heat of the
Cayette plains//Broad paths/full of people full of people/full of
people/in exodus from everywhere/broad paths toward closed
horizons/nonetheless paths/paths open above and beyond/the
impossibility of the reach//Bonfires/dance/tom tom/rhythm//
Rhythm in the light/rhythm in the color/rhythm in the sound/
rhythm in the movement/rhythm in the bloody fissures of bare

feet/rhythm in the fleshless nails/but rhythm/rhythm.//Oh doleful voices of Africa!)

Whether or not Neto accomplishes the effects of sound and movement he strives for, he does, both in the poem's rhythm and in its graphic composition, establish an ascending beat that goes from the slower, longer lines of the first two stanzas, to the one-word lines of the third (with a graphic stairlike effect that culminates in the musically suggestive word *ritmo*), to the quickened tempo of the fourth stanza with its anaphora of "ritmo." The rhythm of the stanza is rapid, but the syllabic patterns give the impression of off-beat phrasing, which Richard Alan Waterman describes as characteristic of African music, whereby "the beat is, so to speak, temporarily suspended, i.e., delayed or advanced in melodic execution, sometimes for single notes (syncopation), sometimes for long series of notes."[32] The poem's final line carries a plaintive, exalted tone, and rhythmically serves to slow down and then end the crescendo with a sound akin to a drum roll.

Lilyan Kesteloot considers Senghor's poetic style to be distinguished by "son rythme et la longuer de son verset—le temps d'une respiration—qui donnent à ses poèmes le mouvement monotone des vagues de la mer"[33] (his rhythm and the length of his line—the duration of a breath—that give his poems the monotonous movement of ocean waves). In "As terras sentidas" (The Grieved Lands) polysyllabic words in long lines and the prevalence of sibilant sounds create a mood of melancholy accompanied by a distant but persistent drum cadence:

As terras sentidas de África
nos ais chorosos do antigo e do novo escravo
no suor aviltante do batuque impuro
de outros mares
sentidos

As terras sentidas de África
na sensação infame do perfume estonteante da flor
esmagada na floresta
pela imoralidade do ferro e do fogo
as terras sentidas

As terras sentidas de África
no sonho logo desfeito em tinidos de chaves carcereiras
e no riso sufocado e na voz vitoriosa dos lamentos
das terras sentidas de África.
Vivas
em si e conosco vivas

(*Poemas*, p. 27)

(The grieved lands of Africa/in the tearful moans of the old and new slave/in the degrading sweat of the impure *batuque*/of other seas/grieved//The grieved lands of Africa/in the infamous sensation of the heady perfume of the flowers/crushed in the forests/ by the immorality of iron and fire/the grieved lands//The grieved lands of Africa/in the dream soon undone in the jingling of jailer's keys/and in the stifled laugh and the victorious voice of laments/and in the unconscious glow of hidden sensations/of the grieved lands of Africa/Alive/in themselves and alive with us.)

Again Neto employs words with a double meaning. As an adjective *sentidas* means grieved, but the verb *sentir* (to feel) has a past participle *sentido* (felt), of which *sentidas* is the feminine plural when used as an adjective. Thus, the African feels or perceives his land in an almost incantatory way. The poet clearly intends this shifting meaning of the word when he uses *sentidas* in the first line of the second stanza and then *sensações* (sensations) in the second line. And, of course, the use of the word *vivas*, in the third stanza, fortifies the designation of "felt" or "perceived."

The English rendition of the poem above does not capture the effect of the Portuguese sibilants, some voiced, others unvoiced, and some harsh in their "sh" sound. Another of Neto's poems, however, retains in translation some of the effect of sound because of the phonemic similarity between the Portuguese *criar* and the English "create":

Criar criar
criar no espírito criar no músuculo criar no nervo

criar no homem criar na massa
criar
criar com os olhos secos
(*Poemas*, p. 32)

(Create create/create in the spirit create in the muscle create in the nerves/create in the man create in the mass/create/create with dry eyes/)

The verb *criar*, in its repetition throughout the poem, combines meaning, connotation, and sound to express Neto's purpose of turning the negative into the positive. The final admonition, to create with dry eyes, signifies the resurrection of a people and their development of a line of progressive solidarity. Neto uses the exhortation to proceed in the task of rebuilding with dry eyes in several other of his poems, including "O choro de África" (The Tears of Africa) in which he suggests that centuries of weeping have come to an end:

Nós temos em nossas mãos outras vidas e alegrias
desmentidas nos lamentos falsos de suas bocas—por nós!
E amor
e os olhos secos.
(*Poemas*, p. 32)

(We hold in our hands other lives and joys/disavowed in the false laments of their mouths—by us!/And love/and dry eyes.)

Neto does not demonstrate "black rage"; instead he exudes a quiet anger in poems of melancholy and lamentation. His poem "Aspiração" (Yearning) picks up the mood of the African's secular suffering, which he elaborates in "O choro de África," but with a black-man-of-the-world commiseration and protest:

Ainda o meu canto dolente
e a minha tristeza
no Congo, na Geórgia, no Amazonas.

Ainda
o meu sonho de batuques em noites de luar.

Ainda os meus braços
ainda os meus olhos
ainda os meus gritos

(*Poemas*, p. 35)

(Still my mournful chant/and my sadness/in the Congo, in Georgia, in the Amazon.//Still/my dream of *batuques* on moonlit nights.//Still my arms/still my eyes/still my cries/)

The adverb *ainda* (still) emphasizes through its repetition and nasal quality the sense of continued, prolonged suffering and oppression.

Another Angolan poet, Manuel Lima, has consciously tried to simulate dance rhythms, particularly in his poem "América," which has a jazz or boogiewoogie beat:

Mas quando chegares a New Orleans
olha para os meus dentes teclas
de jazz
minhas pernas múltiplas
de jazz
minha cólera ébria
de jazz,
olha os mercadores da minha pele,
olha os matadores ianques
pedindo-me
jazz,
one
two
three

jazz,
sobre o meu sangue
jazz,
milhões de palmas para mim
jazz.[34]

(But when you get to New Orleans/look at my piano key teeth/ of jazz,/my multiple legs/of jazz,/my drunken fury/of jazz,/look at the merchants of my flesh/look at the Yankee killers/asking me for/jazz,/one/two/three//jazz,/over my blood/jazz/millions of palms beat for me/jazz.)

Lima effects grotesqueness and caricature in his images and rhythm, but his efforts are a rather belated response to the techniques of the Harlem Renaissance poets, particularly Countee Cullen and Langston Hughes.

A more serene attempt at African musicality is Mário António's 1961 poem "O tocador de dicanza" (The *Dicanza* Player). The *dicanza* is a long, hollow gourd which the player scrapes with a short stick. By alternating dentals and bilabials and the high front vowel "i" with the low back vowel "a," he captures the high and low tones of the African musical instrument:

> Será monótono o ritmo da dicanza?
> Toca, ó tocador, tua música estranha!
> Burdona o teu bordão bordões ecoando
> Ora em estrídulo grito, ora em afago brando.[35]

(Can the rhythm of the *dicanza* be monotonous?/Play, oh player, your music mysterious!/Bass-ing your bass echoing basses/Now in strident screech, now in soft caresses.)

One important aspect of a poetry that conveys the sounds, rhythm, and spirit of Africa is that of social awareness and political protest. For the Angolan writer the sense of négritude contained in awareness and protest was a step toward defying Lusotropicology.

From Cultural Nationalism to Combative Verse

In the late 1950s toward the end of the period of the most intensive literary activity in Angola, and particularly during those years immediately before and after the armed nationalist revolt, poetry became increasingly more "committed" in theme and representation. Regionalism and cultural nationalism stemmed from a growing social consciousness and *consciencialização* (process of self-awareness) among postwar Angolan intellectuals. The

evocation of childhood innocence and ancestral rites, the invocation of Mother Africa, the insistence on African cultural values,
and the exposure of the oppression of the black masses carried
an undeniable note of protest that would grow in intensity as
the fateful year of 1961 approached.

The narrative, often balladlike technique espoused by *engagé*
poets has several significant ramifications in the total context of
Angolan literary expression. First, it demonstrates a desire to
make social statements by means of a progression that avoids
obscurity. Secondly, the poet most likely sees this form as an
approximation of an African oral, storytelling tradition, and
thirdly, this structure permits a dramatic effect.

Between 1947 and 1950 Viriato da Cruz, thought by some to
be the initiator of the nationalist literary movement, wrote such
poems as "Serão de menino" (Child's Evening Entertainment)
and "Rimance da menina de roça" (Ballad of the Farm Girl).
The first two scene-setting stanzas of "Serão de menino" make a
subtle statement of acculturation:

> Na noite morna, escura de breu,
> enquanto na vasta sanzala do céu
> de volta de estrelas, quais fogareiras
> os anjos escutam parábolas de santos . . .
>
> na noite de breu,
> ao quente da voz
> de suas avós,
> meninos se encantam
> de contos bantus . . .[36]

(On the tepid night, black as pitch,/while in the vast village of
the sky/around the fiery stars,/angels hear parables about the
saints . . .//on the pitch black night,//to the warmth/of their
grandmothers' voices,/children sit charmed/by Bantu tales . . .)

The poet, rather than rejecting them, incorporates European
religious myths into the fabric of an African institution wherein
the old transmit cultural and moral values to the young through
the telling of ageless legends.

In spite of Viriato's role as supposed initiator of cultural nationalism in Angolan letters his poetry—all or most of which was written before the more rebellious stage of cultural and political awareness in Portuguese Africa—has none of the outspoken protest of the poetry composed later by other committed writers. Much of this later, explicitly pamphletary poetry, while usually sincere in its intent, is overburdened by rhetoric and clichés that diminish its artistic value. This is particularly true of the combative verse, even though it represents only a tiny part of what can be considered Angola's period of awareness. More common are poems that reveal and protest in exalted tones against the black man's historical condition, and in this regard Angolan poets differ little from those in other Afro-Portuguese regions or indeed from black writers anywhere. Vindication as a prelude to confrontation poetry saw Angolan writers treating such subjects as slavery and its legacy.

Alexandre Dáskalos, like other sympathetic white poets, expresses his consternation at the horrors of slavery's legacy in the poem "A sombra das galeras" (The Shadow of the Sailing Ships): "Oh! Angola, Angola, os teus filhos escravos/nas galeras correram as rotas do Mundo"[37] (Oh! Angola, Angola, your children slaves/ have traveled the World in sailing ships). The exaltation and the exploitation occasion images of inhumanity and grotesqueness inherent in the Atlantic slave crossings, and these images recall the romantic, nineteenth-century abolitionist poetry of the Brazilian Castro Alves who gained fame for such works as "O navio negreiro" (The Slave Ship). Dáskalos reaches Castro Alves's bombastic heights in his "A sombra das galeras":

> Escravo! Escravo!
>
> O mar irado, a morte, a fome,
> A vida . . . a terra . . . o lar . . . tudo distante.
> De tão distante tudo tão presente, presente
> como na floresta à noite, ao longe, o brilho
> duma fogueira acesa, ardendo no teu corpo
> que de tão sentido, já não sente.
>
> (p. 56)

(Slave! Slave!//The angry sea, death, hunger,/Life . . . land . . . home . . . all distant./But all so present though distant, present/as in the forest at night, far off, the glow/of a bonfire, burning in your body/which having felt so much, no longer feels.)

Differences in poetic conventions and diction, and a distinct historical stance, separate twentieth-century Angolan poets, like Dáskalos, from nineteenth-century abolitionist poets. Looking back in time, however, the contemporary poet can measure the present by the past and thus poeticize new evils created by old horrors.

Black and *mestiço* Angolan poets, no less than their white compatriots, speak of shackles, chains, and the terrors of the ocean crossing when describing the oppression of the slaves' heirs. But for some of the black and *mestiço* poets the implicit protest often carries more force than the shocking but conventional images. Manuel Lima, for example, rages in his poem "América" against the hypocrisy of the United States where slaves toiled on southern plantations. Lima, in the same poem, mentions several southern states and repeats the words *Ku Klux Klan*, all as a pretext to increase the intensity of his protest. But when he deals with Africa in his poetry he comes closer to originality in the images he creates and to a more subtle turn of meaning. When, in a poem called "África," he declares his land to be without name and without men, he exhibits a subtle use of inverse negativism as he leads up to the final stanza in which he says that the story of the archetypal African has to be told in the flames, plantations, *batuques*, chains, and slave ships that await him.[38] Despite the overworked images, the idea of the African constantly being born into his legacy has a more dramatic effectiveness than the fixed point in the present that looks back into history.

The problem of realizing a socially oriented poetry while maintaining a lyrical soliloquy obviously concerned Agostinho Neto when he wrote his poem "O choro de África." He incorporates the theme of the "cry of centuries" into a personal poetic statement:

Sempre o choro mesmo na nossa alegria imortal
meu irmão Nguxi e amigo Mussunda
no círculo das violências
mesmo na magia poderosa da terra
e da vida jorrante das fontes e de toda a parte e de todas
    as almas

e das hemorragias dos ritmos das feridas de África
e mesmo na morte do sangue ao contacto com o chão
mesmo no florir aromatizado da floresta
mesmo na folha
no fruto
na agilidade da zebra
na secura do deserto
na harmonia das correntes ou no sossego dos lagos
mesmo na beleza do trabalho construtivo dos homens

o choro de séculos
inventado na servidão
em histórias de dramas negros almas brancas preguiças
e espíritos infantis de África
as mentiras choros verdadeiros nas suas bocas.
                                    (*Poemas*, pp. 30–31)

(Always the cry even in our immortal joy/my brother Nguxi
and friend Mussunda/in the circle of violence/even in the powerful magic of the land/and of life gushing from the springs and
from everywhere and from all our souls/and from the hemor-
rhages of the rhythms of the wounds of Africa/and even in the
death of blood in contact with the earth/even in the aromatic
blossoming of the forest/even in the leaf/in the fruit/in the
zebra's agility/in the desert's aridity/in the harmony of the currents or in the calm of the lakes/even in the beauty of men's constructive work//the cry of centuries/invented in servitude/in
stories of black dramas white souls indolences/and infantile spirits
of Africa/falsehoods are real cries in their mouths.)

Neto uses the motif of camaraderie and familial oneness in this
poem just as he does in "Mussunda amigo." He also employs his
favorite devices of asyndeton, parataxis, and polysyndeton to

enhance the accumulative, magical images; in fact, he comes close to the surrealistic language of Aimé Césaire in his metaphors (for example, "hemorragias dos ritmos das feridas de África"). Despite the glaring, often flamboyant imagery, Neto's message of protest remains inference because of the aesthetic appeal of his words.

In their identification with the suffering of their brothers Neto and other Angolan poets cultivated the theme of the contract worker in several poems. Mário de Andrade's Kimbundu-language poem "Muimbu ua Sabalu" (Sabalu's Song), apparently the only poetry Andrade ever published, has become a minor classic among the poems that lament the plight of the contract worker. Presumably based on an anonymous Kimbundu lament, the poem tells of the sorrow of an African family whose son has gone to São Tomé:

> Nosso filho caçula
> Mandaram-no p'ra S. Tomé
> Não tinha documentos
> Aiué!
>
> Nosso filho chorou
> Mamã enloqueceu
> Aiué!
> Mandaram-no p'ra S. Tomé[39]

(Our youngest son/They sent him to S. Tomé/He had no papers/Aiué!//Our son cried/Mamma raved/Aiué!/They sent him to S. Tomé)

The second line of the first stanza, "mandaram-no p'ra S. Tomé," is the refrain for all the other stanzas except the fifth. *Aiué* is a Kimbundu interjection of distress, and in all but the first and fifth stanzas it precedes the refrain line. In this way the lament maintains an appropriate repetitious monotony while the variations on the young man's fate and the family's reaction give the poem a basic note of protest. For example, the reference to the fact that the youngest son had no papers means that the "uncivilized" or semi-assimilated African was constantly in danger of being pressed into forced labor if he lacked official documents and was unable to prove gainful employment.

Andrade's poem is a lament, however, and makes no pretense of violent protest against an oppressive institution in Portuguese Africa. And, as a matter of fact, the sadness of departing and the melancholy of prolonged absence would act as compelling elements in the Angolan poets' treatment of contract labor just as it would for the Cape Verdeans. Arnaldo Santos's poem "Contratados" (Contract Laborers) emphasizes the dislocation of the laborer and the distance he must travel:

> Vinham ao longe
> Aglutinados
> Baforada de sussurros no horizonte
> Como ressonâncias fundas de uma força.
>
> Força que é penhor de gemidos
> De levas passadas
> Que arrastaram pobres.
>
> Vinham ao longe
> Em conversas vagas
> Na tarde baixa ressonando dobres.[40]

(They came on afar/Agglutinated/Gust of murmurs on the horizon/Like deep resonances of a force.//A force that is the pawn of moans/Of past recruitments/That dragged off the poor.//They came on afar/In indistinct dialogue/On that lowering afternoon trickling knells.)

Santos's hushed and delicate imagery creates a picture of an anonymous, enigmatic group silently passing as other equally anonymous groups have passed before it. Aural imagery in the whispered sounds is captured by onomatopoeic words such as *baforada*, *sussurros*, *ressonâncias*, and *ressonando*, which all contribute to the sense of a debilitated force.

In a poem that also does not make a direct statement of protest, António Cardoso uses an approach similar to Andrade's Kimbundu lament. Cardoso's "Saudade é onça" (Yearning Is a Jaguar) has a popular, narrative point of view in which a villager tells of his experiences as a contract laborer, among other things, and his longing for a woman left behind during his forced wanderings:

> Fui monangamba, fui no contrato,
> Não custou nada, não me doía,
> Mas onça danada no meu coração,
> A saudade de lá não saía.[41]

(I was a *monangamba*, went on the contract,/Did not bother me, I did not mind,/But that damned jaguar in my heart,/The yearning would not go away.)

The Kimbundu word *monangamba* (*mona-ngamba*) has come to mean porter or stevedore, but by extension it can be applied to a man who does odd jobs. Because of his unstable economic situation the *monangamba* would frequently find himself the victim of police raids, which were a pretext for recruiting cheap labor for the plantations.[42] So the word has social and political connotations, and in a sense it became a symbol of oppression, while in a poetic context it offered, both in meaning and in its euphonious quality, a sentimentalized identification with the dispossessed African. Cardoso's poem humanizes the anonymous *monangamba* who, though resigned to his fate as a contract laborer, expresses his love sentiments with the felicitous jaguar metaphor.

The rural migration to the cities and the contract emigration to São Tomé strongly touched the urban Angolan poets, but they also found ample subject matter for their cultural nationalist and protest art in the black *musseque* existence. António Cardoso wrote social ballads about *musseque*-dwellers, such as this poem about "Sarita":

> Sarita mora no musseque,
> sofre no musseque,
> mas passeia garrida na baixa
> toda vermelha e azul,
> toda sorriso branco de marfim,

e os brancos ficam a olhar,
perdidos no seu olhar.
Sarita usa brincos amarelos de lata
penteado de deusa egípcia
andar de gazela no mato,
desce à cidade
e sorri para toda a gente.
Depois, às seis e meia,
Sarita vai viver pró musseque
com os brancos perdidos no seu olhar![43]

(Sarita lives in the *musseque*,/she suffers in the *musseque*,/but downtown she promenades/all red and blue,/all ivory white smile,/and the whites stop to look,/taken by her look,/Sarita wears yellow tin earrings/the hairdo of an Egyptian goddess/her gait is that of the wild gazelle./She goes down to the city/and smiles at the people./Then, at six-thirty,/Sarita goes back to the *musseque* to live/with the whites lost in her gaze!)

In the first line Cardoso uses the verb *mora* which properly means "dwells"; in the next to the last line he uses *viver* which connotes "to live" in the sense of "to pursue existence." By means of this sort of contrast he flaunts *musseque* life in the face of the European lower city. Sarita's bright colors and cheap, garrish earrings adorn the enigma of an Egyptian goddess as the *musseque* girl moves gracefully through the urban crowds. And the whites are lost in her countenance ("perdidos no seu olhar"), but when she returns to her *musseque* she banishes the lower city from her eyes ("com os brancos pedidos no seu olhar!"). This glorification of the *musseque*-dweller fits into a natural pattern of cultural nationalism, and the occasional touches of satire and irony attempt to destroy the arrogance of the white lower city.

Ernesto Lara Filho combines nostalgia and audacity in his two small collections *O canto do martrindinde* (The Song of the Martrindinde, 1963) and *Seripipi na gaiola* (Seripipi in the Cage, 1970). Lara's praise of the *musseque* has a note of social protest, and his introduction to the first volume of poetry offers a quote from Frantz Fanon's *Les damnés de la terre* (*The Wretched of the Earth*, original, 1961; translation, 1963) which is an explicit protest against colonialism. It deals with Fanon's assessment of the "native" writer's awareness which causes him to reject his assimilation into colonialist society; and Fanon calls the third and final stage of this evolution the "fighting phase."[44] Understandably, *O canto do martrindinde* was "withdrawn from circulation," as the authorities euphemistically put it. But Lara's poetic flirtation with the idea of a black proletarian social awareness is tempered with exoticism, and he remains on the periphery of a "fighting phase."

After the armed revolt of 1961 the voices of the great majority of committed Angolan writers were either subdued or silenced. Some continued to write and publish under the vigilant eye of the censor, and a few who had fled into exile expressed their anger and resolve in poetry and prose that was both combative and independent. Chief among the poets is Agostinho Neto who, along with others in a similar situation, gives some credence to the statement made by the editors of *Modern Poetry from Africa* that "much of the poetry from Portuguese Africa is little more than a cry of sheer agony and loss."[45] It is hoped that it has already been shown that such is not entirely the case. In fact, even in Neto's most doctrinal poems he does not lose sight of the fact that he is a poet, for poetry at the service of a cause also has to give aesthetic depth to meaning.

Neto dedicates the poem "O içar da bandeira" (The Hoisting of the Flag) to the heroes of the Angolan people, and the first few lines read:

> A coragem dos soldados
> os suspiros dos poetas
> Tudo todos tentavam erguer bem alto
> acima da lembrança dos heróis
> Ngola Kiluanji
> Rainha Ginga
> Todos tentavam erguer bem alto
> a bandeira da independência.[46]

(The soldiers' courage/the poets' sighs/Everything, and all sought to raise on high/higher than the memory of the heroes/Ngola Kiluanji/Queen Ginga/All tried to raise on high/the banner of independence.)

This poem represents the closest Neto would come to pure independence rhetoric. True to a technique he had already established in his earlier stage he uses the sentimentality of fraternity and camaraderie, as was seen in the poem "Mussunda amigo." In "O içar da bandeira," the allusion to friends and comrades comes in the context of the dispersal of those who symbolize the hope and strength of a new Angola. The poet brings together heroes of the past and present. A reference in the same poem to Liceu (Carlos Vieira Dias), founder of the musical group Ngola Ritmos, helps to enforce the nostalgia of returning to the land:

> Quando voltei
> as casuarinas tinham desaparecido da cidade
>
> E também tu
> Amigo Liceu
> voz consoladora dos ritmos quentes da farra
> nas noites dos sábados infalíveis.
>
> Também tu
> harmonia sagrada e ancestral
> ressuscitada nos aromas sagrados do Ngola Ritmos.
> (p. 104)

(When I returned/the casuarina flowers had disappeared from the city// And you too/Friend Liceu/consoling voice of the hot rhythms of our sprees/on infallible Saturday nights.//You too/ sacred and ancestral harmony/resuscitated in the sacred aromas of the Ngola Ritmos.)

Neto demonstrates, in this poem, his penchant for strong images and for using such devices as synesthesia, the latter specifically in "aromas sagrados do Ngola Ritmos" (sacred aromas of the Ngola Ritmos). But the poem itself is a personal message; the outsider can safely assume, however, that Liceu is not there when the poet returns, and the fact of his absence gains more emotional force for those who know that he is a political prisoner, or was when the poem was written.

Much of the poetry of this phase has to be seen more strictly from the standpoint of the persons for whom it was intended, and although many would object that art should have a universal appeal that transcends time and place, the historical moment and circumstance, as well as the listening, viewing, or reading public, can and do determine the historical validity of a given work or works. In this regard, the poets of this combative-independence phase elaborate certain themes, which, although they presuppose an ideological sympathy on the reader's part, do have a place in the development of Angolan literature.

Several of Neto's poems deal with the return to an Angola redeemed. The committed Angolan wants to return not only to an independent country, but also to the authentic traditions of the people. In "Havemos de voltar" (We Are to Return), Neto writes:

à frescura da mulemba
às nossas tradições
aos ritmos e às fogueiras
havemos de voltar

à marimba e ao quissange
ao nosso carnaval
havemos de voltar.
(p. 136)

(to the freshness of the *mulemba* tree/to our traditions/to the rhythms and to the bonfires/we are to return//to the marimba and the *kissange*/to our carnival/we are to return.)

Earlier in this chapter I referred to Aires d'Almeida Santos's poem "A mulemba secou" (The Sycamore Withered), which was interpreted as a symbol of the passing of a way of life. Neto's poem, which marks the return of the native sons of Angola to the freshness of the sycamore and to their carnival, takes up the fallen banner of the initial phase of contemporary Angolan literature. Unfortunately this signifies a retrogression in the search for the proper framework and ambient in which to develop a more profound literary expression. The combative phase represents, then, a hiatus, albeit a necessary one, in the development of Angolan literary expression; but even so the poetry and prose of this phase represent a valid part of the total phenomenon.

Inevitably, the rhetoric and clichés of an independence movement would occasion the slogan-type poem, such as António Jacinto's "O povo foi na guerra" (The People Went to War) in which a wife says of her husband:

> Kaianga foi na guerra Kaianga foi na guerra
> não sei se vai voltar.
>
> O povo foi na guerra o povo foi na guerra
> Eu sei: o povo vai voltar.[47]

(Kaianga went off to war Kaianga went off to war/I do not know if he will return.// The people went off to war the people went off to war/I know: the people will return.)

Moving from the individual and personal to the collective and patriotic the poet accomplishes his parallelistic effect.

Costa Andrade, perhaps the most aggressive of the combative poets, nevertheless seeks to cultivate effective poetic language in his "Canto de acusação" (Song of Accusation) which angrily accuses the world of having ignored the armed conflict that erupted in northern Angola on February 4, 1961:

> Há sobre a terra 50.000 mortos que ninguém chorou
>   sobre a terra
>   insepultos
>   50.000 mortos
> que ninguém chorou
> Mil Guernicas e a palavra dos pincéis de
>   Orozco e do Siqueiros

do tamanho do mar este silêncio
espalhado sobre a terra

    Como se as chuvas chovessem sangue
    como se os cabelos rudes fossem
       capim de muitos metros
    como se as bocas condenassem
    no preciso instante das suas 50.000 mortes
    todos os vivos da terra

Há sobre a terra 50.000 mortos
que ninguém chorou

ninguém . . .

As Mães de Angola
    cairam com seus filhos[48]

(There are on the land 50,000 dead that no one mourned/On the land/unburied/50,000 dead/that no one mourned/A thousand Guernicas and the word of the brushes of/Orozco and Siqueiros/a silence as broad as the sea/spread over the land//As if the rains had rained blood/as if the rough hair were/many meters of grass/as if the mouths condemned/at the precise moment of their 50,000 deaths,/all of the living of the land//There are on the land 50,000 dead/that no one mourned//no one . . .//The Mothers of Angola/fell with their children)

This is the "poema quarto" (fourth poem) of a three-part work that begins with "poema terceiro" (third poem). Perhaps Andrade begins with a third poem in keeping with Mário de Andrade's assertion that this is the third and political phase of Angolan poetry.[49] Political and revolutionary slogans are eventually replaced by others and the time-honored rhetoric, such as "morrer de pé pela liberdade" (to die standing tall for freedom) which Costa Andrade uses in "poema terceiro," may serve a purpose purely as a slogan but it detracts, in its hackneyed nature, noble though its sentiment may be, from the poem's political and artistic intent. Still, in "poema quarto" Costa Andrade does show that he can use politically pregnant images with a dramatic and aesthetic intensity. The metaphor of the sea of silence effectively enhances the theme of the world's indifference before the holocaust of the war in a sort of universal conscience-jogging, such as Picasso's painting *Guernica* was meant to bring about.

Most of the writers directly involved in the liberation struggle ceased to write altogether, some perhaps for lack of time and others because they were, in exile, removed from the sources of their artistic motivation. A few poets who remained in Angola or in other areas under Portuguese rule continued to write cryptic protest verse or produce works for the desk drawer. Tomás Jorge, for example, has an unpublished volume of poems called "Tala-mungongo" which contains a number of poems he wrote since 1961, as well as some earlier ones. Jorge witnessed the events of 1961 (specifically, the attempt to free political prisoners from a Luanda prison) and their aftermath, and he himself fell victim to the widespread arrests carried out in Angola at the time. After his short stay in a Luanda jail he composed what he calls "prisoner" poems which combine his personal feelings of desolation with a universal call for peace and harmony. In the third of these poems he uses an extended metaphor of a ship to convey the prisoner's isolation, and he makes a comment on freedom that could be construed as a call for independence:

> E o coração timoneiro
> Que bate teima e se comove
> Negando ser ilha morta
> Em cada peito
> Em cada romeiro da Liberdade![50]

(And the helmsman heart/That beats persists and stirs with emotion/Refusing to be a dead island/In each breast/In each pilgrim of Freedom!)

In his poem "Força" (Force) Jorge exhorts, on the primordial premise that if someone takes something from you you are entitled to use force to get it back; he makes his verse forceful with short, direct, imageless lines, an excessive use of the nasal *ão*, and the repetition of the word *força*. The poem concludes with the following lines:

> Para abrires
> A mão
> Do ladrão
> Cria força
> Tens de ter força.
> (p. 27)

(To open/The hand/Of the thief/Gain force/You must have force.)

Despite the suggestion that the Angolans must use force to wrest their lost freedom from the hand of the oppressor, Jorge more often emerges as a conciliatory rather than a combative poet. His poem "Ressurreição" (Resurrection) resurrects, so to speak, the old but perennial theme in Angolan poetry of racial harmony in the best of all possible worlds. Jorge writes, using the metaphor of swords being turned into plowshares, about what will happen after the napalm and the killing:

> Depois de tudo isto
> Ainda pode ser que
> As catanas se cruzem em parada
> Empunhadas por braços vários
> Com as charruas
> E outras máquinas de trabalho
> Numa Ode à Fraternidade!
> (p. 29)

(After all this/It may yet be that/The *catanas* will be crossed at rest/Held by different hands/Along with the plows/And other work implements/In an Ode to Brotherhood!)

The *catana*, a kind of machete used by the poorly armed Angolan rebels, has come to be viewed as a symbol of what is popularly called the "terrorist" movement.

The effectiveness of Jorge's more militant poetry is weakened because he lacks a sense of rage and utters no cry of agony.

Continuity, Verticality, and the Poet Mário António

Tomás Jorge, who presently lives in Lisbon, continues to write and plans to publish both old and new poems. He is one of a small number of poets who keep alive, to a greater or lesser degree, the literary current that started in the 1940s, ran full in the 1950s, and trickled into a rather stagnant pool in the 1960s. Along the way a sort of bifurcation has taken place whereby those writing sporadically and hastily from exile are the continuation of the current's mainstream that flows from a source of nationalist inspiration. António Jacinto, from his jail cell in Tarrafal on the Island of Santiago in Cape Verde, sends a poetic message to his wife telling about his return:

> Iremos, amor
> dizer-lhes
> voltei e voltamos
> porque nos amamos
> e amamos
> as sepulturas sem fim dos homens sem fim.[51]

(We shall go, love,/and tell them/I have returned and we have returned/because we love each other/and we love/the endless graves of the endless men.)

This stanza from "Poema de amor" (Love Poem) attempts to convey sentiments of nationalism, of love of humanity, and of the ethereal moment of romantic, familial, and celestial love. As an epigraph to his poem Jacinto quotes the famous Chilean poet Pablo Neruda on altruistic love; that the Angolan should turn to Neruda for "inspiration" indicates that not only do they share similar political attitudes, but also that Jacinto probably admires this poet of recognized artistic genius. In other words, Jacinto belongs to a group of Angolan poets who are concerned about both the aesthetics and the social utility of their work.

Some of the poets interested in "poetic" poetry constitute a second current in Angolan literature. Personal lyricism has existed in Angolan poetry, of course, since the beginning of the "Let's Discover Angola" movement. Arnaldo Santos's small book of poetry, *Fuga* (Flight, 1960) contains verse that lyricizes the landscape in the area of Uíge where he lived during the late fifties. A lyrical tropicalism characterizes the poem "Uíge":

> Um sonho vesperal me torna
> Sonolento
> E traz-me o peso enorme das montanhas
> Azuis
> Como céus profundos.
>
> E esse abraço de terra, húmus e sonho
> Como meditando na distância
> Ergue mansamente a mão fechada
> E escurece o sol
> Que vai morrer.
>
> Irá assim para lá da noite . . .
>
> E de repente
> O instinto azul da serra estende-se solene
> E esmaga as luzes da cidade.
>
> Na minha mão
> Fica uma cova de sombra . . .[52]

(A vesperal reverie grips me/With somnolence/And brings to me the enormous weight of the mountains/As blue/As deep skies.// And that embrace of land, humus, and dream/As if meditating in the distance/The hand meekly rises/Blotting out/The dying sun.//Thus it will sink to beyond the night . . .//And suddenly/The mountain range's blue instinct solemnly extends/And crushes the city lights.//In my hand/Remains a hollow of shadow . . .)

Arnaldo Santos's mood poems of delicate images transmit a tropical lethargy and African melancholy combined with a hint of spiritual restlessness; and restlessness would develop into a kind of tension for those poets who vacillated between regionalist awareness and personal lyricism.

Mário António (Fernandes de Oliveira), perhaps the outstanding talent of the "Let's Discover Angola" generation, has failed the promise of the nationalist surge of the fifties, but he continues to write what could easily be considered the best intimist poetry of an Angolan thematic. Tracing Mário António's development as a poet (and he started very young), we see, even in his early stage, a preference for a more personal lyricism. António Cardoso appraises Mário António as "unquestionably a poet" and then discusses how his personal anxieties as a *mestiço* determine the nature of his art.[53] A reading of António's verse, presented in chronological order in his *100 poems*, offers the opportunity of following his poetic development from 1950 through 1962. The duality of his work derives from his conscious dependence on a European tradition and his irrepressible desire to bring his Angolanness into perspective. It also comes about through a suppression of the regional in favor of the universal expression of an individualistic reaction to the human condition; but the juxtaposing of his condition as an African with his Western attitudes causes the ambivalences of a man caught between two cultures.

Many of António's poems treat the theme of love, from adolescent awakening to the ineffable moment of the first romantic experience. In "Poesia de amor" (Love Poetry), written in 1951, he sets forth the theme of idealized adolescent love:

> Vou fazer um poema com olhos e com flores
> Para oferecer ao meu amor-menina.
> Poema de regresso, romagem de saudade
> Àquele que eu fui no começo da estrada.[54]

(I am going to make a poem with eyes and with flowers/To offer to my little girl-love./A poem of a return, of a pilgrimage of longing/To that which I was at the beginning of the road.)

It has already been seen how the nostalgic return to childhood characterizes much of the Angolan poetry written during the fifties. António's journey back into childhood means more than romantic escapism or the attempt to recapture a lost creole reality; his re-creation of childish daydreams brings out the uneasiness and tensions of the *mestiço*'s cultural and psychological confusion. The poem "A sombra branca" (The White Shadow), written when the poet was eighteen, is an oneiric fantasy replete with erotico-racial anxieties:

> A menina branca nascida na Lua
> Na noite de infância foi-me assombração.
> Menina de branco, toda em branco nua
> De branco pintada na imaginação!
>
> Quando choraste, Rosa, nos meus braços,
> Quando, vencida, me rogaste amor,
> Forçados foram todos os abraços
> Porque a branca entre nós se veio pôr!
>
> Ela, a branca, tolheu o meu desejo
> Da Lua vinda numa noite igual,
> Quando arfante, sem pejo, descobriste
> O tropical maboque do teu seio.
>
> Sim, foi ela, a assombração. Perdoa
> Que deixasse o teu desejo insatisfeito
> E odiasse a tua carne boa
> E os teus lábios colados no meu peito!
>
> Foi ela, essa fantasma-luar
> A branca, a inexistente, a sombra
> Que em cio me matou
> E me afastou falhado, sujo, do teu corpo fremente!
>
> Foi ela, a assombração, a branca
> (Perdoa!) o meu fracasso múltiplo, brutal!
> Foi ela . . . Mas insiste, vem, arranca
> De mim esse fantasma e faz-me ver real!
>   (p. 33)

(The little white girl born on the Moon/On that childish night for me was an apparition./Little girl in white, all naked in white/Painted in white in my imagination!//When you, Rosa, cried in my arms,/When, in surrender, you pleaded for my love./ All of my embraces were forced/Because the white one had placed herself between us!//She, the white one, impeded my desire/Having come from the Moon on a similar night,/When breathlessly, without modesty, you bared/The tropical aroma of your breast.//Yes, it was she, the apparition. Forgive me/That I left your desire unsatisfied/And hated your good flesh/And your lips pressed to my chest!//It was she, that phantom-moonlight/ The white one, nonexistent, the shadow/Who in heat slew me/And drove me defeated, sordid from your tremulous body!// It was she, the apparition, the white one/(Forgive me!) my brutal, multiple failure!/It was she . . . But insist, come to me, tear/The phantom from me and make me see what is real!)

Costa Alegre, the black poet from São Tomé (see page 380), and the Angolan Cordeiro da Matta also dealt with the theme of love and black psychically intruded upon by white, but not in the same context of racial and sexual pathology as seen in Mário António's poem, and certainly not with the same handling of imagery. The phantomlike ideal does not exist except as a part of the adolescent's moonlit fantasy world, and by extension Western aesthetic values impinge on his complete surrender to an accessible reality. Psychologists and psychiatrists, including Frantz Fanon in his book *Black Skin White Masks*, have assessed the subjective conflict involved in the black man–white woman relationship, and Mário António's poetry, by means of erotic metaphor, transmits the anguish of self-hate struggling with self-affirmation in a way that gives new dimension to the Angolan's problem of alienation.

A preoccupation with the color white occasionally forces dated conceits on António's love poetry. "Simples poema de amor" (Simple Love Poem), written in 1959, begins with the line "O marfim das tuas coxas o mesmo é dos teus dentes" (The ivory of your thighs is like that of your teeth) (*100 poemas*, p. 117). The title carries ironic intent, however, in view of the violent eroticism of the poem, and the use of the Petrarchan conceit of ivory-colored skin exaggerates the distinctions between black and white as the imagery becomes surrealistic: "Colocas duas estrelas no fundo negro do espaço/E assustada me apertas, mordes-me o peito e o braço" (You place two stars in the black depths of space/And alarmed you squeeze me, biting my chest and my arm). M. António's (many of his books mention only the initial of his first name) irony and surrealistic distortion of conventional love images could be a manifestation of his cultural ambivalence that allows him to use almost angrily the language of the traditions he so readily accepts. His sense of his Africanness may lie in the background of much of his poetry, but it seems constantly in conflict with the obvious presence of Europe.

The use of erotic imagery in António's love poetry shares prominence with the theme of the fortuitous encounter. In a poem entitled "De desencontro e espera o amor se tece" (Love Is Woven of Waiting and Missed Meetings), he conveys the feeling of reluctant emotional involvement, perhaps as a reflection of a certain reticence toward the very European romantic conventions he elaborates in his poetry.

Mário António's move to Portugal in the mid-sixties prompted him to publish a book of poems significantly titled *Rosto de Europa* (The Face of Europe, 1968). His first direct contact with the Europe that hovered over his formative years resulted in poems that give the tension of the "cultural mulatto" (and here we use the term to mean the acculturated African intellectual) a new dimension. The awe that he experienced before the geographical reality of Europe was tempered with the nostalgia of the physically uprooted. Africa comes to stifle the exhilaration the poet first feels before the spectacle of Europe. In the first stanza of "Para depois" (For Afterwards) António confesses:

> Outrora, vias coqueiros e escrevias: "Pinhos."
> Hoje, sob os pinhais, um vento corre
> De África sobre o teu pensamento.[55]

(At one time, you would see coconut palms and you would write:

"Pine trees."/Today, under the pine groves, a wind from Africa/ blows across your thoughts.)

The contrast between perception and education, in the internally rhyming words "vias" (you would see) and "escrevias" (you would write), along with the contrast between the palm and the pine, captures perfectly the condition of the child of a black and *mestiço* bourgeois elite. In this same poem António writes:

> Outrora, cresciam vinhas no teu sonho
> Sem que as houvesse visto
> —Pura fermentação no teu sangue
> Misto.
>
> Entre coqueiros, rias
> Sob pinhais de amor.
> Sangravam araucárias
> Choupos da tua dor.
>
> Porque convocas paisagens
> Para as sobrepores
> À que hoje te é dada?
>
> —Adia
> Para depois
> A harmonia.
>   (pp. 12–13)

(At one time, vineyards would grow in your dreams/Without your having seen them/—Pure fermentation in your mixed/ Blood.//Among coconut palms, you would laugh/Under pine groves of love./Araucaria trees would bleed/Poplars of your grief.//Why assemble landscapes/To superimpose them/On what today is yours?//—Postpone/The harmony/For afterwards.)

The use of the word *vineyards* and the idea of pure fermentation seem somewhat contrived, but the sum of the dissimilar images imparts the problem of cultural and racial duality. In the last stanza the poet seems to be saying that for the time being the twain shall not meet. On another level of interpretation this statement could be extended to include António's rather cynical attitude toward the possibility of a harmony that might solve the fundamental political and racial problems of his native Angola. This attitude may explain in part his passive position on the issue of Angolan independence, a position which has been viewed by some as tacit acceptance of the status quo.

Whatever the case, Mário António's art, though it may suffer from his being a passive supporter of the dictatorial regime, continues to provide a measure of excellence in the temporarily stagnant pool of contemporary Angolan letters. His latest book of poetry, *Coração transplantado* (Transplanted Heart, 1970), gives added evidence of his ability to translate his artistic perceptiveness into compelling images. The twenty-three poems that make up the collection's first, and most extensive, part are really one long work that grew out of the poet's experiences during his brief stay in London. There is an obvious significance in the topicality of the volume's title, as can be seen in the first poem of the series:

> Transplantado coração
> Nem só distância:
> Um mar ou outro
> A faz. Passaram mares
> E ares—contudo, noutros,
> A carapinha cresce
> Em novo tempo.
> Ei-las, crianças negras
> Cruzando a rua, em Londres.
> Ei-las correndo, como
> Eu barrocas: soltas.
> Não há distância entre
> Céu baixo e alto
> Arranha-céu, cubata.[56]

(Transplanted heart/Not just distance:/One sea or another/does that. Seas have passed by/And climes have too—yet, in others,/kinky hair grows/At a new tempo./There they go, black children/Crossing the street, in London./There they go running,

quaint/Like me: free./There is no difference between/low sky
and high/Skyscraper, hut.)

The transplanted, and therefore foreign, heart risks rejection by
the new organism which metaphorically suggests the African in
the alien cold of a European city, and in its conventional, figurative usage the heart is the seat of sentiment, in this case the
homesickness of the uprooted. Homesickness defies geographical
distance, for the poet identifies with the black children in their
quaintness.

António's existentialist anxieties in an alien, ultimately hostile
world cause him to feel guilt for his being removed from his real
sources. Thus, in the second part of *Coração transplantado* he
goes back to his origins, in a manner of speaking. This section
contains four poems composed in Kimbundu with the help of
António's mother-in-law Mrs. Maria da Conceição Abreu; Portuguese-language versions are provided. The poet gives his personal
lyrical touch to the chantlike, incantatory formulas of traditional
African poetry. The second of the four poems illustrates this
traditional stylistic:

> O leão morreu, o campo ficou livre!
> Deixem-me que beba os meus copinhos
> Com os meus amigos!
>
> O leão morreu, o campo ficou livre!
> Deixem-me que brinque com os meus amigos
> Na minha noite!
>
> O leão morreu, o campo ficou livre!
> Deixem-me que olhe a lua com os meus amigos,
> Na minha estrada!
>
> O leão morreu, o campo ficou livre!
> (p. 41)

(The lion has died, the way has been cleared!/Let me have a few
drinks with my friends!//The lion has died, the way has been
cleared!/Let me jest with my friends/On my night!//The lion
has died, the way has been cleared!/Let me watch the moon with

my friends,/On my road!//The lion has died, the way has been cleared!)

The repetition of the first line has a celebratory, ritualistic aspect to it, while the plea for relaxation, diversion, or tranquil communication with nature in the company of friends counterpoises the ceremonial with the element of personal lyricism, which in a sense represents António's coming to terms with a cultural duality.

A few other poets, living in Angola, have in the last few years cultivated lifeless verse, imbued with neo-exoticism or naïveté, art poetry with an occasional cryptic note of protest, or outspoken, and therefore unpublishable, poems destined for a small circle of sympathizers. Jorge Macedo, a young black poet of Luanda, has written three slim volumes of poetry, *1° Tetembu* (1965), *As mulheres* (The Women, 1971), and *Pai Ramos* (Father Ramos, 1971). Macedo revives the theme of the "black Venus," and like a voice crying in the wilderness he calls for universal harmony and love.

Another poet, who writes under the name of Jofre Rocha, has been praised by the few members of the original "Let's Discover Angola" group still left in Luanda as one of a few promising poets of a truncated tradition. Rocha has published on a more or less regular basis in the Luanda press and even has an occasional poem turned down by the censor. Little else of note remains, however, except for some official poets and other unpublished ones such as the young woman from the Dembos region who writes under the name of Marilu Dionísio and also under the more provocative pseudonym of Hende Ngola Ginga. Although a white Angolan, Marilu Dionísio has composed humanistic and politically aware poetry which she dedicates in her unpublished collection "Reencontro" (Reencounter, 1970) to those who know how to suffer with pride and dignity.

Africa and its traditions play only a symbolic role in most of the present poetry of Angola, for there has been a breach in the cultivation of a truly autochthonous Angolan literature insofar as the initial regionalist direction has been greatly weakened.

CHAPTER 5

Prose Fiction
in Angola

The short story rapidly became a popular genre in Angola as writers took cognizance of their cultural and literary circumstances in the 1950s. For a number of reasons, lack of resources and time being two, the novel was little cultivated by the generation of aware writers. More novels would probably have been written if the literary thrust had not come to an untimely end in the 1960s. And because the short story offered them a more reflective vision of their reality than did poetry, some of the writers began to experiment with the longer novella. Another reason for the popularity of the short story was that it could carry the dramatic urgency of the theater, and this suited the social purposes of many of the committed writers.

In 1960 the Lisbon-based Student Empire House published an anthology of stories reprinted from *Mensagem* (both the one published in Luanda and the one brought out in Lisbon) and *Cultura*; it also included offerings by Castro Soromenho and Óscar Ribas. Introductory comments by Fernando Mourão, director of the student group's overseas studies section, acknowledge the urbanism and the European formation of the *Mensagem* and *Cultura* contributors, but recognize as well their efforts to shape neorealist techniques to an African dynamic. Most of the stories written during this period fall into three general categories: the largest number are neorealist tableaux or chroniclelike reportage that employ the device of an ironic twist to expose the conditions of the dispossessed *musseque*-dweller; the second group consists of modified and stylized traditional African tales whose aphoristic and incantatory tones exalt black culture and values; philosophical and artistic stories, by far in the minority, seek to give psychological depth to characters through the development of social situations.

By the early 1960s Angolan writers had produced enough stories and established enough of a direction to warrant the publication, by the Student Empire House, of small volumes by individual authors. Also, Garibaldino de Andrade and Leonel Cosme edited two anthologies, *Contos d'África* (Stories of Africa, 1961) and *Novos contos d'África* (New Stories of Africa, 1962), which were published in Sá da Bandeira, Angola, by the Imbondeiro Press. The preface to the first volume speaks of two trends in the contemporary Angolan short story: the aesthetic; and a new point of discussion. These vague groupings include the three categories mentioned above; the aesthetic story encompasses the third category and the new directions merely relate to the attempt to expose, in realist-naturalist terms, the social reality of urban Angola. Four of the six writers represented in *Contos d'África* are white, and two of these four were born in Portugal but settled in Angola as young adults. This is significant in that it indicates a weakening of the strong regionalist, nativistic impetus of the 1950s. The literary scene in Angola was becoming more diffuse in a political climate averse to the direction some of the original "sons of the land" had set for Angolan culture.

Essentially the same ratio of Portuguese and Angolan (black, white, and *mestiço*) writers is found in the second anthology, although it includes a few stories by some of the original "sons of the land" as well as Alfredo Margaridos's "A osga" (The Lizard), a story which defies categorization in any of the three groups mentioned above, because of its experimental, *nouveau roman* techniques and its lack of any African stylistic or thematic features. *Novos contos d'África* also contains Reis Ventura's "O drama do velho Cafaia" (The Drama of Old Cafaia), a piece that makes propagandistic use of the first moments of the 1961 rebellion in northern Angola. Cafaia, the old and faithful servant, rather than betray his employer at the urging of guerrillas, forces his master to kill him. Melodramatic effects and neocolonialist paternalism characterize this story whose inclusion in the anthology demonstrates, and this despite the editors' good intentions, the loss of the original thrust of creole and African regionalism in the literature of Angola.

Several Writers of Note

"Of note," in most cases, does not necessarily mean outstanding, but rather of some significance in the development of recent Angolan prose fiction. In some instances we see a continuation of the Soromenho-type approach to native African societies. In this respect, Orlando de Albuquerque's short novel, *O homem que tinha a chuva* (The Man Who Had the Rain, 1968), treats not so much traditional myths as the African's existence in a supposedly narrow, superstitious world.

Some white writers demonstrate a highly sophisticated knowledge of African customs, language, and institutions, which they apply to their generally neocolonialist stories. For example, Candeias da Silva's knowledge of the Umbundu language and the customs of the Ovimbundo people has permitted her to fashion stories that exploit those same exotic elements that appeal to Western curiosity, but on a higher plane of authenticity. Maria Perpétua Candeias da Silva Afonso was born in the Huíla district of Angola, and she uses her linguistic abilities to reconstruct Umbundu speech patterns in her African characters' Portuguese-language dialogues. Her novella *Navionga, filha de branco* (Navionga, White Man's Daughter, 1966) sociologically describes a mixed-blood girl and her relationship to her African environment. In an earlier short story, "O homem enfeitiçado" (The

Hexed Man, 1961), she tells of a "semicivilized" African who, because he has not been circumcised, finds himself something of a pariah among his people. Salupassa, the hero, feels impotent in the presence of women because he has not submitted to the important manhood rite. The story's purpose of depicting the semi-assimilated African's cultural and psychological dilemma may be a good one, but the author's insistence, in overly dramatic scenes, on the protagonist's "disability" soon becomes ludicrous.

What writers such as Albuquerque and Candeias da Silva do provide is a base which helps to keep the flagging narrative tradition alive in Angola. When, for example, the Portuguese writer Garibaldino de Andrade tells in his story "Tesouro" (Treasure, 1960) how a white administrator marvels at the way an African describes a situation, he actually succeeds in preserving in the fiction of Angola a small measure of an African narrative technique. The administrator listens dumbfounded to a story told by an African and translated into Portuguese by a *cipaio*. Overwhelmed by the accumulation of detail in the African's account, the European remarks to another administrator that "they [the Africans] are not selective. They include everything that happened, was said, and is perfectly obvious. Would you call this a defect? But what about the dryness of our narration? It kills the story, takes away all its spice . . ."[1] Although these stories may be artistically mediocre, their scientific exoticism and discursive commentary do form a base that complements, even if negatively so, the stories of an African thematic written by the committed Angolan. Costa Andrade, for one, in his "Os regressados das ilhas" (The Returnees from the Islands) incorporates traditional African elements, from an interiorized point of view, despite the story's third-story narrative, into an old man's thoughts: "He was old, he had learned a lot about life. He had to pass this knowledge on to someone. Since ancient times it has been true that a man should die among his people. The forces that cause him to think, walk, tell good from evil, he must pass on to those who remain. And after, he should be mourned by those who have benefited by his life force. A man who is never grieved by his loved ones has neither lived nor has he been fulfilled."[2] Although not foreign to Western mentality, these thoughts transmit some Bantu philosophical concepts. The reference to "life force" calls to mind Jahn's analysis of Bantu philosophy in which he says that "man is force, all things are forces, place and time are forces and the 'modalities' are forces."[3] Andrade may not have had clearly in mind the principles about which Jahn writes, but he did attempt to allow the African psyche to reveal itself.

The aforementioned Mário Guerra (Benúdia), his brother Henrique, and Henrique Abranches all wrote ritualistic narratives which treat etiological or genesis legends, extol the force of the land and the people, and convert such mythic subjects as the exodus theme into minor epics. Benúdia, in fact, wrote several poetic legends centered on archetypal heroes. His "Dumba e a bangela" (Dumba and the Bangela Maiden) tells of a young Kioko (Kwokwe) chief who leads his people on an arduous journey in search of a new land: "They came under the command of the young nephew of Ndjila, Dumba Kiowa—'he who was born with the people on march'—descended from lions, and it was by his order that they were there, waiting for eight long moons, while the children cried for milk."[4] Dumba had met the Bangela maiden in the marketplace and had resolved to wait for her to come to him at the encampment. He thus had to choose between his personal feelings and the salvation of his people. Finally, heeding the advice of the elders, he raised the cry "walla," meaning the time had come to resume the trek. Benúdia offers, in this story, a lyricized and personalized rendition of the exodus theme.

The socially committed urban writer benefited both by the exteriorized depictions of African society by writers such as Albuquerque and by the archetypal narratives of Benúdia and Henrique Abranches. Those writers who gave to their stories an urban setting attempted to expose racial and social conflicts and to see their characters not just as forlorn victims but also as types who function within a social situation and from an African viewpoint.

The African point of view meant for a few writers a combination of the three categories mentioned earlier. Essentially, these authors cultivated neorealist stories in which situation dominates all else, but some used the aphoristic and incantatory, or at least tried to re-create a sense of black values generated in an urban environment. Some were even able to temper their sense of social urgency with a greater attention to artistic technique and philosophical content.

The Luanda of Luandino Vieira

Born in Portugal in 1935, José Graça was taken to Angola as an infant, and so thoroughly has he identified with the area and its culture that his pseudonym Luandino Vieira has become synonymous with contemporary Angolan prose fiction. Luandino has adopted an artistic technique and a stylistic approach appropriate to the didactic optimism of the social reformer. But while he frequently approaches socialist realism in his stories, he also cultivates a social humanism using Luanda's *musseques* as his setting. Luandino employs as well the conventional format of the situational plot with an ironic twist.

The name Luandino is part of a façade that the author seems ultimately to have come to believe in. Similarly, his depiction of the *musseque*-dweller from a folk point of view indicates that, to avoid the label of déclassé, he uses a kind of parable, fairy-tale approach in his re-creation of episodes and types. In other words, he tries to avoid the trap that other well-intentioned, upper-class, white authors, like Soromenho, fell into by attempting to reveal the black man's soul. Luandino draws a fine line between what can be called sociological art and fantasy art. Sometimes the two merge to produce a kind of socialist realism, but at his best Luandino champions the poor in stories that synthesize in a framework of folk philosophy the life style of the *musseque* and certain African traditions. Luandino employs a technique of controlled flamboyancy that saves his stories from being labeled as sentimentalized slice-of-life sketches.

Before discussing individual stories by Luandino, we should consider the controversy surrounding his best-known book

Luuanda (1964). In 1965 the Portuguese Writers Society awarded *Luuanda* first prize for the best prose fiction of the year produced in Portugal and the overseas provinces. The fact that at the time of the award the author was in prison for subversive activities no doubt caused much of the opposition by official Portuguese literati to the society's choice. Finally, the authorities banned the book and the society itself was dissolved. Opposition to the awarding of the prize to *Luuanda* had to do, ostensibly, with negative judgments on its literary value. Luandino makes use of a fictional language that combines standard Portuguese with black speech patterns, the latter being known as black Portuguese or *pequeno português* (literally, "little Portuguese," meaning a bit of Portuguese); he also utilizes a smattering of Kimbundu words. Some critics have taken issue with this dialectal deformation just as certain Cape Verdeans have rejected the use of creole or creolized Portuguese as a literary language. With specific regard to Luandino, some critics have commented that the speech patterns in his stories represent the way whites think blacks talk.

It is true that certain white Angolan writers who attempt to simulate black Portuguese exaggerate the obvious, such as gender and verb tense discordances; often they employ orthographic deformation to suggest peculiarities in pronunciation. Inevitably, such exotic devices detract from the work, for the reader is constantly aware of a stylistic contrivance which has potentially condescending racial and social overtones. Luandino seems to depend more on a stylized re-creation of *musseque* speech patterns than on demeaning exaggerations. His technique involves incorporating black Portuguese phrasing into the indirect free style so that no contrast exists between standard language and dialect. Problems regarding the use of Kimbundu usually concern the extent to which these African words or phrases inhibit the reader's comprehension. Generally, Luandino's use of Kimbundu phrases does not present any more difficulties for the reader of standard Portuguese than, say, Brazilian regionalisms would, and, in the case of *Luuanda*, the African words seem to be employed more for poetic effect. By way of example, in the story "Vavó

Xíxi e seu neto Zeca Santos" (Grandma Xíxi and Her Grandson Zeca Santos) the narrator describes the old lady's growing consternation as she confronts Zeca, and in the following passage the context tells the reader what effect the two Kimbundu words connote: "Grandma Vavó Xíxi shook her head slowly, and her thin face, weatherbeaten by many seasons, began to take on that look that those who knew her feared; because she was going to get *quisseme*, she was going to get *quissende*, for sure. She was known for her temper . . ."5 Then comes the grandmother's outburst introduced by the interjection "sukua!" The Kimbundu words, *quisseme* and *quissende*, besides their pleasing alliterative effect, subtly enhance the character's personality by linking her with an African verbal expressiveness.

All three of the long short stories in *Luuanda* borrow techniques from the craft of the teller of tales. Two of the stories bear the word *estória* in their titles rather than the usual *história*; both words basically mean "story," but *estória* can be defined more properly as a popular, epiclike tale of oral tradition, and like the Brazilian novelist Jorge Amado, who no doubt influenced him, Luandino is a spinner of yarns. Also like Jorge Amado, Luandino creates colorful characters, cultivates a verbal virtuosity, and uses a popular and iconoclastic humor in his stories.

The narrator of "A estória da galinha e do ovo" (The Story of the Hen and the Egg) begins by saying that he plans to tell a story based on the title and that the events he will relate took place in the *musseque* of Sambizanga in this "our" Luanda. At the end of the story the narrator, in the style of the African *griot*, leaves the judgment of the story's worth up to the reader (listener), and only affirms that he has put forth events that really did happen in "our" Luanda. The simple tale the narrator tells is about a woman whose hen wanders into a neighboring yard and lays an egg. The pregnant neighbor craves the egg. A dispute ensues over the egg's legal owner, and what we have is the makings of a fundamentally primitive tale similar to Sancho Panza's commonsense justice or Brecht's reworking of the Old Testament story of the child claimed by two mothers. Luandino portrays various *mus-*

seque types and establishes, with humorously iconoclastic intents, the dichotomy between the exploited and the exploiter.

Neighbors enter into the dispute, and those most respected for their sagacity are asked to help resolve the dilemma. The disputants go first to a local shopkeeper who, the narrator says with humorous irony, should know what to do because he is white. But because the shopkeeper supplied corn on credit to the hen's owner, he feels justified in claiming the egg for himself. Next, the women turn to Azulinho, a sixteen-year-old boy respected in the *musseque* for his cleverness and knowledge of Catholic liturgy. Azulinho enunciates a modified version of the biblical dictum, "I cannot give unto Caesar that which is Caesar's, nor to God that which is God's" (p. 149). He maintains that only Father Júlio can speak truth on the matter, and he proposes to take the egg to the priest. Social satire emerges in Azulinho, for he represents the semi-assimilated African who can manipulate the language but remains a ward of the system.

The women, by then accompanied by a crowd, confront next a "slum lord" who reasons that because the egg was laid on property he owns, it belongs to him. Someone then suggests consulting an elderly drunkard who had once worked in a notary's office. This colorful character envelopes his listeners in turgid legal prose involving ownership titles and receipts for corn to feed the hen. Finally, several policemen arrive and, with thoughts of a meal in mind, they demand the egg and the hen. A small boy intervenes by imitating a rooster's mating call, and the hen literally flies away. This prodigious feat (for a chicken) signifies that the humble and powerless slum-dwellers win out over the arrogant and insensitive authorities. The two women settle their problem amicably, indicating that *musseques* will unite when confronted by interlopers. By using character types—the skinflint shopkeeper to represent the economic exploitation of the *musseques* and the landlord in his pith helmet, leering at women, to symbolize the colonialist—Luandino accomplishes his purposes of protest and satire. Even in his characterization of the *musseque*-dwellers, verbosity turns some of them—Azulinho and the old drunk—into caricatures, but from the standpoint of oral expression Luandino stylizes an important aspect of African values in the urban environment.

Luandino Vieira also wrote eight short stories collected in a volume titled *Vidas novas* (New Lives), published in Paris sometime in the mid or late sixties. Because he was in prison at the time, he could not revise the proofs, for which the editors apologize. All the stories revolve around political repression and the torture of prisoners. Obviously, Luandino had entered into a phase of literary dogma, which for some would destroy the artistic and philosophical value of his work. The stories contain ideological rhetoric combined with the author's conception of traditional African storytelling patterns. "Cardoso Kamukolo sapateiro" (The Shoemaker Cardoso Kamukolo) begins with an "if": "If they do not kill all of them, the children of our land will be able to tell stories to their grandchildren in those better days ahead."[6] The narrator then projects the story into those better days and depicts, with socialist-realist images, bountiful harvests, happy, industrious people, and progress measured by the hum of machinery. After this introduction by the narrator-implicit author, an elderly storyteller entertains a rapt audience of children with tales of the supernatural, but the children, on that particular night, demand a story about the history of their people. Obligingly, the grandfather relates the story of the shoemaker Cardoso Kamukola who one day defied his boss's exploitation and then defended a black child against an irate mob. Luandino adapts an explicitly proletarian example to the African oral tradition whereby a *griot* tells and retells epic events.

The idea of the hero or of the hapless victim who becomes the hero of the people preoccupies Luandino in many of the stories in *Vidas novas*. In "O fato completo de Lucas Matesso" (Lucas Matesso's *fato completo*) the narrator uses an anecdote to champion the cause of the oppressed. Lucas Matesso, imprisoned for suspected terrorist activities, receives a visit from his wife whom he reminds to bring him a *fato completo* when she comes again. A guard overhears the conversation and reports to his superior that the prisoner has requested a full suit of clothes, which is the obvious interpretation of *fato completo*. The prison warden and the guard immediately suspect that Lucas Matesso will receive a message, sewn into the suit's lining, from a "terrorist" contact. On the next visiting day Lucas's wife appears with food and a clean change of clothes, but no full suit. Still, the suspicious guards make a thorough search of the clothes with no success in finding a hidden message. Frustrated, they beat the prisoner in an effort to force information out of him. After the merciless torture, which the narrator describes in some detail, Lucas is returned to his cell where, through pain, tears, and broken teeth, he roars with laughter. The joke is on the prison authorities, for in the *musseques* the dish of fish, bananas, and palm oil is affectionately known as *fato completo*, and it was this that he had requested of his wife. Once again Luandino champions the cause of the *musseque*-dweller by using an African dish, unknown to the white prison guards, as a mark of cultural solidarity.

Luandino displays a talent for poetically descriptive passages of nature as it contrasts with the harshness of the urban setting of his stories. In his glamorization of the *musseques* the sun shines and the moon glows in a special way on the shacks and muddy streets as a kind of vindication of the slums disdained by the European city. And in "O fato completo de Lucas Matesso" the hero's laughter merges with the sound of heavy rain as he savors his plate of fish and bananas. Obviously, Luandino seeks to equate the freedom and force of nature with the people's indomitable spirit in his proletarian stories. In the introductory paragraphs of another story, "O exemplo de Job Kamukuaja" (Job Kamakuaja's Example), he again employs the rain as a motif. The "good water" of the rain washes the leaves and creates muddy rivers in the streets while Mário João, who under torture has revealed information to the police, cries muddy tears of shame. In this story Job Kamakuaja, a member of the proud Cuanhama people, stands as an example of the revolutionary hero who knows how to withstand torture. And, all the stories of *Vidas novas* are exhortations to the Angolan to persevere in his struggle against colonialism.

Despite the didacticism of *Vidas novas*, the collection demonstrates that Luandino continued to develop his artistic techniques; for example, the stories make no obvious use of black Portuguese, yet the flavor of *musseque* speech has not been lost. The stories in *Vidas novas*, at any rate, represent a transitory phase both in Luandino's artistic development and in the development of Angolan prose fiction. For when Luandino won first prize for the best prose fiction written in Portugal and the provinces in 1964, he represented the maturity of Angolan literature. Now that José Vieira Mateus de Graça (Luandino's full legal name) has been released from the Tarrarfal prison, he plans to resume his literary career (in fact, a new edition of *Luuanda* was issued in 1973 but withdrawn from circulation almost immediately). A moderation in censorship and the encouragement of free expression by the Spínola government mean that Luandino will perhaps publish new works and reedit old ones. Depending on political developments in Portuguese Africa, both the poetry and prose fiction of Angola may progress at a new and faster rate.*

The Mestiço Luanda of Mário António and Arnaldo Santos

One of the other directions in Angolan prose fiction is found in several short stories by two people who participated in the first period of contemporary literary awareness. Unlike Luandino Vieira's myth-building, committed stories, those of Mário António and Arnaldo Santos are chroniclelike sketches designed to expose a more synchronic vision of the social and psychological reality of urban Angola.

Mário António, better known as a poet, made his debut as a short story writer in the 1952 issue of *Mensagem* with "O cozin-

---

* Since the fall of the Caetano regime Luandino has published four more stories, written during his imprisonment, in the volume *Velhas estórias* (1974).

heiro Vicente" (Vicente the Cook). Already in this early effort, written during a period of high social awareness, António displays a bent for psychological portraiture. By the time he had published *Crônica da cidade estranha* (Chronicle of the Singular City) in 1964, he had nearly divested his prose of the immediacy and spontaneity of social revelation. His stories had become almost esoteric nonstory stories in which characters grope about in search of meaning in their existence. António cultivates his fictional language with the same sense of craft that characterizes his poetry. He utilizes the techniques and themes of contemporary Euro-American prose fiction, but his characters' intimist search for self does have a special significance in the development of modern Angolan fiction. The theme of the marginal *mestiço* and his sense of belonging to a Europeanized city that still retains the resilience of black Africa places *Crônica da cidade estranha* and António's most recent collection, *Farra no fim de semana* (Weekend Spree, 1965), well within the context of modern African literature of European expression. This most recent work represents the author's best efforts as a chronicler of *mestiço* society in Luanda.

It would be wrong to define chronicler as an observer of day-to-day events when speaking of António's stories, since he subordinates everyday happenings to the personal relationships of characters who move existentially, and at times aimlessly, through their urban environment. The bus appears in António's stories as a symbol; public transportation depersonalizes and is therefore a fitting means of conveyance for the alienated characters as they wend their way through the city. In the first story ("Farra no fim de semana"), Pedro tells Elsa that humanity can be divided into those who depart and those who stay; they are traveling by bus within the prisonlike confines of the city, and the bus ride, as a vicarious journey, supports Pedro's observation that "we are all traveling toward a determined end. There is a moment in our lives which the whole Universe demands and imposes on us. This moment is unique for each one of us . . . All our travels, except one, count for nothing. That moment can come when a city conspires for a bus to make its rounds with only two passengers."[7] This sort of philosophical pronouncement gives António's stories a reflective, static quality.

Anonymity and alienation are suggested by the commonplace names of all António's characters: Mário, Pedro, Carlos, Elsa, Margarida, none of whom has a middle or last name. In this opening story Mário first narrates, only to give way to a third-person narrator and to imaginary diary entries by his friend Pedro. Elsa and Margarida reveal their thoughts through streams of consciousness, and then Mário picks up the narration again in the third and final part of a relatively long story made slightly chaotic by its shifting point of view. The story begins to gain a more obvious linear progression when another friend named Antunes calls to invite these nebulous characters to a weekend party. Margarida and Mário travel by taxi out of the city to the seaside home of Silva Marques, the party's host. The act of leaving the confines of the city by automobile contrasts with the image of the bus circulating within the city limits. And the more personalized car adds to the idea of escape represented by the trip out of the city.

In the congenial but artificial setting of the social gathering the guests lose themselves in alcohol and the music of the guitar. During the dancing an older woman asks Mário, "Don't you find these songs very lovely, carefree, really the image of a people who still maintain joy as an elevated value?" (p. 49) This and similar observations, such as Mário's remark that Alberta sits as only women, boy scouts, and primitives know how, reveal the author's intention of picturing bourgeois *mestiços* in the tension of their alienation from the Africanness that hangs on the periphery of their existence.

The relationship between Mário and Margarida (husband and wife) and Pedro (Mário's traveled friend) reaches its symbolic zenith on the beach at dawn after the all-night party. Mário crosses the sand on which lie exhausted revelers like so many battle casualties; he comes upon his wife and Pedro sitting on an upturned dugout canoe, and he announces that they are the only survivors. All three are the survivors of an experience that has stripped them of their bourgeois façade as they contemplate each other in the unerring light of dawn. The meaning of this scene is not entirely clear, but its *dolce vita* effect fortifies the idea of the mulatto who, in his cultural alienation, escapes from the stifling civilization of the city, seeks catharsis in music, drink, and an imagined freedom in touch with nature, and then falls weakened and graceless from the effort. Mário had thought himself the only survivor as he walked among the fallen guests, including Albertina who, though gracefully primitive the night before, now lies awkwardly in her soiled shorts. But Pedro and Margarida have acted out the entire charade as they sit victoriously, smiling on an African canoe.

António does not use terms of racial identification, except for a passing reference to Elsa's brown arm, but the cultural mulatto's social alienation is suggested in the story's structure and tone. In the second story, "Álvaro," the physical and psychological closeness of an African ancestral presence imposes itself on the hero's thoughts in lyrical-realist reminiscences: "And the mystery hidden beyond the trees that completely surrounded my Father's house—living quarters, small stores, lodging for those who come to consult the American mission doctor. I have a varied but vague recollection of my Mother: I could see her in the many women with babies slung on their hips when they came to buy pieces of cloth, beads, and other things in my father's store" (p. 59). The merchant-settler Father and the unassimilated African Mother became archetypes or mystical abstractions to the *mestiço* offspring who must leave behind the separate worlds of the crude settler and the "native" woman to enter a reality that, because of their legacy, is both foreign and familiar.

António again avoids the sociological in favor of the lyrical and mystical in "Samba," which tells of a white man and a black woman (Samba) who interact through a kind of wordless ritual in the cool morning water of the ocean—a primordial symbol of mythic origins. The author leaves the circumstances of their relationship to the reader's imagination, for his focus is on the poetically imagistic and sensuous unity of water, sky, sand, and

Samba's seminude body. As the sun starts its ascent Armando, in his fascination with the enigmatic Samba, engages in lyrical fantasy, and the author brings the rhapsody to a conclusion in which the girl's dark thighs become confused with the dawn: "the morning was Samba's two black thighs, from between which the first triumphant rays of the Sun fell full upon his [Armando's] face" (p. 80). António contrasts the plastic images of the lithe, dark form with the white opaqueness of the wet, cotton swim suit to capture the eroticism of the scene. The hint of lugubrious fascination is tempered by the notion of Samba as an abstraction of the mystery of eternity: "perhaps the thought had occurred to him that those two dark thighs outlined against the dawn had suggested to men of all times, from the Occident to the Orient, the sense of their religiosity, their search for eternity" (p. 80). The author clearly employs Samba as an embodiment of mystery and timelessness, but he does so on a level that transcends the usual mystification of exotic Africa and the "thingification" of the sensuous black female.

As in his poetry, António in his short stories displays a greater interest in aesthetic form than in sociological content, which, while it may detract from the dynamism and immediacy of his art, offers a compelling tension in its understatement. His concern with Angolan traditions resulted in the Kimbundu "art" poems in his collection *Coração transplantado*, and in fiction he made his concessions with a book of stories based on an African oral tradition. According to António, the fables and tales of *Mahezu* (1966) come from various written sources, such as Chatelain's *Folk Tales of Angola*, to which he went for the outline of an action, for a psychological trait, or for a concept; but he declares, somewhat defensively, "I also have a grandmother who told me stories."[8] He confesses, however, that what remains with him is the memory of the sentiment that these stories caused. His purpose, then, was not to record, but rather to reconstruct and capture the essence of an oral tradition. And this in a sense sums up the duality of Angolan cultural "mulattoism" of which Mário António is the most artistically talented representative.

Arnaldo Santos's background resembles Mário António's in several respects: both are *mestiços*, although António is the off-spring of two mulattoes and Santos is the son of a white father and a black or *mestiço* mother; both write "art" poetry; and both interpret a *mestiço* psychology in their prose fiction. Unlike António, however, Santos has never left Angola; in Luanda, he continues to draw on an experience unsullied by direct outside influences.

Santos has published two small collections of short stories. The first, *Quinaxixe* (1965), contains stories set in and around Luanda *musseques*, including the neighborhood of Quinaxixe. All the stories deal with social ironies stemming from race prejudice and color distinctions as seen from the point of view of children, mainly *mestiços*, and particularly from the perspective of Gigi, a mulatto boy who appears in three of the collection's six stories. In Santos's stories we do not see childhood evoked nostalgically by an adult, but rather the often confused preadolescent struggling with the usual problems of that time of life and with the added tensions created by the anomalies inherent in a multiracial society. Often the stories suggest the dilemma of "cultural mulattoism": what is the place of black Africa in the life of the *mestiço* child who must come of age in a society that puts a premium on lightness of skin color and on European civilization? In the story "Exames da 1.ª classe" (First Form Exams) Gigi passes the final examination but his black friend Arlindo fails. Arlindo knows stories and songs, but his African lore gains him only the approbation of his peers in a school where performance is measured by purely Western standards. In "A menina Vitória" (That Girl Vitória), a sequel to "Exames da 1.ª classe," Gigi goes to another school where the students come mainly from the white lower city. Adults caution Gigi to work on his pronunciation which has been corrupted by black servants and *musseque* children. Vitória, the *mestiço* teacher, refreshes her light-colored face powder with exaggerated frequency and runs her fingers affectionately through the blond hair of the children from the *baixa* whom she invariably seats at the front of the class. She picks on Matoso, a dark boy whose denim school smock identifies his family's lower-class status. Gigi finds his position to be a perplexing one as he attempts to emulate the manners of the white children in order not to incur the wrath of the teacher who humiliates those students who let slip an occasional Kimbundu word. Despite his best efforts Gigi infuriates Vitória when he writes a composition which, in her opinion, treats a high government official with less than the respect due him. "Look here," she snaps, "do you think that he [the official] goes about dirty and ragged like you, and that he eats *fungi* in a native hut?"[9] Baffled and hurt, Gigi, on his way to the anxieties of cultural marginality, reacts with the ironic, under-the-breath insult that Vitória is not even a light-skinned *mestiça* but just an ordinary *mulata*.

The psychological processes found in child characters such as Gigi become refined in the vignettes and chronicles of Santos's collection *Tempo de munhungo*, published in 1968. Santos himself defines the Kimbundu word *munhungo* as vertigo, and thus the title could be translated as Vertigo Time. The author subtitles his sixteen stories *crônicas* (chronicles), and in line with the characteristics of this Luso-Brazilian literary subgenre he does give a quotidian, often anecdotal commentary on the seemingly commonplace. A certain social pungency and irony, absent in António's stories, place Santos in the forefront of contemporary observers of the social contradictions of Luanda's *mestiço* "aristocracy" and its multiracial culture.

The theme of the first story is revealed in a small boy's question to his father: "why don't working class neighborhoods have electric lights?" The narrator-father hesitates and then stammers a complicated but unsatisfactory explanation. Father and son walk down the dark streets while the adult formulates, more for himself than for the child, involved sociological and alternately romanticized answers, but in the final analysis "working class neighborhoods don't have lights because they are working class neighborhoods."[10] The irony of an explanation that is no explanation at all comments on an elusive social problem, and Santos

enhances a subject that other Afro-Portuguese writers have frequently treated in a clumsy, sociological manner.

Santos's style varies from the tersely ironic statement to pretentious verbosity. Pretentiousness seems a studied means of arriving
at social satire. In "Um encontro qualquer" (A Chance Meeting)
the narrator is on his way to a painting exhibit at the Museum of
Angola where he knows bourgeois ladies will exclaim over the
captivating pictures while he will cast a critical eye on the forms
and colors of an overnurtured metaphysic made possible by the
desperation of leisure. As he walks toward the museum a black
urchin interrupts his thoughts with an oddly put question: "Mr.,
can you tell me if it's my time?" (p. 16) Santos displays some technical weakness at this point when he has his narrator ask a series
of rhetorical questions in order to extend the idea of the man's
bewilderment and to delay, for dramatic effect, the obvious explanation behind the boy's question. Could the child be afraid of the
supernatural after dark (the *cazumbis* and *quifumbes*)? he asks
himself; then as he notes the look of urgency in the boy's eyes, he
suddenly visualizes the motorized patrol enforcing the curfew for
"natives." By contrasting the two levels of social expression and
thought Santos creates an abstract juxtaposition between the
visceral anguish of Luanda's black citizenry and the metaphysical
anguish portrayed in the museum exhibit.

A certain pattern of mental gymnastics permeates the stories
in which the narrator ruminates on small, commonplace absurdities within a larger social framework. When a woman enters the
office of a public bureau and asks if there are any mulatto girls
employed there, the surprised male clerk replies that one has
just stepped out for a moment. In this story, "Jingondo para
mulata" (Costume Jewelry for Mulatto Girls), the woman
peddler reveals her bag of gaudy wares and comments knowingly
that they, meaning mulatto girls, like this sort of thing. The narrator imagines how perhaps this cheap jewelry descends directly
from the mystic *missangas* worn alluringly by sensual African
women of long ago, and that maybe there did remain an atavistic,
aesthetic vestige in the *jingondo* sold by a peddler on whose

snowy but fleshy neck a strand of diamonds would be inappropriate. Juca, the mulatto girl, enters the office with her "artistically straightened" hair and a choker of pearls that are as artificial as the smile she flashes when she replies that "no, there are no mulatto girls here" (p. 39). And the narrator says, "We looked at each other and stood about with idiotic smiles on our lips, each one dwelling on his own frailties. For my part I considered that those *jingondo* were no longer subversive" (p. 39). In an earlier reference to the female peddler, the narrator ponders the fact this woman "trafficked subversively in the symbols of a dominated tradition" (p. 38). The narrator's imaginative sarcasm helps to portray the two women as caricatures: the peddler, crude in manner and gross in appearance, comes face to face with the overly sophisticated *mestiço* woman whom she ironically does not recognize as a mulatto because of the façade of her make-up and artificial pearls. Behind this nonconfrontation lie the narrator's almost, but not quite, frivolous thoughts of tenuous symbols of lost African traditions. Myths and symbols do exist in the psychic constitution of the "cultural mulatto," and therein rests the profundity of Santos's commentary. The ultimate irony is summed up in the narrator's mental observation that the cheap jewelry really was not destructive and artificiality and subversiveness take on new connotations within the idea of the lack of a substantive African, or for that matter, *mestiço* mythology in an ethnically unacculturated society such as that of urban Angola.

Arnoldo Santos adeptly describes the *mestiço's* feelings of guilt that make him accept the African intellectually and exotically but not racially and socially. "Bessa-nganas de mentira" (literally translated, "make-believe African maidens") presents one of Santos's best examples of bourgeois *mestiços* who precariously flirt with their cultural ambivalence by vicariously identifying with the outward appearances of their African heritage. A social gathering at the home of João Manuel provides the setting for the slowly unfolding action in a rarefied atmosphere of Wagner, middle-class gentility, and pretentious discussions of such topics as the earthy singing style of Sammy Davis, Jr., which, according to one guest, is flawed only by his simian grimaces. The host disagrees with the narrator's contention that the "pain of music has no face" and counters with a solemn dissertation on the traditional suffering of black people as represented in their songs. This pompous sympathy carries an unemotional detachment that occasions mental ramblings by the narrator that resemble those of his counterpart in "Jingondo para mulata." The highpoint of the soiree occurs when the two *mestiço* women, in African robes, pose for photographs, and the narrator comments dryly, "We exoticize our own people" (p. 57). Shortly after, the group returns to its discussion of American music and Sammy Davis, Jr. In this story Santos successfully makes his artistic statement on the duality and detachment among Angolan *mestiços* forced to accept and reject a part of themselves simultaneously.

With *Tempo de munhungo* Arnaldo Santos takes his place alongside Luandino Vieira and Mário António as an important figure in the development of Angolan prose fiction.

Santos Lima and the Seeds of Freedom

Santos Lima has the distinction of being the only novelist to emerge from the "Let's Discover Angola" group. Under the name of Manuel Lima he also contributed poetry to the first thrust of Angolan contemporary literature. Born in Bié, Angola, in 1935, he studied in Lisbon and has lived for several years in Brazil where his one novel, *As sementes da liberdade* (The Seeds of Freedom, 1965), was published. In volume two of his anthology *Literatura africana de expressão portuguesa* Mário de Andrade includes the story "O sapo e o mocho" (The Frog and the Owl) which he excerpted from Lima's novel. Andrade obviously selected this story because it is a self-contained episode which could be printed in its entirety. But he also must have found it to be a good example of African oral tradition (there is a similar fable in European lore), and in this respect the fable offers a kind of commentary on the novel's main theme.

The story of the frog and owl is told while some "native"

policemen are leading a group of prisoners through the forest to a compound jail. One of the prisoners, to break the monotony of the march, tells the story of a frog who nurses a wounded owl back to health. In return the owl promises to grant the frog's fondest desire, which is to marry a celestial star. Owl, however, puts the lovesick frog off by saying that the marriage can only come about after the princely amphibian has been crowned king of the frogs. To accomplish this the frog leads an uprising, kills the king, and sells his brothers into slavery. All the frogs who inhabit the land come to the coronation of the new frog king. The storyteller makes a long, dramatic pause, and the anxious guards ask if the frog did indeed marry the star, to which the prisoner replies with the question, "Did you ever see a frog with wings?" Frog had forgotten this fact in thinking himself superior to other frogs. "Then what happened?" the guards asked. "Then the owls ate so many frogs they nearly wiped out the entire race," the prisoner replied. The march continues in silence until the prisoner who told the story manages to untie his hands and kill the guards with a knife. He frees the other prisoners and they all go back to their villages where they tell the story of the frog, who is like the "native" policeman, and the owl, who is like the white man. When news of the killings and the escape reaches the Portuguese administrator, he sends for the district *soba*, demands the surrender of the prisoners, and then metes out the usual punishment. The episode ends with the rebellious villagers being shipped off to forced labor camps.

Santos Lima draws a parablelike analogy but then takes a circuitous route to the story's conclusion. The message of the *cipaios* who forgot that they were equal to the other powerless Africans is well expressed in the fable. By describing the aftermath of the slaughter of the guards the author establishes a tone that characterizes the novel. The novel's tone is one of defiance, resignation, and an openendedness that encompasses optimism and pessimism. Although the frogs rebel against their despotic king, the owls eat them anyway. The recaptured prisoners go off to plantations or mines from which they will probably never return; at least they are morally vindicated. The seeds of freedom are, in a sense, planted by their act. And this seems to be the novel's central theme.

As sementes da liberdade has much of the narrative looseness of Assis Júnior's *O segredo da morta*. Like its early predecessor, it discourses in episodic fashion on customs and social realities in an acculturated situation. But it has less to do with creolization than does Assis Júnior's work and more to do with the clash of cultures in an African rural setting. In this respect the work shows some similarities with certain of Castro Soromenho's novels, particularly *Terra morta* and *Viragem*, except that, because Lima is a black Angolan, he re-creates the realities of social and racial animosities from a somewhat different perspective. If Soromenho understands the black man's soul, Lima can better express what black men feel in their souls.

Oddly enough this Angolan story begins on São Tomé where the elderly, black *filho da terra* Guilherme has earned his fortune in cocoa. His favorite son, Ricardo, the novel's hero, turns down the opportunity to study in Lisbon and decides instead to go to Angola where the family originated. Ricardo's decision to leave for Angola reverses a classic pattern of the São Tomé *filho da terra* and in a sense has to be seen as a retrogression for the upward climbing black man or *mestiço*. Nevertheless, the author maps out a curious course for his protagonist. In Angola Ricardo scores high on a government exam, but instead of a comfortable assignment in Luanda he is sent to Catu, a small outpost close to the Congo border. There he is confronted by the double standard that exists between black and white administrative employees. He describes his position as that of a glorified errand boy. Only one white employee, Adolfo, treats Ricardo as an equal, and he, in turn, incurs the disdain of other whites. On one occasion Adolfo remarks that because Portuguese men have no qualms about sleeping with black women they believe this makes them especially qualified to understand the African. Succinctly and sardonically this observation demystifies two aspects of the Lusotropicalist mythology.

Against Catu's historical and contemporary backdrop the narrator tells a story of racial and social conflicts that is interspersed with philosophical, moralistic, and didactic commentary. Catu had experienced bloody fighting during the Angolan wars of pacification, so symbolically the area stands for one of the last outposts of African resistance to European domination. The loss of old traditions and the erosion of cultural values preoccupy the protagonist who begins to move toward a separatist attitude as the author traces a sociological and cultural history of the area. He relates that the black consorts of the Portuguese settlers taught them how to judge the best beeswax and to select the quality peanuts, and the black men worked in the fields only to increase the white man's profits. Reviewing the intricacies of a social stratification that sees Portugal-born whites as superior to Angolan whites, *mestiços* looking down on blacks, sometimes within the same family, and semi-assimilated Africans scornful of "natives," the narrator recounts episodes, some of them melodramatic, others humorous, ranging from incidents that recall patterns of de facto school segregation to the staged spontaneity of a celebration to welcome the provincial governor.

As the narrator reviews the events that characterize the life of Catu, Ricardo himself draws closer to an African existence. He falls in love with a semi-assimilated woman named, significantly, Ginga, who bears him a son and inspires him to till the soil. After rain assures the success of the crop the narrator exults in the lifegiving force of the land: "In the life of the *quimbo* [farm] the sowing and harvesting were the primary occupations and they marked the seasons and events. The people saw the land as the mother of all things and this feeling was a strong cord that bound them together in a mutual and authentic brotherhood that was marvellous, ancient, and almost legendary. Kaluímbi [Ricardo's helper] felt a sense of well-being. He felt like a giant and an ancient tree of his people with roots in his blood."[11] The idea of spiritual links with the earth, with Ginga as the archetypal medium between Ricardo and the land, fortifies the theme of the African at one with the forces of nature.

Back once more in São Tomé to visit his ailing father, Ricardo again refuses to remain on the island of his birth. He tells Guilherme that he now has roots in Angola. But after several years in Catu Ricardo agonizes over the little progress he has made and decides to assure a better future for his son by sending him to study in Portugal. Paradoxically, then, Ricardo carries through the same plan that his own father had in mind for him. But Ricardo first had to return to his African roots as if to renew his spirit in an ancestral, ritualistic, and incantatory way. This explains the romanticized, almost poetic scenes in which Ricardo, under Ginga's tutelage, communes with nature by adopting the simple life of a farmer. But after finding his roots he cannot remain in this pristine state. Spiritually fortified he must move through the process which the exigencies of a new social and economic order have termed progress. And here the parable of the frog and the owl begins to assume greater significance, for although he exults in the land Ricardo essentially fails economically as a tiller of the soil even though he vindicates himself as an African. The prisoners who killed their guards but were shipped off to forced labor camps won one battle although they remained victims of the larger socioeconomic order. Ricardo, by returning to an African way of life and to African values, rejects assimilation in the spiritual and psychological sense but then sees Western education as a viable means of progress for his people.

For all its optimism and faith in a new generation of Angolans, represented by the son, there persists in the novel's final message an openendedness that contains resignation and pessimism. In the epilogue the son, Almi, reveals himself as the story's narrator. When he returns from Portugal on vacation he and his parents engage in a contrived dialogue that sums up the ideals of the black Angolan whose moral values and work ethic generally coincide with those of the Judeo-Christian tradition: Ricardo and Ginga decide to marry in the church; Almi professes his admiration for his self-sacrificing father; both parents express pride in their son's accomplishments in school; Ginga, somewhat out of character, makes sententious pronouncements on humanity. The three then discuss the changes, or lack of change, in Catu; they note that the mulatto population continues to grow, that the Eastern European Marxist visionary Samuel has prospered in certain capitalistic endeavors, and that the devoted black Catholic Agostinho was buried in a segregated, native section of the cemetery. Still, the idealistic Almi can say with conviction that this is the African's era, a century of freedom; and Ginga tells her husband to rejoice in their extraordinary son. Minor absurdities crop up during the family discussion as an indication of cultural and sociopsychological ambivalences: Ginga admonishes her son to marry either a black or a white girl but not a *mestiça*; Almi retorts, in a display of racial solidarity, that *mestiços* are of their race and thus victims of the evils of colonialism. Finally, the novel rambles to a close with Almi's statement that "when a people can bear no more, something happens. For five centuries the seeds of freedom have been germinating in this land" (p. 160).

For all its technical flaws and bombastic, utopian statements of cultural nationalism, *As sementes da liberdade* occupies a significant place in modern Afro-Portuguese literature. As the first contemporary novel by a black *filho da terra* it tells a story of cultural clash and social change, with the important components of the incantatory and ancestral, from the point of view of a descendant of the so-called assimilated African. Lima's approach to a "back to roots" process, with the metaphor of the seeds of freedom strengthening the motif of the land, permits an insight into the Westernized African's psychology, mythologies, and ambivalences.[12]

Domingos Van-Dúnem and a Creole-Kimbundu Revival

The Van-Dúnems of Luanda form the nucleus of an extended family whose roots go deep into Kimbundu tradition.[13] This tradition has been sustained by a set of moral and cultural values that have given old African families a sense of pride and identity in a larger societal framework that generally denies the philosophical validity of an African tradition. The Van-Dúnems place a premium on formal, Western education, but, along with other extended African families, they reject the condescending categorization of assimilation. In effect, their attitudes and life style resolve some of the ambivalences displayed by the family in Santos Lima's novel.

Of the several Van-Dúnems who grew to adulthood at the time of the contemporary cultural and literary movement in Angola, only Domingos has cultivated the family's sense of cultural resilience through writing. Small and unpretentious as this writing and research may be, Domingos Van-Dúnem has a historical importance in the development of Angolan prose fiction. He continues a literary tradition and demonstrates a purity that brings a certain freshness to the type of story set in Luanda's *musseques*. In his unpublished story "Uma história singular" (An Unusual Story, 1957), he employs a familiar subject and technique. The story concerns Nha Moça, a *mestiço* woman who, unable to pay her rent, submits to the lust of the white landlord. She gives birth to a son, Xiquito, and the landlord, Florentino, abandons her. Xiquito grows up the physical image of his father, and he excells in soccer and charm, but because of his dissipations he falls ill and dies of tuberculosis. On the day of the funeral Florentino drives by the cemetery in his big American car and stops to watch the burial with more curiosity than grief. Despite its banality the story reveals a form, structure, and use of language that give it a significant place in Angolan prose fiction. First of all, the author works against his linear narration by inserting extraneous material and asides that reflect, as in the case of Assis Júnior's novel, the influence of an African narrative aesthetic. Specifically, Van-Dúnem appears to simulate an oral technique whereby a story is slightly different every time it is told. In other words, the reader gets the impression that he is listening to a story based on facts generally known to everyone and therefore dependent in their dramatic effect on the improvisatory ability of the teller. At the same time, the author very consciously uses and even exaggerates conventional nonoral literary techniques. He builds up a tension between the somewhat stilted Portuguese of his third-person narrator and the black Portuguese, sprinkled with Kimbundu phrases, of the story's characters. A synthesis of the two occurs at the end when an elderly man delivers a eulogy over Xiquito's grave. While Christian in vocabulary, the eulogy has elements of the African praise song in that it presents a rambling, detailed, and imagistically picturesque account of the dead boy's life. The eulogizer points out the flaws in the boy's character but calls him a rogue rather than a ne'er-do-well. Also, he passes lightly over the usual images of the Heaven-bound soul and discourses on the communal spirit of Xiquito as revealed in his social contributions: he had founded the Angolan Literary Center, a group which, in the old man's words, "afforded a certain intellectual level to the people of our land and aided in the struggle against the degrading situation in which we find ourselves."[14] Phrases in the eulogy such as "he who founded the Angolan Literary Center" parallel mnemonic and rhythmic designations found in the African praise song.

Also significant is the fact that throughout the story Van-Dúnem seems to be parodying his own style of writing. A line in the story's first paragraph reads, "The imperious necessity of the struggle for existence obliged them, men and women, to tread the sandy soil of Cabilango beneath a blazing sun" (p. 2). Even if not consciously, Van-Dúnem exaggerates, and therefore ridicules, the exotic descriptions of colonial literature. Later, he seems deliberately to attempt burlesque language when he describes the *cipaio* Kubindama's search for Nga Moça's shack in the maze of *musseque* dwellings: "Kubindama stuck his forefinger in his nostril; one would say that he was seeking a solution to his distressing problem" (p. 8).

The story's many examples of sententious phrases and modified proverbs give evidence of an African talent for improvisations and indirect statement. At one point a character recalls that a victim of the landlord took legal action against him, but to no avail because "Dimanda dia ngulu kudifundilé kiombo": "one should not complain of the swine to the wild boar, because they are brothers and will always support one another. A proverb the old folks tell, and the old folks are always right" (p. 5). Verbal play, as a part of a people's psychological survival, comes out in this otherwise simple story with an aesthetic appeal that demands rereading.

Social abuses, so belabored by writers of Portuguese Africa, surface with a disarming unpretentiousness in "Uma história singular." The question of color distinctions, for example, while treated insistently but tastefully by writers such as Arnaldo Santos, flashes unexpectedly in the pages of Van-Dúnem's story with devastating statements. During his illness Xiquito dreams that Marcolino, an elderly black man, is strangling him: "He awoke, breathing heavily. Old man Marcolino never forgave him for striking him because he [Xiquito] would not permit a black man to live with his mother. But Marcolino was stubborn. He would wait for Xiquito to die in order to realize his amorous desires" (p. 9). This matter of fact comment on the reality of distinctions based on color makes a dramatic impression in the context of Xiquito's dream and of Marcolino's morbid patience.

Van-Dúnem admits that he often thinks in Kimbundu and then translates into Portuguese when he writes, and this perhaps explains certain stylistic peculiarities in his few short stories and two or three plays. During 1970 and 1971 Domingos Van-Dúnem gained the opportunity to proselytize, in a manner of speaking, for the concept of a creole-Kimbundu aesthetic and a revival of native Angolan folklore. He edited a section in the popular Luanda magazine *Noite e dia*, and in the April 1971 issue he published a vignette entitled "Oh! o Sporting destruiu tudo" (Oh! Sporting Destroyed Everything). The story can be taken as a clever preface to his subsequent articles on Angolan folklore which is being replaced by imported diversions. The narrator tells of how on a trip to the City of Novo Redondo he encounters a slightly inebriated old woman singing a European folk song. When asked if she knows any Angolan songs she retorts that Sporting has destroyed everything, Sporting being a local soccer team. When the team was formed, the young men stopped listening to the old songs and then the young women stopped singing them; the men played soccer instead, and the women cheered them.

Van-Dúnem uses this vignette to introduce his appeal for a codification and restitution of a dying urban folklore. Not a folklorist himself, Van-Dúnem does little more than report on those vestiges of African and popular forms that still survive in Angola's urban areas, and he sees his role as that of a voice of a people who are losing touch with their culture. The small monthly section he edits in a slick, cosmopolitan magazine, devoted mainly to the European scene, especially movies, music, sports, and the arts, may have little impact on the collective conscience of white-oriented Angola, but his efforts do maintain a link with the ideal espoused by the committed Angolan writers and intellectuals of the "Let's Discover Angola" generation.

Finally, note should be taken of Van-Dúnem's endeavors as a playwright, an activity which he began to develop during the fifties when he belonged to the Experimental Theatre Group of Luanda about which, unfortunately, we have scant information. It is known, however, that he launched his own career as a dramatist in 1967 with the unpublished, unstaged, three-act melodrama "Kioxinda" (Fate).[15] In 1972, he published and staged his one-act *Auto de Natal* (Christmas Play). The Catholic priest Father Alexandre do Nascimento, who wrote the preface for the published version, attests to the play's popular appeal and to the author's religious devotion. At first reading, *Auto de Natal* seems in fact to be a curious mixture of Christian piety and naively contrived African folk customs. The play resembles the type of religious didacticism clothed in simple parable that the early missionaries concocted to catechize their African and Indian charges. But Van-Dúnem is not a missionary, and he has something other than religious indoctrination in mind in his bilingual (the text has face-to-face Portuguese and Kimbundu pages) dramatization of the Nativity. In his version of the Christian myth he condenses events and simplifies miracles with incredible rapidity and amazing equanimity. His treatment of Christian myths may appear to be tremendously naive to the Westerner, but in reality all myths are inherently naive. In effect, then, Van-Dúnem's modifications of the story of Jesus' birth are naive only in that they make the Westerner more acutely aware of the element of the improbable and the absurd in the original Christian myth, a myth which we either take for granted, as part of our cultural-ethical background, or perhaps respect with reverent awe as part of our religious training.

In Van-Dúnem's play Joseph tells the medicine man that just that morning he had noticed that his wife Mary was in an "interesting state," which rather perturbed him because he had always shown her the same respect he had for his own mother. The medicine man's reply that we cannot understand everything may strike us as somewhat ludicrous or at least unacceptable as a theological explanation. On the other hand, the Africans before whom this play is performed are familiar with the Christmas story, and the playwright can thus feel free to truncate the action into one day and to pass lightly over the theological explanation of parthenogenesis. In truth, the play seems more a pretext for affirming some African institutions and values than for celebrating the Nativity. Thus, an old hunter and a *kimbanda* or medicine man play important roles with their sententious, moralizing pronouncements, and the *griot*-narrator embellishes the story with his descriptions of village life and his references to local customs.

The play ends on a note of Christian exaltation with the birth of the child, but true to the play's syncretic essence the strains of "Silent Night" merge with the beat of African drums as the narrator calls for harmony and understanding in the spirit of brotherhood. The author undoubtedly strikes this note of solidarity in deference to Lusotropicalist multiracialism. But in spite of the play's defects Van-Dúnem did succeed in bringing an acculturated, African-oriented spectacle to a segment of Luanda's population that had reason to feel culturally alienated or at least not adequately represented in their own land.

It is fitting, then, that this section end with Domingos Van-Dúnem who, while not an outstanding writer, has kept alive a spark of that original zeal that may some day be rekindled in the development of a viable literary expression in Angola.

PART TWO

MOZAMBIQUE

CHAPTER 6

Portugal's
East African Province

In his book *Luanda, "ilha" crioula* Mário António speaks of the
Cape Verde archipelago, the Guinea Gulf islands of São Tomé
and Príncipe, Angola, and Brazil as Atlantic regions that share
certain cultural aspects. He excludes Mozambique obviously because of its location on Africa's east coast and also because its
historical and cultural development differs from that of the Atlantic areas, particularly as far as patterns of acculturation and
civilization are concerned.

Mozambique lies in southeastern Africa, bordered on the north
by Tanzania and Malawi, on the south by South Africa and Swazi-
land, on the east by the Indian Ocean, and on the west by Zambia
and Rhodesia. Although geographically smaller (303,073 square
miles) than Angola, Mozambique has a larger population, about
7,500,000. As in Angola, several Bantu ethnolinguistic groups constitute the bulk of the African population: the Makua-Lomwe
and Makonde in the north, the expert musicians, the Chopes, in
the southeast, and the Tongas in the south and south-central
regions. Mozambique also has a sizable Muslim population as
well as a small, but significant, group of Asians, mainly East
Indians and Chinese, in the coastal cities.

Since the Portuguese presumably have applied the same "native policies" in Mozambique that they did in Angola, we might wonder why the eastern colony has had a unique development. Part of the answer lies in Mozambique's earlier links with Goa (Portuguese East Africa was under the authority of the viceroyalty of Portuguese India until the mid-1700s), its very small European population (about 150,000), and its economic, political, and cultural contacts with the Republic of South Africa, and in recent years, with the independent state of Rhodesia. Since the nineteenth century these and other factors have tended to exacerbate the troubled racial situation in Mozambique. On the other hand, an equally unusual situation developed in Mozambique during the late sixteenth and early seventeenth centuries. In the Zambezi River valley region the local territorial chief, or Monomotapa, had begun to grant Portuguese merchants and soldiers large tracts of land in exchange for their support in tribal wars.[1] These Europeans took African women as their mistresses, and by the time the Portuguese Crown had joined in the enterprise through the granting of *prazos* (land titles lasting for three generations), the white settlers and their *mestiço* descendants had attained great economic and political power and had undergone a process of Africanization in contrast to the creolization of west-central Angola.[2] The period from the seventeenth through the nineteenth centuries might be called the golden age of race relations in Mozambique; still, harmonious multiracialism has been spotty and of little consequence for the 7,000,000 Africans living under the control of 150,000 Europeans.

The principal impetus of the modern literary activities in Mozambique came in the ostensibly European port city of Lourenço Marques where in relatively recent times small numbers of white, black, and *mestiço* intellectuals have begun to take stock of their situation, but not necessarily in concert with one another.

A Tripartite Development

Three social and cultural organizations, basically divided along racial or color lines, emerged in Lourenço Marques about the second decade of this century. The history of these groups provides some clues to the present literary ambient in Mozambique. The Grémio Africano (African Union), founded July 7, 1920, started out with an exclusively black and *mestiço* membership. But according to some who have followed the history of the organization, white instigators, particularly officials of the Fundação de Negócios Indígenas (Foundation for Native Affairs), convinced black members that the *mestiço* leadership of the Grémio did not have the best interests of their darker brothers at heart. As a result, some black members left the Grémio and in 1932 established the Instituto Negrófilo (Negrophile Institute), which was soon renamed the Centro Associativo dos Negros da Colônia de Moçambique (Associative Center of the Negroes of the Colony of Mozambique), it having occurred to someone that the original title was better suited to a nonblack group. Meanwhile, the Grémio Africano, now almost completely *mestiço*, had also adopted a new name, Associação Africana (African Association). Then, in 1935, some native-born whites organized themselves into the Associação dos Naturais de Moçambique (Association of the Native Sons of Mozambique). Sometimes referred to as "second-class whites," these native sons set as their goal the attainment of political and economic equality with metropolitan-born Portuguese, or "first-class whites." About 1960 this organization reversed its whites-only policy and launched a campaign to recruit black and *mestiço* members, this being a means, of course, of gaining greater political and economic power in a changing social climate.

Despite these attempts at alliance, harmonious multiracialism seemed doomed to failure by already hardened lines of color and social distinctions. Black Mozambicans tell the anecdote of two African couples who accepted an invitation to a dance sponsored by the previously all white group. Perplexed whites pointed out to the black couples, as they took to the dance floor, that they may have been invited to the dance, but not necessarily to dance. Official policy, it would seem, does not always determine social practices in Mozambique.

More damaging are the divisive attitudes among black and *mestiço* Mozambicans. Depending upon the source, we get varying accounts of who caused the rift. According to some black observers, a mulatto elite had ruled the Associação Africana and excluded blacks from policy-making decisions. Some *mestiços* argued, to the contrary, that the Albasini brothers and Dr. Karel Monjardim Pott, all important figures in the early years of the association, were conscientious mulattoes who had the interests of the less fortunate black man at heart. Whatever the truth of the matter, accusations have flown back and forth, obviously to the delight of the white power structure. *Mestiços* have claimed, for example, that blacks have generally refused to dance the popular *marrabenta* and to eat typical African foods, while they, the mulattoes, have done more to preserve authentic African culture.

Amidst the accusations and counteraccusations, the gathering forces of nationalism in the early sixties helped to bring about the founding, within the black association, of a secondary school studies nucleus led by Dr. Eduardo Mondlane who, until his death, directed FRELIMO (Mozambique Liberation Front). José Craveirinha, the *mestiço* poet, and Luís Bernardo Honwana, an important young, black short story writer, participated along with other artists and intellectuals in the nucleus which was generally opposed to the conservative policies of the Associative Center's leadership. Eventually, several of the members of the nucleus were arrested and sentenced for alleged subversive activities connected with FRELIMO, and in 1965 the Centro Associativo dos Negros itself was ordered closed by the authorities.

In regard to artistic activity, members of the three organizations found an outlet for literary and cultural expression in *O Brado Africano* (The African Roar) and *A Voz de Moçambique* (The Voice of Mozambique), both being newspapers still in publication. In 1916 João Albasini established *O Africano*, which two years later became *O Brado Africano* and has served as the official organ of the Associação Africana. Besides its regular section written in the Ronga language of the southern Tonga people, it has printed stories, poetry, and articles by many of Mozambique's most important writers and intellectuals. *A Voz de Moçambique*, the official newspaper of the Associação dos Naturais de Moçambique, likewise has afforded writers the opportunity to see their poems, stories, and articles in print. The Centro Associativo dos Negros has had no official publication, but within the secondary school studies nucleus aspiring writers have received encouragement to pursue their literary and artistic endeavors.

The *mestiço* and white groups have continued to exist without interruption, and the black organization reopened in 1969 as a strictly social center. But the experiment in racial cooperation has mainly failed despite the present superficial harmony among certain members of the three more or less distinct groups. Racial separatism and traditional Portuguese paternalism have resulted in a climate of artistic production in which nonwhites must frequently depend on a white, albeit liberal, protector. This system of patronage has, in some cases, facilitated the publication of some significant works and the showing of paintings by blacks and *mestiços*, but it has inevitably stymied an independent development and a critical philosophy similar to those in Angola. As we consider the question of literature in and of Mozambique, this last statement will receive further qualification.

CHAPTER 7

Mozambique's Modern Literary Climate

Rui de Noronha, who died in 1943 at the age of thirty-four, left a collection of poetry called *Sonetos* (Sonnets), which was published posthumously in 1949 and apparently was considerably revised by the editors. This *mestiço* poet borrowed from a European tradition of Parnassian-like verse, and within the fixed metrics of his poetry he occasionally rose to heights of exhortation. This is exemplified in "Surge et ambula" (Arise and Walk), one of his most frequently quoted and anthologized sonnets in which he calls on a supine and somnolent Africa to stand up and march shoulder to shoulder with the rest of the world. The Mozambican critic Eugênio Lisboa has written that Noronha is "a more or less mediocre poet, not because he is not very representative of a specifically African set of problems, but very simply because his poetry, as poetry, is little more than mediocre."[1] Lisboa is right on both counts, and more will be said presently on poetry as poetry, but the fact that Noronha did use an African thematic, of sorts, makes him historically important in the context of Mozambican literature.

It would be redundant, however, to evaluate Noronha's poetry, since technically and thematically it differs little from much of what can be considered representative of Angolan poets. His poem "Quenguelequeze" (a Ronga salute to the moon) has the same contrived exoticism found in many of Bessa Victor's pieces, to draw but one comparison. Bessa Victor achieved much of his exotic effect with Kimbundu words, while Noronha depended on the Ronga language for the same effect.

Similarly, João Dias, the black author of one book, *Godido e outros contos* (Godido and Other Stories, 1952), while of some historical significance in the development of Mozambican literature, exhibits the same technical defects as those of some Angolan writers. During his short life (1926–49) he experienced the frustrations of the black man in a hostile, white society. His stories contain a note of bitterness that will be observed as an important factor in the writings of several authors from the islands of São Tomé and Príncipe. In an autobiographical piece entitled "Em terras do norte" (In Lands of the North), the black protagonist disembarks from a train in rural Portugal to face the curiosity, derision, and even the animosity of the local villagers. He ruminates about the repulsion whites feel toward his color and then considers that when Portuguese mariners first reached Africa they reacted to the people's color with such envy that as a defense they assigned the negative label of black to the skin hue they in reality admired. The narrator then says, "Today, nobody seems to notice that our color is not black. 'Coal is black' the offended children of my neighborhood used to retort."[2] In the turgid prose of his essayistic stories Dias reveals a bitterness and sarcasm that reflect the hypersensitivity of a black Mozambican reared in a society where racism has generally lacked the veiled subtleties of São Tomé and Angola.

Dias's stories, like Rui de Noronha's sonnets, represent early manifestations of the types of tensions that would continue during the more recent decades in Mozambique. Although many parallels exist between Mozambique and the other regions of Portuguese Africa, Mozambique also offers a uniqueness of literary expression, both in the works of individual authors and in its polemical aspects.

Mozambique's Regional Consciousness

The move toward a regional, literary consciousness in Mozambique gained impetus in the early 1950s. One indication of a new literary and cultural awareness came in the form of a few pages of poetry published in 1952 under the title *Msaho* (a type of song of the Chope people); then in August 1957 appeared, in the Mozambican city of Beira, the first issue of a monthly magazine called *Paralelo 20* (the twentieth parallel passes very close to Beira) which was to continue until February 1961. These coordinated efforts by Mozambicans themselves signaled the beginning of a sometimes soul-searching consideration of the province's cultural autonomy. To *Msaho* eight poets each contributed one to three poems. Some of the contributors can be identified as genuine poets while others are first and foremost members of a generation which saw poetry as a valid means of participating in a heightened cultural and artistic awakening. Thus, *Msaho* can be said to have at least a symbolic importance.

From 1959 to 1963 the Casa dos Estudantes do Império published poetry anthologies from three regions of Portuguese Africa, including *Poetas de Moçambique* (Poets of Mozambique, 1962), which consists of poems published previously in such newspapers as *O Brado Africano*, *A Voz de Moçambique*, and *A Tribuna*. The anthology brings together samplings of the works of twenty-six poets; it also includes some traditional Chope songs as proof of the same interest in an African oral tradition displayed by the Angolans in *Poetas angolanos*.

Along with the anthologizing of poetry came, in *Paralelo 20* and in a special supplement of the Angolan journal *Mensagem*, articles and appraisals of the literary phenomenon in Mozambique. But it was Alfredo Margarido who set off a significant, and somewhat bizarre, debate with his appraisal of poetry in Mozambique.

Polemics and the Question of
Poetry in Mozambique

Alfredo Margarido, who has written on all areas of Afro-Portuguese literature, applied, in his introduction to *Poetas de Mozambique*, a modified Marxist approach to Mozambican poetry. Among his several declarations is the assertion that "we therefore should enunciate some problems linked to Mozambique's socioeconomic structure, because this poetry must have as its primary objective a didactic function, and in order to accomplish this end it has to structure and radicalize the needs of the masses so as to reveal, with its basis in these very elements, the essentially historical objectives toward which the social current flows."[3] Such statements could not help but elicit a reaction from those members of the Mozambican cultural and literary elite who considered poetry as an end in itself.

The white Mozambican poet Rui Knopfli issued a mild protest, without mentioning Margarido by name, in the arts and letters section of *A Tribuna*, a Lourenço Marques newspaper. Margarido in turn replied to Knopfli in the April 1963 issue of *Mensagem*, a journal published in Lisbon by the Casa dos Estudantes do Império and named after the then defunct Angolan cultural and literary review. To Margarido's sarcastic article, entitled "A poesia moçambicana e os críticos de óculos" (Mozambican Poetry and the Bespectacled Critics), Knopfli responded with the first installment of a three-part essay published in *A Voz de Moçambique*. He made these major points: (1) too much importance has been given to the incipient phenomenon of Mozambican poetry; (2) anthologies and certain critics have limited themselves to problems concerning only the black man; (3) poetry anywhere is a specific aesthetic phenomenon and should be treated as such; (4) Mozambican poetry can only be defined in all its diversity as suggested in item two; (5) all other considerations, speculative or not, have to be approached and developed around the basic themes outlined in these points.[4] "A small oracle of Mozambican culture," Margarido termed Knopfli in "Do poeta Knopfli à cultura moçambicana" (From the Poet Knopfli to Mozambican Culture), published in the June 1963 issue of *Mensagem*.

The debate was rapidly reaching the level of derisive comments and ad hominem attacks as Margarido and Knopfli assailed one another. Margarido, in a short note entitled "Outra vez o poeta" (Once Again, the Poet), defended the ranking of poets according to their importance as representatives of the praxis of black Mozambique. "Praxis," used in its Marxist sense, appears several times in Margarido's writings, and Knopfli makes it a point to ridicule him for his insistence on the word. Knopfli indeed has the last say in the controversy with his article "Ainda o diletante Alfredo Margarido" (Still the Dilettante, Alfredo Margarido), which appeared in *A Tribuna*. From the standpoint of wit and a compelling argument Knopfli emerged the victor in the protracted debate. Still, the major question remains unresolved: what can be considered Mozambican poetry, and who should be considered a poet of Mozambique? Knopfli himself admits to having engaged José Craveirinha, a fellow poet, in friendly debate on the matter, and, of course, the two differed on whom they would include in the category of poet of Mozambique.

Before attempting to reach some conclusion on the question of poetry in and of Mozambique, we must discuss another participant in the debate. Eugênio Lisboa, a perceptive and provocative critic, has contributed several articles on the subject of poetry in Mozambique. One such article is the preface to Rui Knopfli's 1969 collection of poetry *Mangas verdes com sal* (Green Mangoes with Salt). Lisboa supports and supplements Knopfli's main points on the subject with the contention that poetry is its own reality, its own universe. Like Knopfli, Lisboa quotes some European theorists to defend his basic thesis, but his most significant reference is to the Mexican poet Octavio Paz. In his book *El arco y la lira* (The Bow and the Lyre) Paz defines poetry, in very poetic prose, as multifaceted, involving many things that have to do with human experience. Poetry, he writes, is the "voice of the people," and Lisboa follows this up with the comment "voice of the people, collective voice—some beautiful poems by Craveirinha

would fit this, also (if her language were up to it) would some of
Noémia de Sousa's poems fit this . . ."⁵ Lisboa categorizes other
Mozambican poets on the basis of Paz's definition: Knopfli, for
example, belongs to the group of those who speak the "language
of the elect."

In a later article, "A poesia em Moçambique" (Poetry in Mozambique), Lisboa states that poets such as Noémia de Sousa
were "invented," meaning that her rhetoric and subject matter
have given her a prestige out of proportion to her talent as a
poet. (More will be said about Noémia de Sousa's poetry later.)
But although Lisboa and Knopfli stand firm on what constitutes
the language of poetry, they exhibit a frustration and impatience
that occasionally result in flippancy when they attempt to demystify the literary situation in Mozambique. Lisboa wrote, for example, that "an infinite number of cartridges has been fired in
Byzantine distortions: José Craveirinha is a Mozambican poet,
Reinaldo Ferreira is a European poet, Rui Knopfli is a complicated mixture of the two . . . Rui Noronha is black in color but
white in his sonnets, Fernando Ganhão is white of skin but black
in content, Rui Nogar is somewhere in between."⁶ Of course, all
are poets born in Mozambique. Under the pretext of denying
rigid classifications of poetry, Lisboa implies that categorization
based on an African thematic or lack of it has no validity, although he himself talks about the "voice of the people" and the
"language of the elect" as separate groupings. It seems even more
likely and necessary to make these distinctions for an incipient
poetic expression (good, bad, and indifferent) than for an established literature, and even more so in Mozambique where social
and racial factors confuse and complicate the cultural scene.
Angolans have wrestled with the problem of poetry *of* and *in*
Angola, and in Mozambique the problem has been aggravated by
the absence of a viable black and *mestiço* bourgeois elite. A relatively small group of white Mozambicans, led by Knopfli and
Lisboa, has grappled with the philosophical and aesthetic questions inherent in the phenomenon of literary expression and culture, and in doing so their own exasperations have occasionally

obscured some of the basic issues that by necessity relate the poetry of Mozambique to the social conditions there. Margarido erred mainly by relegating poetry to a position subordinate to its artistic value, and he left himself open to the censure of those who understand that form cannot be divorced from content.

There are many kinds of poetry, as the critic David Caute points out in his introduction to the English translation of Jean-Paul Sartre's *Qu'est que ce la littérature?* (*What is Literature?* 1967). He takes issue with Sartre on some fundamental points concerning poetry:

Prose, he [Sartre] argues, is capable of a purposeful reflection of the world, whereas poetry is an end in itself. In prose, words are significative; they describe men and objects. In poetry, the words are ends in themselves. It is doubtful whether Sartre's radical distinction is a tenable one. Many kinds of poetry exist, ranging from the communicative and discursive (as in 18th-century England) to the most "poetic" and symbolist (as with Rimbaud and Mallarmé). Although criticism of a poem must pay close attention to its immanent structure of words and symbols, it is obvious that the reader enters the poem through word associations and references which are linked, however indirectly, to everyday significative language.[7]

Lisboa indicates, in his enthusiasm for Octavio Paz's openended, inclusive description of poetry, that he too accepts the fact that there are many kinds of poetry. As was already mentioned, Knopfli maintains that poetry in Mozambique should be seen in all its diversity and not just in the assemblage of problems relating to the black man. The trouble is that even though Mozambique may also be the 150,000 or so whites who run the province, it is still valid to approach the question of Mozambican poetry from the standpoint of a literature of Portuguese expression that makes use of an African thematic. This approach will naturally exclude some of the more purely European poets, but it will include others who, often indirectly, enhance and give form to the phenomenon. Likewise, those black, white, and *mestiço* poets who sing, often discursively and even artlessly, of an African

Mozambique deserve inclusion in the framework of a literature of Portuguese expression. Universal tenets and the primal cry of poetry notwithstanding, good, even excellent, poets such as Alberto de Lacerda and Reinaldo Ferreira warrant less attention than does, say, a lesser poet such as Noémia de Sousa. And, it is not so much that too much attention has been paid to Mozambican poetry, but rather that the individual poet, representative of this incipient movement, has been projected into a position of importance he does not fully deserve as an artist.

The black and *mestiço* poets who write from or within a black psychology and who assume a committed or militant stance constitute a category—obviously of significance to anyone interested in an African literature of Portuguese expression in Mozambique. White poets who attempt to write from an African perspective or who display a committed sense of regionalism form another group that can be further broken down into subdivisions, such as those who merely exteriorize and those who identify. If a poetry *of* Mozambique means anything, then those who consciously write from a European perspective, and who, for want of a better designation, are called Euro-Africans, play a role in our consideration only insofar as they take part in the two categories just identified. So, expanding on the allusion to Alberto de Lacerda and Reinaldo Ferreira, it can be said that they are poets who write almost exclusively within a European tradition and should therefore be viewed in the context of contemporary Portuguese poetry; on the other hand, that element in their poetry which reflects any discernible aspect of a Mozambican reality, even an acculturated or Europeanized one, does deserve passing commentary in this study. To contemplate briefly how the varied Mozambican reality affects a Euro-African writer, we might mention one white Mozambican critic's contention that the poet Rui Knopfli is presently going through an identity crisis. Presumably, then, Knopfli does have ambivalent feelings toward the question of poetry *in* and *of* Mozambique. And Eugénio Lisboa is no less ambivalent than Knopfli when he implicitly rejects the idea that Knopfli is a mixture of the European and the African, if by mixture is meant a sensitivity to his place in the mainstream of European poetry and his consious relationship to non-European thematic elements as represented in his art. Indeed, Knopfli has shown that he can be sensitive to the black reality around him even if he neither fully comprehends nor completely accepts it.

Northrup Frye has written that "in literature man *is* a spectator of his own life, or at least of the larger vision in which his life is contained."[8] This larger vision includes not only the universal but also the microcosmic immediacy of a regional experience. In the case of the Mozambican poet who aspires to capture the essence of the word, extraliterary factors conspire frequently to lend an artistic tension to his work. Subliminally or otherwise, some white Mozambican poets are aware of the so-called African praxis, and this awareness contributes to this tension in form and content. A white Mozambican intellectual has said that for some of his group there remains one of two alternatives: either to paint themselves black or to join the ranks of those in power, the latter being the ultraconservative wing that currently controls the destiny of the province. In its flippancy this remark neatly sums up the dilemma of the white intellectual who, while ideologically and philosophically opposed to the political and social status quo in Mozambique, does not see himself as expendable in any radical alternative. Such a situation may be at hand with the change of government in Portugal. For the time being, however, only the literary scene as it appears before April 1974 can be assessed.

No less ambivalent than his Euro-African colleagues, the *mestiço* poet José Craveirinha commands the respect and admiration of those who uphold the idea of poetry for poetry's sake. Craveirinha pays for this acceptance in that he must always be the protégé. The "clever black lad" has become a negative catch phrase for the paternalism of the colonialist mentality which is played out in the patronage of promising writers or artists by white intellectuals. Certainly, in the practical sense, the good offices of a white elite have afforded some blacks and *mestiços* an opportunity that the general racist structure of Mozambican society would ordinarily deny them. But the lack of a certain self-determination has the disadvantage of a kind of vassalage which means that when the non-white becomes more than just a clever black lad he represents a threat to the white fief. The painter Malangatana, the poet Craveirinha, and the short story writer Luís Bernardo Honwana have been at once the victims and the beneficiaries of this set of circumstances. Craveirinha has reacted with a certain bitterness to the offhanded racism of some of his colleague-protectors, and maybe his hypersensitivity makes him resent such relatively minor, but sociologically significant, incidents as the casual remark of a white friend that he had sent the "black" to get his suit from the cleaners; the black being the houseboy (*moleque*). On the other hand, Craveirinha reacts to what is inherent in such otherwise innocent comments; he reacts to the fact that the black masses on the periphery of the white city have been depersonalized, even when they perform their function as domestics in the homes of Europeans.

Even more significantly, Craveirinha rejects the inclusion of a host of poets in the category of poets of Mozambique. And this brings us back to the basic dilemma of poets *in* and *of* Mozambique. Both sides of the issue present problems: to deal with only those poets who reflect an African thematic is to reduce the field to a very few, while to include those who display a strictly Western viewpoint is to blur the picture of an Afro-Portuguese literary phenomenon in Mozambique. The literary climate is confused and amorphous, but certain patterns have evolved to the point where some semblance of a direction can be seen.

CHAPTER 8

Euro-African Writers

I have chosen to adopt Euro-African as a term that applies both to those writers who shun the regionalistic for a more universalist expression and to those who, while they may employ a regionalist thematic, do so more as spectators to the incipient events of an Afro-Portuguese literary expression in Mozambique. Euro-African writers can be identified in the other areas considered, particularly in Angola, but in Mozambique they are more in evidence, because of the lack of a more or less coordinated cultural and literary movement equivalent to the "Let's Discover Angola!" group.

Alberto de Lacerda and Reinaldo Ferreira represent some of the best Portuguese-language poetry of the last few decades. It could be said, however, that their poetry would be essentially the same if they had been born and raised in Lisbon, or in the metropolitan province of Tras-os-Montes, instead of in the overseas province of Mozambique. (Ferreira was not born in Mozambique but lived much of his life there.) The following fragment from one of Ferreira's three poems included in *Poetas de Moçambique* demonstrates the extent of his nonregionalism:

Eu, Rosie, eu se falasse, eu dir-te-ia
Que partout, everywhere, em toda parte,
A vida égale, idêntica, the same,
E' sempre um esforço inútil,
Um voo cego a nada.[1]

(I, Rosie, if I were to speak, I would tell you/That *partout*, everywhere, *em toda parte*,/Life is *égale*, *idêntica*, the same,/It is always
a useless effort,/A blind flight to nothingness.)

Ferreira's universal ennui that crosses language barriers (only
European languages) in its sameness may in some way reflect the
poet's condition as a European cut off, geographically, from Europe—and this has something to say about poetry *in* Mozambique.

Alberto de Lacerda dedicated his collection of poems, *Exílio*
(Exile, 1963), to his native city of Ilha de Moçambique, but a
promotional band on the book's cover bears these words by the
poet and critic René Char: "In Europe, the poetry of today and
tomorrow is represented by some fifteen names. Alberto de
Lacerda, whose voice is universal, is one of them." The landscape
of Mozambique makes subtle imagistic appearances in Lacerda's
intimist poetry, and this may be reason enough to include him
in a consideration of poetry in Mozambique. But the earth from
which Lacerda's art springs is not that of the place of his birth.
He left Mozambique at the age of eighteen and has lived mainly
in Portugal, Great Britain, and the United States; thus, it is easy
to understand how, despite his formative years in Africa, he could
detach himself from all but the nostalgic home, landscape, and
occasionally shadowy, black figure that one sees in a very few of
his poems. A close analysis might reveal, of course, that his poems
contain in their internal structure the cadences of Mozambique
or some other subtle feature that would identify him as Mozambican, but generally speaking he falls outside of the context of this
study.

Here I shall consider those Euro-African writers who either
vacillate between a strictly Western tradition and an African colonialist romanticism or, in fewer cases, espouse a perspective that

reveals something about the conflict of which they find themselves a part. Admittedly, some nonwhite writers may fall within this category. In Mozambique, however, the overt racial animosities seem to have created a distinctive body of literature by white writers.

To be sure, a number of Euro-African writers represented in such anthologies as *Poetas de Moçambique* express the same regionalist invocation and evocation, childhood nostalgia, alienation, and identification found in Angolan literature. In the category of regionalist tags, for example, *monangamba*, the word for contract laborer, used by the poet António Jacinto, for one, identifies the poetry as Angolan. In much Mozambican literature *magaíça* is used to label the worker who goes to the Rand gold mines of South Africa.

Fernando Ganhão, whom Alfredo Maragrido has called the only white Mozambican poet to assume a black praxis, uses Ronga words for their exotic sound in his lyrical ballads. His "Ronda da infância" (Childhood Round Dance) has a soft musicality that accompanies the nostalgia in free-verse stanzas which are literally overloaded with African words beginning with the letter "m": *Malanga, Mafalala, Mamanas, malimune, machope, mafurreira, moleques,* and *mufanas.* The capitalized words are place names or proper nouns, and most of the others refer to foods or to certain human types. Ganhão demonstrates his familiarity with that African world that moves on the outskirts of the white city of Lourenço Marques, a world which he sentimentalizes and exoticizes in lines punctuated with exclamations; he strives to capture the elusiveness of an essence he can only reconstruct as an observer without the aesthetic sensitivity of José Craveirinha.

Another Euro-African poet, novelist, dramatist, and short story writer, Orlando Mendes, declared himself to be Mozambique's first mature poet, much to the consternation of Rui Knopfli who wrote a generally unfavorable review of Mendes's poetry collection *Clima* (Climate, 1959). Miffed by Knopfli's evaluation, Mendes asked for a clarification, which Knopfli offered in the May 1960 *A Voz de Moçambique* in an article humorously entitled "Clima instável" (Unstable Climate): "Any sensible person with good taste knows that this [Mendes's] supposed grandeur is a speck of dust at the door of the true grandeur of a Reinaldo Ferreira, that his *métier* is an anecdote at the feet of the formal grandeur of a Cordeiro de Brito, that his *Moçambicanismo* is laughable in comparison with the genuine, radical expression of a Craveirinha or a Noémia de Sousa. All of them are much, much greater, much more authentic than any O. Mendes."[2] With his usual verve Knopfli overstates his case, for even he would agree that Mendes is a better than average poet. Perhaps, though, his criticism says something important about the dilemma of the Euro-African writer. Where indeed do many of these writers fit in the realm of a literature of Mozambique? If they possess the talent of a Reinaldo Ferreira or an Alberto de Lacerda, they can compete in the broader arena of European poetry. If they have a regionalist bent, but genuinely so, they must compete with the authenticity of poets who feel a sense of the land and the culture. Mendes calls himself a mature poet because he generally avoids overt exoticism while adopting a regionalist thematic. But he runs the risk of being neither fish nor fowl; he remains on the periphery of the more or less committed regionalism of a Fernando Ganhão, and he does not achieve the level of expression of a Reinaldo Ferreira.

If Mendes's poetic voice is constrained, then the language of his prose fiction is exaggerated and analytical. His novel *Portagem* (Toll, 1965) treats a recurring theme in Mozambican literature: the tribulations of those with mixed blood. The novel's mulatto protagonist, João Xilim (Xilim being a corruption of shilling and reflecting the influence of South Africa in Mozambique), travels from his interior village to a coastal city, and along the way he is faced with the consequences of being neither black nor white. This theme of the marginal man is described in a ponderous, naturalistic manner as the author dramatizes in bizarre episodes the antipathy toward the mulatto by both whites and blacks. João Xilim's problems begin in childhood, for he is the unhappy prototype of the *mestiço* who must constantly bear the shame of a wanton mother and the blemish of a licentious father. A leavening of incest—João's white half-sister seduces him—adds to the social pathology, and a lack of verisimilitude occurs when the half-sister reappears years later as the wife of João's employer. During João's trial for the murder of his wife, the defense lawyer declares the mulatto to be as underdeveloped and simpleminded as the black. All in all, Mendes paints a bleak picture of deplorable and irremediable racism. This sociological novel may give a true, dramatized account of the dispossessed mulatto, but it is unconvincing as a work of art because of the mock tragic tone of its exalted seriousness.

Other Euro-African writers present cul-de-sac racial situations in their works of fiction. Vieira Simões's *Vagabundo na cidade* (Vagabond in the City, 1959) is subtitled *Crónicas e histórias quase verdadeiras* (Chronicles and Almost True Stories), and in three of the sixteen narratives he treats the black man's plight as a symbol of the demise of a people. In literal terms Simões goes beyond the theme of the end of a way of life to deal directly with the theme of death. In "O mar chama por mim" (The Sea Calls to Me) a small boy, drawn by his native fishing village, leaves his job in the city to continue the family tradition even though he knows that he will one day be swept out to sea like his father before him. Death also appears as a theme in "Pequenino" (Little One) which tells of a houseboy from the backlands who lives a forlorn existence in the city and on Christmas night dies of a broken heart, symbolically on the road that leads to the backlands. With rather gross sentimentality the author heightens the sense of the separation of two worlds by having the boy die of longing for his African village on the most important of Christian holy days. And, not content with that note of irony, Simões becomes mawkish with a final statement on the social and racial climate of Mozambique when the narrator reminds his readers that only they know the boy did not really succumb to alcoholism. The houseboy (*moleque*) becomes a tragic figure in Mozambican prose fiction because as a child, signifying innocence and defenselessness, and as an often semi-assimilated African, living in close proximity with Europeans, he offers the writer the opportunity to delineate dramatic situations of racial exploitation.

Simões uses a journalistic approach to document commonplace incidents in his collection *Cidade dos confins* (Border Town, 1963). One of the so-called "small plots" tells the story of a white public employee who plans to marry a mulatto girl. His fellow worker, Henrique, terms him a liberal who would have second thoughts about his sister sitting next to a *moleque* on the bus. The progressive Alberto finally marries the mulatto girl, and it is suggested that they would live somewhat happily ever after. What the author really conveys is the virulent racist attitudes of many lower- and middle-class white Mozambicans. Economics, particularly the competition for jobs, has helped make the Mozambican brand of racism more visceral than that found in Angola. Simões documents this fact through a series of dialogues between Alberto and the white supremacist Henrique who does not even pay lip service to the Lusotropicalist myths of racial harmony and miscegenation. At one point during the discussion on race, Alberto produces from his wallet the clipping of a letter sent to a local newspaper by a black taxi driver. The man apologizes for his "bad" Portuguese, saying that he would prefer to write in *landim* (a popular designation for the Ronga language of southern Mozambique) to express his feelings better. He tells the readers that his livelihood depends on his being a careful driver, but that occasionally everyone, regardless of race, commits a traffic infraction. When it happens to be a "person of color" he has to bear insults and racial epithets. The cabbie ends with the sarcastic observation that in Europe, where there are few blacks, there must be practically no automobile accidents. In a footnote Simões verifies that the letter did appear in a local newspaper. This kind of reporting marks the young prose fiction of Mozambique with a stamp of social documentary, more so than in the case of the Angolan short story which, while revelatory, is more imaginative and identifies more closely with the black characters with which it deals.

One of the more prolific and better known Euro-African writers is Rodrigues Júnior who was born in Lisbon and raised on the Island of Madeira. Rodrigues Júnior represents an officially sanctioned African literature of Portuguese expression and therefore is the heir to the colonial crown of black Mozambican culture. Gerald Moser includes him in the category of the Angolans Reis Ventura and Henrique Galvão, colonialists whose "attitude oscillates between ideal brotherliness and practical paternalism."[3] Moser quotes from a letter sent to him by Rodrigues Júnior in 1961, which proudly proclaims: "I carry Africa in my blood, and in my flesh and in my soul. I understand Africa better than I do Europe" (p. 16). Moser characterizes Rodrigues Júnior well, but later in the same essay he writes that "Rui Knopfli in poetry and Rodrigues Júnior in essays and novels cut the umbilical cord [with Europe] and asserted their Africanness" (p. 28). Knopfli and Rodrigues Júnior make strange bedfellows in that their political stances as well as their approaches to the question of Mozambican culture are diametrically opposed. Knopfli unleashed a scathing attack on Rodrigues Júnior in an article entitled "Uma nova teoria racista da poesia: Poetas em escala Júnior" (A New Racist Theory of Poetry: Poets on a Júnior Scale) which appeared in *A Voz de Moçambique* (14 September 1963). In another newspaper, *O Diário* (8 September 1963), Rodrigues Júnior had put forth some attitudes on Mozambican poetry which Knopfli termed inverse "Margaridismo." Alfredo Margarido and Rodrigues Júnior stand left hand in left hand as supporters of concepts that run counter to the Knopfli-Lisboa concern with the multifaceted poetry of Mozambique. If Margarido excludes those poets who do not express an African infrastructure, Rodrigues Júnior, in Knopfli's view, makes contradictory and racist rankings: in the article cited above, he calls Rui de Noronha a highly representative Mozambican poet and Knopfli a minor poet, but then rearranges his order, placing Knopfli second and Noronha sixth on his scale of poetic values. Knopfli concludes that because white poets occupy the first two positions in Rodrigues Júnior's rankings, *mestiços* the next three, and Noronha, who is presumably a mixture of East Indian and African, the sixth, race must have been a criterion. According to Knopfli, Rodrigues Júnior upholds pseudoscientific theories on vocational suitability based on race. What we can gather from Knopfli's attack is that he, in all his frustration and anger, expressed in sarcasm and biting witticisms, represents a more honest position in the total panorama of Mozambican literature.

Rui Knopfli and the Essence of the Word

Rodrigues Júnior, for all his professions of Africanness, has a condescending attitude toward the black reality he re-creates in his works; Rui Knopfli, for all his "poetry for poetry's sake" stance, gravitates toward a meaningful position in relation to that same black reality.

Knopfli takes derisive exception to Margarido's assertion that "Knopfli is not really a European poet but rather a European born in Mozambique who denies Europe not only as a cultural unit but also as a region with a landscape that has nothing to say to him, for he prefers the *micaia* flower to roses." And further, "the poet Rui Knopfli is a symbol: he belongs to the group of those who do not know the richness of the language of the great populational masses and therefore creates a poetry that is more and more idealistically subjective."[4] The poet Rui Knopfli is what he is as a poet, and his work should be evaluated, for the purposes of this study, within the context of the poetry of Mozambique. The poem "Naturalidade" (Birthright) must certainly have inspired, in part, Margarido's assessment of Knopfli. But rather than seeing the poet as a symbol of anything, we should consider his poem as an artistic unit whose content has something to say about the psychic dilemma of the white man in Mozambique:

> Europeu, me dizem.
> Eivam-me de literatura e doutrina
> europeias
> e europeu me chamam.
>
> Não sei se o que escrevo tem a raíz de algum
> pensamento europeu.

E' provável . . . Não. E' certo,
mas africano sou.
Pulsa-me o coração ao ritmo dolente
desta luz e deste quebranto.

Trago no sangue uma amplidão
de coordenadas geográficas e mar Índico.
Rosas não me dizem nada,
caso-me mais à agrura das micaias
e ao silêncio longo e roxo das tardes
com gritos de aves estranhas.

Chamais-me europeu?
Pronto, calo-me. Mas dentro de mim há savanas de aridez

e planuras sem fim
com longos rios langues e sinuosos,
uma fita de fumo vertical,
um negro e uma viola estalando.[5]

(European, they tell me./They vitiate me with literature and doc-
trines/from Europe/and they call me European.//I do not know
if what I write has the root of some/European thought./It's
probable . . . No. It's certain,/but African I am./My heart
throbs to the mournful rhythms/of this light and this spell.//I
have in my blood an amplitude/of geographical coordinates and
Indian Ocean./Roses tell me nothing,/I feel more the sadness of
micaias/and the long, purple silence of afternoon/with cries of
strange birds.//You call me European? Fine, I don't deny it./But
within me there are savannahs of aridity/and endless plains/with
long, languid, winding rivers,/a ribbon of vertical smoke,/a black
man and a guitar being strummed.)

The poet moves from the cerebral—Europe is doctrines, ideas,
thoughts—to the sensual and the sentimental to represent the
African he feels himself to be. His claim that Africa dwells within
him controverts the exteriorization found in the static visual images of landscape. The defiance in the final rhetorical question,
"chamais-me europeu?" and the resigned acceptance of the fact

are then contradicted by the poet's link with an anonymous black man strumming a guitar.

Along these lines of representing a theme that brings a sociological truth or social problem into focus, Knopfli's poem "Mulato" escapes conventionality through the distillation of the encounter between European and African. The terse, economical language transmits the brusqueness of the meeting in which physical appetite, determined by social conditions, prevails over tenderness:

> Sou branco, escolhi-te.
> Hoje durmo contigo.
> Negro é teu ventre,
> porém macio.
> E meus dedos capricham
> sobre o aveludado relevo
> das tatuagens.
> Denso e morno é o luar,
> cálido o cheiro húmido
> do capim, acre o hálito
> fundo da terra.
> Venho cansado e tenho
> fome de mulher. Sou branco.
> Escolhi-te. Hoje durmo contigo:
> Um ventre negro de mulher
> arfando, a meu lado arfando,
> o cansaço, o espasmo
> e o sono. Nada mais.
> Amanhã parto. E esqueço-te.
> Depressa te esqueço.
> E teu ventre?[6]

(I am white, I chose you./Today I sleep with you./Your stomach is black,/but smooth./And I run my fingers/over the velvety relief/of tattoos./Dense and tepid the moonlight,/warm is the humid smell/of the grass, acrid the deep/breath of the earth./I arrive tired and I am/hungry for a woman. I am white./I chose you. Today I sleep with you:/A woman's black stomach/heaving, heaving at my side,/the lassitude, the spasm/and sleep. Nothing

more./Tomorrow I depart. And I forget you./Quickly I forget
you./And your stomach?)

Only a capricious curiosity and the headiness of the personified,
earthy ambient mitigate the arrogance and expediency of the
sexual encounter in which the dominant male chooses from
among the submissive females. But from this soon forgotten encounter will result the mulatto (the Portuguese word *ventre* can
mean stomach, abdomen, and womb), and the question posed at
the end of the poem confronts the reader with the essence of a
social problem.

Rui Knopfli's individualist art presents a poetic tension between
personal lyricism and social content. The essence of the word, the
concern with technique and style help the poet to represent
aesthetically a multifaceted cultural reality in Mozambique. From
the apex of the urban Euro-African world Knopfli externalizes
the African quarter of Xipamanine and the amorphous area where
African and European come together. And he invents his poetic
world from disparate elements that in the final analysis all come
to bear on his condition as a Mozambican sensitive to his environment and capable of transforming his sensitivity into sometimes
subtle, sometimes dynamic imagery.

The famous Portuguese poet Fernando Pessoa wrote that

> O poeta é um fingidor.
> Finge tão completamente
> Que chega a fingir que é dor
> A dor que deveras sente.[7]

(The poet makes believe./He makes believe so completely/That
he comes to make believe that the pain/He really feels is pain.)

This applies to many poets, but particularly to one like Knopfli
who cultivates the word with such felicitous care. Thus Knopfli's
own ambivalence, toward his identity, his cosmopolitan attitudes,
and even his defensiveness all translate into the inventiveness of
his art. He also displays a certain linguistic tension in his art in

that he writes poetry in English, and indeed, he demonstrates a penchant for things English and American. And as Knopfli developed as a poet, from his first collection, *O país dos outros* (The Others' Country, 1959), to his latest, *Mangas verdes com sal*, it can be seen that even in those poems that make no direct allusion to his being a Mozambican, there exists a point of reference to his Mozambicanness. In poems written between 1965 and 1969 he ranges over a variety of allusions, from Johannesburg to Hamlet, from concretist verse to a lyrical epistle to the Soviet poet Evtushenko. Using the first line of the stanza by Fernando Pessoa quoted above, Knopfli entitles one of his poems "O poeta é um fingidor," in which he plays on the sound, meaning, and sentiment of words. The collection *Mangas verdes com sal* contains two poems entitled "Ars poética," and in the one dated 1966 Knopfli demonstrates his sensitivity to the power of words and to his search for an expressiveness that in its sophistication denies the provinciality of the ambient in, and from which, he must function. The poem begins:

> Os meus versos nem sempre são
> aquilo que parecem e nunca
> dizem o que parece estarem a dizer.
> Nestas coisas de poesia,
> desde a pontada do lado esquerdo
> ao tenente russo que passeia
> no azul, mirando as nuvens
> do avesso, o mínimo detalhe
> pode ter uma importância máxima.[8]

(My verse not always seems/that which it appears to be and never/does it say that which it appears to be saying./In matters of poetry,/from the sudden sharp pain in the left side/to the Russian lieutenant who goes for a walk/in the blue, looking at clouds/from the other way around, the smallest detail/could have the greatest importance.)

Knopfli's concentration on the lyrically expressive and the imagistic value of fragments of reality allows him to move away almost completely from the regionalist landscape, and at the same time his poetry incorporates suggestive aspects of Mozambique life into universalist art.

The poet seems even to want to rectify the earlier, more direct references to his regional ambient. "A descoberta da rosa" (The Discovery of the Rose) bears the epigram "Rosas não me dizem nada . . ." (Roses tell me nothing), which, of course, comes from his "Naturalidade." In this soliloquy Knopfli says that during his ten years of writing poetry he has never seriously used the conventional image of the rose. The last lines of the poem read:

> Salvo o devido respeito por tudo quanto é útil
> e estimável na terra, faltam-me o tempo
> e o ânimo para as empreitadas mais ingentes.
> E o pouco que me sobra tenciono aplicá-lo
> em tarefas humildes como o cultivo
> destes versos, algum súbito amor inadiável
> e a lenta e minuciosa descoberta da rosa.
>   (p. 107)

(Except for the due respect for all that is useful/and worthy of esteem on earth, I have no time/nor energy for the more immense tasks./And what little time I have free I intend to use/in humble chores such as the cultivation/of these lines, some sudden urgent love/and the slow and meticulous discovery of the rose.)

The idea of the slow and meticulous discovery of the image of the rose reflects this phase of Knopfli's poetry in which he primarily seeks the subtle lyrical expression, whether it comes in the conventional rose of the European tradition or in the more exotic *micaia*. But he seems to be rejecting the contrastive effect of the rose and the *micaia* which appears in his earlier poem.

As Knopfli seeks to capture the essence of the word, he effects a conversational tone when he treats subjects which by their very cosmopolitanism and sophistication seem to suggest an attempt on his part to rise above provincialism. Knopfli has long been an aficionado of progressive jazz, as can be seen in several of his poems. The first lines of "Hackensack" offer a discourse on the

great pianist Thelonious Monk who composed the jazz piece that
lent its title to Knopfli's poem:

> Você compreende Thelonious Monk?
> Não. Você não o entende.
> Até lhe desagrada e o inquieta
> aquela forma esquisita
> de ter o passo obliquo e trópego
> e de deixar tombar a nota
> não quando você a espera
> mas um momento antes ou depois,
> sempre depois se a espera antes,
> sempre antes se a espera depois.
>   (p. 81)

(Do you comprehend Thelonious Monk?/No. You don't understand him./You're even bothered and disquieted/by that strange
form/of having an oblique and unsteady step/and of letting fall
a note/not when you expect it,/but a moment before or after,/
always after if you expect it before,/always before if you expect
it after.)

And this of course represents perfectly the sophisticated offbeat
phrasing of Monk's music. Many of Knopfli's poems contain a
kind of arrogance as if the poet, who can appreciate the highly
refined music of the Modern Jazz Quartet and Thelonious Monk,
had a half derisive, half affectionate eye on his own European
provincial and agitatingly African milieu. But in other poems,
such as "Auto-retrato" (Self-Portrait) and "Então, Rui?" (What
Now, Rui?), he appraises himself as a combination of haughty
aloofness, almost self-effacing humility, and Latin roguishness,
as well as an extreme of sentiments. The third stanza of "Auto-
retrato" reads, "De português, o olhinho malandro, concupis-
cente/e plurirracial, lesto na mirada ao seio/" (p. 91) (From the
Portuguese, the narrow roguish, concupiscent, and pluri-racial/
eye, swiftly focused on a breast/ /). These lines pay tribute, in a
humorous way, to an aspect of Lusotropicology, but more im-

portantly they offer a comment on the Euro-African in his tropical surroundings.

In the book's title poem, "Mangas verdes com sal," Knopfli uses the tropical fruit to evoke childhood memories:

> Sabor longínquo, sabor acre
> da infância a canivete repartida
> no largo semicírculo da amizade.
>
> Sabor lento, alegria reconstituída
> no instante desprevenido, na maré-baixa
> no minuto da suprema humilhação.
>
> Sabor insinuante que retorna devagar
> ao palato amargo, à boca ardida,
> à crista do tempo ao meio da vida.
>
> (p. 121)

(Distant taste, pungent taste/of childhood divided by pocket-knife/in the broad semicircle of friendship.//Slow taste, reconstituted joy/at the unaware instant, at low tide/at the moment of supreme humiliation.//Ingratiating taste that slowly returns/to the bitter palate, to the burning mouth,/to the crest of time in the middle of life.)

The taste of the mango becomes an abstraction of the flavor of childhood, and it might be said that this pungent flavor characterizes the totality of Knopfli's poetry.

Knopfli progressed then from poems, such as "Naturalidade," that show an obvious concern with an interpretation of a Euro-African dilemma to individualist poems that treat of a variety of subjects unrelated to Africa, but which somehow retain that pungent flavor that marks them as Mozambican. Knopfli the intellectual, the quick-witted, often sharp-tongued critic has captured the inner, sometimes imperceptible tension of the social and cultural scene in his native Lourenço Marques without compromising his own sense of artistic probity. Thus, his second collection of poetry, *Reino submarino: Cancioneiro de Moçambique* (*Underwater Kingdom: Mozambique Songbook,* 1962), includes

a poem with its title in English, "Winds of Change," which subtly
suggests that the calm of the white neighborhood Polana covers
impending turmoil:

> Ninguém se apercebe de nada.
> Brilha um sol violento como a loucura
> e estalam gargalhadas na brancura
> violeta do passeio.
> E' África garrida dos postais,
> o fato de linho, o calor obsidiante
> e a cerveja bem gelada.
> Passam. Passam
> e tornam a passar.
> Estridem mais gargalhadas,
> abrindo umas sobre as outras
> como círculos concêntricos.
> Os moleques algaraviam, folclóricos,
> pelas sombras nas esquinas
> e no escuro dos portais
> adolescentes namoram de mãos dadas.
> De facto como é mansa e boa
> a Polana
> nas suas ruas, túneis de frescura
> atapetados de veludo vermelho.
> Tudo joga tão certo, tudo está
> tão bem
> como num filme tecnicolorido.
> Passam. Passam
> e tornam a passar.
> Ninguém se apercebe de nada.[9]

(No one perceives anything./A sun as violent as madness shines/
and shouts of laughter burst forth in the violet/whiteness of the
pavement./It is the flashy, postcard Africa,/the linen suit, the
oppressive heat/and the ice cold beer./They go by. They go by/
and they go by again./More strident peals of laughter/opening
one over the other/like concentric circles./The *moleques* jabber
away, folklorically,/along the shadows of the corners/and in the
darkness of doorways/adolescents woo holding hands./Indeed,
how meek and good/is Polana/in her streets, tunnels of coolness/

carpeted in red velvet./Everything comes out so certain, everything goes/so well/like in a technicolor film./They go by. They go by/and they go by again./No one perceives anything.)

The repeated line, "Ninguém se apercebe de nada," frames the poem in an ominous suggestion of impending change, as do the lines "Passam. Passam/e tornam a passar." Life goes on in tranquillity for the residents of the white, upper middle-class neighborhood. A colonialist, picture postcard Africa, complete with white linen suit, and the comparison of Polana with a technicolor film convey a sense of an illusory reality of paper and celluloid. Black houseboys (*moleques*) conversing incomprehensibly in Ronga add a quaint note of folklore to the tropical scene. And very effectively Knopfli combines the idea of life as usual and the fact that no one perceives anything into a three-line unit at the poem's end. Even the contrast between the image of the violent sun and the tunnellike freshness of Polana supports the view reflected in the words of the title.

Rui Knopfli's sensitivity to the tensions inherent in the situation of Mozambique and his ability to express the essence of the word make him both a poet of universal appeal and a poet who figures importantly in a regionalist movement which by the nature of the times and the social conditions in Mozambique is multifaceted.[10]

CHAPTER 9

Poetry and Prose from a Black Perspective

Despite his opposition to the idea that Mozambican poetry should express an African frame of reference to the exclusion of other points of view, Rui Knopfli recognized the genuineness of what he himself has called *Moçambicanismo*. This Mozambicanness refers specifically to the use, by poets and writers of prose fiction, of thematic and stylistic approaches that translate, in artistic terms, the essence of an African social reality. As is the case with the literature of Angola, the urgency of social and racial consciousness often turns the poems and stories of the committed Mozambican into guileless expressions of concern. Still, taken in its totality, the *engagé* poets and writers, few though they are, have helped to set a course that here and there contains a note of promise for a genuine regionalist expression with universal appeal.

The Collective Voice

Borrowing Eugénio Lisboa's application of the term *collective voice* to that poetry of Mozambique which enunciates a people's shared social reality, we can identify several poets who sing in exalted, occasionally négritude tones of Mother Africa and the other themes common to a committed literature.

The painter Malangatana Gowenha Valente, better known simply as Malangatana, plays a minor role in the total development of the socially conscious poetry of Mozambique, but he also offers, by virtue of his lack of artistic pretentiousness, an opportunity to observe how the unrefined voice of the people might sound. None of Malangatana's poems—and he has apparently written very few—appear in the anthology *Poetas de Moçambique* or in Mário de Andrade's anthologies of African poetry of Portuguese expression. Two of his poems, in English translation, do appear in Moore and Beier's *Modern Poetry from Africa*, and two others, in the original, are published in *Présence africaine*'s "new sum of poetry from the Negro world." Ulli Beier, who has visited Mozambique, may be responsible for bringing Malangatana to the English- and French-speaking worlds, and some have suggested that the Austro-Nigerian was perhaps more inspired by Malangatana's audacious paintings than by his poetry. Nevertheless, the painter's feel for vivid colors and raw, fantastic images occasionally comes through in his otherwise uninspired poetry. "O mineiro sobrevivente" (The Surviving Miner) tells of a *magaíça* who lives to return from the hardships of a South African mine:

> Sou sobrevivente dos milhões
> mortos por falta de ar puro
> não estavam êles habituados
> ao ar condicionado
> e à mina que os entupiu.
>
> Morreram morreram sem se despedirem
> debaixo daquela mina de ouro
> debaixo de aquela caverna
> onde não chiava galinha
> onde só há homem.[1]

(I am a survivor of the millions/dead through lack of pure air/ they were unaccustomed/to the air conditioning/and to the clogged mine.//They died they died without a farewell/down in that gold mine/down in that cavern/where not even a hen clucked/where there are only men.)

The survivor relates the horror of the mines in direct and prosaic language punctuated with hyperbole (millions died) and contrastive imagery. Particularly imposing in the midst of the references to the underground existence of the mine is the allusion to the chicken, which, along with the idea of artificial air and the presence of only men in the cavern, has the effect of counterpoising, with just fragmented images, the natural, open world of the African with the closed, stifling world of the miner. What the poet seems to be doing is transmitting this sense of artificiality to his African listeners who can identify with the importance of the chicken as one small, but symbolic, element of village life.

Malangatana speaks to the people and tries to simulate their voice. Other poets, while directing their verse to a limited readership, strive to express themselves in what they conceive of as a collective voice. Marcelino dos Santos, who writes under the African name Kalungano, echoes his aware Angolan counterparts in poems of evocation and identification. His direct, familiar language contains the poetic conceits of the committed writer. Images such as those in his "Oferenda: A minha mãe" (Offering: To my Mother) and "Sonho da mãe negra"(Dream of the Black Mother) are almost identical to those that appear and reappear in the modern poetry of all Portuguese Africa. These images accompany, of course, the themes of an identity phase, and in the hands of a generally untalented poet they appeal more to the reader's sense of sympathy with a social situation or cause than to his aesthetic appreciation.

The white poet Francisco Rui Moniz Barreto, who goes by the name Rui Nogar, composes his verse in a collective voice that frequently thunders in effective declamatory passion. Not unlike the Angolan poet Ernesto Lara Filho, he has taken part in the way of life of the African suburbs. His forceful verse stands out amidst the more plangent poetry of Mozambique. One of his favorite motifs is the battle scene in which bullets and grenades serve to emphasize his condemnation of man's inhumanity toward man, and the suggestion of gunfire and bursting shells has an important purpose in those poems in which loud and blatant sounds figure prominently in his oratorical style. The line "balas que o ódio calibrou" (bullets calibrated with hate), or variations thereof, appears in at least two of Nogar's poems as a figurative expression of man's callousness. In the unpublished poem "De antes que expirassem os moribundos" (Before the Dying Expired) Nogar uses the bullet motif and the idea of hate to cry out in commiseration and solidarity with suffering comrades:

As balas doem companheiros

Não a dor física
de chumbo percutido
que o ódio calibrou
no almofadado socego
dum gabinete qualquer

Não a presença agónica
dessa infalível certeza
que irredutível se insinua
nas fracções de segundo
que os séculos devoram

As balas doem sim
o tempo que nos faltou
para salvar os companheiros
nossos velhos companheiros
de novas humilhações
novas rotas de cacau
cacau oiro e marfim
novos escravos a leiloar
nos aerófagos da hipocrisia
novos deuses crucificados
na subversão das micaias
que a nossa África abortou

Oh as balas doem sim irmãos

As balas doem

(Bullets hurt, comrades//Not the physical pain/of the beaten lead/that hate has calibrated/in the cushioned quietude/of some study//Not the agonizing presence/of that infallible certainty/ that irreducibly forces its way/into the fractions of a second/that the centuries devour//Yes bullets hurt/the time we needed/to save our comrades/our old comrades/from new humiliations/ new routes of cocoa/cocoa gold and ivory/new slaves to auction off/in the aerophagies of hypocrisy/new gods crucified/in the subversion of the *micaias*/that our Africa aborted//Oh bullets hurt, yes brothers//Bullets hurt)

Nogar's attempts at linguistic virtuosity result in the forcefulness of rage despite the preciosity of such phrases as "aerófagos da hipocrisia." His directly stated images drift toward the surrealistic, and the antithesis of present and past merges in an epic sweep that gives an exclamatory freshness to the common theme of the solidarity of the collective voice.

Rui Nogar receives Eugénio Lisboa's rather constrained endorsement as a poet who has contributed in some small way to the poetry of the collective voice. But Nogar continues to write and, it is hoped, to develop his talent even during times not particularly conducive to his brand of militant verse.

Eugénio Lisboa has written that "Noémia de Sousa is a myth not worth sustaining, no matter what sympathy her prolix and stammering poems may deserve."[2] But both Lisboa and Knopfli, despite their urgent need to deflate the myths perpetrated by leftist and rightist elements, have had to pay some homage to Noémia de Sousa's place in the phenomenon of social literature in Mozambique.

Noémia de Sousa cultivated a sort of high-pitched emotional tone and full-throated passion in her verbose poetry. And in the fifties, when most of her poems were written, she seemed to raise her voice at the right time to echo the collective spirit among a handful of *mestiço* and black Mozambicans who were in the process of developing a self-awareness. One distinguishing feature of her poetry is that her poetic persona declares her African identity with such vehemence, as if she were impelled by some sacred force back to ancient origins. The poet transmits this sense of urgency and contrition toward Mother Africa in "Sangue negro" (Black Blood):

> O minha África misteriosa, natural!
> minha virgem violentada!
> 　Minha Mãe! . . .
>
> Como eu andava há tanto desterrada
> de ti, alheada distante e egocêntrica
> por estas ruas da cidade engravidadas de estrangeiros
> 　Minha Mãe! Perdoa!
>
> Que a força da tua seiva vence tudo
> e nada mais foi preciso que o feitiço impar
> dos teus tantãs de guerra chamando.
> 　dum-dum-dum-tam-tam-tam
> 　dum-dum-dum-tam-tam-tam
> 　para que eu vibrasse
> 　para que eu gritasse
> 　para que eu sentisse!—fundo no sangue
> a tua voz—Mãe
> 　E vencida reconhecesse os nossos erros
> 　e regressasse à minha origem milenar . . .[3]

(Oh my Africa, mysterious and natural!/my violated virgin!/ My Mother! . . .//How I have been so long exiled/from you, distantly and selfishly alienated/through these city streets teeming with foreigners/My Mother! Forgive me!//Because the force of your vigor overcomes all else/and nothing more has been needed than the unmatched enchantment/of your war tom-toms calling./ dum-dum-dum-tam-tam-tam/dum-dum-dum-tam-tam-tam/for me to thrill/for me to cry out/for me to feel!—deep in my blood/your voice—Mother/And subdued, to recognize our errors/and return to my millennial origins . . .)

Once again we see the fecund land symbolized in the abstract figure of the mother. Noémia de Sousa's stammering (as Eugénio Lisboa would have it) and her exoticism tempered by the self-

righteousness of exultation in an ancestral, unsullied Africa actually make the theme of the delirious daughter of the betrayed
mother more effective as a metaphor. The road back to origins,
as represented in Noémia de Sousa's poetry, demands verbal thrash-
ing about and hyperbolic proclamations of self and people. Her
dynamism, unstudied as it is, allows her a certain illusion of spontaneity combined with contrivances that just barely save her verse
from banality. The poem "Se me quiseres conhecer" (If You
Would Like to Know Me), for example, exudes an aggressive
insistence in these first two stanzas:

> Se me quiseres conhecer,
> estuda com olhos bem de ver
> esse pedaço de pau preto
> que um desconhecido irmão maconde
> de mãos inspiradas
> talhou e trabalhou
> em terras distantes lá do Norte.
>
> Ah, essa sou eu:
> órbitas vazias no desespero de possuir a vida,
> boca rasgada em feridas de angústia,
> mãos enormes, espalmadas,
> erguendo-se em jeito de quem implora e ameaça,
> corpo tatuado de feridas visíveis e invisíveis
> pelos duros chicotes da escravatura . . .
> Torturada e magnífica,
> altiva e mística,
> África da cabeça aos pés,
> —ah, essa sou eu!
>   (*Nouvelle somme*, p. 467)

(If you would like to know me,/study with well-seeing eyes/that
piece of black wood/that an unknown Maconde brother/with
an inspired touch/carved and worked/in distant lands to the
North.//Ah, that is I:/empty sockets desperate to possess life,/
mouth rent in wounds of anguish,/enormous, broad hands,/
raised as if imploring and menacing,/body tattooed with scars
visible and invisible/from the cruel lashes of slavery . . ./Tor-

tured and magnificent,/haughty and mystic,/Africa from head to foot,/—Ah, that is I!)

Identification with a wood sculpture, with a representation that contains a life force, gives the poetic persona the iconlike dignity of the static, black figure. And Noémia de Sousa, if she has accomplished nothing else, has wrought an incantatory symbol in verse.

Noémia de Sousa also cultivated a solidarity of the black man of the world, invoking in the poem "Deixa passar o meu povo" (Let My People Go) Marian Anderson and Paul Robeson whose radio-transmitted voices merge with the sound of the Mozambican marimba. But it seems almost natural that Noémia de Sousa's own collective voice should wear thin and then finally fade away, to be echoed, however, in the poetry of others who instill their art with audacious rhythm and spirituality.[4]

José Craveirinha, Poet of Mozambique

Out of the sparse landscape of a poetry *of* Mozambique has emerged the formidable figure of José Craveirinha. Craveirinha's poetry contains the declamatory force, the vivid images, and the commitment of the best of a Rui Nogar or a Noémia de Sousa; but it also possesses a sense of craft and a feeling for the power of the word that make this *mestiço* poet of Lourenço Marques the foremost interpreter of Mozambicanness and a durable artist whose work transcends the regionalist context in which it is conceived. What in Noémia de Sousa's poetry is forceful yet conventional, is in Craveirinha's poetry bold and unique.

Craveirinha's slim volume *Chigubo* (1964), the title being the name of a traditional Ronga dance, includes poems written during the early and mid-fifties, and, like Noémia de Sousa's poems of the same period, they convey an African regionalist fervor that was beginning to take hold in Mozambique. Racial affirmation comes in Craveirinha's "Manifesto":

> Oh!
> Meus belos e curtos cabelos crespos

e meus olhos negros´
grandes luas de pasmo na noite mais bela
das mais belas noites inesquecíveis das terras do Zambeze.[5]

(Oh!/My beautiful and short curly hair/and my black eyes/great moons of wonderment on the most beautiful night/of the most beautiful, unforgettable nights of the lands of the Zambezi.)

Although not one of his best poems, "Manifesto" displays Craveirinha's sense of poetic rhythm in his accumulative technique that goes from the initial exclamation to the last long and flowing line. In the rest of the poem Craveirinha employs metaphors and similes that defy their own exoticism because of his timing and control of a spontaneity that continuously takes the reader by surprise.

Nevertheless, the shock of contrasting images seems natural in Craveirinha's poetry; he takes the conventional image or poetic phrase, gives it sometimes a bold, sometimes just a slight twist, and carries it to its ultimate point of representation and meaning. The poem "Africa" contains this stanza of compelling imagery:

Em meus lábios grossos fermenta
a farinha do sarcasmo que coloniza minha Mãe África
e meus ouvidos não levam ao coração seco
misturada com o sal dos pensamentos
a sintaxe anglo-latina de novas palavras.
(p. 12)

(On my thick lips ferments/the grain of sarcasm that colonizes my Mother Africa/and my ears do not carry to my withered heart/mixed with the salt of my thoughts/the Anglo-Latin syntax of new words.)

The first two lines treat the oft-used theme of the long-suffering African made to swallow the bitter bread of oppression, but Craveirinha gives the conventional an original cast. Through the verb *fermenta* (ferments) he suggests the slow, inebriating growth of anger; and the image of ears that hear the colonizer's language but reject its syntax accompanies Craveirinha's own artistic deformation of Portuguese syntactical and lexical expression.

Craveirinha takes the image of coal, used timorously and defensively by the Angolan Geraldo Bessa Victor and ludicrously by the São Tomé poet Costa Alegre (see p. 380), and converts it into a defiant symbol of négritude:

> Eu sou carvão!
> E tu arrancas-me brutalmente do chão
> e fazes-me tua mina, patrão.
>
> Eu sou carvão!
> E tu acendes-me, patrão
> para te servir eternamente como força motriz
> mas eternamente não, patrão.
> Eu sou carvão
> e tenho que arder, sim
> e queimar tudo com a força da minha combustão.
> Eu sou carvão
> tenho que arder na exploração
> arder até às cinzas da maldição
> arder vivo como alcatrão, meu irmão
> até não ser mais a tua mina, patrão.
> Eu sou carvão
> Tenho que arder
> queimar tudo com o fogo da minha combustão.
> Sim!
> Eu serei o teu carvão, patrão!
>
> (p. 29)

(I am coal!/And you tear me brutally from the ground/and you make me your source of wealth, boss.//I am coal!/And you ignite me, boss/in order to serve you eternally as motive force/but not eternally, boss./I am coal/and I must blaze, yes/and burn all with the force of my combustion./I am coal/I must blaze in exploitation/blaze into ashes of malediction/blaze live like tar, my brother/until I am no longer your wealth, boss./I am coal/I must blaze/burn all with the fire of my combustion./Yes!/I will be your coal, boss!)

Much of the poem's effectiveness depends on the repetition of the nasal sound represented by the graph -*ão*, which appears no less than nineteen times in the words *carvão, chão, patrão, combustão, exploração, maldição, alcatrão, não*, and *irmão*. Generally, the frequent and close repetition of this sound is thought to be displeasing, but obviously Craveirinha takes advantage of the shock appeal and the resonance inherent in the stressed nasal syllable to wed aural quality with the idea of released energy. In the style of négritude, he converts the negative into the positive, on the level of language and on the level of symbol; the lump of coal, which has been a bonanza for the exploiter who tears it brutally from the earth, becomes a burning force that will turn into ashes of vengeance. The poet, then, effectively captures a sense of black rage through a combination of sound, symbol, and rhythm. In fact, rhythm figures very importantly in much of Craveirinha's poetic forcefulness. If we consider, for example, how he arranges the words ending in -*ão* throughout the poem, we see how he uses beat and pauses for dramatic emphasis. The lines seem to grow and recede like waves, and if we follow the nasal sound throughout the poem we become aware of how he captures something akin to a slow, ominous, reverberating drum beat. For the sake of illustration, let the word *boom* represent the nasal sound as it appears internally and at the end of lines and the word *shish* those few lines that end either with the high nasal of the word *sim* or with some other stressed consonantal, non-nasal sound; in this way we get an idea of the use of sound and beat in the rhythm of the poem: boom/boom/boom//boom/boom/shish/boom, boom/ boom/shish/boom/boom/boom/boom/boom, boom/boom . . . boom/boom/shish/boom/shish/boom, boom.

Craveirinha, in his attempt to imitate the rhythms and sounds of African drum beats, went even further than Agostinho Neto by exaggerating the obvious to the point of creating a surrealistic, incantatory, magical effect. His "Quero ser tambor" (I Want to Be Drum) first seems a little too contrived, but the sense of contrivance rapidly dissipates under the emphatic beat and syllabic stresses:

Tambor está velho de gritar
ó velho Deus dos homens
deixa-me ser tambor
corpo e alma só tambor
só tambor gritando na noite quente dos trópicos.

E nem flor nascida no mato do desespero
Nem rio correndo para o mar do desespero
Nem zagaia temperada no lume vivo do desespero
Nem mesmo poesia forjada na dor rubra do desespero

Nem nada!

Só tambor velho de gritar na lua cheia da minha terra
Só tambor de pele curtida ao sol da minha terra
Só tambor cavado nos troncos duros da minha terra!

Eu!

Só tambor rebentando o silêncio amargo da Mafalala
Só tambor velho de sangrar no batuque do meu povo
Só tambor perdido na escuridão da noite perdida.

Ó velho Deus dos homens
eu quero ser tambor
e nem rio
e nem flor
e nem zagaia por enquanto
e nem mesmo poesia.

Só tambor ecoando como a canção da força e da vida
Só tambor noite e dia
dia e noite só tambor
até à consumação da grande festa do batuque!

Oh, velho Deus dos homens
deixa-me ser tambor
só tambor!

> (*Poetas de Moçambique*, p. 71)

(Drum is old from crying out/oh ancient God of men/let me be drum/body and soul just drum/just drum crying out in the hot night of the tropics,//And neither flower born in the forest of despair/Nor river running to the sea of despair/Nor spear tempered in the live flame of despair/Nor even poetry forged in the

crimson pain of despair//Nor anything!//Just drum old from
crying out in the full moon of my land/Just drum of hide tanned
in the sun of my land/Just drum carved from the hard trunks of
my land!//Me!/Just drum breaking the bitter silence of Mafa-
lala/Just drum old from bleeding in the *batuque* of my people/
Just drum lost in the darkness of the lost night.//Oh ancient God
of men/I want to be drum/and neither river/and neither flower/
and neither spear for now/and neither even poetry.//Just drum
echoing like the song of force and of life/Just drum night and
day/day and night just drum/until the consummation of the
great festival of *batuque*!//Oh, ancient God of men/let me be
drum/just drum!)

The Portuguese word *tambor* has an onomatopoeic quality suggestive, naturally, of the reverberations of a drum. Craveirinha's
techniques of repetition have some features that bear comment. He uses anaphora (E nem . . ./Nem . . ./Nem . . ./
Nem . . .) and epistrophe, or the repetition of the same word or
words at the end of successive lines (. . . desespero/. . . deses-
pero/. . . desespero), and he continues this procedure in the
third stanza; but just when he seems to have established a pattern,
he abandons the device of epistrophe in the fourth stanza. He
returns to the repetition of the word *nem* (which can be translated as either "nor" or "neither") in successive lines in the fifth
stanza, but this time the lines are shorter lines and the technique
of polysyndeton is used with the conjunction *e* (and), all for the
purpose of emphatic reiteration.

The rhythmic flow and the sometimes methodical, sometimes
shifting beat of the poem create the necessary ambient for the
poet's incantatory metamorphosis. And it should be remembered
that in African religions the drum performs a sacred function; it
summons the gods. Thus the drum assumes a more immediate
symbolic importance than the nature symbols of the flower and
the river, and even, for now, the spear in its bellicose defiance.
First, through the power of the word, must come the drum
echoing the song of force and of life.

Gerald Moser, in speaking of the cultivation of a regional identity through language in Portuguese Africa, cites a number of African or African-sounding terms used by some Mozambican poets: "We can be sure," Moser comments, "that the writer uses these terms to identify his writing as Mozambican."[6] He goes on to quote, in English translation, a stanza from José Craveirinha's "Hino à minha terra" (Hymn to My Land) in which the poet accumulates African place names. According to Moser this incantatory technique has a Whitmanesque ring, but he sees this as an attempt at differentiation, meaning that the poet merely seeks to distinguish his regionalism from that, say, of an Angolan poet. The invocation of the land in exalted verse sprinkled with exotic-sounding words of course characterizes much of Mozambican identity poetry; Noémia de Sousa and Fernando Ganhão, to name only two, make ample use of the technique. In the case of Craveirinha, however, and particularly in regard to his "Hino à minha terra," the technique serves far more than identification through the use of regionalisms. Craveirinha takes the conventional and exaggerates it to an almost baroque point in the poem's profusion of polysyllabic African place names. The following stanzas from "Hino à minha terra" illustrate his purposes of defiance, convocation, and incantation as conveyed through the use of sound:

> O sangue dos nomes
> é o sangue dos nomes.
> Suga-o também se es capaz, tu
> que não os amas.

Amanhece
sobre as cidades do futuro.

E uma saudade cresce no nome das coisas
e digo Metengobalame e Macomia
e é Metengobalame e cálida palavra que os negros inventaram

e não outra Macomia.

E grito Inhamússua, Mutamba, Massangulo! ! !
E torno a gritar Inhamússua, Mutamba, Massangulo! ! !
E outros nomes da minha terra

afluem doces e altivos na memória filial
e na exacta pronúncia desnudo-lhes a beleza.
Chulamáti! Manhoca! Chinhambanine!
Morrumbala, Namaponda e Namarrói
e com o vento a agitar sensualmente as folhas dos canhoeiros
eu grito Angoche, Marrupa, Michafutene e Zóbuè
e colho as sementes do cutilho e a raiz da txumbula
e mergulho as mãos na terra fresca de Zitunde.
    (*Chigubo*, pp. 32–33)

(The blood of names/is the blood of names./Drink it in also if you are able, you/who do not love them.//Dawn comes/over the cities of the future.//And a longing grows in the names of things/ and I say Metengobalame and Macomia/and it is Metengobalame and burning word invented by black men//and not another Macomia.//And I cry Inhamússua, Mutamba, Massangulo! ! !/And again I cry Inhamússua, Mutamba, Massangulo! ! !/And other names of my land/flow sweet and arrogant in my filial memory/ and in their exact pronunciation I lay bare their beauty./Chulamáti! Manhoca! Chinhambanine!/Morrumbala, Namaponda and Namarrói/and with the wind sensually rustling the *canhoeiro* leaves/I cry Angoche, Marrupa, Michafutene and Zóbuè/and I gather the seeds of the *cutilho* and the root of the *txumbula*/and I plunge my hands into the cool earth of Zitunde.)

The epigrammatic first stanza, with its reference to the blood of names, fits well within Janheinz Jahn's definition of the Bantu concept of the power of the word: "The driving power, however, that gives life and efficacy to all things is Nommo, the 'word,' of which for the moment we can only say that it is word and water and seed and blood in one."[7] The place names, and later the names of African peoples, plants, and fauna of Mozambique, do more than point up differences among regions in "Hino à minha terra"; the poet's purpose is to infuse these names with life by giving them the "magic power of the word," to quote again from Jahn's comments on Bantu philosophy. It becomes clear that Craveirinha conjures up the life-giving force with his profusion of words, for he talks about the "burning word" that black men invented, and Jahn has written that *magara*, which is "the life of intelligence," is realized through the concrete entity of Nommo, the word (*Muntu*, p. 127).

In "Abstração" (Abstraction) Craveirinha paints a vivid word picture, using hot colors and sensuous, tropical images for a surrealistic, oneiric effect:

> No meu delírio
> Há uma cor de pesadelo em cada imagem
> E verde-limos
> Num fundo de algas e conchas.
>
> Soluços sobem em bolhas lentas
> Das gargantas de afogados surrealistas
> E dançam sinfonias de búzios à beira-mar
> Enquanto desfrizados cabelos de mulatas
> Acorrentam os pés de marinheiros bêbedos.
>
> . . . No meu delírio azul-jacarandá
> as rosas não são rosas nem pão nosso
> Todos os meus gritos não são sonhos
> Nem gaiolas de arame para aves de estimação.
> E os seios das prostitutas não são seios
> São flores
> E o delírio não é delírio
> Nas virgens grávidas
> E apenas a minha raiva é abstraccionismo puro
> Num aquário de poesia com peixes listrados
> E botões de cravos inconformistas
> Floridos espasmos de sangue
> Nos olhos voluptuosos
> Dos poetas enforcados.[8]

(In my delirium/There is a nightmare color in every image/And seaweed green/On a bottom of algae and conches.//Sobs rise in slow bubbles/From the throats of drowned surrealists/And they dance symphonies of cowrie shells on the shore/While the straightened hair of mulatto girls/Entwines the feet of drunken sailors.//. . . In my delirium of rosewood-blue/Roses are not roses nor tepid bread/All my cries are not dreams/Nor wire cages for prized birds./And prostitutes' breasts are not breasts/They are flowers/And delirium is not delirium/In pregnant virgins.// And only my rage is pure abstraction/In an aquarium of poetry with striped fish/And nonconformist carnation buds/Blossoming spasms of blood/In voluptuous eyes/Of hanged poets.)

Craveirinha dedicates this poem to "Bertina, pintora mulata" (Bertina, mulatto painter), and like the abstractionist paintings of Bertina, it is a kind of surrealistic collage of images. A reference to drowned surrealists and hanged poets suggests stifled rage, and, in fact, when the poet refers to his rage as pure abstraction, the poem can be seen as a delirium of passion, a passion of social protest, perhaps, and a passion of the artist restricted by his own use of words. The social protest, or awareness, appears in the otherwise sensual images of prostitutes, mulatto girls, drunken sailors, which in more realist terms depict a social scene perhaps witnessed abstractly. And the sea images call to mind the port setting of Lourenço Marques. But whatever the intimation of social protest and black rage in this and other of Craveirinha's poems, it is the power of the word that establishes his artistic predominance in the poetry of Mozambique.

Craveirinha not only cries out his words; he also sings them, especially in "Velha cantiga" (An Old Song), a poem that deals with the theme of the mulatto:

> Canto
> Cantiga que cocuana cantou à lua em cima da palhota
> E mãe ensinou nome que avô chamou
> Tempo de passarinho amarelo morrer
> Na ratoeira de flor
> Sol puxando sombras na esteira
> As raparigas no caminho do rio e cantando.
>
> (Ah, mulato, nascer é bom?
> E' bom, nascer mulato?)
>
> E canto
> Cantiga velha de passarinho de mato verde
> Que mãe ensinou nome

> Que mãe ensinou nome
> E sangue não esqueceu!
> (*Paralelo 20*, p. 17)

(I sing/A song that grandfather sang to the moon over the hut/ And mother taught the name that grandfather called/Time for little yellow bird to die/In the snare of the flower/Sun pulling shadows over the straw mat/The girls on the river road and singing.// (Ah, mulatto, is it good to be born?/Is it good to be born mulatto?)//And I sing/An old song of the little bird of the green forest/That mother taught me name of/That mother taught me name of/And the blood did not forget!)

The wistfulness and nostalgia captured in folkloric allusions to an African, rural childhood become more socially poignant in the parenthetical question by means of which the poet combines the problem of the mulatto with the more universal, metaphysical concern of human existence.

Craveirinha continues to publish an occasional poem in newspapers of Lourenço Marques and Beira, and the editors of the *Colecção N'goma* plan to bring out a collection of his poems under the title *N'goma*.* Some of his more recent poetry will be considered in chapter 10. Meanwhile, although his most recent verse may lack some of the virility of his earlier poetry, Craveirinha continues to be the master of the power of the word and the most important cultivator of African thematic and stylistic features in the poetry, not only of Mozambique, but of all Portuguese Africa.

Luís Bernardo Honwana, Short Story Writer of Mozambique

Luís Bernardo Honwana dedicated his one book of short stories, *Nós matamos o cão tinhoso* (We Killed Mangy Dog,

---

* Soon after the coup in Portugal and the installation of a black, provisional, liberation government in Mozambique, Craveirinha published his collection *Karingana ua karingana* (a Ronga phrase meaning "Once upon a time"). See the bibliography for further information.

1964), to José Craveirinha, the "true expression of the poetry of Mozambique." It was Craveirinha, along with Rui Knopfli and Eugénio Lisboa, who first encouraged and helped the young Honwana to launch his career as a writer. Honwana, like Craveirinha, owes much of his projection to the patronage of a bourgeois elite in Lourenço Marques. An architect, Pedro Guedes, and his wife aided Honwana with the publication of his book in an English edition. Dorothy Guedes translated the stories into English and the African Writers Series published the volume under the title *We Killed Mangy-Dog & Other Mozambique Stories* (1969). Thus, Honwana gained some publicity outside of the Portuguese-speaking world, and a small but significant group of foreign critics has acclaimed his stories for their poetic sensitivity.

It would be premature to say that Honwana has established himself as a writer on a par with, let's say, the Nigerian novelist Chinua Achebe; but by virtue of his one modest collection, he has set a direction for the modern prose fiction of Mozambique. For the time being, Luís Bernardo Honwana is *the* short story writer of Mozambique. Honwana was born in 1942 in Lourenço Marques but raised, until the age of seventeen, in Moamba where his father was an official interpreter. After high school he engaged in journalistic activities, writing his first stories for the young people's page of the newspaper *Notícias*. During this formative period he became exposed to books and films, and discovered that he had a talent for painting. He also claims, in the course of his biographical remarks, that he does not know if he is really a writer. This modest attitude toward his writing reflects a concern with the problems of craft to which the young Honwana had become sensitive when he was being introduced to the cosmopolitan intellectual and artistic life of Lourenço Marques. But as the beginning writer struggled to gain control over technique, his work revealed a visible natural talent for storytelling. And because Honwana upheld certain attitudes and standards of a Western tradition, he avoided the temptations of the picturesque and the direct, pamphletary social statement of an African reality. In retrospect, however, Honwana himself realizes that much of his narrative style and point of view do reflect an early exposure to an African oral tradition.

The story of the mangy dog, told in the first person by a preadolescent boy, offers some striking examples of Honwana's stylistic method. First of all, the decrepit animal is introduced through a series of repeated descriptions that qualify as formulas such as those used in oral poetry. The narrator describes the dog's large head and tearful blue eyes; then he emphasizes mangy dog's sadness and loneliness by comparing him with the other neighborhood dogs who indulge in the usual group ritual of running, playing, and sniffing under one another's tails. The narrator repeats his childish observations with a refrainlike sameness and regularity. The head of this old and indolent dog sways like an ox's and his slow, uneven gait gives him the appearance of a dilapidated cart in motion. To use a musical analogy, it can be said that such descriptive "refrains" give the first eight pages of the story an "offbeat" rhythm and a sense of "call and response" because of an overlapping of repeated images. What we are suggesting here is that consciously or not the author was employing some storytelling techniques that reflected African stylistic features.

Toucinho, the youthful narrator, tells the story with a deliberate repetition of detail and a spontaneity that counteracts the slow narrative pace. Mangy dog, Toucinho, and Isaura, a mentally retarded girl, relate to each other in a series of incidents leading up to a main episode that reveals, in dramatic fashion, the cruelty and innocence of childhood. The fact that Toucinho is black seems to determine in part his lower position in the pecking order of a youthful band consisting of whites, *mestiços*, and East Indians, but Honwana treats racial juxtapositions in a matter-of-fact manner and thus achieves artistic unity in the story while making a meaningful social comment. Because of Touchino's inferior status in the gang, he somewhat reluctantly forms an emotional alliance with the outcast dog and the retarded girl who herself becomes mangy dog's self-appointed protectress. Psychologically the boy is torn between his low, but still socially

acceptable position among his peers and his being almost an outcast with Isaura and the dog. When money rests on the weekly
soccer game, the other boys exclude Toucinho, probably because
of his small size or lack of ability rather than because of his color.
Mangy dog, a regular spectator at the Saturday afternoon event,
appears on this particular day along with Toucinho on the
veranda of the clubhouse where some of the town fathers,
including the administrator and the veterinarian, have gathered
for their regular card game. In bad humor because of heavy
losses, the administrator becomes irritated when it seems that
Toucinho and mangy dog are laughing at his run of bad luck. As
if trying to decide which one to vent his wrath on, the administrator spits between the boy and the dog. Eventually the pariah
dog becomes his victim, and he complains to the veterinarian that
the disgusting creature should be put to death as a menace to
public health.

The veterinarian, not wanting to be bothered, convinces
Toucinho and his eleven companions that they should be mangy
dog's executioners. In a clearing in the woods the boys gather
with their fathers' rifles and the intended victim. They play out a
protracted ritual of bravado and fear in an attempt to screw up
their courage for the deed. Quim, the leader of the group, lam-
basts and taunts the sniveling Toucinho who finds himself emotionally and physically allied with the dog who stands trembling
against his leg. Then Honwana employs the graphic technique of
boldface type and capital letters to emphasize not only Toucinho's impassioned plea but his swallowed shouts of anger and
his unspoken desperation as well: "QUIM, WE DON'T HAVE
TO KILL THE DOG. I'LL KEEP HIM. I'LL TAKE CARE
OF HIS SORES AND HIDE HIM SO HE WON'T GO
AROUND TOWN WITH THOSE DISGUSTING SORES!"[9]

As the tension mounts Quim orders Toucinho to fire the first
shot as proof that he has overcome his cowardice. Meanwhile,
several *moleques* employed by a nearby property owner spy on
the strange ritual, and Quim scatters them with racial epithets
and threats. But the sudden appearance of the retarded girl

strengthens, by intimidation, Quim's resolve. Isaura compulsively embraces the frightened animal, and Toucinho rushes to pull her away. At the sound of the first shot Toucinho and Isaura, clasped in each other's arms, fall to the ground in mutual despair. The boyish executioners then engage in mock heroics while reconstructing their individual roles in the shooting of the dog. This incident offers a contrast between compassion and cruelty, and the following day, in the aftermath of what amounted to a manhood rite, the boys, including Quim and Toucinho, commiserate and seek to assuage their guilt feelings by agreeing that "WE KILLED MANGY DOG" because the veterinarian ordered them to do so. Thus the several refrains culminate poetically in the admission and rationalization of guilt, and the author completes the picture of innocence and cruelty with the intrusion of the callous adult world on the impressionable world of childhood.

Most of the stories in Honwana's collection take place in a small, provincial town, probably modeled on Moamba where the author spent his childhood. Autobiography, as might be expected from a beginning writer, also would seem to be present in some of the stories. But even in his nonfictional sketches Honwana displays a talent for artistic selectivity. On the back cover of the book he explains that "Inventário de imóveis and jacentes" (Inventory of Property and Household Effects) is just what the title states. The description of crowded living quarters, makeshift furniture as well as foreign news magazines (*Time* and *Life*), but all in orderly and clean arrangement, offers an effective social statement on an aspect of African life in transition.

In "Papá, cobra e eu" (Papa, Snake, and I) the author focuses on an episode in the domestic life of an African family. It seems to be the Toucinho, though now a little older, of "Nós matamos o cão tinhoso!" who tells of the unfortunate occurrence that illustrates the precarious condition of an African family with aspirations for social betterment in a white-dominated world. The story unfolds in the home and backyard of this family of modest means, but of a certain economic stability afforded it by the father's steady employment, probably as a low-level civil servant. Honwana, by concentrating on the domestic setting, succeeds in defining individual roles as the characters face the outside world. The strong mother rules over her household with a firm hand and the father defers to her in matters of disciplining the children and seeing to their personal and health needs.

Because the parents speak both Ronga and Portuguese interchangeably, depending on the situation and whom they are addressing, they illustrate their position between an African cultural reality and the realities of an imposed, if not readily adopted, set of values. A strictly enforced code of conduct in the household, where orders are given in the two languages, reflects the parents' resolve to overcome economic social odds that stand in the way of their children's success. The use of language follows certain patterns of social and cultural sensitivities within the household: the mother speaks Ronga to Sartina, the cleaning girl, who understands little Portuguese, but when she is angry or excited she lapses into the African language. On one occasion the strong matriarch alternates between Ronga and Portuguese while chiding Sartina in the former language and giving instructions to her children in the latter. Although the children know Ronga, the parents do not encourage them to speak it; obviously, within their pattern of social values they see the perfection of their offsprings' Portuguese as an avenue of greater opportunity to excel or just as an assurance of survival in a culturally and linguistically racist society. But every night after supper the father prays aloud in Ronga with a fervor that he presumably would not be able to generate in Portuguese. So even though he entreats a Christian God, the language he uses to do so offers a link with an African spirituality.

After giving the reader glimpses of the domestic routine and after having unobtrusively, yet compellingly, established the theme of cultural ambivalence, the narrator tells how one day a snake gets into the family chicken coop and then kills a neighbor's favorite hunting dog. The outside world has intruded on the domestic tranquillity of the household. Mr. Castro, the dog's owner, arrives and in short words demands indemnity from the family. Toucinho, or Ginho (as he is referred to in this story), witnesses the confrontation during which his father humbly accepts the vituperation and threats hurled at him by the white man. The universal theme of the son discovering that his revered father has clay feet is magnified, for the father must try to retain a semblance of human dignity in the face of inalterable social and racial patterns. When later that night father and son discuss the incident, the father explodes in a sententious lecture about love and faith in God as a means of existing while passively suffering daily humiliations. At the end of the story mother, father, and son redefine their familial roles almost as a way of recapturing a measure of lost dignity. When the mother appears she finds her husband and son laughing uproariously at a joke they are sharing at Mr. Castro's expense; she becomes irritated at not being apprised of the source of their amusement. But father and son have come together in a spirit of traditional male solidarity, and after their laughter has subsided the father placates his wife with a parablelike explanation: "It's nothing, woman. But our son thinks that no one rides mad horses because it is easier to ride tame and hungry ones. Do you understand what I'm saying? When a horse goes mad you shoot him, and that's that. But tame horses die every day. Every day. Do you understand what I'm saying? Day in and day out, as long as they can stand!" (p. 104) This change of tone, from the pious pronouncement of "turn the other cheek," to the shared amusement in derisive defiance of Mr. Castro, to the parablelike philosophy, helps to reestablish positions within the family structure even though the father's pronouncement gives added insight into the moral dilemma of the African attempting to affirm his dignity. Mr. Castro is out of earshot, the hostile world is still there, but the father can act out his rage which will make his "tameness" that much easier to bear.

The mother goes back to bed satisfied with her husband's exalted explanation, and as an afterthought she promises to administer a purgative to Ginho the next morning to reaffirm her role as the protective matriarch. The father derives contentment from his ability to instruct his son on the larger moral issues that will be of aid to him when he leaves his parents' home to face the world alone. Ginho himself retires that night with thoughts of Sartina, which dissipate any nightmares of snakes and dogs. Tranquillity, representing a certain security in the family's unity, returns to the household, and the author attenuates his implicit comments of a sociological nature with the final reference to Ginho's adolescent concerns.

Honwana never preaches, nor does he inveigh against social conditions; instead he often adopts an anecdotal approach to reveal social irony. In the short vignette "As mãos dos pretos" (Black Folks' Hands) he uses the pretext of a small boy's curiosity to review several etiological versions of why black people have white palms. First, the boy's teacher explains that because it has been only a few centuries since blacks walked on all fours, their palms have not had time to darken by exposure to the sun. This mock-scientific thesis is balanced by the local priest's pious explanation that black people kept their palms hidden from the sun by clasping their hands in prayer. Another adult offers the boy a populist, visceral theory which postulates that God made blacks that way so they would not soil white folks' food when they prepared it for them. Finally, the boy's mother combines the scientific, the religious, and the philosophical in a more convoluted explanation: God repented having created black people because white people derided them, enslaved them, and made them perform menial chores; but God could not undo what he had done because whites were accustomed to having blacks around; so God made the palms of blacks' hands white as a reminder that what man accomplishes is merely the work of man. Thus, black men have palms equal to those of men who clasp their hands in prayerful thanks that they were not born black.

Etiological stories abound in African oral tradition, and Honwana, with tongue-in-cheek humor, parodies the European versions of the origin of the black man's white palms. His intent, however, is not purely humorous, for he also has social satire in mind. And he adds a final touch of defiant humor to the story by including a full-page picture of a black man's palm. On the book's back cover Honwana says of this picture that "the hand of 'As mãos dos pretos' is mine," and with this he transcends his otherwise humble biographical statements by affirming that the hand of a black man wrote these stories.

The remaining three stories in the collection resemble, in theme and presentation, the socially aware, revelatory stories of Angola. But as in the case of Honwana's stories, they never become doctrinaire, for Honwana, at the age of twenty-two, was already struggling to develop as a writer and not just as an observer of social reality.

CHAPTER 10

Contemporary Trends and Prospects

Mozambique's combative literature parallels Angola's in that during the mid- and late-sixties a small number of militant poets wrote verse while in exile. However, no poet of the caliber of the Angolan Agostinho Neto has contributed to this phase of Mozambican literature. Mário de Andrade's anthology includes, under the general heading of "War," selections by the Mozambican poets Sérgio Vieira, Armando Guebuza, and Jorge Rebelo. All three are members of the independence party FRELIMO. Vieira's "Tríptico para estado de guerra" (Triptych for a State of War) documents the cruelties of combat. Slogans are dispersed throughout his poem, such as the one at the end of the final stanza: "Frelimo e Moçambique/Para que um povo viva/e estado de guerra morra"[1] (FRELIMO and Mozambique/So that a people might live/and a state of war might die). As the title indicates, the poem is divided into three parts, and perhaps the poet means to suggest that the book of war should be closed just as the triptych tablets may be folded shut. Despite this "artistic" touch Vieira's poem has little to recommend it either aesthetically or as a combative poem. Guebuza's "As tuas dores" (Your Sorrows) has a better overall sense of technique but even more exhortative rhetoric than Vieira's verse, and Rebelo's "Poema de um militante" (Militant's Poem) gives just a hint of the aesthetic didacticism sometimes well developed in guerrilla theater.

Whatever our sympathies may be for the cause represented by Mozambican combative poetry, we must turn to that literature still being written and/or published in Mozambique for any cogent assessment of the future of that phenomenon. Writers such as Luís Bernardo Honwana, José Craveirinha, and Rui Nogar served prison terms as political dissenters; upon release they followed separate and necessarily cautious paths in their literary and cultural activities. Honwana presently studies law at the University of Lisbon, but he also plans to revise his *Nós matamos o cão tinhoso* and perhaps to publish a second book of stories. As mentioned previously, Craveirinha and Nogar continue to live in Lourenço Marques where they write and publish an occasional poem. More will be said shortly on the participation of both poets, particularly Craveirinha, in the recent literary effort.

The bizarre arrest and trial of Duarte Galvão (pseudonym of Virgílio de Lemos), because he wrote a poem which allegedly insulted the Portuguese flag and was therefore subversive, stand as proof of the sensitivity that attended the cultural and literary scene in Mozambique during the mid-sixties. Galvão's *Poemas do tempo presente* (Poems of the Present, 1960) includes "Poema à cidade" (Poem to the City) which he wrote in 1954. One reference in the poem irked the zealous authorities: "bayete bayete bayete/à capulana vermelha e verde"[2] (*bayete bayete bayete*/to the red and green *capulana*). *Bayete* is a Ronga phrase equivalent to "long live!" and *capulana* is the long flowing robe worn by many African women in Mozambique. Red and green are colors of the Portuguese national flag, but during the trial it was pointed out to the prosecution that these colors also have a symbolic significance for the Ronga people.

Although Duarte was acquitted, the incident, besides its political implications, speaks to the problem of how ignorant many white Mozambicans are of African culture. But in the midst of this racist reality and during the period of relative calm that settled over the literary and cultural world of Mozambique in the late sixties and early seventies, some scattered, but significant occurrences of a cultural, literary, and scholarly nature have given at least a hint of continuing activity. Newspapers such as *A Voz de Moçambique* and *O Cooperador* have continued to carry news of local cultural happenings. In 1971 *A Voz de Moçambique* reported on a unique event that caught the imagination of the intellectual and literary community: Lindo Hlongo, a young black man, had written a play which a Portuguese, Norberto Barroca, produced and directed in Lourenço Marques.

The play, *Os noivos ou conferência dramâtica sobre o lobolo* (The Newlyweds or a Dramatic Consultation on the Lobolo), treats a subject of cultural and economic importance to the African population. Similar to the *alembamento* in Angola, the *lobolo* is the practice whereby the groom compensates his father-in-law for marrying his daughter. In modern times hard cash has become the usual tender in such matrimonial transactions, and as a result certain hardships have been forced on the male who must often go to the diamond mines of South Africa to earn the necessary money. Social problems arise from the often long separation of the groom from his bride, and the play treats these questions as part of the general theme stated in the subtitle *A tribo em trânsito* (Tribal Life in Demise).

None of the actors in the production had had any previous experience, but despite its overall amateurishness the play succeeded in conveying a message aesthetically clothed in social satire and musical folklore and comedy. The very naïveté of the acting frequently achieved a pleasing effect of slapstick and caricature that served to satirize the internal and external forces that had contributed to the general demise of tribal values. But tribute was paid to the tenacity of an African musical culture. Between every scene a traditional or popular dance was performed, and at the play's end the entire cast, including the director, danced the *marrabenta*.

The first performance of *Os noivos* took place on April 28, 1971, in a theater in the downtown area of Lourenço Marques.

A note on the event published in *A Voz de Moçambique* makes quite a bit of the heterogeneous composition of the audience, which is considered revolutionary in a city where the races live separate and unequal existences. The writer of the note then thanks the playwright and praises the director who, as an outsider, has done more for theater in Mozambique than any native son. In May 1971 the performance was repeated in an East Indian–owned theater in the African suburb of Xipamanine before a largely black and *mestiço* audience.

The play has dubious importance in the development of theater in Mozambique; as a spectacle and a cultural event it has symbolic significance even though it may not quite herald an African renaissance in Lourenço Marques. Indeed, while there may be evidence of a renewed interest in things African on the part of a segment of the white intelligentsia and a reappraisal of their Africanness by black and *mestiço* youth, much of what is expressed in literature is either relegated to the purely ethnological or viewed as purely decorative.

As an example of the decorative, in 1971 the first issue of a small poetry magazine called *Caliban* was organized by J. P. Grabato Dias and Rui Knopfli. The cover features an African mask from the region of Angoche in Mozambique, and on the inside cover is a quotation from Act I, scene 2, of Shakespeare's *The Tempest*. Caliban, the slave, tells Prospero: "You taught me language, and my profit on't/Is, I know how to curse. The red plague rid you/For learning me your language! . . ."[3] These lines and others spoken by the two Shakespearean characters are repeated by Janheinz Jahn in his development of theses originally put forth by O. Mannoni and George Lamming.[4] Grabato Dias and Knopfli obviously had in mind similar attitudes toward the language of the colonizer, but the contents of their magazine have a very cosmopolitan flavor. Besides a short article by Eugénio Lisboa on T. S. Eliot, there appears a translation of "Ash Wednesday" by Rui Knopfli, plus an anthology of poems by Jorge de Sena, José Craveirinha, Rui Nogar, Sebastião Alba, Jorge Viegas, Grabato Dias, and Knopfli. What for Jahn was a method of solving the aesthetic and stylistic, as well as psychological, problems of an African literature written in a European language has become for the organizers of *Caliban* the broader issue of the tension of poetic language per se. This tension seems to be the one unifying theme in the publication's four issues; but the Mozambicans' awareness of the more sensitive problem of an African awareness and their use of African masks as decorative illustrations constitute a kind of integration that perhaps reflects Knopfli's views on the question of poetry in and of Mozambique, and poetry anywhere for that matter.

A close-up of the facial portion of a *mapico* mask adorns the second issue of *Caliban*, and the cover of the combined third and fourth issue has on it the bulging headlights and the grillwork of an automobile, which the editors entitle "Land Rover Mask." Along with the humor they probably intended to represent traditional Africa and the technological West combined, and the meaning of the title is emphasized in the depiction of the savage Caliban in the grotesque beauty of the masks. The tension of poetic language is seen in the translations of the Polish poet Zbigniew Herbert and the American Marianne Moore, the original poems by a small number of mostly Euro-African poets, and the selection from Lindo Hlongo's play *Os noivos*. Translations, particularly of poetry, always pit one language against another, and in the case of *Caliban* they aid in giving the magazine an audacity under its seemingly sophisticated façade.

Jorge de Sena, one of the better contemporary Portuguese poets, has been a kind of distant mentor of Knopfli and Lisboa. His critical acumen has aided the Mozambicans in their efforts to demystify the literary situation in their province. A reading of Jorge de Sena's contributions to *Caliban* demonstrates to what extent he shows a sensitivity to the cultural significance of language. Two of his poems in the first issue are in English, and another, in the joint issue, is called "Noções de linguística" (Ideas on Linguistics). De Sena's children, born to the Portuguese language but raised mainly in the United States, now prattle naturally in their adopted English. This observation leads to a reflection on the paradox of language, its durability, and its cultural inheritability:

> As línguas, que duram séculos e mesmo sobrevivem
> esquecidas noutras, morrem todos os dias
> na gaguês daqueles que as herdaram;
> e são tão imortais que meia dúzia de anos
> as suprime da boca dissolvida
> ao peso de outra raça, outra cultura.
> Tão metafísicas, tão intraduzíveis,
> que se derretem assim, não nos altos céus,
> mas na merda quotidiana de outras.[5]

(Languages, which last for centuries and even survive/forgotten in other tongues, die daily/in the stammering of those who have inherited them;/and so immortal are they that a few years/can suppress them from the mouth fragmentized/under the weight of another people, another culture./So metaphysical, so untranslatable are they,/that thus they mollify, not in the heavens on high,/but in the quotidian crap of other tongues.)

The poet speaks with irony of the vulnerability of languages and cultures, and he contrasts the idea of language as a purveyor of philosophical thought and untranslatable sentiments with the idea of insidiousness of an imposed language and culture. This poem relates obliquely, but not remotely, to the problem put forth in the Caliban-Prospero metaphor.

Other poems in *Caliban* relate even less directly to the problem of language and culture, but most selections in some way have a bearing on the magazine's unifying theme of integration and poetic tension. The magazine's co-editor adopts the Latinized name Frey Ioannes Garabatus and writes verse in the style and language of the sixteenth century. A kind of experimentation pervades the magazine, and even Rui Nogar contributes to the spirit of the sound and feel of language in his poem "Do himeneu vocabular" (Of Vocable Hymeneal) in which he says, "Eu amo a frescura das palavras adolescentes/sinto prazer em desnudá-las/sílaba a sílaba/lentamente" (*Caliban* 1, p. 26) (I love the freshness of adolescent words/I take pleasure in undressing them/slowly/ syllable by syllable). The poet manipulates his words with sensual pleasure and a feel for their purity.

But it is José Craveirinha who best plays out the conflict of language in a manner which speaks to the problem of an African poetry of European expression. It has been seen how in his earlier poetry Craveirinha achieved an African stylistic through the use of words and rhythmic patterns. In the poems he contributes to *Caliban* he still demonstrates a preference for vivid, surrealistic images, but less of a concern with the ancestral element of an African thematic. Still, the angst and the escape into erotic dreams are characteristics in this phase of Craveirinha's development that present a portrait of the African confined to the European city. The poem "Escape" illustrates this theme:

> Na noite açulada de nervos
> as línguas
> uma na outra furiosas
> húmidas afiam-se os gumes no beijo
> e os ásperos mamilos
> dos teus seios masoquisam-me o peito.
>
> Ah, sonho!
> única maneira
> livre de existir
> enquanto ferozes as manhãs
> no langor das urbes
> sanguíneas florescem nas acácias
> (*Caliban* 1, p. 23)

(In the night incited by nerves/our tongues/one furiously on the other/humidly whet their sharpness in the kiss/and the rough nipples/of your breasts rub masochistically against my chest.// Ah, dream!/only way/to cease to exist/while ferociously the mornings/in the languor of metropolises/sanguineously blossom in the acacias)

A motif of violence comes out in the erotic, tactile imagery of the first stanza with its metaphor of the knife and the rough texture of the nipples, while in the second stanza the visual imagery dominated by allusions to the color red converts the violent eroticism into a passion of feeling. Awaking from the dream in the crimson light of dawn, the poet identifies this sentiment of escape with the freedom of nature—the crimson acacias—that covers the languid, stultifying city.

If the general cast of *Caliban*, as a cosmopolitan Mozambican magazine, is unilateral integration from a Euro-African point of view, then Craveirinha offers another direction to the multi-faceted literary scene. White writers may make occasional forays into the black and *mestiço* suburbs and hinterland of Mozambique for the decorative or even for a suggestion of a cultural or psychological truth, but Craveirinha comes from that rural reality to meet the dominant group on equal terms. Symbolically, Craveirinha is Caliban, and his distortions of Prospero's language constitute an aesthetically formulated curse. The urbanized poet voices his denial of the city, not with romantic invocations of Mother Africa, but with totemic images; in this respect "Lustre à cidade" (Brightness Comes to the City) represents some of Craveirinha's best poetry:

> Velha quizumba
> de olhos raiados de sangue
> sorve-me os rins da angústia
> e a dentes de nojo
> carnívora rói-me a medula infracturável do sonho.
>
> E nas quatro costas
> do horizonte reaccionário das paredes
> uma exactidão de féretro tem precisamente
> as passadas infalíveis dum recluso.
>
> E a vida
> a injúrias engolidas em seco
> tem o paladar da baba das hienas uivando
> enquanto no dia lúgubre de sol
> os jacarandás ao menos ainda choram flores
> e de joelhos o medo
> puxa lustro à cidade.
>
> (*Caliban* 1, p. 22)

(Old *quizumba* [the hyena]/eyes streaked with blood/sucks my
kidneys of anguish/and with loathsome fangs/carnivorously
gnaws on the unbreakable marrow of my dreams.//And on the
four coasts/of the walls' reactionary horizon/a coffinlike exact-
ness has precisely/the infallible footsteps of a recluse.//And life/
with its insults unflinchingly borne/tastes of the slaver of hyenas
screeching/while on the gloomy, sunlit day/at least the jacaran-
das still cry flowers/and fear, kneeling,/pulls brightness toward
the city.)

A repulsive beast of carrion in the folklore of some African cultures, the hyena comes in the dark of night, with pusillanimous
audacity, to eat defenseless creatures and decaying flesh. Craveirinha uses this element of African folklore along with images of
darkness, loneliness, decay, and death to represent the anguish of
the urbanized African; and in the last stanza combines the surrealistic image of the hyena with the idea of the indignation
heaped on him by the city, which even in the sunlight contains
gloom. Nature, in the form of trees "crying" flowers, and the
poet's cautious apprehension bring the only ray of hope for his
survival in the city.

Caliban in no way offers a comprehensive sampling of all that
has occurred recently in Mozambican letters. On the other hand,
the magazine's synthesis and integration, to say nothing of its
high artistic standards, offer some sense of the general literary
climate in Lourenço Marques where more than likely any future
development in Mozambique will take place. For the time being,
important writers and critics such as Lisboa, Knopfli, Craveirinha,
and Honwana, to mention a few of the small elite, will constitute
a viable base for whatever coordinated literary movement may
develop in the future. But as is the case in Angola, the future is
nebulous.

PART THREE

THE CAPE VERDE ISLANDS

CHAPTER 11

Ten African Islands

About the year 1460 Portuguese and Genovese mariners came upon the uninhabited Atlantic island subsequently named Santiago. In the years immediately following, the Portuguese, with the aid of the Genovese navigator Antonio Noli, discovered the remaining, likewise uninhabited, islands of the Cape Verde archipelago: Fogo, Maio, Boavista, Sal, Santo Antão, São Vicente, São Nicolau, Santa Luzia, and Brava. Some scholars, notably Jaime Cortesão, have contended that, long before the arrival of the Europeans, Senegalese had journeyed regularly in large canoes to collect salt on the appropriately named Island of Sal, which lies some two hundred and eighty miles west of Africa's Guinea coast.

Whatever the truth of the matter, Cape Verde became a permanent settlement only after the arrival of the Portuguese and the slaves they brought with them from nearby Africa. This unequal meeting of African and European formed the basis of Cape Verdean society. But without going into the details of Cape Verdean history, a task already undertaken by a number of scholars,[1] a rapid look at some of the archipelago's cultural realities will help to lay a foundation for an understanding of its modern literature.

Although no one can be sure of the origin of all the Africans brought to Cape Verde, a sizable contingent must have come from the relatively close Guinea region. The European, mainly Portuguese, settlers were, in the early period, *donatários* (recipients of royal land grants), plantation overseers, artisans, and not a few exiles, all of whom set about extracting a profit from the land by exploiting slave labor on the sugarcane and cotton plantations. Only on Santiago, however, did anything approaching the New World latifundium system develop, and in comparison with Brazil productivity was short-lived, eventually giving way to the more favorable conditions of Bahia and Pernambuco.

Economic decline set in about the second half of the seventeenth century and contributed to Cape Verde's isolation and to the progressive formation of a creole society. Francisco José Tenreiro, in describing the creation of this creole society, speaks of the black woman's role as one that blunted the "sharp edges of inequality based on social conditions between black and white, while out of a strictly slave society emerged one based on servitude."[2] Tenreiro was referring to the African woman's frequent status as consort to the European settler and mother of racially mixed children.

Even though the archipelago, because of its convenient location between two continents, served as a stopping-off place for slave ships and later as a refueling point for merchant vessels, its contacts with the outside world did not greatly alter the process of creolization. In his essay "Do funco ao sobrado ou o 'mundo' que o mulato criou" (From the Shack to the Mansion or the "World" That the Mulatto Created) Gabriel Mariano discusses some of the peculiarities of Cape Verde's creole society. He compares its particular brand of creolization with that of the Guinea Gulf Island of São Tomé and of the Brazilian city of Bahia (Salvador). According to Mariano, the miscegenation that occurred in all three Portuguese areas took on some special features in Cape Verde because of its relative isolation. In other words, Cape Verde was left to its own racial and cultural homogenization. Mariano lists a number of Brazilian terms of racial identity which, he concludes, prove to what extent color consciousness exists in that South American country. On the other hand, cultural and racial dissolving and integrating factors imposed themselves with extraordinary force on Cape Verdean society, to paraphrase Mariano.[3] Presumably, then, the nearly homogeneous aspect of Cape Verdean society did away with the need for terms that distinguish on the basis of race or color.

The question of racial and cultural amalgamation in Cape Verde has to be qualified, but in any case the result has a measure of fact mixed with myth, especially as it pertains to the islands' elite. Of Cape Verde's population 70 percent is *mestiço*, 20 percent is black, and 10 percent is white. If American terms of racial identification are applied to Cape Verde's population, it must be said that it is overwhelmingly black. But in Cape Verde, as in Brazil and other Afro-Portuguese regions, the category of *mestiço* does have cultural, social, and psychological significance. It should also be noted that Cape Verde appears to surpass even Brazil in the degree to which widespread miscegenation has created a real or imagined climate of racial harmony, and this gives credence to Lusotropicalist idealism.

But there are extenuating economic factors behind any society's ethos. Henrique Teixeira de Sousa, after paying homage to the concept of the racial melting pot in his article "A estrutura social da Ilha do Fogo em 1940" (The Social Structure of the Island of Fogo in 1940), divides Fogo's population into four classes. In descending order on the social scale are the whites, the mulattoes (offspring of a white father and a black or mixed-blood mother) who for convenience' sake can be called *mestiços*, the true mulattoes (children of two *mestiço* parents), and the *povo*, poor people of any color but usually black. Teixeira de Sousa assures us that this is not a strictly racial or ethnic division but is based largely on social stratifications. He observes, however, that on Fogo it is difficult and rare for a *mestiço* or mulatto to be accepted into a white family, whereas the reverse is a common occurrence.[4] Despite the possibility of upward social mobility the mixed-blood has to contend with a reticence brought about by the stigma of color and racial background.

Historically, then, color consciousness and an elitism determined by the "purity of blood" have accompanied social classifications on the Island of Fogo. Teixeira de Sousa tells of situations
in which the illegitimate *mestiço* haughtily bears the name of a
white father he perhaps never knew or who never recognized him
as his offspring. And because he was frequently of illegitimate
birth and abandoned by his father, the *mestiço* formed a marginal class while the upward-moving mulatto challenged the
white's economic and social dominance. It is apparent, then, that
racism based on class and ethnic origin did, and does, exist in
Cape Verde. In "Sobrados, lojas e funcos" (Mansions, Stores, and
Shacks), published in 1958, eleven years after his first study,
Teixeira de Sousa gives a more detailed appraisal of the shift of
power from the white landowning class to the ascending mulatto
class. This transition began to evolve in the postabolition period,
during which whites controlled the island's economy, and a popular saying was that the monkey lived among the rocks, the black
man in the shack, the mulatto in the store (where he was employed as a clerk), and the white man in the mansion.[5] The day
would come, however, when the monkey would run with the
black man, the black man with the mulatto, and the mulatto with
the white man. On the Island of Fogo as well as on other islands
of the archipelago social change can be attributed to such factors
as the breakdown of the plantation system, the decline of certain
economic institutions, the emigration of traditional white families, and the resulting ascension of the mulatto class. Teixeira de
Sousa and others see these factors as having contributed to the
racial democratization of Cape Verdean society. And indeed a
homogeneous, mixed-blood population in the upper stratum has
helped to assuage traditional racial antipathies, although the
legacy of distinctions determined by color and the presence of a
black population, mostly lower class, still serve to maintain race
consciousness. Cape Verde does not have the visceral racism and
tensions of other multiracial societies, but traditional attitudes
and socioeconomic factors do make color an important consideration throughout the archipelago.

"*A Romance Experience in the Tropics*"

Cape Verde's modern cultural awakening emanated principally from the intelligentsia on the windward islands of São Nicolau, Santo Antão, and especially São Vicente where in the mid and late thirties members of the elite declared their regional uniqueness and began to seek a way of expressing their autonomy. Uniqueness for many members of this generation was their special position in a generally Latin cultural infrastructure. One of the first and most important statements on these attitudes came from the pen of Baltasar Lopes da Silva in his essay "Uma experiência românica nos trópicos" (A Romance Experience in the Tropics). The author, a novelist, poet, philologist, and teacher, intends to demonstrate his native Cape Verde's distinctive membership in the family of Portuguese tropical diversity. After affirming the Portuguese base of the islands' creole speech, he contrasts Cape Verde's racial harmony with the segregated conditions of the United States' deep South and its northern ghettos. With the United States capturing world headlines in the thirties for lynchings and other manifestations of blatant racism, Lopes could not have chosen a more vulnerable society to illustrate his point. Unfortunately, this contrast somewhat obscures the real point, which has to do with the problem of ethnic identity as it reflects the question of an African consciousness within Cape Verdean regionalism.

The Cape Verdean intellectual feels, of course, that he has come to terms with the problem of ethnic identity and he takes pride in the racial and cultural integration of his creole society. By their titles alone several books and treatises by Cape Verdeans and admirers of Cape Verdean society attest to the pride, protectiveness, and romantic devotion some feel for island life. Pedro de Sousa Lobo wrote, for example, an article entitled "A originalidade humana de Cabo Verde" (Cape Verde's Human Originality, 1959), and I have already quoted from Gabriel Mariano's "O mundo que o mulato criou" (The World the Mulatto Created). Nuno Miranda's "Integração ecuménica em Cabo Verde" (Ecumenical Integration in Cape Verde, 1959) and Manuel Ferreira's *A aventura crioula* (The Creole Adventure, 1967) might also be mentioned. All these works emphasize integration and originality. Complete outsiders have also been impressed with Cape Verde's character; for example, the English writer Archibald Lyall's *Black and White Make Brown* (1938) tells of racial amalgamation and lyrical creole expressions such as *morabeza* (affability) and *cretcheu* (love).

Manuel Ferreira, in his *A aventura crioula*, offers this declaration of Cape Verdeanness: "A melting pot of Afro-European values, there is in Cape Verde a new type of *mestiço* being formed. He is taking on a culture that tends toward differentiation, although predominantly European, which is perfectly understandable if we consider that after the initial period of settlement the umbilical cord with Africa was severed while throughout the centuries a European human stream continued to come along with an infiltration, through many routes, of Portuguese culture . . ."[6] The arguments put forth by Ferreira and others asserting that Cape Verde's society is more European than African need not be contradicted but rather put into a perspective that takes into account the historical confrontation between a dominant and a subjugated group. In other words, the so-called severing of the umbilical cord with Africa and the continuing infusion of European values into Cape Verdean society also have to be seen as a process of progressive deculturation. Quite naturally, however, the elite has systematically isolated, emphasized, and exaggerated those aspects of their culture which not only distinguish it from other cultures, but also lend their society prestige in the eyes of the Western world. In some respects Cape Verdean ethos rests on a defensive attitude that views the islands as a successful biological and cultural melting pot (more so than Brazil and Hawaii, for example) and on a conscious diminution of an African heritage.

Africanisms in Cape Verde

Manuel Lopes, one of the pillars of Cape Verdean literature, wrote that "it is common to see foreigners, avid for the exotic, disembark on these African islands, principally São Vicente, with that sick curiosity of those who have visited Africa, the land of mystery. At the end of a half-hour of sightseeing they reembark disillusioned and irritated because they have encountered nothing new nor uncovered any mystery. They have seen no idols nor have they attended any sessions of black magic."[7] In a later interview, carried by a Lisbon newspaper, Lopes again refers to the cliché of African mystery and calls for a radically African literature, presumably not in Cape Verde, that will contribute to an understanding of the African.[8]

Like many of his contemporaries Lopes eschewed the yen of tourists for the exoticism of tropical lands. In the case of Cape Verde the elite's indignation has often resulted when the Negroid aspect of the population has occasioned outsiders to assume that they were in the presence of Africans. And no more indignant a reaction to the label of African can be found than Baltasar Lopes's reply to Gilberto Freyre, the Brazilian sociologist, who, in his books *Aventura e rotina* (Course and Adventure, 1952) and *Um brasileiro em terras portuguesas* (A Brazilian in Portuguese Lands, n.d.), makes some offhand observations on Cape Verde's place in the Lusitanian family of tropical regions. He declared the Island of Santiago to be quite Negroid, "an indication that, contrary to what is happening more and more in Brazil, the bulk of the population retains the elements of African origin."[9] Because the Cape Verdean elite seems willing to allow for the presence of African survivals in Santiago, Freyre's statement had only mild shock appeal. But he struck a sensitive nerve when he observed on the Island of São Vicente the same predominance of the African over the European that he had seen in Barbados or Trinidad, and more than he had seen in the most obviously Negroid areas of Brazil. First, Freyre attached great importance to physical type and, secondly, he denigrated São Vicente where the European-oriented elite flourished. He then added insult to injury by characterizing the Cape Verdeans as a people who in "seeking to be European have repudiated their African origins and found themselves in a precarious state or situation of not only economic but also cultural instability."[10] Whatever the precipitous aspect of Freyre's overview of the situation during his rapid trip through the islands, this last point would have some validity if he had never left his native Pernambuco.

We should make the point that it is not so much the predominance of European values in Cape Verde as it is a question of the sensitivity displayed by some members of the elite when reminded of the Africanisms that persist there. Paradoxically, Freyre's outmoded notions on Portuguese adaptation to the tropics clashed with the latent Eurocentrism of a Cape Verdean elite self-consciously aware of their society's measure of Lusotropicology. In "Cabo Verde visto por Gilberto Freyre" (Cape Verde as Seen by Gilberto Freyre, 1956) Baltasar Lopes asserted that the "messiah" has disappointed us, meaning that he, like others, had expected the champion of Lusotropicology to celebrate Cape Verde as an outstanding example of acculturation and of race mixture.[11] Baltasar Lopes's firsthand knowledge of the archipelago put him at an advantage in the debate, and Freyre's declaration that he found the creole speech of Cape Verde ugly detracted from his credibility when he proffered more scientific observations.[12] The emotional response by some Cape Verdeans to Freyre's abrupt pronouncements did not, however, enhance their valid criticisms of his appraisal of island life.

On the subject of Africanisms in Cape Verde, Lopes made certain statements some thirty-five years ago that he would, in all likelihood, repudiate today. But in 1936 he wrote, with regard to creole speech, that "the allotropisms and metaphorical language contain an elementary psychological explanation. The African, who shaped creole speech, conveys a certain poetry of the marvelous stemming from his concept of life and his *intellectual virginity*" (italics added).[13] He then compared the speech of children with that of savages, both of whom, he maintained, use a limited vocabulary to express the emotions that fill their world, and there-fore they by necessity speak poetically. The concept of the pre-logical primitive cropped up with some frequency in the early period of Cape Verdean awareness. To pick a flagrant example, in 1936 the Portuguese José Osório de Oliveira wrote that "the inhabitants of Santiago demonstrate the lowest intellectual devel-opment because they are more purely African and because the process of miscegenation was less intense on that island where the 'ethos' of black Africa still has some influence."[14] There exists, then, ample evidence that Cape Verdean society of that period was prone to misgivings and ambivalences on the question of the archipelago's African heritage. In part, the strong expression of a creole ethos was an attempt to overcome a sense of the inferiority of an African presence.

The price of declaring Cape Verde's European heritage has often been the belittling of this African presence. If the African element has become less visible in its unadulterated form, African cultural survivals and adaptations show a vitality obscured only by the desire, on the part of some, to diminish their importance. Because, however, a creole society means the union of disparate ethnic, physical, and cultural elements, some of these same mem-bers of the elite often recognize and even emphasize the survival of African elements and the black man's contributions to the Cape Verdean mystique. Gabriel Mariano, for one, in his article "A mestiçagem: Seu papel na formação da sociedade cabover-diana" (Race Mixture: Its Role in the Formation of Cape Ver-dean Society), focuses on Africanisms and their significance in the development of Cape Verdeanness. Writing about the proveni-ence of slaves brought to Cape Verde, Mariano considers that he himself may have had ancestors from Guinea, the Sudan, Angola, or even Martinique.[15] And he comments that "from what I can gather, the social formation of the Cape Verdean worked more on the basis of an Africanization of the European than it did the reverse."[16] As the title of his article indicates, Mariano tempers his argument for Africanization by steadfastly accepting the notion that miscegenation and racial democratization make the islands unique. With regionalist pride he supports Cape Verde's particular brand of Lusotropicology, but he also romantically makes a case for the African origins of cultural and social elements which some have taken to be purely of creole origin, meaning that they were generated in Cape Verde with no discernible African sources. According to Mariano, the black man and the *mestiço*, rather than merely being assimilated into a strictly European cultural pattern, took what was imposed on them and molded it to their own world view. This idea differs fundamentally from the concept that an intrinsically inferior people became "civilized" through contact with a superior society.

Quoting Aimé Césaire's contention that colonialism has provoked a juxtaposition rather than a harmony of cultures, Mariano seems to suggest that Cape Verde has to be seen as an exception to this truth.[17] Although Mariano's article, published in 1958, presents more enlightened ideas than those expressed in the thirties, it still forcibly constitutes a declaration of Cape Verde's unique situation in the Portuguese space: "It is significant that a civilization of whites, created by whites, should have accommodated itself to expressions of black culture. What has come to pass in our times is a *mestiço* culture where whites, blacks, and mulattoes follow common paths of realization and feel equally responsible for the destiny of their community. This fact gains even more significance when we remember that in other areas of Portuguese colonization, such as Brazil, São Tomé, Angola, and Mozambique, the black man and the mulatto feel, in a way, like guests of the societies that they helped or are helping to create."[18] After reaffirming Cape Verde's singularity and modifying the defensive contention of "more European than African," Mariano calls the formation of the creole society the work of Africans. He makes some passing references to an African legacy in dance, song, a few musical instruments, and certain implements such as the mortar and pestle used to grind corn. He agrees with Francisco José Tenreiro that the black woman has softened the harshness of Portuguese speech and made popular Catholic saints more festive and magical.[19] There is a basic contradiction in Mariano's view in that he sees the African's role as mainly lyrical in the formation of Cape Verdean society.

Even before Mariano's generation, however, members of the elite had set about documenting Cape Verdean folklore. With the detachment of the social scientist doing his field work and with the concern of the "son of the land" seeking to know the full extent of his cultural reality, these intellectuals, while they may have seen African survivals as minimal, turned their attention to the Island of Santiago where, paradoxically, a visible black heritage was conceded to exist. Baltasar Lopes collected specimens of traditional songs from Santiago and wrote an essay on the African-inspired "Folklore poético da Ilha de Santiago" (The Poetic Folklore of the Island of Santiago). Another amateur ethnologist, Félix Monteiro, did a two-part study on the *tabanca*, an African religious rite still alive in the interior of Santiago. Some investigators no doubt believed that they were merely recording for posterity that which was destined to disappear, and one fairly recent observer wrote that Africanisms in the interior of Santiago were "tenuous reminders of black Africa in folk poetry and in an occasional survival of proto-religions imported with the contingents of slaves."[20]

Despite the importance of the elite's research, they have generally demonstrated the lack of a true concept of African survivals, particularly in their modified or assimilated forms. Whether the dominated group, that is, the enslaved African, adjusts that which is imposed upon it to its own psychological or aesthetic scheme or whether the dominant group absorbs and borrows from the culture of the subjugated people, the latter is the important contributor. Popular American music is a case in point; and jazz, although born in America, carries the indelible mark of Africa. The presence of the readily identifiable is not the only manifestation of an African survival. This last statement definitely applies to Cape Verdean society, and although the determination of these survivals is better left to the trained ethnologist, anthropologist, and folklorist, we, as a means of better understanding the creative writing of the islands, must turn our attention, however briefly, to a consideration of popular music, creole speech, and folklore.

The Morna and the Coladeira

The *morna* belongs as uniquely to Cape Verde as jazz does to the United States. And although the *morna* resulted from the black man's and the *mestiço's* modification of European musical forms to suit their creole culture, many, such as Jean-Paul Sarrautte, have preferred to see this expression of island song and dance as wholly Lusitanian in origin.[21] Others have argued that the *morna* is similar to the Afro-Cuban béguine, and the Brazilian João Condé has compared it with the music of his country: "it has always seemed to me that the *morna's* relationship to the samba is unmistakable."[22] Condé may find it difficult to prove a direct kinship between the *morna* and the obviously African-influenced samba, but he would have no more difficult a task than those who have offered theories on the *morna's* descendance from the music of Portugal's Algarve region. And it might be added, parenthetically, that those who see the *morna* as Portuguese, and thus totally European in origin, possibly ignore the fact that there was black African music in the Iberian peninsula, and especially in the Algarve, since the time of Moorish occupation. The origins of the *morna* require more extensive research by ethnomusicologists, but it is difficult to believe that any form of native Cape Verdean music does not have a link with West Africa, particularly since this region, through jazz and Latin American rhythms, has influenced the popular music of much of the world.

The Cape Verdean writer Luís Romano places the *morna's* beginnings at the end of the nineteenth century, and he emphasizes its non-African elements such as melodic qualities and the use of European string instruments. Romano sees the more syncopated *coladeira* as having reached its level of popularity about 1930.[23] Although he offers nothing new on the question of the *morna's* origins, he does intimate that the *coladeira* derives from an African musical tradition. If this is true, the *coladeira* probably predates the *morna* as the islands' basic and dominant musical style, despite its relatively late popularity. Félix Monteiro, long a student of Cape Verdean folk institutions, expressed a similar view during a conversation I had with him in Santiago on June 8, 1971. With all due respect to those who emphasize European musical elements, and their presence obviously cannot be denied, it is not necessary to scratch the surface very deeply to discover a continuing African musical heritage in Cape Verde—in the nostalgic *morna*, obviously in the traditional *coladeira*, and in the islanders' preference for such highly syncopated dances as the Brazilian samba.

Cape Verdean Creole Speech

The creolized Portuguese spoken in various dialects on all the islands has served since the first decades of the twentieth century as a rallying point for Cape Verdean regionalism. Much of the credit for creole's present prestige goes to Baltasar Lopes da Silva whose monograph *O dialecto crioulo de Cabo Verde* (Cape Verde's Creole Dialect, 1957) culminated his shorter studies and pronouncements on the regional dialect's status as a viable language. Lopes's impressive work reflects his training in Romance philology. In fact, he goes to great lengths in explaining the degree to which *crioulo* approximates standard Portuguese, whether phonetically, syntactically, morphologically, or lexically. In an earlier article Lopes had verified that "Cape Verdean creole is clearly a Romance language."[24] But while stressing the obvious Romance aspects of Cape Verdean creole, he admits a lack of precise information on the African linguistic influence, and he calls for an analysis of the "dialect." The survival of Portuguese-language archaisms and the presence of a small percentage of identifiable African words in creole should come as no surprise, even to the nonlinguist. What applies linguistically to Cape Verdean creole holds true, to some extent, for such widely separated creoles as the patois of Haiti and the *forro* of São Tomé, or even certain dialects of Brazilian Portuguese and the black English of the United States. The latter two are, of couse, dialectal variants largely comprehensible to speakers of the standard language. Lopes speaks of Cape Verdean creole as a dialect of Portuguese, but it might be better to draw a distinction between a dialect and a creolized language: the former is a regional variant readily understood by those who use other dialects of the same language, while the latter may be completely incomprehensible in its spoken form to those who know the "mother tongue."[25] And no speaker of any dialect of Portuguese, be it peninsular or Brazilian, can follow a conversation in Cape Verdean creole without some intensive initiation into the peculiarities of the language.

Recalling Lopes's reference to the African's "intellectual virginity," one can understand why he would seek to establish creole's linguistic legitimacy on its strictly Romance origins and at the same time relegate any African influences to a secondary folkloric, metaphorical level. Lopes wrote that "I have never found any linguistic trace that necessarily originates from an African substratum."[26] But the Portuguese dialectologist Jorge Morais-Barbosa, considering the presence of temporal verb conjugations in Cape Verdean creole, has written the following: "But even in these cases a careful analysis of the facts suggests the existence, in a previous phase of creole, of an aspectual type of conjugation, later progressively influenced by the European model, which in the case of Portuguese never ceased to be present and to impose itself on the speakers of creole. This is sufficient reason to see as precipitous the claim that in these creoles [of Portuguese Africa] there exist no traces of African languages."[27] Another linguist, Marius Valkhoff, took up Morais-Barbosa's point with these words: "When I visited St. Thomas [São Tomé] and Príncipe in 1958, Creole had already died out on the latter island and I had great difficulty in finding a few people who still knew the dialect and whom I could question. Hence it is urgent that these Creole varieties be recorded and studied; the longer we wait the more lusitanized (hispanized in the case of Annobón Creole) they will become."[28]

In a discussion of Portuguese Guinean creole, which bears a

close resemblance to that spoken in Cape Verde, W. A. A. Wilson praises Baltasar Lopes's contributions to the study of the latter language. But Wilson laments that in Lopes's concern with words of Portuguese origin, "one is left to infer that there is an obvious gap in his word list."[29] This gap stems from Lopes's approach to the subject from the standpoint of Romance philology. And additional gaps in the scholarly knowledge of Cape Verdean creole have resulted from minimal research on possible syntactical and morphological elements from West African languages.

As I have intimated, the elite, by disclaiming an African substratum and erasing the pidgin stigma, contributed to creole's respectability among the upper classes of Cape Verdean society. Creole's few detractors have been overwhelmed by the prestige of those who argue in favor of the language's validity. Understandably, one of the arguments against the cultivation of creole is that it is a link to the speech of "uncivilized" Africans. Essentially on this premise José Maria da Costa wrote his article "Devemos evitar o crioulo: O crioulo é uma inferioridade" (We Must Avoid Creole: Creole Means Inferiority), in which he states that "creole is a legacy of the untutored and uncouth slave who was incapable of learning the Portuguese of his masters."[30]

A more significant polemic has revolved around the use of creole as a literary language. Basically, the polemic can be reduced to one question: can creole serve as a vehicle of Cape Verdean literary expression? Gabriel Mariano would maintain that creole has already proven itself to be such a vehicle, especially for poetry. For Mariano, Cape Verde stands out as a region where a creole has become an erudite as well as a popular literary language, in contrast to Portuguese Guinea, Angola, and Mozambique. In the main, Mariano relegates the problem to such queries as to what degree creole art poetry differs from popular verse and to what extent these works, when composed by "educated" individuals, approximate those expressed in Portuguese.[31]

Writing in the *Cabo Verde: Boletim*, the poet Nuno Miranda rejects the notion that creole has a future as a literary language. In his view the dialects of standard Portuguese spoken on the

islands have sufficient richness to express Cape Verdean regionalism. Miranda likewise repudiates the use of a creolized word or
phrase inserted into a Portuguese-language work; he calls for an
end to esoteric stylizations and criticizes the Portuguese writer
Manuel Ferreira for combining creole and Portuguese. Ferreira
himself, although he champions the cause of creole, also contends
that Cape Verdeanness can be effectively expressed in the Portuguese language. This assertion has been borne out by the fact that
most noteworthy Cape Verdean poetry and prose fiction has been
written in a more or less standard Portuguese. Virtually all Cape
Verdeans speak and write Portuguese, and those writers who also
know creole can and do translate that regional expressiveness into
a stylistic vitality through the medium of the standard tongue.
As for so-called "esoteric stylizations," they can contribute to the
aesthetic value of a work if the usage does not deteriorate into
picturesqueness and exoticism.

To this day creole, as a language of common usage, continues
to affirm the Cape Verdean's sense of regional independence.
With regard to creole's literary viability three general alternatives
can be identified: a more or less standard Portuguese only subtly
influenced by creole expression; a creolized Portuguese or a mixture of Portuguese and creole; a literature written entirely in
creole. In the section that immediately follows, and indeed
throughout the remaining chapters on Cape Verdean literature,
I shall have occasion to test the validity of these alternatives.

Folklore and Popular Literature

As far back as the nineteenth century samples of creole poetry
and even some African legends were collected and transcribed
in the original in such publications as the *Almanach luso-africano
para 1899* (Luso-African Almanac for 1899).[32] The inclusion
of these African and creole samplings seemed to serve the purpose
of entertaining curiosities. It was not until the 1930s that members of the intelligentsia undertook a more analytical and ethnographic approach to the popular creole poetry of the islands.

Throughout Cape Verde's history creole had been the language of the people and therefore the vehicle of folktales, popular literature, and song. And it was in honor of this tradition that Eugénio Tavares compiled *Morna* (1932), a collection of creole poems and songs, some of which were written by him. Whatever Tavares's value as a translator of and spokesman for the popular poetry of the islands, his efforts on behalf of creole earned him a historically important place in the development of Cape Verdean literature.

In 1933 appeared Pedro Cardoso's historically significant *Folclore caboverdiano*. Born on the volcanic Island of Fogo, the *mestiço* Cardoso revealed a pride in his African heritage and at the same time he defended his status as a Portuguese citizen. That both Cardoso and Tavares saw fit to express often fervent Lusitanian patriotism testifies to the processes that had long been at work on the Cape Verde islands and which blossomed in the late nineteenth century with high-flown proclamations of civilization versus backwardness. Cardoso has to be considered as one of the first intellectuals to be caught in the psychic dilemma of being devoted to Western civilization as well as attracted to African cultural dynamics. And his investigations in Cape Verdean folklore were unprecedented during a period in which Africanisms and creole carried an unquestionable stamp of inferiority.

Symptomatic of the times in which he lived, Cardoso, in explaining African-influenced traditions, employed an unacceptable, often amusing terminology, from our point of view. He observed that "in Cape Verdean folklore one certainly finds the reminiscences of heathen rites and beliefs, particularly on the Island of Santiago (*batuque*, *tabanca*, etc.) where an unmixed Ethiopian element predominates."[33] Although he insists on the traditional Portuguese base of Cape Verdean folklore, he stresses the need for a study of regional sources, a study which he undertook himself. At the beginning of his book Cardoso offers some elementary notions on creole speech; he then defines several terms originating in African languages or applicable to African cultural survivals. He explains such words as *batuque* (the music, dance, and song of which the *torno* is a part), *torno* (a dance of obscene movements and attitudes), *jabacoso* (a word of African origin meaning witch doctor), and *manduco* (a short, wooden club used by the peasants of Fogo, which derives its name from a type of tree found in Guinea). Cardoso spontaneously records *batuque* songs taken from the lips of popular singers (*cantadeiras*), and he demonstrates both his attraction and his revulsion for the primitive when he avers that "these improvisations give evidence, in their ingenuous rudeness, of the lyrical-satirical nature of that patient, heroic, humble, and strong race, which for millennia has been dispossessed and martyred despite these and other excellent qualities, only because of one defect—that of being black."[34] Colonialist attitudes emerge in his allusions to obscene dances and in the fatalistic image of the resigned but noble savage. Yet Cardoso's poetry presents the slave (or rural worker) and the master (or landowner) in situations where the powerless reveals his humanity with satire and irony.

Norman Araújo, in his study of Cape Verdean literature, comments in passing on Cardoso's concern with economic and social exploitation tinged with racial overtones.[35] Irony gives these racial overtones a note of social protest, as can be seen in this creole-language poem:

> Morgado de unha reado,
> Dunde bêm tanto requeza?
> Sê tràbalho que ta dà,
> Nhô ê ladrom de probeza.
>
> Nhô ê rico, mi ê probe,
> Ma mi m'ca probe ninguêm.
> Mi ê probe de Nhór-Dés,
> Que pa dà, só êl que têm.[36]

(Stingy landowner,/How'd you get so rich?/All you do/Is steal from poverty.//Master's rich, I'm poor,/But I'm nobody's poor man./I am a poor man of God the Lord,/Who is the only one who has something to give.)

The narrator uses color distinctions to underscore the gap between poor and rich in the eighth stanza when the singsong antithesis changes from rich-poor to white-black: "Nhô ê branco, mi ê préto" (Master is white, I am black); and in successive stanzas, of which the following is an example, appear metaphors illustrative of a folk philosophy:

Nhô ê branco, mi ê préto,
Nhôr sim; ma nhô considrá:
Branco ê papel, mas sim tinta
Ê mudo, êl ca ta papiâ.

(Master is white, I am black,/Yes sir, but think of this:/Paper is white, but without ink/it is mute, it can't talk.)

Sardonic, equalizing humor also carries a note of self-effacing bitterness when poor and black again become synonymous in this four-line *finaçon* recorded by Cardoso:

"Probe na dimanda co branco
Ê cima cópo sem garafa,
Ê cima bóca sem bocado,
Ê cima sáia sem cordon."
(p. 92)

(Poor man disputing white man/Is like drinking glass without bottle,/Is like mouth without mouthful,/Is like skirt without sash.)

In other creole poems and songs collected by members of an emerging elite in the 1930s the antithesis of poor man-rich man as synonymous with black man-white man confirms the social and racial confrontations in the lore of the people. And significantly, as far as cultural survivals are concerned, the form and structure of the songs and music (i.e., *finaçon*, *torno*, and *batuque*) prove to be African in origin.

The *finaçon*, a word which Baltasar Lopes describes as possibly deriving from the Portuguese *afinação* (tune), has as its main characteristic "the expression of moral rules, norms of behavior, and concepts elaborated through experience."[37] A social concept is detailed in the following poem-song which translates the popular saying quoted by Henrique Teixeira de Sousa in his essay on the Island of Fogo:

> Branco ta morá na sobrado,
> Mulato ta morá na loja,
> Nego ta morá na funco,
> Sancho ta morá na rotcha.
>
> Ta bem um dia,
> Nhô Tasco Lambasco,
> Rosto frangido
> Rabo comprido,
> Ta corrê co nego di funco,
> Nego ta corrê co mulato di loja,
> Mulato co branco di sobrado,
> Branco ta ba rotcha, el ta tomba . . .[38]

(White man lives in the mansion,/Mulatto lives in the store,/ Black man lives in the shack,/Sancho lives on the rock.//A day will come,/Mr. Tasco Lambasco,/Wrinkled face,/Long tail,/ Will run with the black man of the shack,/The black man will run with the mulatto of the store,/The mulatto will run with the white man of the mansion,/The white man will go to the rock, and off he'll jump . . .)

In his commentary on this *finaçon* Baltasar Lopes calls attention to the construction and the descriptive sobriety which, in his opinion, represent a counteracculturative attitude. A repetition of the verb *ta morá* (lives or, better, dwells) in the first stanza suggests a static social situation, while in the second stanza *ta corrê* (runs) connotes motion and rapid social change, and *ta tomba* (falls) depicts the social and economic descent of the landowning class. But rather than presenting counteracculturative attitudes, the poem, with its effects of social mobility and inversion, gives an artistic stamp of communal folk documentation to a socioeconomic reality. And just as the verbs used convey the idea of social stability followed by ascending (and descending) change, the humorous portrayal of the monkey serves a structural and aesthetic purpose. In the poem's rhythm the second through fourth lines of the second stanza offer a rifflike expansion among the otherwise unadorned references to the three social-racial types. Serving as a break between the stability of dwelling and the mobility of running, the lines that describe the monkey mark the inversion with irony.

Baltasar Lopes collected several *finaçons* sung at *batuques* celebrated on the Island of Santiago. With intellectual honesty he admits to having never attended a *batuque*, which makes his documentation all the more impressive. From informants he was able to gather some basic data on the *finaçon*, and in an essay he describes the musical instruments that accompanied the singers and discusses the role of the soloists and chorus. In considering the satirical, occasionally obscene nature of the *finaçon* and the *desafio*, or their challenge-rebuttal element, Lopes theorizes on the etymology of certain specialized words. Not surprisingly he minimizes the importance of the African nature of the *batuques* with hypotheses on the influence of Iberian poetic forms such as the medieval *cantigas de maldizer* (slander songs) and satirical Portuguese poetry. No one would dismiss these possibilities without the benefit of research and careful stylistic analysis. In the case of the *cantiga de maldizer*, however, it seems unlikely that this courtly Galician-Portuguese poetry of Provençal origin would have come in the cultural baggage of the Portuguese who had most contact with the slaves in Cape Verde. At any rate, the *cantigas* had practically ceased to be cultivated by the fourteenth century, long before the discovery of Cape Verde. Other types of satirical poetry, some of it popular, continued on the peninsula and no doubt found their way to the various regions of Portuguese overseas dominion. One can safely speculate that convergences occurred between the peninsular *desafio* and a similar challenge-rebuttal tradition from West Africa.

Striking examples exist of African-like praise songs in the *finaçons* improvised for Dr. Honório who was a lawyer born in Portuguese Guinea and who, because of his prestigious position and rapport with the common people, became a celebrated person in the interior of Santiago. Lopes's informant reported how the venerated lawyer would visit a *batuque* terrain and announce himself in improvised creole verse:

> Nhâ guênti, nhâ guênti, nhâ guênti!
> Es cusa ê Honório di nha Branquê di Balanta
> Qui djâ bêm bu coraçam pâ nhôs . . .

(People, people, people!/This that you see before you is Honório, son of Branquê of Balanta/Who has come to open his heart to you . . .)

The people would then respond to Dr. Honório's greeting:

> Corpo ca birâ runho di nhô qui chigâ
> Pamó di nhô sabê cuma sô preto qui nhô ê;
> Cabéça nhô tênê grandi
> E dinhêro nhô tênê sô branco . . .[39]

(I don't feel bad about your being here/Because though you are black/Your head is big [a good mind] /And only the white man has more money than you . . .)

When in 1941 Dr. Honório met with an untimely death, he immediately became the object of a series of praise songs that combined improvised eulogy with a glorified reconstruction of his life. This sort of folk poetry clearly illustrates the link between Cape Verde and Africa long after the so-called umbilical cord had been severed. And it would be rash to say that the form, structure, and spirit of the African praise song do not continue to influence the popular poetry of Santiago even to this day.

One other manifestation of improvised song lyric was documented by Félix Monteiro in his article on the mulatto singer Ana Procópio. This popular singer, who died in 1957 at an advanced age, "had so much faith in her capacity to improvise that in instances of great enthusiasm she would challenge the players to vary the rhythm and the tonal intensity because she knew they could follow without losing her."[40]

The usual theme of Ana Procópio's songs dealt with love complaint or just the power of love, and Monteiro òbserves that there were no vestiges of Africa in her songs. An ignorance of the kind of music that accompanied her lyrics prevents us from commenting on their rhythmic structure, but the fact that she improvised and, in doing so, varied the rhythm and tonal intensity lead us to suspect some influence of African syncopation and offbeat phrasing. Whatever the origins of Ana Procópio's music, Monteiro succeeds in drawing attention to a significant chapter in popular lyric poetry on the archipelago, and with a spirit of regionalism he has helped to counter the belief, held by some such as Gilberto Freyre, that Cape Verde was barren of cultural originality.

A few members of the educated elite cultivated popular, creole poetry as an expression of their sense of regionalism. Jorge Pedro and Gabriel Mariano attempted to re-create popular themes in creole, and their success, or lack of it, depends to a great extent on whether or not we accept creole as a literary language, even in simulated folk verse. Mariano's creole poetry adheres to authentic folk techniques and traditional themes. Baltasar Lopes has noted a faithfulness to popular origins in Mariano's use of asyndeton and the "elliptical tone characteristic of the creole of Santiago, a tone that closely follows the conceptual and proverbial base of the island folk poetry."[41] Jorge Pedro, on the other hand, has generally allowed himself greater freedom in thematic and stylistic elaborations of popular poetry. These liberties and stylizations led a critic to call Jorge Pedro's poetry the "fooling around" of an educated man who waxes ironic with that which he obviously considers inferior.[42] Jorge Pedro did fall into the trap of African exoticism in his effort to capture the feel of "native" society in transition. He chose a condescending glorification of the good old days that misinterprets natural cultural change. Both Gabriel Mariano and Jorge Pedro only sporadically cultivated creole verse and have written very few poems.

The critic Arnaldo França has named Mário Macedo Barbosa and Sérgio Frusoni as poets who tried to elevate creole to an artistic plane. In "Caco-lecó" Barbosa uses a ballad style to depict, in lyric fashion, the existence of the common folk. In his study of Cape Verdean literature Norman Araújo devotes several pages to Sérgio Frusoni, the Italian-born poet of popular creole verse. Perhaps because of his foreign birth Frusoni was extremely attached to Cape Verde; his sparse production of creole verse, much of it unpublished, contains a strong note of nostalgia and dedication to a popular mystique.

Creole as a literary language received its test in the writings of poets such as Mariano, Pedro, Barbosa, and Frusoni. But very few, despite the so-called artistic elevation of creole, have cultivated "art" poetry or prose fiction in the popular vernacular. For whatever prestige creole may have as a socially acceptable means of communication and oral expression, it lacks vitality as a language of contemporary Cape Verdean literature. First, as already suggested, the use of creole severely limits the work's reading audience, and, secondly, it runs the risk of imparting a ludicrous, pidgin effect to those works, particularly prose, that do not aim at representing cultural regionalism. As I shall demonstrate in chapter 12, something of a compromise on the use of Portuguese and creole has been reached by a few writers; but the debate continues, and Nuno Miranda has been joined by other Cape Verdeans who object to even the hybridized or stylized use of creole. Creole poetry centered on popular themes does seem aesthetically viable when cultivated by those educated writers who can avoid the condescension of the interloper. Furthermore, as a nationalistically inspired artistic consciousness creole poetry is an inevitable part of the identity phase in Cape Verdean literature.

That segment of the Cape Verdean oral tradition represented by fables and other types of folk literature has also attracted the attention of members of the elite. Examples of this literature that have been published are "O lobo e o chibinho" (The Wolf and the Kid), which is a popular legend from São Nicolau, and two folktales from the Island of Santo Antão;[43] and Baltasar Lopes collected from Fogo a version of the popular story "João que mamou na burra" (John Who Was Suckled by a Donkey) which he published in 1940. Manuel Ferreira contributed to the *Grande fabulário de Portugal e Brasil* (Great Fable Book of Portugal and Brazil, 1962) comments on and a sampling of Cape Verdean oral literature.

An extensive and curious collection was compiled by an American, Elsie Clews Parsons, who in 1923 published her two-volume *Folklore from the Cape Verde Islands*, which contains fables, stories, proverbs, sayings, and riddles. The curious aspect of the work stems from the fact that Parsons did all her collecting in the United States among Cape Verdean immigrants and their descendants in Rhode Island, Connecticut, and Massachusetts. In her preface she observes that the greatest number of stories are European in origin, while others, though European in essence, are adapted to an island or African setting, and still others are completely African. In Cape Verde an African oral tradition probably had much to do with the preservation of this popular literature, whatever its origin. And it must be stressed that the didacticism of fables and folktales offers universal moral tenets which, in their illustrative form, make for the convergences that allow a merging and blurring of origins. Thus, the Guinean hyena and *ganga* appear alongside the European wolf in Cape Verdean fables that translate lessons that know no ethnic boundaries. And significantly, Elsie Clews Parsons has recognized that European fables were often transformed and adapted in the African milieu of Cape Verde.

Finally, it should be noted that the Cape Verdean intelligentsia's interest in the folklore, popular poetry, language, and music of the islands accompanied the birth of a regionalist awareness that blossomed into a literary movement in the 1930s. How this literary movement developed will be the concern of the next chapter.

CHAPTER 12

The Birth
of a Literature

The comment by the seventeenth-century priest António Vieira on the jet black but refined clerics he observed in Santiago suggests the degree of early nonwhite participation in certain institutions that the Portuguese established in Cape Verde.[1] Because of their numerical superiority and the opportunities for a certain amount of upward social mobility, blacks, and particularly *mestiços*, found themselves by the nineteenth century in a position to take advantage of newly installed educational facilities, such as the high school founded in Praia in 1860. By 1894 there were 4052 students, 90 percent of whom where "of color," enrolled in Cape Verde's schools—an impressive figure for that period and for a total population that probably did not exceed 100,000.[2]

Along with an educational system that contributed to a relatively high rate of literacy, the mid and late 1800s saw the beginning of dramatic societies, literary clubs, and social-cultural associations, all modeled on their European counterparts. A perusal of the curriculum offered at the seminary secondary school in Mindelo in the 1890s, with its courses in Latin, rhetoric, and classical literatures, gives some indication of how a growing *mestiço* and black elite was exposed to Western values.

A curious testimonial to this process of institutionalized and psychological Europeanization came from the pen of Juvenal Cabral in his *Memórias e reflexões* (Memoirs and Reflections, 1947). The author, a black Cape Verdean born in 1889, explains that his father named him Juvenal because he so admired the "sublime" Latin poet. In describing his early school experiences Cabral tells how he started to perfect his Portuguese in his god-father's home "where I did not hear the creole they speak where I come from and which is no more than the fragmented remains of corrupted, archaic Portuguese mixed with a number of barbarous terms."[3] At school the young Juvenal stood apart from his forty white (and *mestiço?*) classmates who at first regarded him with derisive curiosity. After spending some time at the Seminary of Viseu in Portugal he returned to Cape Verde, on the advice of a superior who doubted that white parishoners would accept a black priest.

Through his reminiscences Cabral demonstrates a Lusitanian pride mixed with the humility of the colonized. When referring to his former classmates he thinks sadly that "my childhood chums, my study and play companions, will not remember me, a poor, forgotten African, without the wherewithal to overcome nor the wings to reach the pinnacles of fame and glory."[4] Despite these humble protestations pompously expressed, Juvenal Cabral did make something of himself. He struggled to excel by the only means available to him: by accepting European values and resolving to help his race to climb from the "depths of ignorance."

Cabral may not be entirely typical of that period, but he does represent an aspect of the mentality of his generation. His son, Amilcar Cabral, the founder and secretary-general of the African Party for the Independence of Guinea and Cape Verde (PAIGC), who was assassinated in 1973, may not be typical of his generation either. Between the two generations, in the 1930s, the winds of change began to blow across the Cape Verde islands. Under the onus of the social formation that shaped Juvenal Cabral's thinking, but also with the influences of a new order, the members of a modern generation began to assess the factors that shaped their destiny as Cape Verdeans.

The Cultural and Literary Journals

Founded in 1936, the cultural and literary review *Claridade* has come to be synonymous with the beginnings of modern Cape Verdean writing. There were some important individual precursors, of course, such as Pedro Cardoso. And brief mention should be made of the imposing figure of José Lopes. The poet José Lopes, owing in part to his longevity (1871–1962) and to his prolific production, became a living legend in his native São Vicente and something akin to a poet laureate of all of Cape Verde. But although Cape Verde and Cape Verdeans occasionally figure in his poetry, he cultivated an uncharacteristic verse fashioned in rigid metrics and studied rhyme. Other poets sought their inspiration in the glories of Europe, but none so provincially and visibly as José Lopes who became a symbol of idyllically anachronistic verse for many members of succeeding generations. Arnaldo França recalls how he and his contemporaries attacked Lopes with a criticism that they later regretted for its harshness.[5]

If José Lopes was a curiosity, the group that launched *Claridade* (they are often referred to as *claridosos*) can be thought of as a phenomenon. Political, social, and cultural events throughout the world during the thirties played a part in awakening the regional consciousness of Cape Verdean intellectuals. Purely literary and cultural movements or currents—namely modernism, both Brazilian and Portuguese, and Brazilian northeast regionalism—aided the Cape Verdean in assessing and writing about his own environment. The iconoclastic Week of Modern Art that took place in Brazil in 1922 had its repercussion in Cape Verde, and a generation of young Cape Verdeans began to look inwardly at those values which made their society unique, even though this self-scrutiny did not always bring about the innovations of their Brazilian counterparts.[6]

The Brazilian Northeast Generation of 1930 had expanded its regionalism to encompass politically motivated, proletarian concerns, while the Cape Verdeans of that period generally limited themselves to exposing the harsh climatic conditions and the resulting social and economic difficulties that plagued the populace. Several Brazilian Northeast writers, such as Jorge Amado, José Lins do Rego, and Graciliano Ramos, approximated the spirit of the angriest contributors to Spanish American vanguardism. All of them, including the *claridosos*, desired to use their local culture as a source and not merely a subject of artistic creation.

Presença, the journal of Portuguese modernism, along with novels, short stories, and poetry from abroad, had circulated among young Cape Verdean intellectuals during those transitional years of the twenties and thirties. Then, in March 1936, a group of intellectuals and aspiring writers brought forth the first issue of *Claridade*, "a review of arts and letters." These Cape Verdeans, living mainly in São Vicente, took advantage of the contact that the port city of Mindelo afforded them with the outside world. They applied new literary techniques to the discovery of their Cape Verdeanness. Only nine issues of *Claridade* were published, and these sporadically: two issues in 1936 and in 1947, one each in the years 1937, 1948, 1949, and 1958, and the latest in 1960.[7] In spite of its sporadic existence, the journal has had more than a symbolic meaning; it has served as the first true outlet for the writings of the members of the elite.

In his capacity as the journal's first director, Manuel Lopes wrote what amounts to a manifesto in the opening issue. Under the heading of "Prudência e expansionismo" (Prudence and Expansionism) he characterized the sterility of the islands and the presence of the sea as invitations to depart. In "Conflito" (Conflict), he commented that the Cape Verdean possessed two opposing attitudes: wanderlust and nostalgia. But, he continued in "Libertação moral" (Moral Liberation), "The Cape Verdean, upon reaching a state of full spiritual development, realizes that the colonial condition of his land has created in him a conviction which allows him to see that his action is limited and restrained. His anxiety to depart is brought about largely by what might be called 'liberation taboo' (taboo in the sense of interdiction). Then, away from Cape Verde, not just in a foreign land, but also in Portugal, he feels more *himself* because he does not see his possibilities of self-realization frustrated."[8] The impact of Manuel Lopes's words possibly surpasses their intent. At the time he expressed these thoughts the term *colonial* did not carry the same political connotations it does today, so Lopes's references have to be seen as being more to the question of the Cape Verdean's insularity and provincialism than to his feelings of colonial wardship. Be this as it may, the "colonial state" of the Cape Verdean has, in truth, influenced the degree to which he can detach himself from a psychological involvement in the concepts of the Portuguese space as well as from the understandable social and economic dependency on the "mother country." Lopes's remark on the contrasting forces of wanderlust and nostalgia heralds a constant theme which invariably speaks, sometimes only by implication, to the problem of the colonized in the modern literature of Cape Verde.

Mixed with the growing awareness and nativism of the Cape Verdean intellectual came a leavening of feelings of defensive inferiority. Thus, Manuel Lopes modestly and resignedly referred to Cape Verde as having a culture of a "small ambient." But, he insisted, instead of being retiring, or seeking its inspiration and sources elsewhere, Cape Verde chose to develop its own language, dance, cooking, and literature. So it was with resolve and a sort of a vengeance that the first contributors to *Claridade* set about studying local customs with an interest in at least recording them before they passed into oblivion.

Not unexpectedly, the first issue of *Claridade* carries on its cover popular creole verse, including a *finaçon*. To the second issue Baltasar Lopes contributed the first of his many statements defending creole speech, and further analysis of the content of the nine scant issues—none of which exceeded one hundred pages—reveals the *claridosos*' commitment to "plant their feet on Cape

Verde's soil." The samplings of popular poetry and stories, the arguments in support of creole as a legitimate language, the long, sometimes passionate essays on Cape Verdean ethos, and the articles devoted to questions of island ethnology all formed a base for the *claridosos'* principal end: the cultivation of an autochthonous literature in Portuguese.

Most of *Claridade's* pages were indeed given over to some one hundred poems and about twenty short stories or excerpts from novels. The creole poetry and cultural documentation served to enhance the nativistic trends in the "art" writing as the themes of departing-staying, wanderlust, and insularity began to emerge in such poems as Manuel Lopes's "Poema de quem ficou (Poem of He Who Stayed Behind), Pedro Corsino Azevedo's "Terra longe" (Distant Land), and Jorge Barbosa's "Emigrante" (Emigrant). Poems and stories dealing with drought, rain, and social conditions started to appear in the first issues of *Claridade.*

Because of the social consciousness inherent in the *claridosos'* writing, Manuel Lopes was right in giving only passing recognition to the influences of Portuguese modernism. In referring to the modernist journal, Lopes states that "the *Presença* message was for us epidermic—it did not penetrate our humanity."[9] But Brazilian literary movements, as has already been noted, did touch a responsive nerve. The critic Mário António Fernandes de Oliveira wrote, citing poems in *Claridade* and elsewhere, that "it is not just a matter of simple literary influences; Brazil, the sentiment of Brazil, emerges as a theme."[10] Oswaldo Alcântara, one of the prime movers of the *claridoso* group, penned the following lines in his "Poema 5": "Amigos, inimigos, onde pára/ Aquele que me prometeu a Estrela da Manhã?"[11] (Friends, enemies, where is/He who promised me the Morning star?) Anyone familiar with Brazilian literature will recognize that Alcântara's lines are based on the modernist poet Manuel Bandeira's "Estrela da manhã" (Morning Star):

> Eu quero a estrela da manhã
> Onde está a estrela da manhã?

> Meus amigos meus inimigos
> Procurem a estrela da manhã.[12]

(I want the morning star/Where is the morning star?/My friends my enemies/Search for the morning star.)

Bandeira's verse represents the anxieties of the poetic persona, while Alcântara's rendition of the same idea seems to reflect more the Cape Verdean reaching out to Bandeira for guidance as the "small ambient" seeks its own regional identity. The relationship between Brazil and Cape Verde in poetry will be discussed in greater detail in the next chapter.

As far as the question of race and Africa is concerned in the "art" writings of the *claridosos*, it can be said that they generally avoided the issue, and, as a matter of fact, seemed to take a certain pride in the absence of color consciousness in their homogeneous society. But even as the *claridosos* delineated social problems brought on by climatic and economic factors, the inevitable racial designation occasionally appeared in their writing. The short story "Titina" by Virgílio Pires serves as an example of the convergence of social condition and color. In this passage the change in the main character's situation quite naturally accompanies a shift in racial perception: "Titina was not the same girl of days gone by. The mulatto woman with opulent breasts whom he had adored and who had made him suffer so much. Now she was just another black woman, with lots of kids, hanging breasts, shabby clothes."[13] Just as in Brazil, there exists a cult of the desirable mulatto woman in the Cape Verde islands, and the prototype creole girl is usually a *morena*, meaning she is brown-skinned. When, however, she loses her physical charms and bearing, as Titina does, she can be relegated to the anonymous category of "just another black woman," in spite of her light skin.

In another story published in *Claridade*, Virgínio Melo's "Beira do cais" (Dockside), the problem of the illegitimate offspring of upper-class men, meaning white, and lower-class women, meaning black or mulatto, comes wrapped in a romantic mantle, indicating the Cape Verdean mystification of miscegenation: "White boys from the village attend the dances on Cor de Rosa Street. They also appear regularly in Caboquinho to move about among the dancers. The sailors let them dance. The boats in the harbor contain many light-skinned lads born to dock women."[14] The question of color did not preoccupy the *claridosos*, but, as has been seen, accepted attitudes on preferred somatic types would emerge in Cape Verdean literature.

With all their ambivalences and their search for identity, the contributors to the first three issues of *Claridade* set the direction for cultural awareness and literary expression in Cape Verde. During the ten-year interval between 1937 and 1947 when no issue of *Claridade* was published, the short-lived review *Certeza* appeared, not to fill the void, but to add a new tone to Cape Verde's cultural and literary consciousness. In many respects, the two issues of *Certeza*, both published in 1944, cannot be considered outside of the purview of *Claridade*. The important difference between the individuals who founded *Claridade* and those who launched *Certeza* is generational. Many of the *Certeza* group were grade-school children in 1936, while most of the original collaborators of *Claridade* were born in the 1910s: the *claridoso* Manuel Lopes, for example, was born in 1907, while Nuno Miranda, one of the founders of *Certeza*, was born in 1924.

Certeza barely escapes classification as an informative bulletin, but what it lacks in content and depth it makes up for in zeal. More so than *Claridade*, it has been labeled as being strongly dependent on outside influences, particularly literary currents such as Portuguese neorealism. Arnaldo França, one of its founders, has credited the Portuguese writer Manuel Ferreira with a catalytic role in its inception. Ferreira, while serving as a military expeditionary in São Vicente, participated in the literary life of Mindelo and shared his knowledge of the contemporary scene in Portugal with Cape Verdean writers. His own captivation with things Cape Verdean earned him easy acceptance among the Mindelo intelligentsia.

The older members of that intelligentsia, despite their claims of regional uniqueness, had only one foot planted on the soil of Cape Verde; the other was just a step away from the pavements of Europe. *Certeza*'s orientation, while basically European, was more open and broadly cosmopolitan or international than *Claridade*'s as would befit the times in which this group initiated its literary efforts. The Spanish Civil War must have had its effect on the *claridosos*, and the Second World War, with its concurrent international crises and ideological upheavals, no doubt made an impression on the *Certeza* intellectuals. Universal involvement in the events of the period and irreversible forces destined to revamp social and political structures instilled the young everywhere with fervor. Arnaldo França wrote of his young compatriot's hope for the future: "Such a temporal contingency molded the youth of the day, even though the ideological consciousness attributed to them was more intrinsically anticipated than it was the fruit of an indispensably careful study."[15]

Cape Verdeans did indeed live outside of the mainstream of the important happenings that tended to bring, by direct contact, an ideological consciousness. But the young *Certeza* intellectuals did sense an immediacy in the events of the day that prompted them to publish such articles as "Wilkie e a paz" (Wilkie and Peace), reprinted from a Lisbon newspaper. They even displayed a progressive concern for the emancipation of women in a short article which attacks the myth of female inferiority and claims that women have been looked upon as flesh and blood bibelots.[16] And the subject of woman's place in Cape Verdean society has particular significance, as we shall note in our evaluation of prose fiction.

Difficulties in getting *Certeza* printed elicited editorial protests in the second issue, and in line with a somewhat rebellious attitude, one article lodged antibourgeois complaints against the press in Cape Verde, which, according to writer Guilherme Rocheteau, wasted precious space on the announcement of the arrival of "our most distinguished and honorable compatriot, Mr. So and So." In another iconoclastic article, Luís Pinto gave a historical overview of the development of the bourgeoisie in Marxist terms. He called for a society in which men and women would fill their hearts with love and solidarity regardless of race and color. The sort of idealism expressed by Pinto occasionally became indignation over the plight of the world's oppressed. And Rocheteau, although he criticized the space given to biographical notes on a black American leader in the newspaper *Notícias de Cabo Verde*, hastened to add that he himself felt a kinship with black men, "our brothers," throughout the world. Sentiments of Pan-Africanism were only mild manifestations of racial solidarity since the spirit of négritude had barely touched the Cape Verdean intellectual bent upon finding his regional identity amidst the turmoil of international social upheaval.

Before *Certeza* the Cape Verdean intelligentsia had paid homage to the idea of a heterogeneous Lusitanian family united under a common banner. And on the occasion of the founding of the Casa dos Estudantes do Império by Angolan university students in Lisbon in 1944, Luis Terry, writing in *Certeza*, employed the usual commonplaces on the Portuguese's ability to transcend race and culture. But the Cape Verdeans' sympathy for the increasingly activist, Lisbon-based organization of African and some Asian students suggested a heightened nationalist consciousness and incipient dissatisfaction with the social and political status quo on the part of the *Certeza* group. The authorities must have detected such a tone in *Certeza*, for the third issue was not allowed to be distributed.

With regard to the literary offerings in *Certeza*, Manuel Ferreira has pointed out the absence of the popular and creole-language elements carried in *Claridade*. Instead of a *finaçon*, the front cover of *Certeza* features a poem, in the neorealist tradition, by Nuno Miranda:

> Dez ilhas. Dez . . .
> E o mar a namorar-lhe as praias
> que não são
> San Sebastián, Carlton ou Palm Beach.
> Tantas
> quanto
> os dedos compridos das mãos.

> Dez ilhas. Dez . . .
> Dez praias lambidas pelo sol sensual.
> Dez ilhas . . .
> Dez mandamentos . . .
> Atentas vigias no mar . . .[17]

(Ten islands. Ten . . ./And the sea caressing beaches/that are not/San Sebastián, Carlton, or Palm Beach./As many/as/the hands' long fingers./Ten islands. Ten . . ./Beaches drenched in the sensual sunlight./Ten islands./Ten commandments . . ./Alert sentinels in the sea.)

Neorealist starkness and the idea of abandonment and isolation combine with romanticist images of tropical sensualness and with the nostalgia that forces the Cape Verdean to obey the call of the ten islands with the faith of one who abides by the commandments. Miranda's poem and Arnaldo Carlos's "Dois poemas do mar" (Two Poems of the Sea) put forth the motifs of the sea and of loneliness and isolation, which pervade modern Cape Verdean literature. The hope for a better tomorrow, voiced in some *Certeza* essays, relates in António Nunes's "Poema de amanhã" (Poem of Tomorrow) to the islands' social and economic crises.

A small journal, consisting of a total of twenty pages in its two issues, would go virtually unnoticed in a large area of distribution (France, the United States, even Portugal). But in the still formative stages of a regional literature, *Certeza* stands out. And Manuel Ferreira has correctly observed that the *Certeza* group contributed, in spirit, to the next phase of *Claridade*, on which, in fact, writers such as Arnaldo França and Nuno Miranda collaborated.

Fifteen years after the publication of *Certeza* a group of secondary school students launched another effort, the *Boletim dos alunos do Liceu Gil Eanes* (Bulletin of the Students of Gil Eanes High School). These students intended to fill the void left by the demise of *Certeza*. Unfortunately, it was another case of brief existence: the first issue was also the last. Despite its sophomoric tone this publication gave further proof of an atmosphere of intellectual and artistic activity among Cape Verdean schoolboys. Like their predecessors these students had wide literary interests, as evidenced by articles in the *Boletim* on the sixteenth-century Portuguese playwright Gil Vicente's *Mofina Mendes* and their use of quotations from the Brazilian novelist Machado de Assis and from the French writer André Gide. *Claridade*'s utilization of popular motifs possibly influenced the organizers of the *Boletim* to adorn its pages with linoleum prints of typical island scenes; certainly the *claridosos*' literary direction continued in the poetry selections. Corsino Fortes celebrated Cape Verde in two poems, one a rather somber profession of the poet's love for the city of Mindelo. This somberness, parenthetically speaking, is one facet of a love-hate relationship that recurs in modern Cape Verdean literature and has to do with the theme of wanting to stay while having to depart.

The *Boletim*'s most notable contributor was Onésimo Silveira who was destined to become a controversial figure. In an introductory note to Silveira's two poems, Rolando Vera Cruz Martins tells of how the former Gil Eanes student left Cape Verde to seek success on the equatorial island of São Tomé. Silveira's first published poems proved him to be a socially aware poet who attempted to write from the point of view of the people. His poem "Frustração" (Frustration) makes use of a narrative technique to dramatize the desperation of the poor Cape Verdean.

At this point mention should be made of another landmark publication, which appeared in 1958, a year before the *Boletim dos alunos do Liceu Gil Eanes*. It was issued as a literary and cultural supplement to the official magazine *Cabo Verde: Boletim de propaganda e informação* (Cape Verde: Promotional and Informational Bulletin). From 1949 until the mid-1960s, this monthly magazine, published in Cape Verde's capital city of Praia, carried a wide variety of essays, articles, and features dealing with the economic, political, cultural, and social life of the archipelago. Because of its regular monthly appearance for nearly twenty years, *Cabo Verde* served the useful purpose of being an outlet for the works of the *claridosos* and the members of other groups when their own literary reviews failed. It disseminated information and served as a forum for polemics on such topics as creole speech and the problem of emigration. Given the cultural and literary climate of the forties, fifties, and sixties, the "Suplemento cultural de Cabo Verde" (Cultural Supplement of Cape Verde) seems a natural result of the magazine's sensitivity to the artistic activities of its most dynamic constituency: the intellectual elite of Praia and Mindelo. In the main, the supplement printed offerings, both literary and cultural, by the same writers and intellectuals who contributed to *Claridade*, *Certeza*, and the *Boletim dos alunos do Liceu Gil Eanes*.

One other literary sheet deserves brief comment in this review of journals and other publications that marked the development of Cape Verde's regional consciousness. "Seló" (presumably from the English "sail ho!") appeared twice in 1962 as a page in *Notícias de Cabo Verde*. One of "Seló's" organizers, Osvaldo Osório, pledged in his editorial remarks that this, the most recent generation, would continue in the spirit of their predecessors of *Claridade*, *Certeza*, and the "Suplemento cultural" because no ideological differences existed between them. This stance resulted in the publication of fourteen poems and five short stories dealing directly with Cape Verdean problems, but perhaps with a greater grimness than the writings of previous generations. Mário Fonseca, in his poem "Fome" (Hunger), used angry images to convey the idea of degradation in Cape Verde's chronic food shortage:

> E a fome a gotejar . . .
> E a fome a escorrer . . .
> Pelos gargalos quebrados
> De garrafas fedorentas.[18]

(And hunger dripping . . ./And hunger draining . . ./Down the broken necks/Of fetid bottles.)

And with his poem "Holanda" (Holland), Osvaldo Osório introduced, to the theme of perennial emigration, the latest country to attract large numbers of Cape Verdeans.

The cultural and literary awareness of this formative period, from the 1930s to the present, developed through a process of regionalistic attitudes, by the elite, toward Cape Verdean reality. Although a few have modified their opinions on Africanisms in Cape Verde, the subject of Africa has to be seen during this period in terms acceptable to groups spurred on by their own elitism in an atmosphere isolated from the tensions and nascent revolutionary furor of the nearby continent. The archipelago's social and economic problems, only indirectly related to the concerns of black Africa, occupied the attention of the Cape Verdean. Thus, Arnaldo França could list the following as factors in the Cape Verdean intellectual's approach to an understanding of the archipelago's problems: drought, bubonic plague, epidemics of pneumonia, the closing of emigration to the United States, a drop in the number of export goods, the decline of the port in São Vicente because of competition from neighboring ports in the Canary Islands and mainland Africa, and other economic and social conditions.[19] There are some more intangible factors that have affected a Cape Verdean elite essentially untouched by such problems as the presence of a white, ruling minority. One such factor is the absence of a consciousness of an African dynamic, whether cultural or political, except in an abstract way.

Francisco José Tenreiro, who with Angolan Mário de Andrade compiled the first collection of African poetry of Portuguese expression, explained why they had excluded Cape Verdean poets from the anthology: "This is because, in my opinion, the poetry of the creole islands, with very few exceptions, does not translate the sentiment of negritude which is the *raison d'etre* of black poetry. Is it of less interest because of this? Is it less valid for a global understanding of the black world? By no means. It is a case of a poetry with deeply rooted regional characteristics, the fruit of the acculturation of the black man on the Archipelago, and, as such, well worthy of a particularized study."[20] Later anthologies of African poetry of Portuguese expression would include selections from Cape Verde, but Tenreiro's comprehensible hedging parallels the confusion of some Cape Verdean intellectuals themselves. A few of the younger Cape Verdean intellectuals have committed themselves to a concept of their unique creole culture without denying their destiny as a people inextricably tied to black Africa. And in this respect the degree, if one can talk of degrees, to which Cape Verdeans can be seen as a colonized people and the extent to which they recognize this state determine the level of their commitment to the alleviation of social ills.

Probably the most vehement opposition to the Cape Verdean elite's basic philosophy has come from the poet and short story writer Onésimo Silveira in his 1963 essay *Consciencialização na literatura caboverdiana* (The Process of Self-Awareness in Cape Verdean Literature). Himself a past contributor to *Claridade* and a member of the Gil Eanes group, Silveira was one of the more politicized of the younger generation, and this attitude, no doubt, came as a response to the nationalist and independence movements that had emerged in the early sixties in other regions of Portuguese Africa. The fact that the politically oriented, anti-colonialist cast of Silveira's essay possibly offended the authorities, and because he was dissatisfied with the elite's reluctance to accept Cape Verde as a case of African regionalism, probably contributed to his decision to go into voluntary exile, first to communist China and then to Sweden.

Born and raised on the Island of São Vicente, Silveira, a dark-skinned *mestiço*, reputedly did not gain the complete acceptance of the light-skinned elite. Nonacceptance on the basis of color alone does not seem likely, but it may be true that Silveira's humble origins did set him apart from those who would differ with his more militant position. Some *claridosos* and others of the established elite have been charged with denying Silveira's authorship of the controversial article, or they have hinted that the intellectual substance of the essay was supplied by another Cape Verdean whom Silveira knew in Angola. Because the essay runs counter to certain aspects of a Cape Verdean mystique, these allegations may be attempts to discredit Silveira. The fact remains, however, that his experiences and the essay written by or attributed to him have an important bearing on modern Cape Verdean literature.

Silveira lived for a time in São Tomé where he witnessed the harsh realities of Cape Verdean contract labor on the plantations of that island; and ironically, Silveira's wanderings both in São Tomé and in Angola induced him to speak out against the "escapism" that became thematic in so much of Cape Verdean literature. The irony lies in the fact that he had to escape from the islands in order not to evade their problems. Silveira's idea of antiescapism meant not evading some basic social issues which, he claimed, had brought his generation around to seeing Cape Verde as an example more of African than of European regionalism: "This inversion of the terms of the problem flows from the influence of the African renaissance, which revitalizes all fields of activity and all instances of spirituality of the black or Negroid man. This represents a move from the old attitude of self-negation to an attitude of integral self-acceptance; an effort is being made to remove that mentality painfully forged in the crucible of limitations and impositions that ignore his human condition. Today he seeks to find the paths of behavior of an authentic human being as Sartre defines one in his essay 'Orphée noir.' "[21] Under the influence of the African rebirth, Silveira and others of his generation began to take a more politically militant view of Cape Verdean regionalism. And the Angolan Mário de Andrade agreed with Silveira in considering the writing of the *claridosos* as lacking in authenticity because it did not reflect an African regionalism. Although Andrade included *Claridade* poets in his 1958 and 1967 anthologies, he wrote that "in his [Silveira's] understanding, this inadequacy in the [*Claridade*] movement, as regards the archipelago's social realities, is a consequence of the *claridosos'* common attitude toward Cape Verde's true place within its regional context."[22] F. J. Tenreiro implied that the idea of an acculturated, creole society could be accepted as the criterion for including Cape Verde within the context of a global understanding of the black world even though that society lacked relevance as far as a black African consciousness was concerned. Both Silveira and Andrade have preferred to see an African consciousness as relevant to Cape Verde's regional context. Related to the question of Cape Verde's regional context, much of the criticism of the *claridosos* has stemmed from a broader polemic on literature's social and political function. But rather than seeing the writing of the *claridosos*, as well as other Cape Verdean members of a literary elite, in the category of a negative example of African literature of Portuguese expression, we should at least accept at face value Tenreiro's contention that this writing has a unique place within the loose confines of black literature.

With the questions of Cape Verdeanness, African regionalism, and conflicting attitudes toward these concepts in mind, we shall now consider some poets and themes from the *Claridade* generation to the most recent groups.

CHAPTER 13

A New Poetry

Janheinz Jahn has declared that all creative writing by persons of African heritage is "under suspicion" until a better critical method of neo-African literature is developed. It might be said, then, that under Western domination any writer of African heritage may express his origins, or even a psychological reaction to his origins, in a subconscious or ambivalent way. The peculiar nature of Western domination in a creole society such as that of Cape Verde means that although writers may relegate an African heritage to a distant, almost forgotten past they still must display some awareness of that heritage—not necessarily in incantatory tones—and deal with it, even if inversely. By understanding that a fundamental tension exists between Africa and Europe in Cape Verdean literature, we can follow Tenreiro's recommendation to approach the subject by acknowledging that deeply rooted regional characteristics are the fruit of the black man's acculturation; at the same time, specific thematic and stylistic elements, when they occur, can be considered as direct reflections of an awareness of an African heritage in a basically creole literature. Poetry, as is usually the case with a developing literature, became

275

the first vehicle of artistic expression for the tensions and the ethos of Cape Verdeanness.

Nearly all of the twenty-five or so published, modern Cape Verdean poets have some link with the *Claridade* and *Certeza* groups. A good number of these poets are represented in the anthology *Modernos poetas cabo-verdianos* (Modern Cape Verdean Poets, 1961), edited by Jaime de Figueiredo.[1] However, António Pedro, who published a book of poems in 1929, can be considered a direct precursor of the *Claridade* and *Certeza* groups because of his Cape Verdeanness. But his poetry possesses an exotic abandon rarely found in the poetry of the *claridosos*. Although born in Cape Verde Pedro spent his formative years in Europe; he returned to Praia at the age of twenty, still impressionable enough to be affected by the more picturesque aspects of his native island. His collection *Diário* contains poems written in a style that incorporates Cape Verdean motifs and reveals his attraction to the island's African heritage. One of his poems, "Batuque," has a kind of Vachel Lindsay, wide-eyed series of visual and sound images depicting the African dance:

> Vi um batuque,
> baque, bacanal!
> E fiquei de olhos cansados
> —pobres selvagens—
> a ver horas e horas
> rolar a mesma dança doida . . .[2]

(I saw a *batuque*,/bam, bacanal!/And my eyes tired/—poor savages—/of seeing the dance roll on/crazily/for hours and hours.)

The poet, in a manner similar to Lindsay's, effects "boomlay boom" rhythm with flagrant exoticism in the alliterative sound of *batuque, baque, bacanal.*

Some of Pedro's other poems picture savage delirium and nubile maidens, but occasionally he displays an aesthetically pleasing irony in lines such as these:

Os brancos daqui
são mais modestos que os pretos:
os pretos chamam-se pretos,
os brancos chamam-lhes gente daqui,
e aqui . . .
há brancos e pretos . . .
(*Diário*, p. 14)

(The whites around here/are more modest than the blacks:/the blacks call themselves blacks,/the whites call them people from here,/and here . . ./there are whites and blacks . . .)

Pedro at least demonstrates verbal ability in his handling of the back and forth references to black and white in order to comment ironically on racial perceptions as they relate to social ethnocentrism.

Three Claridade Poets

Chronologically, the first to emerge as a poet of a newfound cultural and social awareness in Cape Verde was Jorge Barbosa. Barbosa's first collection of poetry appeared in 1935, one year before the first issue of *Claridade*. Significantly entitled *Arquipélago*, it covers the range of characteristic island themes. The first poem, "Panorama: Destroços de um continente" (Panorama: Remains of a Continent), carefully establishes the idea of abandonment and loneliness:

> ilhas perdidas
> no meio do mar,
> esquecidas
> num canto do mundo.[3]

(islands lost/in the middle of the sea,/forgotten/in a corner of the world.)

In the second stanza the poet creates a vision of the vast surrounding sea whose waves alternately caress and castigate the resigned shore, and he expands the sea motif by invoking the fifteenth- and sixteenth-century Portuguese caravels with their adventurers, noblemen, criminals, priests, and cargoes of slaves. Barbosa's concept of the genesis of the archipelago and its civilization romantically recalls the days of "sunburnt mariners," and this nostalgia becomes wistfulness as he contemplates the empty expanse of the sea from the context of the slow pace of island life.

Images of vicarious experiences through contact with the outside fill Barbosa's poetic world. A German freighter puts into port, and "ouvem-se notícias de longe . . ." (one hears news from afar). Words such as *longe* (far) and *terra-longe* occur with frequency in Cape Verdean literature, and in Barbosa's poetry they are often charged with his physical immobility and his fantasied wanderlust. In "Irmão" (Brother) he romanticizes Cape Verdean wanderlust, which has carried creole speech and the morna to distant lands, but emigration to America has come to an end and "essas aventuras pelos oceanos/já não existem . . ." (those adventures over the seas/exist no more). In the same poem nostalgia goes hand in hand with the theme of the Cape Verdean resigned to live out his existence on the drought-plagued islands. Yet there is a sense of solidarity in the Cape Verdean's shared destiny, which Barbosa captures in these lines from "Irmão":

> Ó caboverdiano humilde
> anónimo . . .
> —meu irmão!
> (*Arquipélago*, p. 16)

(Oh humble Cape Verdean/you are anonymous . . ./my brother!)

When Barbosa uses such words as *humilde* and *anónimo* he explicitly states what the body of his poetry implies: an escapism based on a fantasy world, and a passive, almost pleasurable acceptance of the Cape Verdean's humility and anonymity.

Simplicity becomes a key element in Barbosa's poetic style and in his artistic pose before Cape Verde's social reality. He composed what amounts to a manifesto of his sense of simplicity in these lines from the poem aptly entitled "Simplicidade": "Eu

queria ser simples naturalmente/sem saber que existia a simplicidade."⁴ (I would like to be simple naturally/without knowing that
simplicity existed.) Barbosa's attitude is similar to that of the
famous Portuguese poet Fernando Pessoa whose heteronym
Alberto Caiero declared, "Sejamos simples e calmos,/Como os
regatos e as árvores"⁵ (Let us be calm and simple,/Like the streams
and trees) and "Assim tudo o que existe, simplesmente existe"⁶
(Thus, all that exists, simply exists). Without necessarily embracing all of Pessoa's poetic philosophy of anti-intellectual "sensation-
ism," Barbosa has applied the idea of simplicity in a way that has
social overtones in the context of a "committed" Cape Verdean
literature.

Jorge Barbosa occasionally lodged some mild protest against
the social conditions of his islands. In "O Poeta" (The Poet) he
"simply defends" all mankind:

> O Poeta pediu aos ricos pão para os pobres
> e defendeu simplesmente o direito de viver
> para todos os homens.
> Isto foi um alarme tão grande
> que o acharam um ente perigoso
> e chamaram-no Poeta revolucionário.⁷

(The Poet asked of the rich bread for the poor/and simply defended the right to life/for all men./So great was the shock/that
they found him to be dangerous/and labeled him a revolutionary
Poet.)

Despite this generalized call for justice, which contains only by
inference a note of more particularized social protest, Barbosa
would never be labeled a revolutionary poet. Onésimo Silveira
scored the collection *Caderno de um ilhéu* (Notebook of an
Islander, 1956) in which "O Poeta" appears as more escapist than
the two earlier collections, *Arquipélago* and *Ambiente* (Milieu,
1941), which he called representative of a more spontaneous stage.
This evaluation has more to do with content than with total artistic worth; as a matter of fact, Barbosa continued to employ the

theme of escapism which, in *Caderno*, reaches an aesthetic high point in his poetry.

"Momento" (Moment), for example, has a thematic profundity in its simplicity, for not only does it express a sense of resigned melancholy, it also depicts a sensation:

> Quem aqui não sentiu
> esta nossa
> fininha melancolia?
>
> Não a do tédio
> desesperante e doentia.
> Não a nostálgica
> nem a cismadora.
>
> Esta nossa fininha melancolia
> que vem não sei de onde.
> Um pouco talvez
> das horas solitárias
> passando sobre a ilha
> ou da música
> do mar defronte
> entoando
> uma canção rumorosa
> musicada com os ecos do mundo.
>
> Quem aqui não sentiu
> esta nossa
> fininha melancolia?
> a que suspende inesperadamente
> um riso começado
> e deixa um travor de repente
> no meio da nossa alegria
> dentro do nosso coração,
> a que traz à nossa conversa
> qualquer palavra triste sem motivo?
>
> Melancolia que não existe quase
> porque é um instante apenas
> um momento qualquer.
>
> (*Caderno*, pp. 17–18)

(Who here has not felt/this our/refined melancholy?//Not the sort that comes/from desperate and morbid tedium./Not the nostalgic/nor the introverted sort.//This our/refined melancholy/ that comes from I know not where./A little perhaps/from the solitary hours/passing over the island/or from the music/from the sea before us/intoning/a clamorous song/instrumented with the echoes of the world.//Who here has not felt/this our/refined melancholy?/that which unexpectedly suspends/a laugh just begun/and which leaves a sudden bitterness/in the midst of our joy/in our hearts,/that which brings to our conversation/any old sad word for no reason at all?//A melancholy that almost does not exist/because it is just an instant/a fleeting moment.)

Within the poem's structure of posing rhetorical questions and offering final statements Barbosa combines images of wistfulness, humility, isolation, the sea, poignancy, faraway land, resignation, and solidarity by means of a simple, flowing lyricism that conveys a sense of the ineffable.

Some Brazilian modernist poets, especially Manuel Bandeira and Carlos Drummond de Andrade, have displayed a kind of fatalistic, sardonic acceptance of their land's socioeconomic underdevelopment. And in the case of Cape Verde, the creoles' limited surroundings, languid tropicality, and fantasied escapism accompany what can be called, for want of a better term, their defensive inferiority. The Cape Verdean intellectual does not feel his culture to be inferior, of course, but the same note of defensiveness that emerges in Baltasar Lopes's reply to Gilberto Freyre also suggests itself in the poetry as a kind of defiance of a small culture overshadowed by larger ones.

Because the *claridosos* were particularly sensitive to the cultural reality of Brazil, Jorge Barbosa quite naturally evoked that setting in several of his poems: "Carta para Manuel Bandeira" (Letter to Manuel Bandeira), "Carta para o Brasil" (A Letter to Brazil), and "Você, Brasil" (You, Brazil). All three poems are consistent with Barbosa's escapist stance, and they fix Brazil, a culture that has successfully defied the cultures of larger (meaning more advanced) civilizations, as Cape Verde's big brother in the Lusotropicalist family. Gabriel Mariano has called Cape Verde a society that has surpassed Brazil in creolization and racial harmony, but Brazil remains as the prototype of Lusotropicalist acculturation. The example of Brazil has permitted a poet like Jorge Barbosa to celebrate Cape Verde's similarities with Brazil in language, foods, music, and general world view. Often this poeticized ethos becomes essentially symbolic. Thus, Barbosa sees the mythologized role of the African in Brazil as a parallel to the black man's presence in Cape Verde. In "Você, Brasil" he poeticizes the same racial clichés traditionally romanticized in Brazilian culture. He writes, for example, of the languid speech patterns of the islands and Brazil:

> E' a alma da nossa gente humilde que reflecte
> a alma da sua gente simples,
> ambas cristãs e supersticiosas,
> sentindo ainda saudades antigas
> dos serões africanos,
> compreendendo uma poesia natural
> que ninguém lhes disse,
> e sabendo uma filosofia sem erudição
> que ninguém lhes ensinou.
> (*Caderno*, p. 58)

(It is the soul of our humble people that reflects/the soul of your plain people,/both peoples are Christian and superstitious,/still feeling ancient longings/for African evenings,/understanding a natural poetry/that no one recited to them,/and knowing a philosophy without erudition/that no one taught them.)

The reference to atavistic memories has something of the ancestralism common to négritude poetry, but it has even more of the racial paternalism found in a bygone era of Brazilian literature.

Barbosa's allusions to African influences in Cape Verde bring us to a consideration of that part of his poetry which makes use of black characters and customs. The exotic lure of African vestiges in Santiago led him to sing, in "Ilhas" (Islands), of "o delírio do batuque no terreiro" (the delirium of the *batuque* terrain). In other poems he evokes tribal rites and remote ancestors from the Guinea coast. In this type of poem Barbosa approaches the subject of Africanisms more with the curiosity of an outsider than with the incantatory awe of the contemporary African removed in time and by circumstances from his origins; and of course he makes no pretensions of fostering an image of Cape Verdean Africanness as anything more than picturesque survivals. What does become incorporated into his Cape Verdeanness is the tropical sensuality of the *pretinha* (black girl) and the *morena* (brown-skinned girl), as can be seen in the poem "A moça que foi ao batuque" (The Girl Who Went to the *Batuque*) in which the adolescent black girl loses her youthful bloom several months after that night at the dance. The poet knows why the girl has lost her dazzling, white smile, and he knows why her small, pointed breasts have begun to sag and why her once lithesome thighs have lost their rhythm. This sort of Lusotropicalist eroticism carries an unavoidable note of condescension.

Generally speaking, however, an innocence of tone and a humanistic simplicity have kept Jorge Barbosa's poetry from becoming merely exotic and patronizing toward the humble Cape Verdean. But even when his concern resulted in poems that literally cry for the suffering humanity of Cape Verde, he produces less an outcry filled with indignation than the sobbing of one who views the misery around him with frustration and pity. His gentle humaneness and his simplicity seem more authentically poetic, despite the psychological and social escapism, in those verses that represent his artistic rendering of the Cape Verdean ethos.

Under the pseudonym Oswaldo Alcântara the already frequently mentioned Baltasar Lopes da Silva published a relatively small number of poems in magazines, newspapers, and anthologies. Alcântara's poetry reflects the duality of the intellectual trying to affirm his artistic sophistication while exposing the popular roots of his culture.

In contrast to Jorge Barbosa, who only traveled to Brazil in his imagination, Alcântara actually visited the dreamed-of mecca.

Out of his experiences in Brazil came the poem "Saudade no Rio de Janeiro" (Yearning in Rio de Janeiro):

> Caminho, asfalto sem fim,
> minha terra longe,
> dondê a tua voz antiga
> in memoriam de Nhã Isabel?
>
> Brancaflor era alva de Lua,
> Passo-Amor era cavaleiro andante!
>
> Caminho, asfalto, pureza violada debaixo das
> rodas assassinas,
>
> Vieste escondida na minha mala
> para Cristo te consagrar
> na altura hierática do Corcovado.
> (*Claridade*, no. 8, p. 1)

(Road, endless asphalt,/my land faraway,/where is your ancient voice/in memoriam of "Miz" Isabel?//Brancaflor bathed in moonlight,/Passo-Amor was a Knight errant!//Road, asphalt, purity violated under murderous wheels./You, my land, come hidden in my suitcase/for Christ to consecrate you/on the hieratic heights of the Corcovado.)

In this short work Alcântara uses popular allusions in the creolism *dondê* and in the invocation of Nhã Isabel, the teller of fairy tales. But the term *in memoriam* and the word *hierática*, as well as the tone of sophistication in the image of "violated purity," at least set this poem apart from the simple directness of Barbosa. Thematically, the inversion of the "imprisoned" Cape Verdean longing to leave is the Cape Verdean pining for his far-off island. The image of the statue of Jesus atop Rio's Corcovado mountain parallels Barbosa's use of the same reference in his "Carta para o Brasil":

> E' que ali no alto do Corcovado
> o Cristo Redentor está de braços abertos
> para a minha recepção na terra amável!
> (*Caderno*, p. 56)

(Because there atop the Corcovado/Christ the Redeemer stands with open arms/to receive me in that amiable land!)

While Barbosa wraps his fantasized voyage to Brazil in religiosity, in Alcântara's poem Cape Verde receives Brazil's consecration as if the modern metropolis of Rio de Janeiro felt, along with the poet, a longing for the quiet of the isolated islands.

In Alcântara's small poetic production, so small that it may be presumptuous to generalize, there seems to exist a kind of escapism different from Barbosa's. Several poems recall, with nostalgia, European werewolves and Guinean *gongons* as well as historical or legendary figures and fairy-tale characters to invoke a childhood lived on the creole islands. Alcântara does not idealize wanderlust, but he perhaps escapes into an idealized Cape Verdean past. According to Onésimo Silveira, the *claridoso* Alcântara atones for the sin of escapism by having written the "Romanceiro de São Tomé" (Balladry of São Tomé), a series of eight poems, in the eighth issue of *Claridade*, on the emigration to the plantation island. Silveira acknowledged that Alcântara did not evade the subject of that degrading emigration in his "Romanceiro" which, notwithstanding their formalist technique, reflect his social concern.

Alcântara did, however, evade the subject of Africa, but in doing so he also avoided the exotic pitfalls of ancestralism and the picturesque images of *batuques* in Santiago. Alcântara's escape into the past is not just an invocation of pristine childhood memories, it is a poetic re-creation of a creole youth filled with fantasy and the supernatural. In an important way his poetry serves as an example of the black man's acculturation, to use Tenreiro's term. Convincing art comes from the ability to simulate authenticity, and Alcântara did not feel Africa, just as Barbosa did not feel Africa in some of his most unconvincing poems. On the other hand, these lines from Alcântara's "Nocturno" (Nocturne) could only have been written by a Cape Verdean, a product of the acculturation of the black man:

> Nas encruzilhadas paradas
> há suspeitas de fantasmas
> que passeiam esbranquiçadamente
> entre as sombras das casas,
> . . . lobisomens andam a chupar
> o sangue das crianças . . .
>
> Os gongons piam da rocha a presença nocturna do medo . . .
>
> (*Claridade*, no. 3, p. 8)

(At the motionless crossroads/there are suspicions of ghosts/ whitely abroad/among the shadows of the houses,/. . . were-wolves are drinking/the children's blood . . .//From the rock *gongons* chirp the nocturnal presence of fear . . .)

Alcântara's European formalism does not alter the deeply rooted regional nature of his poetry in this representation of a creole child's fear-filled night.

Manuel Lopes, the third member of the *Claridade* triumvirate of poets, is more properly a novelist and short story writer than a poet. As a poet he does offer yet another variation on the theme of escapism in his small production of verse, most of which originally appeared in *Claridade* and other journals but was later brought together in two collections, *Poemas de quem ficou* (Poems of He Who Remained Behind, 1949) and *Crioulo e outros poemas* (Creole and Other Poems, 1964). Many of his poems display a personal lyricism, and several intellectualize the social themes that preoccupied the Cape Verdean of his generation.

"Poema de quem ficou," like several of Barbosa's and Alcântara's poems, deals with the theme of remaining or departing:

> Eu não te quero mal
> por êste orgulho que tu trazes;
> por êste ar de triunfo iluminado
> com que voltas . . .
> . . . O mundo não é maior
> que a pupila dos teus olhos:
> tem a grandeza
> da tua inquietação e das tuas revoltas.

. . . Que teu irmão que ficou
sonhou coisas maiores ainda,
mais belas que aquelas que conheceste . . .
Crispou as mãos à beira-do-mar
e teve saudades estranhas, de terras estranhas,
com bosques, com rios, com outras montanhas,
—bosques de névoa, rios de prata, montanhas de oiro—

> que nunca viram teus olhos
> no mundo que percorreste . . .
> (*Claridade*, no. 3, p. 1)

(I bear you no ill/because of your haughtiness/because of that
air of triumph/with which you return . . ./The world is no
larger/than the pupils of your eyes:/they possess the grandeur/of
your restlessness and your rebellions.//. . . Because your brother
who remained/dreamed even greater things,/more beautiful than
those you saw . . ./By the seashore he clinched his fists/and had
strange longings for strange lands,/with forests, with rivers, with
other mountains,/—cloud-ringed forests, rivers of silver, mountains of gold—/that your eyes never saw/in the world you
traveled . . .)

Jorge Barbosa escaped in his fantasies to Brazil; Manuel Lopes
intellectualized the idea of a fantasy world with an escapist rationalization that evaded the issue of the necessity of leaving. In
Lopes's escapism can be seen abandonment in the sense that the
future really holds no hope for the Cape Verdean. This feeling of
hopelessness characterizes the third part of *Crioulo e outros
poemas* in which the poem "Crioulo" depicts the Cape Verdean
as a man who holds an "undeceived hope." In "Encruzilhada"
(Crossroads), the poet, who had himself left the islands, looks
back at Cape Verde and asks:

> Que disse a Esfinge
> aos homens mestiços de cara chupada?
>
> Esta encruzilhada
> de caminhos e de raças

onde vai ter?
Por que virgens paragens se prolonga?

Aonde vão nas suas andanças
os homens mestiços de cara chupada?

Que significa para êles o amanhecer?
(*Crioulo e outros poemas*, p. 55)

(What did the Sphinx say/to the *mestiço* men with gaunt faces?//This crossroad/of routes and races/where does it lead?/ through what virgin places will it be prolonged?//Where go they in their wanderings/the *mestiço* men with gaunt faces?//What does daybreak hold for them?)

Lopes makes a strange transition from the Sphinx to Sputnik, in a later stanza, to state his desperation at the poor, underfed creole man's never ending misery. What difference do Sputnik and cosmonauts make, he asks, when hunger sweeps the naked islands of Cape Verde? Perhaps the meaning of this poem was prophetic for the *claridosos*; perhaps they saw Cape Verde at a crossroad in its social and economic development, and in their poetry they sought to deal with the problem in a way that would be a matter of social escapism for more politically committed writers.

The fundamental tension between Africa and Europe in the poetry of Jorge Barbosa, Oswaldo Alcântara, and Manuel Lopes manifests itself indirectly through the paternalism and exoticism of the first, the representation of an acculturation that evades the subject of Africa in the poetry of the second, and the objectification of the *mestiço* in the third. More importantly, how these poets accept or resign themselves to the deeply rooted characteristics of an acculturated society has a psychological bearing on the theme of escapism.

Amílcar Cabral wrote, in 1952, that the message of the *Claridade* and *Certeza* groups had to be transcended in favor of a poetry that would discover "another land within our land."[8] Headed himself toward a state of nationalist consciousness, Cabral considered Barbosa, Alcântara, and Lopes to be pioneers of an event, an important event to be sure, but one that was only a step toward cultural and artistic autonomy in Cape Verde.

The question of evasion or escapism lies at the core of the dissidence between those intellectuals of the *Claridade* generation and those who came after them. Often these younger intellectuals have praised the "old guard" for having initiated a concept of Cape Verde's autochthonous culture. They criticized the older generation for their social passivity. Gabriel Mariano, speaking for the younger elite, flatly stated that *evasionismo* is the condition of the Cape Verdean; it is the condition of a *mestiço* people, descended from slaves, and who are poorly fed and poorly educated.[9] No doubt economic conditions have made Cape Verdean patterns of emigration necessary, and racial, historical, and climatic factors have only exacerbated this necessity. The almost exclusively white inhabitants of Portugal's economically depressed Azores Islands have also emigrated in large numbers, but they have gone chiefly to the Americas and certainly never to the plantations of São Tomé.

Mariano offers a basically socioeconomic assessment of escapism; Silveira goes further in his insistence on Cape Verde as an African region. He asks, in effect, how and to what extent the individual Cape Verdean intellectual interprets the problem of emigration and his own reasons for leaving the islands. The common people suffer from a kind of imposed emigration, while some intellectuals, frustrated by the constraints of a small region, abandon the islands for a larger, more diversified ambient. Given the elements of class and race, the distinction between evasionism and antievasionism has no real meaning in Cape Verdean literature unless it accompanies considerations of the question of African regionalism and the issue of nationalist sentiment. Whether or not Cape Verdean intellectuals avoid the question by relegating Africa to remote origins and tenuous survivals or express their regionalism with sentiments of a new land within the land determines more the distinctions between the older and younger generations than the question of whether these intellectuals actually leave or remain in Cape Verde.

It seems valid to consider the younger, antievasionist writers not only with the idea in mind that they have their feet planted on the soil but also from the standpoint of how they emphasize Cape Verdean regionalism. The *claridosos* attempted to reveal and uphold at all costs their reality as an acculturated people; antievasionist writers began to develop and project a new cultural and social dynamism, as the technique and content of their poetry clearly demonstrate.

Ovídio Martins's poem "Anti-evasão" (Antievasion) served as a rallying cry for Onésimo Silveira's essay on Cape Verdean self-awareness. Published in Martins's book *Caminhada* (Long Journey), the poem's final lines read:

> Gritarei
> Berrarei
> Matarei
>
> Não vou para Pasárgada.[10]

(I shall shout/I shall roar/I shall kill//I shall not go to Pasargada.)

Pasargada, the ancient capital of Persia, was depicted by the Brazilian poet Manuel Bandeira as a mythical land to which he could escape to live out his romantic and hedonistic desires. For the antievasionists Pasargada came to symbolize the elite's objectification of Cape Verde's pressing problems. The poetic persona of Martins's poem pledges that he will face these problems with vigor and resolve. The dynamism, as contrasted with the quiet resignation and pity of some older poets, gains force with the use of the verbs *gritarei*, *berrarei*, and *matarei*; and the future, emphatically expressed in the verb forms, holds hope and defiance for the committed Cape Verdean poet:

> Pedirei
> Suplicarei
> Chorarei . . .
>
> Atirar-me-ei ao chão
> E prenderei nas mãos convulsas

Ervas e pedras de sangue
Não vou para Pasárgada.

(I shall plead/I shall entreat/I shall cry . . .//I shall throw myself to the ground/And with convulsive hands I shall cling to/
Bloodied plants and rocks/I shall not go to Pasargada.)

The exaltation and the realistic images of blood mixed with the
soil of the land are in marked contrast to the preciosity of the
escape into fantasy, and Martins's poem gave rise to Silveira's
bold slogan: "Esta é a geração que não vai para Pasárgada!" (This
is the generation that will not go to Pasargada!)

Amílcar Cabral apparently extracted the phrase "another land
within our land" from Aguinaldo Fonseca's poem "Sonho"
(Dream), in which Fonseca anticipated the younger generation
in their refusal to abandon the islands:

> Mamã,
> já não vou partir,
> vou ficar aqui.
> Esta terra é pobre, mas é minha terra.
>
> Mamã,
> êste sonho meu,
> é de nova vida
> é de outra terra dentro da nossa terra.
>   (*Cabo Verde: Boletim*, no. 15, p. 8)

(Mother,/No more do I think of departing,/here I shall remain./
This land is poor, but it is my land.//Mother,/ this my dream,/is
of a new life/is of another land within our land.)

Rather than presenting carefully worked images, poets such as
Fonseca and Martins fashioned nonlyrical, identity verse filled
with verbal gestures of regionalist, and implicitly nationalist,
commitment.

For the younger poets the image of the faraway land (*terra-
longe*) also became a symbol of the Cape Verdean's painful emi-

gration to the plantations of São Tomé; Martins employed this theme in "Terra-longe":

> Tuas lágrimas na Terra-Longe
> têm que ser de esperança
> Canta amigo
> canta
> e põe no teu canto
>   o encanto
> de qualquer crioula.
>   (*Caminhada*, p. 55)

(Your tears in the Faraway Land/have to be of hope/Sing friend/ sing/and in your song put/the charm/of some creole girl.)

Linking the song of hope with the image of the creole girl Martins effects a note of Cape Verdeanness in his poem of defiance and commitment. And always with a sense of the future, he composed another poem centered on the theme of the faraway land. In this poem, "Voltarás serviçal" (You Will Return, Laborer), he approaches a biblical tone as he exhorts the contract worker to return to his home like a prodigal son and to ask the forgiveness of the land he abandoned:

> Que voltarás
> não numa manhã de nevoeiro
> de morbidez alquebrada
> mas num dia de sol quente
>   ébrio de saudade
>   da terra que ficou
>   sedento do perdão
>   da terra que entregaste
> sòzinho quase nas mãos dos Cains.
>   (*Caminhada*, p. 57)

(For you will return/not on a misty morning/of fatigued morbidness/but on a day of blazing sun/drunk with longing/for the land you left/and eager to be pardoned/by the land you relinquished/almost into the hands of Cains.)

Presumably, the Cains are the evasionists who would sell out their brothers by avoiding the islands' social problems. And in Martins's poems are seen an added emotionalism and regionalist fervor that expose the self-awareness of the antievasionists.

Terêncio Anahory, in his collection entitled *Caminho longe* (Distant Road, 1962), also cultivated the motif of the faraway land with emotional pledges of devotion to the islands. "Carta para a ilha" (Letter to the Island) advances the idea of antievasion with a sense of solidarity and common destiny:

> Sou teu irmão que vem de longe!
> Todas as histórias que te podia contar
> ficaram coladas no meu corpo . . .
> Mas quando te acenarem quimeras
> de fartura
> de evasão
> de viver melhor . . .
> Vira o teu rosto e cumpre aqui
> o teu destino ilhéu![11]

(I am your brother who comes from afar!/All the stories I could tell you/remained rooted in my body . . ./But when they wave chimeras/of abundance/of escape/of a better life at you . . ./ Turn away and seek here/your island destiny!)

The motif of the faraway land is accompanied by the theme of fraternity, and in some poems, such as Anahory's "Canção da roça" (Plantation Song), brotherhood becomes racial solidarity:

> Roça tem sol
> roça tem água
> café maduro
> e cacau gostoso . . .
>   Roça tudo tem!
>
> Mas roça também tem
> sangue de negro e mulato
> correndo nas ribeiras
> saltitando nas lavadas
> gritando
> gritando sempre:

"Fugi di roça
Fugi di roça!"
E na ânsia de levar o grito
para o vale e para a montanha
corre por todos os cantos da roça!
(*Caminho longe*, pp. 57–58)

(Plantation has sun/plantation has water/ripened coffee/and tasty cacao . . ./Plantation has everything!//But plantation also has/ black and mulatto blood/running in the streams/bounding in the water courses/crying out/always crying out:/"Flee plantation/ Flee plantation!"/And in its desire to carry the cry/to mountain and valley/it flows throughout the plantation!)

Besides the terms of racial identity, which establish more fully the idea of the African's continuing servitude, the poet uses creole syntax and words (*Fugi di roça*) as a means of attaining a tone of communal populism.

Critics have credited Silveira with being the first to experiment with alternating lines of Portuguese and creole in poetry, specifically in his poem "Saga," which appeared in the eighth issue of *Claridade*. In a later poem, "As-aguas" (The Rains), he was more successful with this technique, using it to capture the effect of communal exaltation at the end of a drought:

E abriram a porta desapontadamente!
Lá fora cantava uma voz estranha . . .

Câ era sô vento . . . Era tchuva também!
Era tchuva mandóde de nom de Nossenhor![12]

(And dejectedly they opened the door!/Outside a strange voice sang . . .//It was not just the wind . . . It was rain too!/It was rain sent in the name of the Lord!)

Significantly, the poet uses Portuguese in the first two lines to describe the Cape Verdeans' dejection; he then switches to creole, in the second couplet, to capture their sense of religious elation at the coming of the rains. But Silveira realized the problem of

being understood by the Portuguese-speaking reader, and he thus
modified his creole so that the meaning of the last two lines is
entirely comprehensible without the inconvenience of decipher-
ing the words. He demonstrated his concern with communication
by supplying a Portuguese translation of the more difficult creole
in the poem's epigram. Generally speaking, he turned to creole
for the fixed phrase, the popular saying, or the more sentimental
expression, and this usually after the poem's main sense had been
established in Portuguese.

In his antievasionist, faraway land poetry Silveira employs the
Portuguese language to argue for a new artistic expression in the
land. After rejecting the crowded boats headed for the plantations
of the south, meaning the equatorial island of the Guinea Gulf,
Silveira calls for a new poetry in "Um poema diferente" (A Different Poem):

> O povo das ilhas quer um poema diferente
> Para o povo das ilhas:
> Um poema com seiva nascendo no coração da ORIGEM
> Um poema com batuque e tchabéta e badios de Santa Catarina
> Um poema com saracoteio d'ancas e gargalhadas de marfim!
> (*Hora grande*, p. 34)

(The people of the islands want a different poem/For the people
of the islands:/A poem with a vigor born in the heart of ORI-
GINS/A poem with *batuque* and *tchabéta* and *badios* from Santa
Catarina/A poem with hip-swinging and ivory guffaws.)

Silveira touches one of the rare moments of négritude in Cape
Verdean poetry when he emphasizes origins and celebrates black
dance, body movements, and laughter. For Silveira the heart of
origins means identifying with, and not merely documenting,
acknowledging, or waxing picturesque about, the Africanisms in
the interior of Santiago, in Santa Catarina where the inhabitants,
nicknamed *badios*, dance the *batuque* to the handclapping *tchabéta*
rhythm.

Antievasion and the defiance and often angry images of the

faraway land were only a short step from the younger generation's contention that Cape Verde was an example of African
regionalism.

Africa, Black Mother, and Racial Harmony

Several post-*Claridade* poets did cultivate a concept of Cape
Verde's African regionalism. Rarely did they achieve what might
be called a sense of black renaissance, but they did struggle to
bring their African heritage into line with their creole identity.

Those few Cape Verdean poems that speak of Africa generally
do so in nature images, in the evocation of ancestors, or in a celebration of Africa, which means, of course, that these poems bear
a similarity in theme to an important stage of black writing in
various languages. The *mãe-terra* and *mãe-negra* (mother earth
and black mother) motifs merge in a telluric symbolism that suits
the ends of Cape Verdean intellectuals preoccupied both with the
suffering of their arid islands and with their ethos.

Some of the *claridosos* used the motif of the mother earth;
Jorge Barbosa, for one, wrote a poem entitled "Mãe-terra." But
Aguinaldo Fonseca may be the first Cape Verdean to publish a
poem entitled "Mãe-negra," in which, alone and destitute, the
black mother rocks her child in her arms and identifies with the
dark sky of the night. The maternal figure often appears in black
poetry as a symbol of the life-giving earth and of a long-suffering
people.

Fonseca makes use of images of darkness in his aesthetically
pleasing poem "Magia negra" (Black Magic). Here he presents
the martyred, archetypal black man, identified with nature,
shrouded in lyrical mysticism, and in contact with his African past:

> Abro
> De par em par, a janela
> Ao convite da noite tropical.
> E a noite enche o meu quarto de estrelas vivas.
>
> Nesta hora morna e calma,
> Profunda e densa como um túnel,

'O rumorejar longínquo das palmeiras
Varrendo o Céu
E' misteriosa voz do negro martirizado.
Prendo os meus gestos e o meu grito abafo.
Silêncio . . .
No poço da paz nocturna
Interceptada
Pela orgia sincopada
Das estrelas e dos grilos,
Arrasta-se o vão lamento
Da África dos meus Avós,
Do coração desta noite,
Feridos, sangrando ainda
Entre suores e chicotes.
E a Lua cheia veio
À voz quente do batuque,
Faz feitiço . . .
E o negro dorme
Sonhando ser Santo um dia.[13]

(I throw open/The window wide/Inviting in the tropical night./ And the night fills my room with brilliant stars.//At this tepid, calm hour,/Deep and dense as a tunnel,/The distant murmur of the palm trees/Brushing against the heavens/Is the mysterious voice of the martyred black man.//I check my movements and stifle my cry./Silence . . ./In the well of nocturnal peace/Intercepted by the syncopated orgy/Of stars and crickets,/The vain lament drags itself/From the Africa of my Ancestors,/From the heart of this night,/Wounded, still bleeding/Amidst sweat and whips./And the full Moon that came/With the fiery voice of the *batuque*,/Casts its spell . . ./And the black man sleeps/Dreaming of becoming a Saint one day.)

This poem possesses the incantatory and audacious metaphorical elements common to négritude poetry, and Fonseca achieves a measure of success by sustaining a representational unity of word and theme through a technique of auditory and visual imagery.

Luís Romano's "Negro" is less successful than Fonseca's poem because the former's images lead to an exoticism and sensuality similar in style to what colonialist literature imposed on Africa. These few lines from "Negro" will suffice to make the point:

> Mistério de sangues e gerações
> Côres
> mistério eterno.
>
> Negros:
> escuto a grita do vosso entusiasmo
> nas noites de orgia
> nos prelúdios das danças pagãs.[14]

(Mystery of blood lines and generations/Colors, eternal mystery//Black men:/I hear the clamor of your enthusiasm/on nights of orgy/in the prelude to pagan dances.)

References to "nights of orgy" and "pagan dances" need no comment, except to say that even the *claridosos*' poetic view of Africa lacks the frivolous exoticism of the lines quoted above.

Those writers who occasionally paid homage to Africa were even more frequently attracted to a celebration of a creole ethos. A poet like Ovídio Martins was at his best when representing a creole exuberance in which a vocabulary of the melting pot took on a special meaning, as can be seen in this poem of rejoicing entitled "Chuva em Cabo Verde" (Rain in Cape Verde):

> Choveu
>   Festa na terra
>   Festa nas ilhas
> Já tem milho pa cachupa
> Já tem milho pa cuscus
> Nas ruas nos terreiros
>   por toda banda
> as mornas unem os pares
> nos bailes nacionais
>   mornas e marchas
>   mornas mornadas
>
> Choveu
>   Festa na terra
>   Festa nas ilhas

que cantam e dançam
e riem e choram de contentamento
soluçam os violinos choram os violões
nos dedos rápidos dos tocadores
"Dança morena
dança mulata
menininha sabe como você não tem"
E elas sabinhas
dão co'as cadeiras
dão co'as cadeiras
dão co'as cadeiras.
(*Caminhada*, p. 22)

(It rained/Celebration on the land/Celebration on the islands/Now there is corn for *cachupa*/Now there is corn for couscous/On the streets on the squares/everywhere/*mornas* join couples/in national dances/*Mornas* and sambas/*mornas* and marches/*mornas* at their *morna* best//It rained/Celebration on the land/Celebration on the islands/so they sing and dance/and laugh and cry with joy/violins sigh guitars wail/under the players' flashing fingers/"Brown skin dance/mulatto dance/no sweeter girl than you"/And deliciously/ they sway their hips/sway their hips/sway their hips.)

This communal poem includes images of Cape Verdeanness which the elite can use without exoticism and with which all islanders can identify. Traditional dishes, *cachupa* and couscous, the national *morna*, the borrowed samba, and Brazilian carnival marches all figure in Cape Verdean celebrations; and the preeminence of the brown-skinned or mulatto girl as the prototype of the desirable creole female vies with Brazil's cult of the *morena*. What makes all these images authentic and meaningful is the real exuberance that unites Cape Verdeans when the rains come. A short anecdotal digression here will perhaps serve to illustrate the sense of shared joy of Martins's poem, which, I might interject, has something significant to say about the sociology of literature, as far as the author and his reading public are concerned. Arnaldo França, Jaime de Figueiredo, and Félix Monteiro recounted to me the contagious joy that gripped them when an unexpected rain poured through the window of a restaurant, just inland from Praia, where they were entertaining a visiting Portuguese. The guest, quite understandably, looked to remedy the situation by closing the window, while the three Cape Verdeans sat transfixed and wet in silent exultation. The vibrance and rhythmic rejoicing of Ovídio Martins's poem carry a meaning that only a Cape Verdean can fully understand.

Martins's attempts to simulate a creole rhythm in his verse parallels António Nunes's more apparent efforts to effect such a beat in his "Ritmo de pilão" (Rhythm of the Pestle) which, with its monotonous pounding, recalls the days of slavery and voices a protest against the continuing servitude and suffering of the masses:

> Bate pilão, bate,
> que o teu som é o mesmo
> desde o tempo dos navios negreiros,
> de morgados,
> das casas grandes,
> e meninos ouvindo a negra escrava
> contando histórias de florestas, de bichos, de encantadas . . .
>
> Bate pilão, bate
> que o teu som é o mesmo
> e a casa-grande perdeu-se,
> o branco deu aos negros cartas de alforria
> mas êles ficaram presos à terra por raízes de suor . . .
>
> Bate pilão, bate
> que o teu som é o mesmo
> desde o tempo antigo
> dos navios negreiros . . .[15]

(Pound pestle, pound/for your sound is the same/since the days of slave ships,/of plantation barons,/of plantation mansions,/and of children listening to slave women/telling stories of forests, beasts, and enchantments . . .//Pound pestle, pound/for your sound is the same/though the mansion is gone,/the white man gave the black man his freedom/but he remained attached to the land by roots of sweat . . .//Pound pestle, pound/and your sound is the same/since the days/of the slave ships . . .)

With the refrainlike repetition of "Bate pilão, bate," the poet pounds home the urgency of a desperate social situation, and in the final stanza the monotonous sound of the pestle appears to grow louder as it punctuates the air and accompanies strong words calling for change and revolt:

> Bate pilão, bate
> que o teu som é o mesmo
> e em nosso músculo está
> —nossa vida de hoje
> feita de revoltas! . . .
> Bate pilão, bate! . . .

(Pound pestle, pound/and your sound is the same/and it is in our fiber/—our life, today/fashioned on revolt! . . ./Pound pestle, pound! . . .)

The aggressiveness expressed in such poems as "Ritmo de pilão" would move a few writers close to more explicit forms of protest.

Protest and Poetry at the Service of a Cause

Although Nunes's use of the word *revoltas* may carry social implications, it does not necessarily suggest that he was calling for political rebellion. In the fifties, however, a heightened social awareness brought some Cape Verdean poets increasingly closer to the rhetoric of political nationalism. The few cases of outspokenly committed or revolutionary literature come from writers living outside of Portuguese territories or from those who write under pseudonyms and publish their works in the exterior.

Luís Romano, while not a political exile, apparently has found it easier to express himself in occasionally vehement "antiracist racism" poetry because he presently lives in Brazil. His "Irmão branco" (White Brother) combines angry protest with a conciliatory plea for racial harmony, and in truth there is no message of political revolt in any of his writing. But this particular poem does lash out at white racism and exploitation of the black man:

Irmão branco

Tuas sementes mortas não poderiam brotar

Misturaste meu sangue negro
na massa de uma terra que desejaste ùnicamente para ti

Empunhaste os membros que te dei—irmão branco—
e extraiste fortunas ño lodaçal onde meus olhos viram a luz
Assim, dia a dia, construiste na destruição
a sepultura dos teus sonhos
hora a hora inoculaste nas minhas veias
o fel que amargamente terias de beber.[16]

(White brother//Your dead seed would not sprout//You mixed
my black blood/with the matter of a land you coveted only for
yourself//You grasped the limbs I put at your service—white
brother—/and you extracted fortunes from the degradation of
earth where my'eyes first saw the light//Thus, day by day you
built on destruction/the grave of your dreams/hour by hour you
injected into my veins/the bitter bile that you would have to
drink.)

Romano's black rage lacks consistency and has instead an incon-
gruously articulated denial of basic humanity that seems even
more incongruous in view of the poem's last lines: "Acolhi-te na
inocência da minha simplicidade/como uma criança" (I received
you in the innocence of my simplicity/like a child). Many négritude poets have exulted in the African's naturalness and in his
nontechnological culture, but what Romano portrays is the stereotype of the childlike native duped by the wily European. Even
though the poem's title somewhat prepares us for it, the crowning
touch of incongruity comes when the poet tells the white man
that there is still time for him to extend his hand in brotherhood.

A young lawyer from Santiago, Felisberto Vieira Lopes, wrote,
under the name Kaoberdiano Dambara, *Noti* (Night, 1965), a
collection of creole-language poetry in which militancy and black
rage are not mere rhetorical devices. In the virile creole of the
interior of Santiago, Dambara launches in his poetry a direct
attack on Portuguese colonialism. His pseudonym is symbolic of

his political and cultural defiance; Kaoberdiano serves as an abstraction for the downtrodden Cape Verdeans, and there is even a sense of black resistance in the poet's consistent use of the letter "k," which in the Portuguese alphabet exists only for loan words, but which is commonly used in the transliteration of African languages.

Ioti Kunti, presumably another nom de guerre, writes in the collection's preface that previous attempts by Cape Verdean intellectuals to penetrate creole problems have been superficial, and he praised Dambara's vigorous and combative collection. The book's epigraph reads, "Noti, oh mai, kontam bo segredo" (Night, oh my mother, tell your secret). With these words the poet quickly establishes the symbolic importance of night and the likewise symbolic nature of the dark earth mother of Africa and the secrets they harbor.

After a dedicatory verse to the early, popular poet Pedro Cardoso, which fixes the collection's debt to a creole ethos, the poet offers thirty-three poems, most of which display a devotion to the people's cause in a mixture of socialist realism and Maoist literary rhetoric. But Dambara softens the revolutionary stiffness of his poetry with an occasional humorous note. In one poem, "Branco" (White Man), he carries invective against the exploiter of the land to such a degree of seething anger that the following poetic insult offers almost comic relief: "No ka kunfia na bó/nem kru, nem kuciado,/nem xuxo, nem labado"[17] (We don't trust you/ neither raw, nor cooked,/neither unbathed, nor washed). I cannot help but observe here that this type of verbal virtuosity, which doubtlessly forms a part of a Cape Verdean oral tradition, resembles the joke style of black America.[18]

Noti was published by the Department of Information and Propaganda of the PAIGC (African Party for the Independence of Guinea and Cape Verde), and its overall intent is anything but humorous. The first poem in the collection, "Pa mund' intêro" (For the Whole World), ends with the pledge: "pa nôs sô tem um kussa: Afrika ô Morti!" (p. 12) (For us there is only one thing: Africa or Death!) In "Purdam" (Forgive Us) Dambara evokes

Mother Africa and calls on her sons and daughters to turn their
backs on the exploiters:

> Dexa branko, dexa splorador di bo Tera,
> kudi mágua, obir dor di bo Mai,
> kudi'l ko bo "amor puro" e forti,
> duedja n'aitar di Pobo: Afrika, purdam!
> (p. 37)

(Turn your back on the white man, turn your back on the exploiter of your Land,/heed the sorrow, hear the painful cries of
your Mother,/heed her with your strong, pure love,/kneel at the
altar of the People: Africa, forgive us!)

This poem of filial contriteness toward Africa possesses the same
element of exhortative religiosity found in Ovídio Martins's "Voltarás serviçal." Dambara goes further than Martins by calling for
a Cape Verdean unification with Mother Africa.

In spite of a theme of African redemption, Dambara demonstrates in several poems an undeniable devotion to creole traditions. With his highly rhythmic "'Leviandod' kaoberdiano"
(Cape Verdean "Levity") he seems to defend what no-nonsense
revolutionaries would term revisionist frivolity. This insistence
on Cape Verdeanness constitutes yet another mitigating element
in his militant poetry:

> Violon tundum, tundum,
> Kiki "sentod ta spiniká"
> notas, posia, tchôro,—patetissa!
> Pueta? Pateta? . . .
> Kiki "sentod ta spiniká"
> morna, koladera, "leviandod" kaoberdiano,
> stranho, passagero
> kussa ki bo ka ntendê ê lebiandadi
>
> Violon tundum, tundum, voz d'aima Kiki,
> voz di nha aima,
> voz di nôs aima kaoberdiano.
>
> Violon tundum, tundum
> tchoro, fomi, adjustissa,

dor kim ka podê fla,
violon di nôs peto, korda di nôs aima!

Kada som ê um dor,
kada nota ê um sufrimento,
kada musga ê um tristessa
na violon di nôs peto.
(p. 41)

(Guitar tundum, tundum,/Kiki "sits strumming"/notes, poetry,
sobs,–nonsense!/Poet? Fool? . . ./Kiki "sits strumming"/*morna*,
coladeira, Cape Verdean "levity";/a strange, fleeting/thing that
you don't understand, is levity.//Guitar tundum, tundum, the
voice of Kiki's soul,/the voice of my soul,/the voice of our Cape
Verdean soul.//Guitar tundum, tundum/weeping, hunger, injus-
tice,/pain that I cannot describe,/guitar of our bosoms, chords
of our souls!//Each sound is sorrow,/each note is suffering,/each
song is sadness/in the guitar of our bosoms.)

Poets before and since Dambara have seen the *morna* as the expression of a people's melancholy: but in concert with his poetry's
militancy Dambara expands the nationalist spirit of the *morna*
to encompass, in its woeful lyricism, the recognition of injustices.

Naturally, that creole institution of pure African origin, the
batuque, receives Dambara's attention. For if the *morna* is the
voice of the Cape Verdean's soul, "batuko ê nôs aima!" (*batuque*
is our soul!) These words come from the mouth of an old woman,
Dunda, who in the poem "Batuko" tells her inquisitive grandchild
what *batuque* teaches the young. Nha Dunda explains that "korpo
ta matado, aima ta fika:/aima ê forsa di batuko" (the body will die,
the soul will remain:/the soul is *batuque's* strength). Dambara
penetrates that surface of exoticism that even some committed
writers have assigned to *batuque*, and in so doing he raises the
ceremonial to the level of a people's world view.

Returning to the central motif of night, the poem "Juramento"
(Vow) further explains the symbolic significance of darkness:

Noti sukuro, mistério na floresta,

mar ta ronka tromento, feras ta guemê
batuko londji ta treme tchom: galo ka kanta inda

Nês noti sukuro di mistério,
Si aima nôs guentis ta papia ko nôs,
nha mai 'm bem jura na bo regás.
(p. 17)

(Dark of night, mystery in the woods,/the sea roars its storm,
beasts howl/a distant *batuque* shakes the earth: the cock has not
yet crowed//On this dark night of mystery,/The souls of our
people speak with us,/my mother I rest my head in your lap as I
make my vow.)

The poet promises to die poor, dark, and black at his mother's
feet so that his soul may be resurrected in the forest where the
storm rages as does the struggle. To the conventional night/mys-
tery relationship Dambara adds incantatory images that move
with a powerful staccato percussion in creole, thus giving a new
dimension to darkness/blackness.

Night also harbors the injustices done to the African, and in
this respect the poem "Mulato" demystifies miscegenation with
such references as "night of carnal sin." The *mestiço*, nevertheless, can undo the humiliation of his conception by joining the
struggle for an African independence. On the positive side, the
blackness of night is the color of rich earth, it is profundity and
eternity. In "Orassan di noti" (Night Prayer) darkness holds the
secret of a race:

Noti, oh Mai,
kubrim ko bo assa,
kontam bo segredo,
stila na nha bida
sufrimento di nha guentis,
dam aima, forsa, koraxi negro!
(p. 28)

(Night, oh my Mother,/cover me with your wings,/tell me your secret,/instill in my life/the suffering of my people,/give my soul strength, black courage!)

This invocation of night and of the abstract Mother is a ritualized prelude to the struggle. Dambara's combative poetry fulfills a psychological and emotional, as well as aesthetic, need. Mário Andrade has written that Dambara has raised creole to the level of a literary language.[19] Whether or not this is the new Cape Verdean poetry Onésimo Silveira called for, *Noti* represents an important and necessary identity phase of an autochthonous African-creole literature.

Cape Verdean Poetry in the Early 1970s

I have neglected to include a number of published poets in my discussion for the simple reason that many of them, because they wrote uncharacteristic verse, do not fit within the general scheme of my approach. Others, while they did compose poems on Cape Verdean themes, were deemed to be less representative than those writers I chose to discuss.

To maintain a continuity in an approach to a poetry that expresses Cape Verdeanness, with its attending themes of antievasion, drought-rain, and its implicit tension between Africa and Europe, I turn in this section to a brief appraisal of two virtually unpublished poets: Osvaldo Osório and Arménio Vieira. No doubt, students and others continue to write poetry of a regionalist nature in Cape Verde, but most of it has not found its way into print in a very subdued literary atmosphere where there exist no arts and letters, journals or literary groups. A survey of the 1971 scene in the cities of Praia and Mindelo revealed only a handful of poets who pursue their craft with anything approaching conviction and constancy.[20]

Osvaldo Osório and Arménio Vieira, who live in Praia, helped to organize the 1962 literary page "Seló," and thus they present a real link with the more active period of the 1960s. Both poets contribute to what can be considered a literary climate under the tutelage or with the encouragement of several members of the

Claridade and *Certeza* groups, such as Jaime de Figueiredo, Félix Monteiro, Arnaldo França, and, in Mindelo, Baltasar Lopes.

Osório's poetry shares with Vieira's a sense of isolation and an intellectual reaching out from the islands. At times their Cape Verdeanness contains a cryptic note of social protest. Osório's still unpublished collection, "O cântico do habitante" (The Inhabitant's Chant), includes poems of fanciful imagery and frequently esoteric sentiments. His themes are aggressively universal in their concern with man's place in the universe. The collection's title poem reduces the earth to a small blue ball as if to put all spaces into equal perspective:

> a terra
> pequena bola azul
> girando
> no espaço infinito
> ela a nossa terra
> não é mais que uma província

(the earth/small blue ball/rotating/in infinite space/it, our earth,/ is no more than a province)

Color photographs of the earth as seen by astronauts must have inspired the image of the "small blue ball" in this 1970 poem. And it may not be farfetched to see some small political implication in the word *província*. Perhaps the poet is implying that Cape Verde, a province in the Portuguese space, is a microcosm of the shrinking world where the destinies of men everywhere are inextricably tied together. Whether or not Osório had this idea specifically in mind, the references in this and other of his poems to the threat of a nuclear holocaust and to the dehumanization of life cannot help but leave the reader with the feeling that his audacious, occasionally hyperbolic images of a universal scope harbor some very "provincial" preoccupations.

Arménio Vieira, less esoteric than Osório in his imagery, applies an intimist lyricism to that classic Cape Verdean theme in his poem "Anti-evasão" (Antievasion), appropriately dedicated to Ovídio Martins:

Percutindo lento
na madrugada insone
brando canto langue . . .
—Recuso o violão que tange
sons de ópio enlangquescente

Para longe o encanto
dos rumos verdes
lá para longe estrelas tretas
(laranjas de ouro
que possam caber
na palma da mão)

As estrelas são bolas quentes
derretendo as bolas da ilusão
Não!
Evasão não quero
—castelos de espuma
são mentiras de água e sabão.

(Percussing slowly/in the sleepless dawn/soft languid chant . . ./
—I refuse the guitar that strums/sounds of enveloping opium//
Far off the enchantment/of green courses/there far off crafty
stars/(golden oranges/that could fit/in the palm of your hand)//
The stars are heated bubbles/melting bubbles of illusion//No!/ I
reject evasion/—foam castles/are soap and water lies.)

In this unpublished poem Vieira reiterates the theme of antievasion with a preciosity of metaphor—perhaps a little too precious,
particularly the image of the "orange"—that has special significance because he is one of the few antievasionists who has physically remained on his island. Vieira's poem exemplifies the continuation of an unresolved problem, both in its cultural-literary and
in its regionalist-political overtones. What is the nature of evasion
as related to emigration and to Cape Verde's future as a cultural
region within or outside of the Portuguese sphere of political
dominance? This question has confronted Cape Verdean intellectuals since the beginnings of their modern self-awareness. By refus-
ing the strumming guitar of enveloping opium, Vieira seems to be
rejecting, as illusory, the mystique of Cape Verdeanness.

Both Vieira and Osório intellectualize the problem of evasion within a "poetic" framework, meaning that they esteem the properties of word and image. But their still regionalist message bodes well for the regionalist tradition in Cape Verde. One gets the impression, however, that poetry in Cape Verde has been momentarily arrested in its development. Nevertheless, the beginnings of an autonomous literary expression in Cape Verde have been too auspicious for the present and future generations not to realize the promise of their cultural heritage. And, this promise extends to the birth and growth of Cape Verdean prose fiction, which will be evaluated in the following chapter.

CHAPTER 14

Cape Verde
in Narrative

Although the currents of négritude and black rebirth flowed far
from Cape Verde's shores, the fact that island intellectuals began
to immerse themselves in a regionalist awareness about the same
time that writers in the Caribbean and Africa were in the process
of discovering their roots gave the literary movement on the
archipelago an impetus and a headstart on the other regions of
Portuguese Africa. Since there is often a time lag between the
appearance of poetry and the beginnings of prose fiction, particularly the novel, in a newly developing literary expression, the
Claridade movement, by virtue of having emerged in the thirties,
with antecedents in the twenties, would be expected to have produced narrative writers in the ensuing decades.

Free from the incursions of Europeans, who in the early twentieth century cultivated exotic, colonialist novels set in the "untamed" territories of Angola and Mozambique, the Cape Verdean
writer could turn his attention to elaborating his own regionalist
reality in prose fiction. Several of the *Claridade* and *Certeza* writers who initiated their literary careers as poets soon after found
the medium of prose well suited to their purposes of exposing
their ethos and dealing with Cape Verde's perennial problems. By

its very nature prose fiction permits description, reflection, and conceptualization. Thus the chronic problems of drought, famine, unemployment, and emigration have offered the Cape Verdean short story writer and novelist the opportunity to treat a subject matter in prose works whose mimetic qualities might well be termed primarily sociological by some. Imitation of reality can imply a "slice of life" or a documentary sketch, especially for prose fiction conceived in the urgency of regional identity. Like the new poetry, Cape Verdean prose was born under the sign of Portuguese neorealism, Brazilian modernism, and Brazilian Northeast regionalism. Thus while the Cape Verdean may have inherited the art of social portraiture from the neorealist, he also had the example of the Brazilian Northeast novel to fashion his regionalist language with lyricism and elements of an oral folk tradition.

Manuel Lopes

In 1936 the *claridoso* Manuel Lopes published an unpolished version of his short story "O galo que cantou na bahia" (The Cock That Crowed in the Bay); this lyrical piece of social commentary, although not Lopes's first prose offering, got the Cape Verdean narrative off to a propitious beginning. By 1958 the author had revised this story of the small-time smuggler Jul'Antone and included it with five other short works of fiction in *O galo que cantou na bahia*.

The 1936 version of "O galo que cantou na bahia" can be considered symbolically as the beginning of the modern Cape Verdean prose narrative because it is the first artistic presentation of folk elements and typical themes built around characters whose delineation reveals some important aspect of island reality. Both Jul'Antone and Toi, the customs guard whose success at apprehending petty smugglers has supplemented his meager income, are poor devils at the mercy of the islands' economic restrictions. But Jul'Antone's downfall, which is Toi's good fortune, becomes enveloped in the Cape Verdean lyricism of a *morna* composed by Toi. Lopes, like most Cape Verdean writers of fiction, fully details creole life through dialogue sprinkled with creolisms, poetic asides, and descriptive re-creations of the regional landscape.

In treating the major themes of evasion and poverty Lopes exhausts the particulars of "wanting to stay, having to depart," and while he shows how this dilemma principally affects poor and uprooted rural people, he tempers his fatalism by celebrating the land in some passages that are purely pastoral. As a matter of fact, Lopes's first published prose piece, "Paúl" (Marshland, 1932), is a quasi-fictional account of a lush, tranquil, bucolic oasis on the Island of Santo Antão. The lush marshland also features in the poetic prose sketch "Ao desamparinho" (At Dusk).[1] In this rhapsody Eduardinho, a student and aspiring intellectual from the city of Mindelo, revels in the idyllic setting of the marsh.

As Lopes directs his literary steps into the hinterland, his main characters, who seem to be diverse models of citified intellectuals, come into contact with a rural culture and with folk types. True to the *claridosos'* interest in all aspects of island reality, these urban narrators have the detachment or the tendency toward mystification of the interloper.

In "No terreiro do bruxo Baxense" (On the Wizard Baxenxe's Land) a black centenarian is encountered who forms a living link with an African past. The narrator describes the wizard's appearance as gorilla-like and frightening, and it is learned that the ancient man has a goatee similar to those worn by African chiefs. This basically unflattering description, complete with the conventional racist assigning of simian characteristics to the "witch doctor," precedes the narrator's explanation of how the old man was capable of causing harm to others when petitioned to do so by a client. The links with Africa are also philosophical as is apparent in Baxenxe's parabolic reasoning on the evil he can do, for he reminds his detractors that "no one condemns the knife that cuts into living flesh. Criminal is the hand that wields the knife."[2] Confounding and exteriorizing an African concept, the narrator becomes involved in Judeo-Christian metaphysics after witnessing an extraordinary pedate demonstration by the wizard's grotesquely deformed son. People in the area contend that the monster, who amuses himself with this foot pantomine, was born as retribution for Baxenxe's evil deeds. "In the wizard's balance of good and evil the tray of good must have been empty" (p. 134), the narrator aphoristically explains. But his intellectual agility prompts him to add that the tray of evil had been filled by others.

This humanistic, albeit condescending attitude accompanies this same narrator when he leaves the wizard's hovel and walks into the story "O 'sim' da Rosa Caludo" (Rosa Caludo Says "Yes"). Arriving at the home of a local administrator, the narrator witnesses a wedding ceremony at an impasse because the bride refuses to enunciate the final sealing word. The narrator-agent cajoles the reluctant girl into saying yes by promising to take her picture. Out of gratitude the bride's patron invites the narrator to the wedding celebration. And at this point the author begins a part of the long short story which, in its use of local color, regional speech, and folk customs, resembles a nineteenth-century realist word portrait of rural life.

Into this living laboratory of folk reality walks Eduardinho, the impressionable student from Mindelo, with pencil and notebook in hand, ready to capture the essence of rural folk unspoiled by outside influence. Engaging the narrator in conversation he explains who he is: "I am a scholar and researcher; I find a purity in all that these people do. My name is Eduardo Miranda Reis, better known as Eduardinho. Indeed, the excessive use of the diminutive is one of our virtues; it reflects our affection, our *morabeza* [affability], our generosity."[3] Eduardinho's enthusiasm and positivist attitude surpass those of even the more committed intellectual when he exhorts his compatriots to sink not only their feet but also their heads in the soil of Cape Verde. The gentleman narrator, a déclassé by design, smiles indulgently at the young man's fervent and somewhat ludicrous expressions of Cape Verdeanness. Later when Eduardinho receives a pummeling while attempting to separate several brawling guests, the narrator sagely advises him that what he has just experienced tells him more about a people's reality than a handful of notes on folklore. With his head buried in the soil Eduardinho fails to see the total reality of the land.

Manuel Lopes, in this and other stories in his collection, deals moralistically, if not allegorically, with the question of Cape Verdean self-awareness. Eduardinho and the narrator represent opposing poles of this awareness; the former wants to record and maintain folk traditions in their pure state, while the latter limits himself to philosophical and psychological ruminations on this reality with no particular desire either to change or to preserve it. Both points of view represent variations on the problem of evasion. Because the narrator allows himself to move naturally with the fluxes and emotions of the common people we might be misled into thinking of him as a member of the enlightened and committed elite. In reality, his pronouncements on the acceptance of the peace and disorder that make up the common folks' natural existence relegate him to the level of a disinterested observer, cynically condescending in his existentialist aloofness. In the bucolic sketch "Ao desamparinho," which bears the subtitle "Do caderno de apontamentos de Eduardinho" (From Eduardinho's Notebook), the idealistic member of the Grupo Literário Renovador (Renovator Literary Group) reveals, in his poetic observations, what the author seems to intend as an unrealistic mystification of Cape Verdean reality.

Eduardinho, as an idealist caught in the fury of the crisis of Cape Verdean identity, forms a link with Lopes's novel *Chuva braba* (Torrential Rain, 1956). In his notebook the young intellectual records with pride the decision of the novel's hero to return to the land. A "return to the land" satisfies Eduardinho's romantic sense of the Cape Verdean's tenacity and resignation, and, as the novel's main theme, the refusal to abandon the land speaks directly to the question of evasion.

Mané Quim, the adolescent hero of *Chuva braba*, courts Escolástica, a country girl one or two cuts beneath him on the social scale. Despite the girl's fears, brought on by a vigilant mother, she and Mané Quim make love in a wooded, idyllic setting. Because the land is a motif, the act takes on a symbolic, ritualistic significance. Mané Quim's godfather, Joquinha, who has recently arrived from Brazil, offers to take the boy away from Santo Antão to live with him in the Amazon. Mané's mother welcomes this escape from the rainless island as a godsend. Wanderlust and the force of his land struggle within the boy, but finally the call of adventure prevails and he sets out on the first leg of his voyage. On the morning of his departure for São Vicente Mané awakens in town to the sound of a driving rain, and rain falling on his island means that the land will yield again. Dripping wet Mané runs to his godfather's room and tells him that the rain has called him back to the land.

Several of Lopes's characters are sociological types or abstractions of a creole essence. The old landowner Lourencinho, who from the beginning opposed Mané's departure, comes forth as the voice of the land warning that to abandon one's native soil is to lose one's soul. Joquinha and Lourencinho confront each other, and the farmer accuses the traveler of seeking to buy Mané's soul. Lopes then imagistically contrasts the attraction of the broad sea to the plot of land where roots extend downward. Joquinha protests that his own soul is broad while Lourencinho's is narrow. According to Lourencinho, taking Mané away from his native soil would be tantamount to murdering him, and to dramatize his point he offers his knife to Joquinha. The author follows through with the symbol when on the morning of his planned departure Mané awakens with the feeling that a knife has been plunged into his head and sunk into the ground.

Not only the illustrative characters but much of the novel's descriptive imagery has a symbolic value that reinforces the theme of the return to the land. The country girl Escolástica identifies with the grace of nature when like a quail taking flight she disappears behind a wall. In effect, she is the embodiment of creole femininity as she runs off flirtatiously with a basket balanced on her head and her hips swaying rhythmically and provocatively. With Lopes's re-creation of the social and cultural landscape comes a sufficient number of creole terms to warrant the inclusion of a glossary at the end of the book. And certain local expressions contribute to the novel's regionalist flavor. One saying that occurs frequently in Cape Verdean writing is "quem não tem paciência não terá filho branco" (he who lacks patience cannot expect to have a white son). For the Cape Verdean this saying has apparently lost all social and racial connotations and is roughly equivalent to "haste makes waste." But from the standpoint of its origin, the saying reveals the historical importance and still lingering significance of skin color in the creole world of Cape Verde.

Turning again to the novel's major theme, we see that in the story "Ao desamparinho" the pedantic Eduardinho characterizes Mané Quim as the "timid, simple, apparently amorphous boy of few words but who is ardent and passionate, and for whom the Ribeirãozinho is not only a piece of land alive like the blood pulsating in the subsoil and the heart palpitating elsewhere but also a kind of symbol, a challenge to the constancy and fidelity of the man of the land" (p. 213). Eduardinho has no less pompously worded an impression of Lourencinho whom he calls an old philosopher, romantic and intolerant, who would rather marry the rain, because the rain gives and a woman only takes.

Eduardinho extols the rain as one who can permit himself the luxury of idealizing its poetry and drama when it drenches the parched land. Safe in his urban surroundings from the ravages of the drought Eduardinho can also make romantic literature of the horrors of the implacable and destructive east wind.

In his second novel, *Flagelados do vento leste* (Victims of the East Wind), Lopes dramatizes, in a manner worthy of Brazilian Northeast writers, the devastation of a prolonged drought fanned by the relentless wind from the east. In keeping with his unsympathetic view of the pretentious researcher, whom he caricatures in Eduardinho, he modestly states in his preface that this novel, like *Chuva braba*, tells a little of the little he knows about Cape Verde.

This "little" represents Lopes's most ambitious work in length and scope. With a sagalike tone the third-person narrator recounts a sequence of events that revolve around José da Cruz and his family who are caught up in the spectacle of hundreds of refugees being decimated by hunger. At the beginning of the story José is the prototype of the constant and tenacious Cape Verdean who patiently awaits the rains while others abandon their homes and land. His patience is rewarded when the rains come, but his joy is short-lived. The wind suddenly shifts, and from the Sahara comes the terrible harmattan bringing locusts and scorching heat. From this point the story progresses from the vertical stability of the farmer rooted to his land to chaotic scattering of the peasants and finally to horizontal movement in the flight of hordes of dirt farmers and their families. Hunger and death accompany the sharecroppers as they make their way to the coastal cities, and in the mountain passes desperate, masked highwaymen attack, rob, and sometimes kill the helpless refugees.

But José steadfastly remains on his plot of land. The embodiment of simple rural pride, he refuses the food, presumably acquired by ill-gotten means, offered to his starving family by Leandro, José's grown son by a previous marriage. Leandro lives a hermit's existence in the mountains because of a hideous scar that disfigures his face. He dominates the novel's second part in which the road leading to the coast stands out as a major motif. The road represents escape for the fleeing peasants and a means of sustenance for the highwaymen.

Lopes fills the pages of this novel with horror after horror: the wind tears a baby from his mother's arms and impales him on a branch; bandits commit heinous crimes, and survivors take horrible vengeance. Men's desperate acts parallel the wildness of nature. All in all, the novel seems to be a tropical Gothic romance, with scenes of the grotesque and the arcane. If *Chuva braba* ends on a note of promise, *Os flagelados do vento leste* ends with the pessimistic proposition that the poor Cape Verdean must resign himself to the inevitable and like Sisyphus continue to struggle with his unhappy burden. When Lourencinho, the conscience of the land from Lopes's first novel, appears on the road, we understand more fully that Manuel Lopes's antievasionism—praised by Onésimo Silveira as he perceived it in *Chuva braba*—is actually an acceptance of that which cannot be remedied. From atop his horse, Lourencinho confronts the miserable José da Cruz who, having lost his three small children and his wife, has finally joined the stream of refugees. The landowner peers down at José, praises him for his previous tenacity, and then severely chides him for losing his dignity in the face of adversity. Mirroring the intractability of the harsh land, the intransigent man of the soil employs an anachronistic military metaphor to tell the dumbstruck José that he must know how to lose a battle. It would seem more apt to think of José and his fellow sharecroppers as having lost the entire campaign. As a social document the novel offers no solutions, and its final message appears to be that the vagaries of island reality have sealed the Cape Verdean's faith.

Baltasar Lopes

Unrelated to Manuel by kinship, Baltasar Lopes shares his fellow *claridoso's* distinction of being a much heralded Cape Verdean writer of prose fiction. Baltasar Lopes, the researcher of creole speech and the poet who writes under the name Oswaldo Alcântara, has only a few prose pieces to his credit: several short stories and one novel in print.

Baltasar Lopes has written technically well-constructed stories on universal themes with an emphasis on a psychological twist. As a regionalist he uses commonplace incidents to capture the poignancy of everyday human situations. In the story "Caderneta" (The Card), for example, a woman, driven by economic privation, turns to prostitution. The owner of a brothel, fearful of "freelance" competition, reports her to the authorities who require her to carry a card which must be stamped regularly as proof of physical examinations. In an effort to regain her sense of dignity, the woman, in a circumlocutory, fawning, yet unpretentious way, asks a doctor, who had once helped her, to intercede with the authorities to remove the stigma of the card.

Stories of this sort have a Chekhovian incisiveness and universality about them, but Baltasar Lopes, the regionalist, also has in mind the social sketch of Cape Verdean life. Another Lopes story, "Balanguinha," has a woman as its principal character. The strong-willed heroine defies her patriarchal father to marry beneath her. After an absence of years she surreptitiously returns at night to the family farm, drawn by nostalgia. Like several important Cape Verdean stories, "Balanguinha" comments on the social situation of women, in this case a woman of the landowning class, on the precariousness of male-female relationships in a world where economic instability represents a threat to marital stability. Later on in this chapter we discuss this problem as António Aurélio Gonçalves treats it in his novellas. As for the heroine of "Balanguinha," her independence is related, by inference, to the self-sufficiency of the Cape Verdean woman often left to fend for herself in a society of high male emigration and clandestine professions.

Although Baltasar Lopes's stories focus on human behavior as it is affected by very special regional conditions, his novel *Chiquinho* deals directly with the major themes of drought and emigration. Perhaps even more importantly, his regionalism becomes infused with a creole ethos free of the mystification parodied in Manuel Lopes's character Eduardinho.

First published in 1947, *Chiquinho* was begun many years before, and, in fact, a chapter appeared in the first issue of *Claridade* in 1936. There are obvious autobiographical elements in this first-person narrative which, divided into "Infância" (Childhood), "São Vicente," and "As águas" (The Rains), concerns Chiquinho's formative years in the area of Caleijão on the Island of São Nicolau, his student days in Mindelo, and his young adulthood back on his native island. It is in the first part of *Chiquinho* that Lopes develops a strong sense of creoleness, which is reminiscent of Oswaldo Alcântara's poem "Nocturno," in which there appear images of werewolves, Guinean *gongons*, and other fantastic creatures that fill a Cape Verdean child's world. The young narrator Chiquinho and his playmates gravitate toward Nhá Rosa Calita, an ancient black woman who both frightens and delights them with legends and tales.

As Chiquinho relates his childhood memories a series of interpersonal and social relationships come to light. The place of Africa in this world of superstition takes on a socially ambiguous role in a context only attached by vestiges and reminiscences to an African heritage. The ancestral heritage exists, but to be directly tied to Africa immediately casts a noncreoleness on the social and cultural reality of a people who, even on the lower social levels, view themselves as a unique amalgamation of the African and the European. In fact, it is seen how the claim of "more European than African" is translated into an artistic framework in the first part of Baltasar Lopes's novel.

The *gente-gentio* (heathen) syndrome surfaces when the old man Nhô Chic'Ana tells the children that his wife's name, Bonga, is pagan, and the old woman angrily replies that she has no master and that there is nothing black about her. In many fixed phrases and popular expressions the stigma of black-heathen-slave persists in Cape Verdean lore. The assignment of aesthetic preferences based on physical appearance falls easily from the lips of Cape Verdeans with a greater or lesser degree of African ancestry. Folks consider Chiquinho fortunate because, like his departed grandfather, he has "good" hair, similar to that of an East Indian. The days of slavery are remembered by Chiquinho's grandmother who tells of an African brought to the island by a cruel master and of how this black man spoke a creole mixed with words of his own language. The grandmother recalls the terrible revenge a mistreated slave took against his master, but she reminds her listeners that usually slaves were treated well, often like members of the family. Slaves could dance their African dances and participate in European festivals which eventually took on an African flavor.

Two points should be made on the novel's portrayal of an African presence in Cape Verde. The first has to do with socioeconomic factors. Because the slave lived cheek by jowl with whites in a nonlatifundium society on the Island of São Nicolau, his acculturation and integration came more rapidly and completely than that of his counterpart on the Island of Santiago. African survivals on the former island became more attenuated so that local folk traditions have often been attributed to European or to sui generis creole origins. The second point has to do with Baltasar Lopes's literary re-creation of Caleijão. In São Nicolau a more or less *mestiço* population functions psychologically on an accepted creole plane that makes allowances for both the African and the European. The creole accepts neither the purely African nor the purely European. This means that he more readily accepts European values even though he prides himself on having successfully controlled and absorbed Africanisms. That which seems more clearly African, such as the black wizard in Manuel Lopes's "No terreiro do bruxo Baxenxe" or the heathen name Nhanga Bonga in *Chiquinho*, represents something of a threat to the cultural solidarity and the psychological self-protectiveness of the creole.

What makes the first part of *Chiquinho* so compelling, more so than the other two parts, is that the child can succumb emotionally to the mysteries and frightening elements of African lore; but in retrospect, for the adult Chiquinho, this lore falls into the category of childish superstitions with only a nostalgic appeal as reminders of a secure and happy boyhood. The adult does not reach back for spiritual sustenance from the African and creole wisdom that infiltrates the entire aesthetic flow of the novel's first part. And that isolated, almost hermetic world of Caleijão has a creole dynamic based on the enchantments and inexplicable possessions, even though the author perhaps did not intend anything more than a nostalgic sketch of a boy growing up in a creole environment.

The enchanting but static world of Caleijão dissipates when Chiquinho leaves the island for São Vicente. During his high school years in Mindelo Chiquinho discovers that the world is not limited to the universe of Nhá Rosa Calita or to the mysterious legends of old Totone Menga Menga. For Chiquinho São Vicente becomes a place where civilization passes in review and where localities like his native Caleijão are considered to be primitive. Andrèzinho, Chiquinho's friend and mentor, takes an intellectual attitude, similar to that of Manuel Lopes's Eduardinho, toward the people of São Nicolau. He admires their purity and condescendingly refers to them as folk heroes. But the serious-minded Andrèzinho has little time for folklore and nostalgia, for his interests are wrapped up in social problems and the formation of an association of young intellectuals. The idealistic intellectual wants to bring Cape Verde into line with the rest of the universe and to foster nationalistic self-awareness among members of his generation. As the students try to school themselves in island customs, there arises a process not only of self-awareness, but also of self-consciousness, particularly if the reality they confront speaks of Africa. At a social gathering in Mindelo a student from Santiago plays a *batuque* that animates the assembly and inspires the narrator to describe the scene with enthusiasm: "The hall is in deepest Africa, the sun blazing on the plateau and the landscape of the savannah, with monkeys frolicking. The *badio* takes everybody with him on his voyage back into the centuries."[4] We need not reiterate the type of Cape Verdean ancestralism found in poetry and prose allusions to Africa, but the presence of the distant "dark continent" at a student party represents an exotic flirtation rather than a spiritual identification. The backlands *badio* acts as guide for his countrymen who are too far removed from Africa to see it as anything more than a series of tropical images and ancestral origins blurred by time.

One of the youth union's principal aims is to organize the workers, and Chiquinho, when he returns to his native island, pledges himself to carry out the group's social and literary-cultural goals. But after his life in Mindelo he finds it difficult to readjust to the people and places of his childhood, and so the narrative looseness of the episodic second and third parts of the novel can be seen as parallel to the protagonist's disorientation and alienation. A variety of one-dimensional characters, including Chiquinho's reprobate uncle, revolves around the hero. These characters are intended to reveal facets of the Cape Verdean's psychic behavior within his small environment. The aberrant social behavior of a certain Mr. Euclides Varanda perhaps discloses one view of the frustrated literary and intellectual aspirations of a petty bourgeois Cape Verdean under the constraints of his surroundings. Mr. Euclides Varanda has spent the better part of his adult life writing a highly erudite book, the title and nature of which he will only allow to be disclosed after his death. Another sketchily drawn character, José Lima, has experienced life as a black Portuguese in the United States, and this humiliating condition causes him to reassess his personal worth. Many of the villagers consider him a revolutionary, and although Baltasar Lopes does not develop this thesis he does suggest that José Lima has had to reevaluate his sense of Cape Verdeanness through his personal contact with an alien world.

The novel's third part prepares for and terminates in Chiquinho's eventual departure from the islands. Memories of creole folklore vanish in the face of moral disintegration resulting from economic stagnation and the inevitable drought as perceived by the adult Chiquinho. The narrator describes scenes of misery with less of a flair, but with no less a sense of horror than Manuel Lopes in his *Flagelados do vento leste*. Mr. Euclides Varanda makes a philosophical case for abandoning the islands; he tells Chiquinho not to be caught in the dilemma because Cape Verde, despite its poverty, holds on to its people. Chiquinho must escape *to* Cape Verde, for the islands live in the Cape Verdean's soul even though they degrade the spirit. The old man's somber pronouncements echo the book's creole epigraph: "Corpo, qu'ê nêgo, sa ta bai;/ Coraçom, qu'ê fôrro, sa ta fica. . ." (The body, which is a slave, departs;/The heart, which is free, remains. . .).

Structurally, *Chiquinho* goes from the homogeneous creole world of childhood where life is a continuing, unbroken circle of social and spiritual stability to the world of intellectual awareness, and finally to the point where intellectual awareness collides with cultural self-awareness, resulting in the protagonist's disorientation. Chiquinho's decision to join his father in New Bedford, Massachusetts, comes directly, then, from Baltasar Lopes's modified treatment of the problem of wanting to stay, having to depart. The protagonist escapes the degradation and stifling atmosphere of the islands, thereby dramatizing Manuel Lopes's words (see page 261) that the Cape Verdean realizes that the colonial condition of his land has fostered in him a conviction which confines and restrains his actions.

António Aurélio Gonçalves

Within the limited ambient of Cape Verdean society António Aurélio Gonçalves has created his impressive literary world. All his efforts are works of short fiction: short stories and novellas, or what the author out of extreme modesty calls *noveletas* (novelettes). Even though his literary production has been small, Gonçalves rightfully figures as one of the pillars of contemporary Cape Verdean prose. In a way, his psychological development of characters—which explains why, perhaps, his short stories usually grew into novellas—and his serene social commentary satisfy his desire to get into the mainstream of world literature. In a 1962 interview Gonçalves mentioned, among those writers who had influenced him, Maupassant, Balzac (whom he translated), Flaubert, and Dostoevski. And his obvious interest in nineteenth-century realism led him to write an essay on the Portuguese novelist Eça de Queirós (1845–1900).

Gonçalves, like the two Lopes, also participated in the initial surge of Cape Verdean regionalist awareness. His two-part short story "Recaída" (Relapse) was published in issues five and six of *Claridade*. Despite a kind of verbal density, which Gonçalves would refine in later works, "Recaída" already demonstrates a skill in emphasizing character over plot, although it represents a social picture of moral and spiritual decay. Gonçalves seems to need the longer novella to develop his talent as a delineator of character. In his short short story "História de tempo antigo" (A Story of Times Past), the focus on the main character's personality lacks both psychological penetration and regionally derived universality.

What Gonçalves does reveal in "História de tempo antigo" (which was published in the ninth issue of *Claridade*) is a penchant for depicting female characters. *Pródiga* (The Prodigal Daughter, 1956), the first of his four novellas, offers a psychological portrait of Xandinha who, as the title suggests, oversteps the limits imposed on her by the norms of a matriarchal family and then returns apparently repentant to the fold. Repentance, however, means for Xandinha a painful concession as she struggles with the conflicting forces of a desire for independence and the attractions of the comfort and relative security of her mother's home. After a severe reprimanding for having left home Xandinha settles back into a family routine in which she and her sisters must abide by a set of confining regulations. She takes a job as a maid in the home of a compassionate and strong-willed woman, but her rebelliousness surfaces when she surrenders her virginity to Toi Nina, a man her mother disapproves of. When rumor of the affair reaches her mother, she orders a woman who specializes in such matters to discover whether her daughter has slept with Toi. A wild scene ensues during which mother beats daughter and daughter again abandons the maternal hearth. In the absence of her employer, who has moved to another island, Xandinha takes a room first with one and then with another female friend. Her child, fathered by Toi, dies soon after birth and Xandinha finds herself nearly destitute after a brief liaison with another man. The comfort of her mother's house beckons. Once more the prodigal returns, and again she only apparently repents; her repentance is concession. At the end of the story Xandinha, accompanied by her sister, goes to retrieve her belongings from a rented room. Suddenly she gives in to the urge to dance down the street and engage in horseplay with her sister, much to the latter's annoyance. A capricious breeze plays with Xandinha's skirt and she accepts the game as her mood becomes one of contentment at the prospect of a restful sleep in her mother's house. This last scene parallels the story's opening when Xandinha, en route to her mother's house, struggles to keep her skirt down and defend herself against the chill of the wind.

The story could be read, perhaps, as a kind of parable in which the mother's home, like Cape Verde for its native sons, holds both an attraction and a repulsion for Xandinha. But viewing it from a different angle, we note that female characters dominate the story. As a matter of fact, the only male character of any importance is Toi Nina, and he is merely a pretext for Xandinha's act of rebellion. No mention is made of Xandinha's father who, it might be assumed, has either emigrated or abandoned his family, or both. The mother, Nhâ Ludovina—and Gonçalves consistently capitalizes *Mãe* (Mother)—looks upon her home as a refuge from the temptations of a São Vicente that can corrupt young women. Another proud female character, Dona Zulmira, has, by virtue of her social status and marriage to a Portuguese, stabilized her position in a society in which women find themselves both socially and psychologically victimized. Zulmira, whose title of respect *dona* contrasts with the *nhâ* usually assigned to women of inferior social rank, shows in her compassion toward her maid Xandinha an implied understanding of woman's plight in social circumstances that can easily rob her of her reputation. The narrator portrays Dona Zulmira as "strong, her African ancestry pronounced and accentuated in her features."[5] Gonçalves occasionally identifies characters by color, and generally with no more in mind than he might have in describing physical features. One of Xandinha's companions is depicted as a black girl while the heroine herself, as well as most of the other characters, are presumably *mestiços*. Gonçalves neither isolates an African reality in Cape Verde nor emphasizes what is not there. Still, he writes authentically within a social reality that fits into the broad category of black or African literature. Like the great, nineteenth-century Brazilian *mestiço* Machado de Assis, Gonçalves often says more by implication than by direct statement, and he celebrates creoleness on a low but meaningful key. Dona Zulmira's strength and her accentuated African features imply, without ancestral romanticism, the resolute position of one who has felt, if only atavistically, suffering and degradation.

A creole reality in Gonçalves's fiction is embodied in Nhâ Candinha Sena in the novella *O enterro de Nhâ Candinha Sena* (The Burial of Mrs. Candinha Sena, 1957). The narrator explains his childhood devotion to Candinha Sena, "a very dark mulatto woman, almost black one might say, with her curly hair always hidden, because even though she was not of the lower class, she always wore a kerchief. She was of average height, but because she was stout and strong she gave the impression of being short."[6]

What applies to Dona Zulmira, regarding the significance of African ancestry, would seem to apply similarly to Nhâ Candinha. She was not of the lower class, yet she preferred the title *nhâ* which when used to address an upper-class woman can connote endearment. As a creole corruption of the more formal Portuguese title *senhora*, *nhâ* also expresses the bearer's *morabeza* (affability). Gonçalves employs Nhâ Candinha as a prototypic creole woman, but he does not limit himself to the delineation of a one-dimensional, purely illustrative character. Through flashbacks and the narrator's efforts to put his own existence as a Cape Verdean into perspective, Candinha emerges as a living being as well as a symbol. She has suffered through the drama of emigration which took her second husband to America where he died. The woman who stays behind, Candinha remains a stable force at her customary place in the doorway of her modest, childless home where she plays mother to all, including the narrator. After the narrator, grown up, returns from his travels abroad, he finds that Nhâ Candinha Sena has aged and her memory is failing; so he avoids her and instead relies on childhood reminiscences to reconstruct the image of the strong Cape Verdean woman with her creole speech and her presents of sweets. Candinha dies, and after the funeral the mourners return to their day-to-day existence as if the woman had never lived. But the narrator makes what amounts to a symbolic gesture of antievasion. He feels remorse at not having gone directly to Candinha upon his return from abroad, and in his imagination he relives his childhood devotion to her as he symbolically asks for her and Cape Verde's blessing.

In *Pródiga* Gonçalves had written that São Vicente ruined Xandinha as only São Vicente knows how. Life in Cape Verde has irrevocably debased the heroine, and this theme of the debased female permits Gonçalves to project the larger corruption in Cape Verde's social and economic structures. A lesser writer might have distorted the delicate subject of Cape Verde's economic decadence, to the degree that it affects the Cape Verdean who remains behind, by gilding the human degradation with romantic mystique. Gonçalves, particularly through his female characters, makes compelling and unobtrusive social comments which capture the substance and the larger vision of Cape Verdeanness.

Gonçalves's third novella, *Noite de vento* (Night of Wind, 1970), also centers on a rebellious, independently minded female character. Nita, the narrator tells us, is very attractive to men, although she has pronounced Negroid features. This mysterious girl rises above the debasement of a woman victimized by Cape Verde society and the stigma of her dark skin to defy the complex conventions governing male-female relationships among the lower classes. Common-law marriages in Cape Verde are accepted arrangements among the lower classes because the individuals involved derive mutual economic benefits from such unions. When emigration or economic crisis occurs the union is dissolved without legal entanglements. Ultimately, however, the man derives the greater advantage, both from the arrangement and from its dissolution, not only economically but also as far as more elusive considerations, such as reputation and self-esteem, are concerned. Nita's first common-law husband, Lela, has the reputation, reprehensible for some but a badge of virility for others, of living with a woman until she becomes pregnant and then abandoning her. Nita leaves Lela and consents to live with the seaman Virgílio who, besides his need of a housekeeper and companion, is fascinated by the heroine's sensuousness and aloofness. Perhaps because she is cynical about these insecure relationships, Nita leaves Virgílio, who confesses to a friend that what hurts most is that it was she who terminated the union, thus wounding his male pride. But by breaking the rules of "companionship" Nita's inexplicable decision, passed off by her friends as capricious, constitutes both personal and female liberation.

Gonçalves created a dark-skinned heroine as if to vindicate and lend more psychological value to the Negroid aspects of the Cape Verdean's biological and philosophical make-up. He obviously uses the female character to elaborate, through her static condition, the monotony and that refined melancholy represented in Jorge Barbosa's poem "Momento."

Just as in *Pródiga*, the wind is a motif in *Noite de vento*. On the night that Nita leaves Virgílio a brisk wind lifts women's dresses, attacks pedestrians, and people have to turn their faces to avoid the onslaught. Besides the conventional use of a storm to represent a character's inner turmoil, the wind also suggests, as in *Pródiga*, female fickleness. But when Nita insists that her decision to leave Virgílio was not arbitrary, the changing gusts of wind can also be seen as emblematic of the inconstancy of life. Some readers, dissatisfied with the enigma of Nita's decision, might be inclined to interpret her move as an indication that she is pregnant by Lela. Even if this were true, and there is no direct proof that it is, her self-assertive decision would still have significance within the context of Gonçalves's re-creation of the restrained ambient of São Vicente.

Gonçalves's apparent fascination with the artistic possibilities of female characters continues in his most recent work, *Virgens loucas* (Crazy Virgins, 1971). In this *noveleta*, which revolves around three prostitutes, Gonçalves also demonstrates his concern for the development of background in his depiction of a regional ambient. He describes, for example, an old, decaying street in the city of Mindelo: "Ancient street, in ill-repair, forgotten in a nook at the city's edge . . . On either side were two long sheds which, one might say, extended from end to end, segmented into dwellings of single compartments. The street had become a long corridor, usually poorly lit at night, flanked by two uniform city blocks, two low-standing monoliths strung out and semi-hidden in the shadows with only a vague clarity from lamp reflections stamped on the walls."[7] Having established a certain mood, the narrator then expands the scene to depict a city that serves as a backdrop for the perambulations of the three prostitutes: "Although poor and unsightly this side street has atmosphere (no one knows what it derives from) that recalls a Mindelo of bygone years with its busy port and tumultuous activity instilling life into an overworked and varied populace of workers raging in their dances to the sound of one-stringed instruments, forming easy liaisons, consuming lives (individuals disappear suddenly)—a Mindelo of toil, of sensuality, of death" (p. 21). Against this somewhat ominous background of arrested vitality unfolds the story of the three prostitutes, especially Betinha, a mulatto girl and the only pretty one of the group.

A passage from the Gospel according to St. Matthew precedes the story and introduces the theme of wisdom versus foolishness or, better still, the quest for dignity among the vagaries of existence. The biblical parable likens the Kingdom of Heaven to ten virgins who go forth with their lamps to meet the bridegroom (Jesus). When the bridegroom does not appear the ten virgins fall asleep during their wait. Suddenly a cry goes up that the bridegroom approaches, and the virgins awaken and prepare their lamps; but five of them, the foolish ones, have no oil so they ask the five wise ones to share theirs with them. The wise virgins tell their sisters to go buy some oil lest there not be enough for any of them. When the five ill-prepared girls finally return, they find the door locked, and the bridegroom answers their cries with the words "I know you not." The moral, of course, is that one must always be prepared for one never knows when he will be called to enter the Kingdom of Heaven.

This parable applies curiously to the story of the three prostitutes who set out one night to buy fuel for their lamp so that they might spend a pleasant evening together conversing in a well-lighted room instead of walking the streets in search of customers. Ironically, they do walk the streets, but in search of a few cents to buy the needed oil. When a young black man steps between two brawling sailors, Betinha seizes the opportunity to praise his heroics and to ask him for the loan of a few coins for the precious fuel. With money in hand the three women attempt to convince a store owner to sell them the oil even though his shop has closed for the night; the man tells them, paralleling the words of the biblical bridegroom, that he "does not know them." Furthermore, he has only enough fuel for his lamp, and in this he parallels the five wise virgins. Light is an important motif in the story, and it becomes an obsession for Betinha who vows to her companions that in the future her first thought upon awakening in the morning will be of her lamp. "I must have light," she declares, "a small one, yes! But it must be all mine. My light!" (p. 36)

In the Portuguese-language Bible, five of the virgins are described as *prudentes* (prudent), and, although prudent may be synonymous with wise, as the King James Version of the New Testament describes the women, it has another connotation in Gonçalves's story. There is irony in the three prostitutes' impulsiveness as they, and particularly Betinha, decide to assume the role of virgins for one night. Their imprudence in not having provided fuel for their lamp points up the failure of their existence. As in previous stories Gonçalves creates aesthetic patterns that mirror the confining social structure of Mindelo; São Vicente can ruin a woman as only São Vicente knows how. Economic privations and attending social relationships have drawn the three "crazy virgins" into their imprudent life. Betinha and her two companions are "crazy" because they seek to defy the role that São Vicente has assigned to them.

Virgens loucas has much to do with the intrinsically social problems of the small island. Implicitly, Gonçalves deals with the problem of evasion, both the type that manifests itself in emigration and the more psychological kind that has to do with how the Cape Verdean views his condition as a person confined in his insularity and ethnic ambivalence. And with regard to ethnic ambivalence, Gonçalves avoids the question of Africa without denying its proximity to Cape Verdean culture. He implies that, within Cape Verdean ethos, racial attitudes, no matter how subtle, in some way determine the creole's concept of self vis-à-vis his position in the world. The young black man who separates the brawling Norwegian sailors and then coolly pats his kinky hair back into place demonstrates a bravado that proves to him his individual worth in a *mestiço* society. And Betinha's indignation before the shop owner reflects her personal degradation as a socially despised woman who attempts to present herself as the prototype of creole femininity.

Gonçalves's sensitivity to a regional psychology can be seen in his habit of reading parts of his stories to unlettered Cape Verdeans who possess attitudes similar to those expressed by Xandinha or Betinha.[8] Gonçalves considers his art to be successful when these ordinary, often semi-illiterate Cape Verdeans perceive aspects of themselves in the characters of the novellas. The female characters, despite their symbolic importance, which may elude the nonliterary reader or listener, lead lives that doubtlessly speak volumes to those who experience a Cape Verdean reality with no means of synthesizing its essence.

António Aurélio Gonçalves has attained a level of artistic maturity that has permitted him to deal effectively with immanent social and psychological patterns rather than present the more relativist portrayal of Cape Verdean society. But Gonçalves also has internalized the regional immediacy and archetypal characters found in the writings of many of his contemporaries.

Fantasy and a Heightening of Social Awareness

Teobaldo Virgínio's novel *Vida crioula* (Creole Life, 1967) employs the symbols and images of Cape Verdeanness in a way that goes beyond the folkloric and becomes fantasy. The author combines reality with myth so that affability, creole speech, emigration, and particularly the prototype creole man and woman take on a fairy-tale quality. Structurally, the novel depends on the repetition of themes expressed in poetic phrases or passages. For example, the second chapter begins, "Toninho's problem could be any Cape Verdean brother's problem, but Toninho's heart is not like just any heart."[9] And this statement is repeated like a refrain several times throughout the novel.

Toninho, the central character, is an archetype whose heart encompasses all facets of creole life. His female counterpart, Celina, is the quintessence of the creole *morena*, and the author uses an erotic, metaphorical parody of a fairy-tale situation to illustrate her demure seductiveness. The lyrical-erotic scene, which is alluded to several times throughout the story, occurs when the protagonist and Celina are out for a walk. Coyly Celina sits on a rock, extends her parted legs, and, calling Toninho to her, says: "Rest in this nice shade, Toninho. Inside the big cave there's an enchanted princess seated on a rock waiting for her prince to come and break the spell so they can be married. But the opening of the cave, as you can see, is surrounded by an angry sea, and there is no young man brave enough to defy the waves and break the princess's spell. So day and night the enchanted princess sits crying because the young man lacks the courage. Would you dare to enter, Toninho?" (p. 22) Celina lives with a strict aunt who discourages all suitors, and the author raises the niece's bold invitation to the mythic level as an expression of the Cape Verdean's social dilemma. At best Virgínio's handling of the erotic suggestiveness is chaotic when applied to the fundamental question of remaining or departing that confronts the Cape Verdean. He analyzes the problem in an aside that combines philosophical musing on the Cape Verdean's dilemma with the image of the enchanted princess: "This interrogative life. This sensation of permanent insecurity. Because the Cape Verdean's problem went beyond the Guincho pier or Corda Road. And, as in a film, he saw the tip of the tongue flicking, the enigmatic smile, the eyes, those sweet eyes of love, half shut, those shapely legs, the image of the fairy inside crying, Celina asking: 'Would you dare enter, Toninho?' This was the crux of the problem, the Cape Verdean entering and not being able to leave" (p. 100). Fortunately, Virgínio tempers the lyricism and ludicrous flamboyancy with tongue-in-cheek humor as he illustrates the binding seduction that island life, represented in its more sensuous aspects by Celina, holds for the Cape Verdean. He carries the metaphor to its logical end when Celina and Toninho consummate their love and produce a child. The creole girl's seduction of the archetypal Cape Verdean is wrapped in the same erotic and lyrical imagery of the passages quoted above: "The sea in fury, and on the rock the enchanted princess lies singing . . . On that profound night of love the creole girl gave herself completely, and the Cape Verdean was born" (p. 111).

Virgínio places the problem of evasion in a context that is both tragic and sentimental; citing works such as Baltasar Lopes's *Chi-*

quinho, Virgínio concludes that those who leave the islands have their reasons. He then offers, in the form of a *morna*, a nostalgic, sentimental, albeit frivolous, justification for the Cape Verdean's physical evasion:

> Se bem é sabe
> bai é magoado
> mas se cá bade
> câ ta birado.
>
> (p. 142)

(If returning is sweet/going is sad/but if you don't go/you can't return.)

As the symbolic nature of the extended metaphors and fantasies becomes obvious, the author's frequently refreshing treatment of Cape Verdeanness deteriorates into gratuitously outrageous episodes in the novel's second part. Unlike Baltasar Lopes's Chiquinho, who follows a traditional pattern when he emigrates to New England, Toninho goes to Los Angeles, somewhat in keeping with the novel's Hollywood-like garishness. After concluding the novel with an exaltation of creole life and a call for solidarity, Virgínio adds a postscript in which he explains that Toninho did return to Celina and to his native island where he became a specialist in the growing of bananas. The incongruity of this profession seems as fitting as the protagonist's emigration to California where he was an indispensable employee of an insurance firm. Exulting in the Cape Verdean's abilities, his capacity for love, and his strong attachment to the land, Virgínio lets the novel come to an end as if exhausted by the banality of its exaltation.

Much of the narrative prose of Cape Verde published in the late fifties and throughout the sixties intensified the problem of emigration and its emotional by-products of homesickness and nostalgia. During the early part of the twentieth century a group of intellectuals and writers in Portugal institutionalized their longing for the past into a current with strong nationalistic overtones known as *Saudosismo*. As part of a broader literary movement in Portugal the concept of *saudade*, a word generally conceded by Portuguese and Brazilians to be untranslatable but which basically means yearning, took on a tone of decadence, particularly in poetry. In Cape Verde in the fifties and sixties a form of *saudosismo*, and not necessarily yearning for the past, embraced all manifestations of Cape Verdeanness and heightened the sentimentality inherent in the problem of leaving the islands.

As might be expected, regionalism has given Cape Verdean prose fiction a certain stylistic and thematic sameness. Several writers have embellished the mystique of Cape Verdeanness in stories that depict the son of the islands about to depart or already departed and longing to return. Some writers, drawing on their own experience, have fashioned stories around Cape Verdean communities abroad. Nuno Miranda, who resides in Portugal, wrote *Gente da ilha* (Island People, 1961), a collection of short stories and chronicles. The section of Lisbon known as Campo de Ourique appears as an island of Cape Verdeanness in Miranda's chronicle "Passagem de ano em Lisboa" (New Year's Eve in Lisbon). *Saudade* and that refined melancholy, captured in poetry by Jorge Barbosa, hover over the New Year's Eve party even during its most animated moments. At midnight a certain Doctor Faustino delivers a passionate speech in which he reminds the gathering that Cape Verdeans have made much progress abroad amidst joy and sorrow. Lips tremble and the women shed copious tears as all share a unifying nostalgia while the radio supplies a *morna* to complete the sentimentality of the scene. But the melancholy is fleeting, for shortly after a piano player attacks the keyboard with a spirited samba march that "cuts into the night, recomposing that passing of the year among Cape Verdeans come together in Lisbon."[10]

The "faraway" land of São Tomé has been a setting for several Cape Verdean stories. For Cape Verdeans in São Tomé, however, the *saudade* and solidarity come to bear not so much on social progress abroad, as suggested in Miranda's story, but on the commiseration of those who share the hardships and humiliations of the contract laborer. Onésimo Silveira has applied his social awareness to the few stories he wrote, the most important of which, *Toda a gente fala: Sim, senhor* (Everybody Says: Yes, Sir, 1960), falls into the category of what A. A. Gonçalves calls *noveleta*, at least in terms of length.

In this story Silveira describes some of the painful realities of contract labor, and like Nuno Miranda he deals with a Cape Verdean world away from Cape Verde. This transplanted world derives from a kind of forced exile resulting directly from the lack of rain, and, as the author says of the main character, "taking a trip was for those who had relatives in Brazil or in North America, or for nice boys and girls and people from São Vicente who don't know how sweet the land can be . . . But the rope that drought has put around his neck has forced him to take the miserable road to São Tomé . . ."[11] Francisco José Tenreiro's monograph *A Ilha de São Tomé* (The Island of São Tomé, 1961) emphasizes those factors that have made the Cape Verdean laborer distinct from his Angolan and Mozambican counterparts. In the first place, all Cape Verdeans are Portuguese citizens by birth, and their creole culture instills in them a certain pride that separates them from the dispossessed Angolan or Mozambican "native." Thus the Cape Verdean in São Tomé remains generally aloof from the other contract laborers and he frequently assumes an attitude of ethnic superiority.

Silveira's story concerns the contract worker Tigusto who after several years on a plantation in São Tomé still hopes that his wife and children in Cape Verde will be able to join him. When he approaches the overseer with this proposition, the man bluntly tells him that women only cause trouble on the plantation and that children bring the owner little profit—the social disruption of a slave economy. Tigusto sums up the contract workers' degradation when he accepts the overseer's decision with a subservient "yes, sir," which, according to his friend Nizinho, must always be used when addressing authority. In a dejected mood, Tigusto leaves for town where he unsuccessfully seeks employment. After several weeks there he is reunited with Nizinho who is visiting the city to attend the September "litany" of a Cape Verdean woman,

Mélia Tavares. Mélia, in payment of a votive promise, has for a number of years offered the religious celebration for her fellow *badios*, and because she is from the Island of Santiago the festivities invariably conclude with a *batuque*. At the end of the celebration everyone joins in the singing of a song which expresses the story's motif of subservience and degradation:

> Oh mundo, oh mundo
> A mim djá'm subi monte—sim, senhor!
>
> Oh mundo, toda gente fala: sim, senhor!
> (p. 28)

(Oh people, oh people/I've already climbed up the mountain—yes sir!//Oh people, everybody says: yes sir!)

Tigusto's voice can be heard over all others, and his participation in the Santiago *batuque* once more illustrates Silveira's insistence on an African revindication for Cape Verde. Nizinho appreciates the *morna*, but he deeply feels the *batuques* of his native Santiago. So while Silveira does not depreciate the *morna*, he sees the *batuque* as a profound, spiritual expression of Cape Verdeanness, much as Kaoberdiano Dambara does in his combative poetry.

Tigusto returns to the plantation where he finds a letter from his wife announcing that it has finally rained in Cape Verde. Elated, Tigusto takes up his guitar and sings a nostalgic *morna*. The *morna*, in works as different as those of Nuno Miranda and Onésimo Silveira, has become a musical motif in Cape Verdean literature expressing *saudade* whether based on socioeconomic factors or on just melancholic pining for the land left behind. But after the *morna*, the Cape Verdeans in Lisbon give vent to joyous emotions in a Brazilian samba, and the contract laborers in São Tomé seek spiritual catharsis in the African *batuque*.

In some respects Miranda and Silveira represent opposite poles of the same problems of Cape Verdeanness. Miranda, on the question of a literary language, condemns the use of creole or creolized Portuguese. Silveira, on the other hand, experiments with creole dialogue in his stories. Both writers deal, however, with Cape Verdeanness from the standpoint of the Cape Verdean away from his islands; Miranda describes the more sentimental, self-imposed exile in Europe, while Silveira portrays the harsh, forced emigration to the faraway land of the south. An equally nostalgic mantle has been draped over those works which depict the Cape Verdean still on his islands but facing the possibility or inevitability of departing.

A number of occasional writers, with stories published in anthologies or magazines, have cultivated what amount to fictional vignettes on the subject of the Cape Verdean faced with the prospect of departing. For example, Ovídio Martins's "Sono na praia" (Drowsy on the Beach), which is included in his collection *Tutchinha* (1962), uses the somnolent atmosphere of a lonely beach as a background for the anxiety-filled thoughts of a teen-age boy about to depart for school in Portugal.

Although the problems of departing or emigration constantly hover over Cape Verdean literary expression, there are several good writers who, in the manner of A. A. Gonçalves, focus their sense of Cape Verdean *saudosismo* on the psychic dilemmas of life in a desolate land. Some among these writers have gone beyond Gonçalves in explicit social concern. Gabriel Mariano obviously intends social criticism in his story "O rapaz doente" (The Sick Boy), which was first published in *Cabo Verde: Boletim* (no. 54) and later reprinted in the landmark *Antologia da ficção cabo-verdiana contemporânea* (Anthology of Contemporary Cape Verdean Fiction, 1960).

"O rapaz doente" falls into the category of nonrural Cape Verdean stories whose regionalism attains universality. Júlio, a boy suffering from a serious illness, probably tuberculosis, arrives in São Vicente from Santiago. A nameless benefactor on Santiago has instructed his wife in Mindelo to see to the boy's treatment, but the woman receives the boy with suspicion and mild revulsion. Dona Maninha fears contagion and feels repelled by the boy's poverty and appearance. This upper-class woman limits her concern for the destitute to the distribution of alms to selected poor people every Saturday between the hours of four and six.

Júlio, who has been physically imposed on her, falls outside of the bounds of her structured charity. Angry at her husband for having encumbered her with this unexpected burden, she quietly attempts to intern the boy in the local hospital. When bureaucratic red tape thwarts her half-hearted efforts she resolutely seeks to free herself of the responsibility by the most expedient means, which is to send him back to Santiago. Dona Maninha's rationalizations mirror the broader reality of society's gestures toward the curing of ills.

By having Júlio contract his illness in São Tomé, the author touches on a major social problem, and he also seeks to dramatize broad social issues through the delineation of a single victim, the sick boy. The boy's dumbfounded expression and his attitude which seems to be apologizing for his existence go hand in hand with an ingrained sense of resignation. Uncomplainingly he sleeps on a bench in the hospital corridor on the night before his return to Santiago. Yet, beneath his beaten appearance lies an adolescent boy eager to enjoy life. He casts approving glances at Dona Maninha's maid, and later he ogles the woman on a movie poster. Mariano uses several techniques to make the sick boy more than an illustration of social ills. While answering Dona Maninha's coldly phrased questions, Júlio drops his beret several times; but later when he discusses the problem of girls with the houseboy Norberto he pulls the cap down on his head at a rakish angle. And before vanishing into the hospital's dark corridor he removes his beret and stuffs it into his jacket pocket. The beret serves as a device to call attention to Júlio's nervousness, to his boyish arrogance, and to his ingrained sense of humility. Mariano's use of a universal situation in his characterization of Júlio supports the theme of social concern and adds to a recognizable flavor of Cape Verdeanness as seen in the boy's quiet melancholy and his tropical roguishness.

In the realm of neorealist treatment of Cape Verdean ethos the name of Henrique Teixeira de Sousa comes to mind. His story "Dragão e eu" (Dragão and I), originally published in 1945 in the Portuguese magazine *Vértice*, resembles Mariano's social commentary and, like other works, portrays characters whose person-alities have been molded by a limited environment. In this story the boy and his dog Dragão share an aggressive spirit of inde-pendence in the confines of a small town. The boy rejects the town's social and physical restrictions, and the dog escapes the castrator's knife to roam virile and free. When the boy names his dog after the fabulous monster, perhaps he demonstrates his own fiery defiance of life. For nine years boy and dog are inseparable companions, temperamentally if not always physically. But the dog disappears one day, and his master accepts the probability that he has been eaten by some of the famished refugees who fill the town during a drought. The boy observes two minutes of silence for his companion of nine years, and a few days later he embarks for America.

The deus ex machina of emigration in Teixeira de Sousa's story enhances both A. A. Gonçalves's thesis that Cape Verde knows how to ruin and the contention of one of Baltasar Lopes's charac-ters in *Chiquinho* that these pieces of land only serve to degrade the spirit. The vigorous, free-spirited Dragão falls victim to a pressing reality, hunger; the young protagonist succumbs to the necessity of leaving.

Teixeira de Sousa has attempted a fictional illustration of his essays on the social structure of the Island of Fogo. He contrib-uted a short story, "Na Corte d'El-Rei D. Pedro" (At King Peter's Court), to a small promotional volume sponsored by a Portu-guese pharmaceutical firm in 1970 to commemorate the Christ-mas season. Like Teixeira de Sousa, the other two contributors to the slim collection are medical doctors, but the Cape Verdean phy-sician proves himself to be a better than average writer and an astute observer of social transitions on his native Island of Fogo. In his story he seems to be following the lead of the Brazilian northeast novelist Lins do Rego who in such works as *Fogo morto* (Dead Fire, 1943) documents the tragic irony of social and eco-nomic transformations. Lins do Rego uses madness as a motif in this process of radical socioeconomic change, particularly through the depiction of a fallen plantation lord who has illusions of a past grandeur.

Raimundo, the central figure of Teixeira de Sousa's story, believes himself to be Dom Pedro, the fourteenth-century king who ruled Portugal with a strong but just hand. Both Raimundo and the story's narrator, Vicente Cardoso, belong to the decadent aristocracy. On Christmas Eve the two men, former boyhood friends, meet by chance and stand together atop the Heights of São Pedro surveying their lost domain. They seem to be at the edge of the cliff, expressed in the saying that "when the mulatto runs with the white man, the white man will run to the precipice and throw himself off." Instead they descend from the heights and go off to Nhô Quirino's bar in search of a Christmas Eve meal. The place is closed, and when Nhô Quirino responds from an upstairs window to the insistent knocking he angrily demands to know the identity of those who have disturbed his sleep. When Vicente Cardoso replies "King Peter and I," the infuriated Nhô Quirino makes an insulting allusion to Vicente's grandmother. As the two men walk away, Vicente ruminates on the irony of having been insulted by the son of one of his grandmother's slaves.

"Na Corte d'El-Rei Dom Pedro," in exemplifying the development of social classes along racial and economic lines, qualifies more as a sociological work than as a story of social awareness. It is unique in that it is set on the leeward Island of Fogo. Most Cape Verdean fiction deals with the windward islands of São Vicente, São Nicolau, and Santo Antão which well illustrate the themes of evasion.

A number of stories included in the *Antologia da ficção caboverdiana contemporanea* and in other collections such as Amândio César's *Contos portugueses do ultramar* (Portuguese Stories from the Overseas Territories, 1969) could be mentioned here. But rather than offer other examples of the variations on the few traditional themes treated in modern Cape Verdean literature we turn in our final two sections to a pair of writers who for entirely different reasons occupy what can be called unorthodox positions in the panorama of prose fiction dealing with the archipelago.

First I shall consider a novelist who while he deals with the usual themes does so in a way that sets him apart as a literary peculiarity, if not a phenomenon.

Luís Romano and a Different
Perspective of Cape Verde

Different may be an understatement when applied to the novel *Famintos* (The Famished, 1962) by Luís Romano. The brother of Teobaldo Virgínio, Romano was born on the Island of Santo Antão but has lived much of his adult life in Morocco and most recently in Brazil. Romano admits that his only novel, published in Brazil, lacks unity. Although it has a theme, it is missing a definite plot and a central character. In fact, characters enter and exit, and sometimes disappear completely with no explanation. *Famintos* possesses, however, an iconoclastic sense of Cape Verdeanness. Technically and stylistically Romano seems to have been greatly influenced by novelists of the Brazilian Northeast, particularly those who carry social protest to proletarian and revolutionary extremes. Some Cape Verdean intellectuals do not consider Romano's work representative of Cape Verdean regionalism. Romano the novelist, like Romano the poet, demonstrates a penchant for ignoring traditional Cape Verdean color-blindness in his literary creations. Also, as he does in his poetry, he leaves the reader slightly confused about the ultimate purpose of his African awareness.

The work has a didactic, quasi-allegorical framework and some descriptive techniques typical of naturalism. The opening scene describes laborers repairing roads on Ilha-sem-nome (No-Name-Island), an appellation that carries the double connotation of anonymity and despair. When one of the workers suffers an incapacitating asthma attack, the foreman kicks him unmercifully. Subsequent episodes have an even greater shock appeal. At the height of the famine that has swept the island a woman dies from malnutrition while giving birth. Ravens swoop down and eat the half-born baby's eyes. Along with a flair for the horrific, Romano displays a gratuitous preoccupation with the scatalogical, offering detailed descriptions of the ravages of dysentery on the populace.

Early in the novel Campina appears on the island of his birth, and, if any character can be considered central, he comes closest. Sometimes known as O Espanhol (The Spaniard) or as O Espanhol de Buenos Aires (The Spaniard from Buenos Aires), Campina is a black man who has lived for several years in Argentina; his life seems to be as bizarre as his nicknames. The politically radical Cape Verdean arrives on his native Ilha-sem-nome in the midst of the populace's suffering, and he immediately becomes the voice of the people. He exhorts his black compatriot Rufino to kill the man who has taken his land and dishonored his daughter. Rufino piously reminds Campina that to kill is a sin. Meekness and complacency, asserts Campina, are the two obstacles to social awareness. He himself had killed a despotic official in Argentina.

Other symbolic characters revolve around Campina and add strength to the theme of proletarian organization. Estudante (Student), a white, upper-class Cape Verdean, idealistically pledges himself to the people's cause. During one episode he, along with other socially aware youth, listens avidly to Campina's stories of proletarian organization and activism. Another member of the group, Diamantinha, composes *mornas* that cannot be sung in public because the authorities consider them subversive, and the businessman Nhambolo complains scornfully of the black music that Diamantinha sings. Carioca, a black Brazilian, tells his companions how he once, while working on a Greek freighter, was the victim of racial slurs from a German crew member against whom he took violent revenge. The politicized Campina analyzes the situation and concludes that the Brazilian should have reacted to his fellow crew member in the spirit of proletarian solidarity.

Villainous characters appear in bizarre array. Mulato, a syphilitic, psychopathic public administrator, makes a habit of deflowering young girls, and he recommends the machine gun as the best solution to the refugee problem. Paradoxically, he has a passion for painting and, even more strangely, for the most proletarian novels of the Brazilian writer Jorge Amado. It seems logical that someone named Crioulo should serve as Mulato's confidant and accomplice in the planning of heinous crimes against the people of Ilha-sem-nome. What might be questioned is Romano's ultimate purpose in depicting characters who, according to their names, are abstractions or allegorical symbols. Perhaps he intends irony and caricature, since Mulato, presumably a mulatto, offers some nineteenth-century racist attitudes when he tells Crioulo that the islanders are a degenerate people who originated on the coast of Africa and who have vices and diseases that give them no right to go on existing.

Ironic symbolism in names continues with the introduction of the priest Santo who excommunicates, en masse, a crowd that listens to Zula, a black student bent on convincing his fellow islanders that hell exists on earth. The cleric chides the crowd for heeding the words of a black man who after having benefited by the white man's education, turns his back on him and blasphemes against God. In a similar far-fetched episode Romano satirizes religious hypocrisy in a scene worthy of a picaresque novel. On a public square a priest delivers a sermon in honor of the birth of a wealthy family's child. During the eulogy a raven passes overhead and deposits his droppings in the priest's declaiming mouth.

Zula, the black student, apparently lost his mind while studying in Portugal. Back on Ilha-sem-nome he appears regularly in public to evoke Africa in fiery speeches, and the author seems to relate Zula's insanity to his prophetic role in the novel. Toward the novel's end Zula delivers an African manifesto. He says in part: "On the plains, the deserts, in the heart of your forests, generate that spark that will unite us and our dreams into one, we who are Africans and bearers of a message that time now brings. Compose, to the glory of this dream, a song replete with the stories of your sorrow. Compose, on behalf of human freedom, a hymn of union, a hymn impregnated with love and justice."[12] Despite the assertion that Cape Verdeans are Africans, Romano mitigates the négritude and revolutionary effects of both Zula's and Campina's declarations by having them evoke a pitiable, downtrodden Africa or mouth commonplaces such as "man should make no distinctions on the basis of race, color, or nationality." Although an admirable ideal, such platitudes tend to turn the characters into allegorical puppets rather than enforce their status as didactic symbols.

Remembering, however, the author's statement that the book's equilibrium derives from the natural disunity of its tableaux, the reader receives a comprehensive and uniquely iconoclastic vision of Cape Verdean reality. Some of the episodes are interpolated stories illustrative of the islands' endemic problems. The story of Rosenda, with its admixture of African exoticism, deals with the problems of prostitution and smuggling. Rosenda, after a brief try at prostitution on the Ilha-da-cidade (Island-of-the-City), returns to Ilha-sem-nome where she meets a man who takes her as his companion. Just as more conventional writers do, Romano treats the subject of precarious paramarital unions in Cape Verde when Rosenda's companion goes to jail for smuggling. Need drives Rosenda back to her original profession. She falls ill and consults a black "medicine man" who cures her with potions. Soon after, she discovers that she is pregnant, and the witch doctor assures her that it is the work of a potion from Africa. He asserts that the child will be the incarnation of the force of Africa. When violent labor begins, Rosenda runs in panic toward the witch doctor's shack but she faints on a lonely path only to have the newborn baby devoured by a pack of roaming dogs. Students of Brazilian literature will recall a similar scene in Graça Aranha's novel *Canãa* (Chanaan, 1902) where wild pigs devour an infant. Aranha's purpose was to illustrate the barbarism and danger of life in the New World. Romano may have had an analogous purpose, but he also seems to have unwarranted shock appeal in mind or perhaps, following the line of the baby's predicted destiny, he suggests that an African force reborn has been cut down at its inception.

In another interpolated story an old woman tells the tale of Miguelinho, an avaricious plantation owner. During the days of slavery the plantation's original owner, Ninho, made a habit of sleeping with young black girls, much to the dismay of his wife, Mãe-Dona, who generally took revenge on the girls by submitting them to harassment and even torture. When Ninho discovers that a particularly attractive girl has gotten pregnant before he has had a chance to deflower her, he orders that the slave responsible for the deed be castrated. Incensed by this cruel punishment, an octogenarian slave woman, Mãe-Preta, brings down a terrible curse on the plantation owner, his family, and his heirs. Ninho promptly contracts leprosy and dies; his wife falls into a vat of sugarcane syrup and drowns; the couple's ne'er-do-well son marries an anemic foreigner, and the two male offspring of this union perish in a shipwreck. The only survivor is Miguelinho, Ninho's illegitimate son by a slave woman, who inherits the plantation but whose obsession with money drives him insane when his buried treasure is uncovered by thieves. This story has an absurd grotesqueness in its emphasis on a human ugliness that becomes nearly humorous in its extravagance. The story's operatic bizarreness and its portrayal of master-slave relations reflect the Northeast plantation society that sociologist Gilberto Freyre describes in his study *Casa grande e senzala* (1933; translated into English as *The Masters and the Slaves*, 1946).

Romano also deals with the motif of the "faraway land" in his novel. The chapters entitled "Os contratados" (The Contract Workers), "Circo" (Cycle), and "Navio negreiro" (Slave Ship) continue his extravagant picture of Cape Verdean reality. Aboard the modern slave ship the crew members express their disdain for their black cargo, and the contract workers themselves voice their fear and distrust of the Africans—that Cabinda race. One worker declares that he dislikes *gente-gentio* (heathen people), and he recites some lines from Cape Verdean folk poetry: "Cavalinho de perna quebrada/que leva gente para Terra-Longe/Terra-Longe tem gente-gentio" (p. 273) (Pony with the broken leg/that carries people to the Faraway Land/Faraway Land has heathen folk). Frantz Fanon's statement on the attitudes of Antillean blacks toward Africans from Senegal offers some insight into the Cape Verdean's dilemma: "I have known, and I still know, Antilles Negroes who are annoyed when they are suspected of being Senegalese. This is because the Antilles Negro is more 'civilized' than the African, that is, he is closer to the white man . . ."[13] And Onésimo Silveira, in his short story "Destino de Bia de Rosa" (Bia de Rosa's Fate), set on the island of São Tomé, captures the feeling of Cape Verdean superiority toward the African in the words of a contract worker whose common-law wife has left him for a Mozambican "native": "If I had money to satisfy Bia's whims she would never have left me, because I know she prefers me to that liver-lip, black 'Moçambique.'"[14] The author of *Famintos* goes even further when one of his characters tells a fellow Cape Verdean that the African is a different kind of person: he goes about in a wild state wearing a red loincloth, and he can withstand rain, sun, mosquitoes, and all sorts of things without ill effects. The Cape Verdean puts the finishing touches on his stereotype when he declares that the African's greatest defect is his laziness (p. 281). Romano exceeds Silveira's portrayal down to the detail of the red loincloth which, in its imagistic flamboyancy, is consistent with the novel's exaggerations.

Compatible with what seems to be the novel's planned disunity is its incongruous criticism of camera-toting tourists in search of the exotic. Perhaps Romano, in his desire to pack as much as possible into his work, wanted to follow up Manuel Lopes's remarks on foreigners in search of African mystery on the Island of São Vicente (see p. 239). Undoubtedly, this curious novel becomes both clearer and more curious still if we consider that Romano makes use of the same motifs, themes, and spirit of Cape Verdeanness cultivated by more serene writers. Manuel Lopes employs Gothic and naturalistic elements in his *Flagelados do vento leste*; Romano exceeds these effects in his descriptions, and, rather than fatalism and social awareness, *Famintos*'s tone is one of socialist realist optimism and revolutionary fervor tempered by a benign spirit of brotherhood. If Manuel Lopes's character Mané Quim and Baltasar Lopes's Chiquinho anguish over whether to stay or depart, Romano's characters deliver diatribes or high-flown speeches on Africanness and antievasion. Aesthetically and structurally *Famintos* is a phantasmagoria of images and episodes that give a different and vivid perspective to the usual elements of Cape Verdean narrative.

In the realm of the different or the experimental, Romano has written a bilingual story entitled *Negrume* (1973) in Portuguese and *Lzimparin* in creole. Both words can be translated as "dusk." Perhaps Romano's own words best characterize the work: "*Negrume* is a sentimental contribution, maybe an isolated case. But there had to be a beginning."[15] Romano foresees other novels and short stories in the language of the archipelago; whether his prediction is right or wrong he himself has taken a bold step in an attempt to affirm Cape Verdean creole as a literary language, and more importantly, as a language of prose fiction.

Romano dedicates *Negrume* to Manuel Ferreira "a 'Portuguese from Lisbon,' my brother who more than anyone has discovered our *amorabilidade* [affability]." Ferreira is probably the most authentic and talented of a number of creolephiles, including the Portuguese José Osório de Oliveira who can be credited with having discovered the poet Eugénio Tavares. Ferreira can be credited with the more creative success of combining Portuguese and creole, and it is with the Cape Verdean stories of that "Portuguese from Lisbon" that we concern ourselves now.

Manuel Ferreira and an Outsider's Perspective from Within

"Much of what I have written deals with Cape Verde. There I lived the intense years of my youth . . ."[16] Manuel Ferreira, who is married to the gracious Cape Verdean Dona Orlanda, spoke these words in a 1961 magazine interview, and the intensity of his feelings for and knowledge of Cape Verde assure his inclusion in any serious discussion of modern literary activity on the archipelago. His active participation in the *Certeza* group and his own talent as a novelist and short story writer have further established him as a legitimate contributor to the major thrust of Cape Verdean self-awareness. However, although I include a discussion of Ferreira's works in my appraisal of Cape Verde's cultural and literary phenomenon, I do not so much consider him a Cape Verdean writer as I do a writer who brings an important perspective to a young literature. Precisely because he does come from another experience Manuel Ferreira puts Cape Verdeanness into a clear, if occasionally romanticized, perspective.

While the members of the *Claridade* and *Certeza* groups were emerging from under a mantle of strictly European cultural imperialism to proclaim their more Western than African regionalism, Manuel Ferreira was in the process of penetrating a reality largely unknown to the Portuguese intellectuals of his generation. When he arrived on the Island of São Vicente in 1941 he met with Cape Verdean writers and intellectuals on a level of mutual discovery; both he and they were discovering a rich cultural reality, an ethos, and a subject matter that would form the basis of an autonomous literature. The already mentioned *Aventura crioula* as well as his numerous articles and essays published in journals, newspapers, and symposia proceedings attest to his fundamental desire to explain and defend Cape Verde as a sui generis case of Afro-European acculturation. In countering the categorization of Cape Verde as an essentially African culture, a view held most notably by Gilberto Freyre, Ferreira has occasionally overstated his argument for the archipelago as a sterling example of a culture more European than African. But as a critic who writes on the entire Afro-Portuguese literary scene Ferreira has somewhat modified his attitudes and brought them more into line with recent theories on Africa, such as those put forth by Janheinz Jahn. And this modification has meant a new twist in his treatment of Cape Verdeanness as seen in his most recent novel, which will be the main concern of this section.

First, however, we should look briefly at Ferreira's development as a writer who cultivates Cape Verdean themes. Ferreira initiated his Cape Verdean phase in 1948 with *Morna*, a collection of short stories; ten years later he published a similar collection entitled *Morabeza*. He rewrote the stories for the 1967 edition of *Morna* and completely revised and expanded the second edition of *Morabeza* in 1968. In 1972 he combined the stories from the two collections into one volume entitled *Terra trazida* (The Land Brought in Me). At this point two observations should be made: Ferreira's habit of constantly revising his stories contrasts with that of Cape Verdean writers like Baltasar Lopes and Manuel Lopes who composed their works with a sense of unrevisable spontaneity and at most had their books reissued when the first printing was sold out; secondly, Ferreira's choice of a less romantically creole title for his 1972 edition of stories perhaps indicates a toning down of his fascination with the labels of Cape Verdeanness. Significantly, then, Ferreira reveals a concern for artistic perfection and he emphasizes his perspective as an outsider who brings a sense of Cape Verdeanness within him.

Several of Ferreira's short stories qualify as small masterpieces in their portrayal of Cape Verdean types. He successfully delineates a certain roguish character who, although slightly marginal, displays some common Cape Verdean values such as the ability to survive by his wits in a society that is miserly in its economic opportunities but compellingly poetic in its sensuous tropicality. In his novel *Hora di bai* (The Time to Depart, 1962) Ferreira brings together a number of the illustrative types found in his short stories. Many of these characters turn out to be personifications of aspects of the Cape Verdean ethos or caricatures of certain attitudes fostered in an acculturated society. Venância, one of the principal characters of *Hora di bai*, personifies *morabeza*, Chico Afonso is a guitar-playing, *morna*-singing embodiment of Cape Verde's free spirit, and the poet Jacinto Moreno appears as the islands' inherent lyricism. Other "flat" or only slightly rounded characters play illustrative roles in the novel's plot and subplots. In the realm of caricature Juca Florêncio, a black administrator, is pedantic and ostentatiously Lusitanian in his patriotism. His pompously European values and rhetoric constitute a satirical comment on the process of over-acculturation on the archipelago, although in view of Ferreira's general treatment of a creole ideal it must be concluded that his intents in depicting the exaggeratedly Europeanized black Cape Verdean do not encompass a criticism of a denial of African heritage. Ferreira does intend, in line with his idealization of Cape Verde's lack of distinctions based on color, to isolate race prejudice as anachronistic in the creole society. Thus he creates in the lawyer França Gil a character who, jealously proud of his Aryan lineage, stands apart from his creole surroundings.

A host of major and minor characters engage in actions that involve plots and subplots centered on love intrigues, adultery, crimes of passion, political schemes, and the misery and hardships of the masses set against the usual themes of drought, the call of the sea, and evasion. Ferreira, in dealing with these themes and motifs, offers a sort of institutionalized nostalgia, but he also demonstrates his ability to create fictional situations with irony, satire, and a sensitivity to the revealing detail in episodes, physical characteristics, and speech patterns. Primarily, Ferreira has shown that he is a teller of tales who has a talent for approaching almost mawkish sentimentality and then saving the situation with outrageous humor or by a well-timed change in narrative tone.

In several respects Ferreira's most recent and most important novel, *Voz de Prisão* (Under Arrest, 1971), contrasts radically with his previous works of fiction. The differences are technical, stylistic, and attitudinal. Told in one breath, with no chapters or other divisions, the story has changing and interchanging narrative points of view. Stylistically it is a linguistic tour de force that combines standard Portuguese and creole to effect a synthetic language, but one that captures a Cape Verdean essence without requiring the reader to share in the intricacies of the archipelago's popular speech. The tension of standard Portuguese juxtaposed with creole, often in the same phrase, accompanies the novel's structural tension which pits the Cape Verdean against himself, in terms of the islands' perennial problems, and against the rest of the world because of Cape Verde's mythology. Structurally the novel can be seen as a series of narrative lines and circles. A linear movement from Cape Verde to Lisbon represents the principal character's emigration from São Vicente to Portugal, but her eventual return to the islands is circular. From Cape Verde lines radiate out in many directions, to Europe, America, Angola, India, even

Timor, to all the places that have attracted Cape Verdeans. From Lisbon, in the stories and reminiscences of Joja, a sexagenarian Cape Verdean woman, lines extend to the same places. Along these lines, or at the point of their origin or at the point where they end, Ferreira, without abandoning a romanticized view of Cape Verdeanness, confronts the islander with a fundamental philosophical problem that can be simply stated as the conflict between the total concept of creole acculturation and the racial and political attitudes of the rest of the world.

Joja is a loquacious, generous, affable creole woman, but unlike the characters in Ferreira's earlier fiction she illustrates more than just one form or essence of Cape Verdeanness. In all her *morabeza* she symbolizes the old order in conflict with itself and at odds with a new generation of Cape Verdeans. The cultural and social mythology of a small ambient expands in Ferreira's novel as Cape Verdean types gain a different perspective on their reality. The outgoing Joja represents, then, a conservative force of culturally and racially *mestiço* Cape Verde. She brings with her to Lisbon a black youth, Vítor, whose apprehensions in Portugal give the novel a point of departure for the question of race as it concerns Cape Verde and the world at large. When Vítor becomes the target of racial slurs in Lisbon, he denies self and harbors the hope that he will some day get possession of a miraculous bleaching preparation from America. Joja laments her ward's difficulties and extols Cape Verde's absence of color consciousness. The idea of Cape Verde as an evolving utopia of racial and cultural harmony reaches the level of controversy in several of the novel's passages. A pivotal narrator, who remains nameless, but who perhaps reflects the author's attitudes, goes in his thoughts from Vítor's specific problem to a debate among Cape Verdean university students in Lisbon. After the usual declarations of cultural symbiosis, a voice speaks out echoing the sentiments of an Onésimo Silveira: "we have denied our African roots and they are fundamental for a harmonious development of our people."[17] What the author implies is that traditional Cape Verdean attitudes have been thrown into confusion by newly emerged black ideologies, African independence, black nationalism, and anti-colonialism, to say nothing of the rising sentiment of pan-Africanism among widely separated intellectuals of African origin. The autobiographical narrator thus finds himself musing on the theories of such contemporary figures as Fanon, Sartre, Cleaver, King, and Carmichael.

For the anonymous narrator and the small circle of Cape Verdeans who gravitate toward Joja to listen to her stories and reminiscences, the creole woman represents a Cape Verdean timelessness that softens the harsh realities of racism and perhaps of the cataclysmic changes that threaten the archipelago. Joja on a homey, folk level and the nameless narrator on an exalted, almost ideological level bring the idea of Cape Verdean ethos into recurring conflict with the ideas of a new order.

From the central setting of Lisbon a line travels to Angola, a promised land for Cape Verdeans from the "stepmother" islands. In Luanda the engineer Vaz, the epitome of the fun-loving roguish type, displays his picaresque audacity in denying his own fair skin and Caucasoid features and declaring that he and his fellow Cape Verdeans, regardless of color, are all black Africans. This link between a traditional type and the precepts of the new order of Cape Verdean ethnic awareness receives impetus from the younger emigrants from the islands. Back in Lisbon some Cape Verdean students appear at one of Joja's gatherings, and she notes disapprovingly that one of the girls no longer straightens her hair. A student fervently explains to his older compatriots that the young generation is fighting imitation and seeking an African aesthetic. A mixture of black pride and regional identity compel the young generation to adopt a new set of cultural values. The basic tension between the new ideals and the traditional ethos reveals itself in Joja's reaffirmation of the Cape Verdean's ability to mitigate racial animosities even while taking a radical stance, and in her reaffirmation she pays tribute to the broader attitude of less exacerbated racial strife within the Portuguese space.

By means of a zigzag course that shifts from narrative line to narrative line within the circular motion of traditional Cape Verdean values, Ferreira defines and refines Cape Verdeanness through the presentation of colorful, but more profoundly delineated and didactically symbolic characters than those of his earlier stories involved in quasi-picaresque, rebellious situations. Following the typical itinerary of the wealthy Cape Verdean, the widowed Joja came to Lisbon to marry off her two daughters and to see her son graduate from medical school. But her fondest wish is to return to Mindelo to live out her days in tranquillity, and as she awaits that moment her timeless, unchanging Cape Verdeanness flows about in a broad space that encompasses and enhances the interpolated narratives that form part of the stories told during intimate gatherings in Lisbon. The tale of one Pedro Duarte Ribeiro, better known as Pidrim, has an important bearing on the revelation of a Cape Verdean personality as it exists for Joja and the others who contribute to the telling of the incidents. It begins in Cape Verde with the A.W.O.L. Pidrim confronting and finally stabbing his despotic commanding officer. After being sentenced and imprisoned Pidrim is turned loose to roam the world. He disappears and then shows up as the hero who has saved lives during a shipwreck. His sense of honor as a Cape Verdean, a special breed of people, comes to the fore when in Bombay a doorman refuses him admittance to a restaurant because he is black. A Cape Verdean in conflict with himself and with a world insensitive to the Cape Verdean ethos, Pidrim points to the color of his skin and to the texture of his hair. He is not black, and by virtue of being a Cape Verdean he is a Portuguese as far as the rest of the world is concerned. Pidrim is a complex illustrative type, strangely out of step with the new order but a reaffirmation of the myths of Cape Verdeanness in his individuality, rebelliousness, audacity, courage, and wanderlust. He is a rogue and a lover, an elusive spirit who seems to be in many places at the same time. He turns up in Luanda, a financial success and an admired figure in the Cape Verdean colony of successful people. Then, in Angola, he dies in a bizarre hunting accident, a fitting end wrapped in mystery and speculation for that embodiment of the Cape Verdean psyche in all its contradictions.

Joja attributes Pidrim's desperate criminal act, his violent nature, and his rebelliousness to an evil spirit that has taken possession of him. In her timeless idealism Joja yields to spiritualism as a means of circumventing the evil in a lopsided world that works against her visceral level of affability. But the anonymous narrator dominates the last few pages of the novel as a prophetic voice tinged with tragedy and romanticism, although orchestrated with a reassertion of Cape Verdeanness—orchestrated in the sense that his words reach a crescendo of creolized musicality in sound and rhythm. He uses an accumulation of adjectives in his apostrophic monologue, telling Joja that her people are "outgoing, ostentatious, merrymaking, impertinent, iconoclastic, outspoken, fiery, garrulous, loud, defiant . . ." (p. 139), and the creole mixed with Portuguese serves as a cry of caution to the old order. For the now abstract narrator tells Joja that some men will enter her home and while she stands there in speechless shock they will take her letters and papers and then will place her under arrest.

This strange ending reflects the muted protest inherent in some contemporary Portuguese prose fiction. Dissatisfaction and restlessness find an outlet in cryptic symbolism in the works of such Portuguese novelists as José Cardoso Pires, particularly in his *O delfim* (The Dolphin, 1968). Some Portuguese write obliquely about the social and political conditions of their country. Manuel Ferreira's position between Third World upheaval and a Luso-tropicalist mythology in a "discontinuous space" may best account for his fictionalized synthesis of Cape Verdeanness in conflict.

Moreover, the extravagance and chaos in form of Ferreira's *Voz de prisão*, and to a lesser extent of Virgínio's *Vida crioula* and Romano's *Famintos*, follow the lines of social disruption in the Portuguese space. Indeed, starting with the Gothic elements of Manuel Lopes's *Flagelados do vento leste* and the magic, static world of Caleijão in Baltasar Lopes's *Chiquinho*, we see the beginnings in Cape Verdean narrative of a refutation of Luso-Brazilian neorealist empiricism. The mythic and symbolic qualities of these novels clash with the objective, positivistic reality inherent in much of Portuguese-language prose fiction. Thus a dialectic exists in the form of Romano's and especially of Ferreira's novels; both works seek a synthesis of Cape Verdeanness and both offer unique models for a somewhat dormant Cape Verdean literature in a Portuguese-speaking world on the brink of a political and social upheaval destined to destroy traditional patterns of Luso-tropicalist ideology.

With *Voz de prisão* Ferreira establishes himself as a Portuguese writer of artistic maturity who has taken up the fallen banner of a committed Cape Verdean literature.

CHAPTER 15

The Case of Portuguese Guinea (Guinea-Bissau)

Most commentators on Afro-Portuguese literature prefer to pass over Guinea. Although there may be little to comment on, even the quantitative absence of a viable literary expression in Portuguese makes the conditions responsible for this situation worthy of consideration within the total phenomenon of creative writing in the five areas. But because of the lack of anything approaching the regionalist thrust of Angola, Mozambique, and Cape Verde, my discussion must be limited to some brief introductory observations and a necessarily short evaluation of that which can be categorized as Afro-Portuguese literature in Guinea.

One justification for including this short chapter in the section dealing with Cape Verde is that until the nineteenth century the tiny territory of Portuguese Guinea (13,948 square miles, or less than half the size of Portugal), situated on the west coast of Africa between Senegal and the Republic of Guinea, belonged to the colonial administration of the archipelago. Cape Verdean creole became the basis for a coastal lingua franca, and many minor government officials and civil servants in Guinea have traditionally come from the islands' *mestiço* elite. As early as 1594 a mulatto sea captain from the Island of Santiago wrote a now classic chronicle on Guinea entitled *Tratado breve dos rios de Guiné do Cabo Verde* (Brief Treatise on the Rivers of Cape Verde Guinea).[1] Of a total population of about 520,000, including fewer than 2000 Europeans, less than 2 percent are classified as "civilized," meaning, among other things, able to read and write Portuguese. Although the Portuguese began their five centuries on the African continent about 1445 when Nuno Tristão sailed from the mouth of the Senegal River to Guinea, their presence in that territory has always been precarious. This fact, along with the ethnic diversity of the area, has contributed to a lack of regional unity. Several ethnic groups, including the Balanta, Manjaco, Papel, and particularly the Fula (Fulani) and Mandinka, do have a rich oral, and in some cases Arabic, tradition. Both written Arabic and oral literature, as such, fall outside the scope of this study, and as I have done with the other areas of Portuguese Africa I deal with the nonliterate tradition only to the extent that it influences the printed word.

The Literature of Portuguese Guinea

Ethnologists or just ordinary Europeans have made attempts at collecting, translating, and recording the stories, fables, and poetry of the diverse ethnic groups of Portuguese Guinea. The *Boletim cultural da Guiné Portuguesa* (Cultural Bulletin of Portuguese Guinea) has carried in its issues or has independently published samples of African oral literature translated into Portuguese. One collection, *Contos bijagós* (Bijago Stories, 1955), was compiled by João Eleutério Conduto, and another Portuguese, Manuel Belchior, has published two works that include essays and samples of Guinean oral literature: *Grandeza africana: Lendas da Guiné Portuguesa* (African Grandeur: Legends of Portuguese Guinea, 1963) and *Contos mandingas* (Mandinka Stories, 1968). Alexandre Barbosa has attained some modest success in Portugal with his *Guinéus* (Guineans, 1962) which contains chronicles and fictionalized adaptations of African legends. Barbosa's book falls somewhere between scientifically collected, authentic oral literature and the writing that for the most part fits into the category of colonial literature.

The novelist Fausto Duarte, a Cape Verdean by birth, stands out as one of the most prolific writers of colonial literature in Portuguese Africa. His 1934 *Auá: Novela negra* (Black Novella) initiated his writing career that included the publication of four more novels and a book of memoirs. In spite of being burdened with many of the misconceptions of the colonialist mentality, and although a mediocre writer, Duarte gives a sympathetic and less ethnocentric picture of Africa than might be expected of an author whose works have become dated as reminders of a past era. Duarte's efforts have appeared in various anthologies and because of his knowledge of Fulani culture his novels are more than the usual colonialist fare. We acknowledge his importance while passing lightly over him as a second-rate writer.

As for poetry little of note has been written either by metropolitan Portuguese or by Cape Verdeans living in Guinea. One Portuguese, Fernanda de Castro, besides one novel and two children's stories, wrote a book-length poem entitled "África raiz" (Africa Roots, 1966) which depicts Africa from a jaded point of view. Castro's poem exploits tropicalism and secular suffering as she evokes the dark continent with its wild beasts, faithful mammies singing to European children, and, of course, the mystery of African nights. With a *tantam* drum roll the poet yields to erotic fantasies of a nubile maiden running naked through the coconut palms pursued by a black man metamorphosed into a magnificent buck. The poem's last two lines sing of Africa the stepmother and Africa the mother, which neatly sum up Castro's maternalistic attitude toward and her exotic feminization of Africa.

In his 1958 anthology of black poetry of Portuguese expression Mário de Andrade includes in the section on Guinea one poem by the Cape Verdean Terêncio Anahory, and João Alves das Neves does likewise in his *Poetas e contistas africanos* (African Poets and Short Story Writers, 1963). Anahory went to Guinea at an early age, but his poetry remains purely Cape Verdean. Alves das Neves's anthology also contains a poem by a black Guinean, António Baticã Ferreira, about whom very little is known except that he is the son of a chief and that he studied medicine in Switzerland. Baticã's "Infância" (Childhood) deviates somewhat from the usual poetic invocations of bygone days. His poem re-creates a rural, almost pastoral setting in contrast to the urban locale of much Angolan or Mozambican poetry. He strives for a rhythmic flow and imagistic sequence simulating West African oral poetry:

> Eu corria através dos bosques e das florestas
> E, como o ruído vibrante de um bosque desvendado,
> Eu via belos pássaros voando pelos campos
> E parecia ser levado por seus cantos.
>
> Sùbitamente, desviei os meus olhos
> Para o alto mar e para os grandes celeiros
> Cheios da colheita dos bravos camponeses
> Que, terminando o dia, regressavam à noite entoando
> Canções tradicionais das selvas africanas
> Que lhes lembravam os ódios ardentes
> Dos velhos. Sùbitamente, uma corça gritou
> Fugindo na frente dos leões esfomeados
>
> Aos saltos, os leões perseguiram a corça
> Derrubando lianas e afugentando os pássaros.
> A desgraçada atingiu a planície
> E os dois reis breve a alcançaram.[2]

(Through the forests and woods I ran/And, like the vibrating sound of a woods revealed,/I saw the beautiful birds flying over fields/And I seemed to be carried along by their song.//Abruptly I turned my eyes/toward the high sea and toward the great granaries/Filled with the harvest of those sturdy peasants/Who at day's end returned at night chanting/traditional songs of the African jungles/That recalled the burning hatreds/of their ancestors. Suddenly, a doe cried out/Fleeing before two famished lions//With great leaps the lions pursued the doe/Pulling down lianas and scattering birds./The ill-fated one reached the plain/And the two kings were soon upon her.)

The poem has a chanting rhythm and an oneiric, almost surrealistic quality despite the vivid realism of its disparate images. Its running movement gives the European pastoral lyricism a dynamism in which the idealization of peasants (hardly a term consistent with tribal socioeconomic structure) and the glorification of the lions seem part of a hymn to the land.

This rather strange poem is the only one Baticã has published as far as I know, and it can safely be stated that an Afro-Portuguese literature has yet to be initiated in Guinea.

PART FOUR

SÃO TOMÉ AND PRÍNCIPE

CHAPTER 16

Two Plantation Islands in the Gulf of Guinea

Historians estimate 1471 to be the year that the Portuguese first reached the two small, uninhabited islands of São Tomé and Príncipe located in the Gulf of Guinea. Príncipe, the smaller of the two equatorial islands, has paralleled and depended on the development of the more important São Tomé. Settlement of the latter began some fifteen years after the arrival of the first Europeans, and by 1554 the population consisted of Portuguese from the metropolis and Madeira, the descendants of 2000 Portuguese Jewish children who had been sent to the island in 1492 to be Christianized, a number of Spaniards and Genovese, and, naturally, African slaves.

With the early cultivation of sugarcane on the islands, the Portuguese imported slaves in large numbers, and as a result of unions between white males and black females a significant, if not sizable, *mestiço* class was formed. This creole population was pretty much left to itself during the seventeenth and eighteenth centuries after the decline of the sugarcane economy. Coffee and later cacao, introduced early in the nineteenth century, brought a new prosperity to the islands. A decline in the slave trade coincided with this period, and when abolition came about in 1869 a

365

labor crisis ensued. By 1876 mainland Africans, the first wave from Angola, were again brought to São Tomé in great numbers, but this time they came as contract laborers. The modern era of the *serviçal* had begun with all its abuses and drama for thousands of people from Angola, Mozambique, and Cape Verde.

With economic changeovers—the decline of sugar and the rise of coffee and cacao—came a stabilization of the islands' population, which in São Tomé reached about 60,000 in 1950, and a definitive social stratification. The term *filho da terra*, which corresponds more or less to *crioulo* as used in Cape Verde, describes the generally *mestiço* descendants of early settlers and slaves. Many *filhos da terra* are of old island families and constitute a kind of aristocracy, which is frequently in a state of economic decadence. The geographer Francisco José Tenreiro, in his treatment of the subject of social groupings in São Tomé, explains the contrasting sociological significance of the terms *filhos da terra*, *Tongas*, and *forros*.[1] In its broadest usage *Tonga* applies to anyone native to São Tomé, be he African or European, rich or poor. Originally, and in a stricter sense, the denomination refers to slaves and the offspring of the contracted laborer born on the plantation. *Forro* means literally "freed" in Portuguese and quite naturally identifies emancipated slaves and their descendants. Among the plantation workers the *Tongas* form a small elite; the *forros* (known in Príncipe as *moncós*), on the other hand, generally have shunned agricultural toil because of its relationship to the servitude of their forebears, and to a large extent they have joined the ranks of the *filhos da terra*. Tenreiro points out that at present *forro* can designate any black person or *mestiço* born on the island (pp. 189–190). Rounding out the population are first the more or less transitory contracted laborers, then the *angolares* who descend from the slave survivors of a sixteenth-century shipwreck, and finally a white landholding, administrative elite.

An African and Creole Society

Of São Tomé's 43,391 "civilized" people, 1152 are white, 1 oriental, 9 East Indian, 4279 *mestiço*, and 37,950 black; of the 16,768 officially classified as uncivilized, 21 are *mestiço* and 16,747 black.[2] According to data collected in 1957, more than 18,000 of the total population consisted of contracted laborers who formed several subcultures depending on their African provenience.

Unlike Cape Verde, the creolized element of São Tomé and Príncipe does not permeate all levels of society. Even the creole speech called *forro*, once widely spoken on both islands, has tended to die out. Still, because of the historical importance of the *filho da terra* class and a certain European influence, acculturation continues to take place on the islands. One of the results of this acculturation is the popular Santomense *sòcòpé*, a dance which Tenreiro calls the product of the fusion of races (p. 188). It would seem, however, that among the imposed European institutions and the acculturated forms there exist many pure or nearly pure African survivals in part because of the presence of the *angolares* who have maintained a modified African culture and principally because of the continuing contacts, until quite recently, with Africa through the contracted workers from Angola and Mozambique. Thus, São Tomé and Príncipe have two cultures, one creole and the other purely African, existing side by side and no doubt influencing one another.

Oral Literature and the Writings of Fernando Reis

Several collections of oral literature, mainly from São Tomé and edited in most cases by metropolitan Portuguese, have appeared over the years. The Portuguese Fernando Reis has compiled Santomense popular verse, riddles, and sayings. Typically, he gives the collection an aura of Lusotropicalist glorification when, for example, he describes one of his informants as that "excellent man whose bronzed skin attests to the Lusitanian presence in his blood, perhaps inherited from some Portuguese poet who went to the island on the wings and dreams of adventure and who there surrendered to the charms of some beautiful creole girl."[3] Despite his impressionistic editorializing, his samplings of poetry in the *forro* language have ethnographic value as do the fables that feature the astute West African tortoise. As is true in all the Portuguese overseas territories, there has been an increase in scientific and scholarly works on São Tomé and Príncipe during the last decade, but much remains to be researched in the literature and folklore of the two islands.

To date only metropolitan Portuguese, white islanders, and Cape Verdeans (notably, Onésimo Silveira), all very few in number, have written works of fiction that delve into the social and cultural conditions of plantation life. Fernando Reis has been relatively prolific in his literary production, having written several books of fiction, a sociological essay, and the collection and study of oral literature mentioned above. He has lived nearly twenty-five years in São Tomé, but, despite his firsthand knowledge of and sympathy toward the people and their culture, romanticism and a colonial mentality have distorted his fictional view into something akin to the nineteenth-century Indianist novel of Latin America. *Roça* (Plantation, 1960), Reis's most ambitious work, has gone through three editions, which would seem to indicate that it has aroused the curiosity of a significant number of Portuguese readers. From the novel's beginning to its happy ending, the author treats the "native" element with paternalistic sympathy. *Roça*'s chronological narrative involves intrigues and conflicts, exploitation and demonstrations of tolerance and brotherly love on the part of certain white administrators. In the final analysis, however, *Roça* and Reis's latest collection, *Histórias da roça* (Plantation Stories, 1970), display ethnocentric attitudes replete with paternalism and exoticism.

The writing that can be called the literature of São Tomé and Príncipe has come from a very small nucleus of *filhos da terra*, and I shall deal with this group in the next chapter.

CHAPTER 17

Filhos da Terra
at Home and Abroad

The few literary works by this small nucleus of *filhos da terra* display, in several cases, a preoccupation with the reaction of the transplanted "man-of-color" to his European environment. Even those whose writings do use island settings and themes show a concern with racial definitions arising from economic and social distinctions. Neither a development of plantation themes nor intimist, lyrical portraits of island institutions and landscapes, in poetry and prose, has reached the level of a cohesive, regionalist projection as is the case of Cape Verde. The reasons for this are apparent: a historical development (including absentee ownership of plantations) dissimilar from that of Cape Verde resulted in the absence of the early establishment of secondary schools and the lack of a literary climate complete with journals, polemics, and a sense of unified purpose. Generally speaking, the São Tomé and Príncipe elites developed their cultural awareness independently of one another—usually in Portugal. Paradoxically, São Tomé's economic importance as a source of agricultural products meant prosperity for a privileged few, but discouraged any sort of cultural and intellectual homogeneity. Because of this lack of focus we cannot talk about a São Tomé and Príncipe ethos. What we

369

can identify are certain recurring patterns in the poetry and prose of the *filhos da terra*.

Humanist Solidarity and an
Incipient Voice of Militancy

There are only six São Tomé and Príncipe poets of some merit, one being Alda do Espírito Santo who has attracted attention with her much anthologized poem, "Onde estão os homens caçados neste vento de loucura?" (Where Are the Men Hunted on This Wind of Madness?) Inspired by the 1953 police massacre of an alleged one thousand Santomense workers who were protesting labor conditions, she portrays the ferocity of the incident, known as the War of Bateba, with powerful images, such as the contrast of the crimson blood on the Ilha Verde (literally, the Green Island). Espírito Santo no doubt irked the authorities when she spoke of voices clamoring for vengeance. But as the poem's final lines demonstrate her militancy is more predicated on humanistic idealism than on ideological combativeness:

> E' a chama da humanidade
> cantando a esperança
> num mundo sem peias
> onde a liberdade
> é a pátria dos homens . . .[1]

(It is the flame of humanity/singing of hope/in a world without shackles/where freedom/is the homeland of men . . .)

The mixed metaphor of the flame singing of hope includes images that are inconsistent with the dynamism suggested in the poem's title and, indeed, present in some of the earlier stanzas.

Alda do Espírito Santo, who was born on São Tomé in 1926, displays in much of her poetry a closeness to the everyday events of island life and she seems to pledge a common cause with the people. She sings of women washing clothes in a stream in "Lá no Água Grande" (There in Água Grande), and her verses often express what amounts to a proprietorial attitude toward the locales she illustrates: she talks of her bay, her land, this African land. The poet sees her island as a microcosm from which she reaches out to include all humanity in what she calls a universal tune in "Em torno da minha baía" (Around My Bay). In spite of an idealistic, sometimes rhetorical tone, Espírito Santo more often than not displays a natural talent for spontaneously conceived images. In "Descendo o meu bairro" (Strolling through My Neighborhood) she records the routine activities of her people, saying, "eu vou trazer para o palco da vida/pedaços da minha gente" (p. 69) (to the stage of life/I shall bring bits and pieces of my people). In the same poem she uses the adjective *estuante* (seething) twice to describe musical rhythms and once to express the action of rain water; figuratively, life seethes in that minute corner of her island.

Except for two years in Portugal Espírito Santo has lived all her life on São Tomé where she teaches school. Another poet of her generation, Tomás Medeiros (b. 1931), surpassed his fellow Santomense in his cries against the injustices suffered by the people. Medeiros, who has published only a handful of poems, carries his sense of outrage to the point of bitterness and sarcasm, as witnessed in the long poem "Meu canto, Europa" (My Song, Europe):

> Agora,
> agora que me estampaste no rosto
> os primores da tua civilização,
> eu te pergunto, Europa,
> eu te pergunto: AGORA?[2]

(Now,/now that you have stamped my face/with the perfections of your civilization,/I ask you, Europe,/I ask you: NOW WHAT?)

"Meu canto, Europa" is an attack on Western technology and institutions that have been used to reduce the black man to a *tabula rasa* on which Europe can imprint the perfections of its civilization. Medeiros launches another attack on Western institutions in "Poema," this time denying the white man's God and asserting through sardonic, humorless guffaws that his own Bantu deities have survived the onslaught of Christianity:

> Sairei à rua
> com os meus sorrisos maduros
> com todos os meus santos vencidos
> para me rir às gargalhadas
> do Deus morto crucificado.
>
> (p. 77)

(I shall take to the streets/with my mature smile/with all my conquered saints/in order to laugh uproariously/at the dead, crucified God.)

Dressed in mourning white the poet sallies forth on Good Friday to flaunt his own spirituality in the face of what he sees as a degenerative force.

Alda do Espírito Santo and other *filho da terra* writers extol and raise to the level of symbol or regionalist emblem such native things as the *sàfu* fruit and the *sòcòpé* dance. Medeiros, on the other hand, in his "Um sòcòpé para Nicolás Guillén" (A *Sòcòpé* for Nicolás Guillén), impregnates the dance song with social irony:

> Conheces tu
> Nicolás Guillén,
> a ilha do nome santo?
>
> Não? Tu não a conheces?
> A ilha dos cafezais floridos
> e dos cacaueiros balançando
> como mamas de uma mulher virgem?
>
> Bembom, Nicolás Guillén,
> Nicolás Guillén, bembom.
>
> Tu não conheces a ilha mestiça,
> dos filhos sem pais
> que as negras da ilha passeiam na rua?
>
> Tu não conheces a ilha-riqueza
> onde a miséria caminha
> nos passos da gente?

Bembom, Nicolás Guillén,
Nicolás Guillén, bembom.

Oh! vem ver a minha ilha,
vem ver cá de cima,
da nossa Sierra Maestra.

Vem ver com a vontade toda,
na cova da mão cheia.

Aqui não há ianques, Nicolás Guillén,
nem os ritmos sangrentos dos teus canaviais.

Aqui ninguém fala de yes,
nem fuma charuto ou
tabaco estrangeiro.

(Qu'importa, Nicolás Guillén,
Nicolás Guillén, qu'importa?)

Conoces tu
la isla del Golfo?

Bembom, bembom
Nicolás, bembom.
(pp. 78–79)

(Do you,/Nicolás Guillén,/know the island of the saintly name?//
No? You do not know it?/The island of coffee plants in bloom/
and of cacao trees swaying/like a virgin's breasts?//Bembom,
Nicolás Guillén,/Nicolás Guillén, bembom.//You do not know
the *mestiço* island,/of fatherless children/whom black women
walk down island streets?//You do not know the island of
wealth/where misery hounds/the people's footsteps?//Bembom,
Nicolás Guillén,/Nicolás Guillén, bembom.//Oh! come see my
island,/come see from here atop/our Sierra Maestra.//Come see
with all your will,/in the cup of your full hand.//Here there
are no Yankees, Nicolás Guillén,/nor are there the bloody
rhythms of your cane fields.//Here no one says "yes,"/nor smokes
cigars or/foreign tobacco.//(What does it matter, Nicolás Guillén,/ Nicolás Guillén, what does it matter?)//Do you know the
Gulf island?//Bembom, bembom,/Nicolás, bembom.)

Medeiros extends his invitation to the famous Afro-Cuban poet Nicolás Guillén, for their respective islands have similar legacies of poverty and exploitation in a setting of wealth and tropical splendor.

Bembom comes from Guillén's "Negro bembón" (Thick-lipped Negro), the first of eight poems that make up the 1930 series called "Motivos de son" (*Son* Motifs), *son* being an Afro-Cuban song and dance form. In his eight poems Guillén uses the black man and the mulatto as the subject rather than the object of his artistic creation. As a member of the so-called *Negrista* movement Guillén, much in the style of the négritude poets, defies the negative label attached to the black man whose human-ity white society ignores and whose physical being it ridicules. Although obviously inspired by Guillén's *Negrista* protest, Med-eiros was also attracted by his use of African musicality. Just as Guillén simulates the rhythm of the *son*, Medeiros's poem sug-gests the beat of the popular *sòcòpé* dance. And in Portuguese the words *bem bom* can mean "nice" or "quite nice," thus reversing the intended sense of racial epithet contained in the Cuban Span-ish word *bembón*. The São Tomé poet employs the word in such a way that he is able to exploit its several associations and its sound quality. In effect, he weds rhythm and theme for dramatic impact in his poetic invitation of social commiseration.

Besides knowing that Medeiros studied medicine in the Soviet Union we have little information about him. It can safely be assumed, however, that his anger and militancy induced him to leave his native island and to become a member of the obscure Committee for the Liberation of São Tomé and Príncipe. Mário de Andrade reports that Medeiros is preparing a critical essay on the evolution of poetry in São Tomé,[3] but apparently he, like so many other writers of Portuguese Africa, has ceased to pursue his art. As a matter of fact, with only a small number of his poems to evaluate, it is difficult to come to any definitive conclusions on his work. However, his social consciousness can be assessed as another significant element of the Afro-Portuguese mood reflected in creative writing.

The *sòcòpé* motif also appears in the poetry of Maria Manuela Margarido (b. 1926), wife of the Portuguese writer and critic Alfredo Margarido, and one of two published poets from Príncipe. Unlike Alda do Espírito Santo, who poeticizes everyday occurrences, Maria Manuela creates in her verse of humanist solidarity an aura of hushed mystery around her images as a means of heightening the effect of an ancestral force ready to burst forth in the people's collective voice:

> Ouço os passos no ritmo
> calculado do sòcòpé,
> os pés-raízes-da-terra
> enquanto a voz do coro
> insiste na sua queixa
> (queixa ou protesta—tanto faz).
> Monótona se arrasta
> até explodir
> na alta ânsia de liberdade.[4]

(I hear the marked rhythm/in the steps of the *sòcòpé*,/the feet-roots-of-the-earth/while the voice of the chorus/insists in its complaint/(complaint or protest—same thing)./Monotonously it goes on/until it explodes/in the lofty desire for freedom.)

Rather than simulate the rhythm of the dance Maria Manuela talks about the rhythm in a poem that contains the themes of the *sòcòpé*, of communality (in the reference to the chorus), and of protest. But in some of her other poems, she uses invocation, African ancestralism, and an incantatory value.

Alda do Espírito Santo, Tomás Medeiros, and Maria Manuela Margarido, along with two earlier poets, Francisco Stockler and the minor figure from Príncipe Marcelo da Veiga, represent the beginnings of a regionalist literature on the Guinea Gulf islands. Also worthy of mention is Viana de Almeida whose collection *Maiá póçon* (Maria from the City, 1937) signifies an early effort by a black or *mestiço filho da terra* to fictionalize some of his views on the question of race and class. Almeida's technically weak and occasionally preachy short stories shed some light on how the colonized could come to grips, psychologically, with the problems of racism, but it is in the works of three islanders who lived most of their lives in Portugal that we gain the best artistic and social perspective of the "man of color" faced with the realities of his identity in Europe.

From Black Disillusionment to Afro-Portuguese Négritude

In the category of literature that reflects the experiences of the *filho da terra* in Europe, Mário Domingues's contemporary novel, *O menino entre gigantes* (The Boy among Giants, 1960), deserves passing reference because of the account it gives of a boy from Príncipe growing up in Lisbon during the 1910s. In this first-person narrative José Cândido, nicknamed Zezinho, tells of how he, the son of a Portuguese administrator and an African woman, is sent by his father to live with his paternal grandparents in Lisbon. The boy's early years parallel those of any normal child growing up in a bourgeois, Lisbon family at the turn of the century, except that his dark skin sets him apart. For many of the people who enter his life Zezinho's family background (on his father's side), as well as his scholastic ability and social graces, compensates for the stigma of his color. His benevolent grandmother tries to make amends for his maternal side by telling him that his mother descended from African royalty.

Throughout his formative years Zezinho struggles to gain some perspective on his African heritage, and, even though the question of race often seems subordinate to the narrator's intentions of depicting the manners of an age, the boys recurring confrontations with the question of color have a cumulative and mildly traumatic effect on his psyche. From his adult vantage point many of the unpleasant childhood incidents fit into a pattern that José Cândido can dismiss as foolish. On one occasion, for instance, Zezinho suffers tremendous embarrassment at a circus performance because of a ridiculous black clown, and on several occasions he studies himself in a mirror in hopes of discerning a greater physical affinity with his Caucasian relatives. Zezinho also learns early that he must excel both physically and academically among his peers; otherwise they will automatically dwarf him. So when an older boy hurls racial epithets at him and declares him his slave, Zezinho must win the respect and admiration of his classmates by pounding his tormentor into submission.

At the age of fifteen Zezinho meets Fuinha, an elderly settler who claims to have known the boy's mother on the island. By this time the mother occupies only a vague place in the twilight zone of Zezinho's consciousness of atavistic links with Africa. He has gained some control over that aspect of his background and can relegate it to a place of romanticized ancestralism. When Zezinho contemplates the lush vegetation of the Sintra mountains outside of Lisbon, he considers that he may be attracted to this place because somehow it reminds him of the tropical rain forest of Príncipe. And when, toward the novel's end, Fuinha reveals with sadistic pleasure the beatings and humiliations suffered by plantation workers, including Zezinho's mother, the boy feels pride for his father's noble defense of the exploited laborers; for his mother he feels only a vague pity.

This novel of social manners would be pedestrian if not for the perhaps unintended view it offers of how Europeanization affects a child cut off from his African identity but still wearing the badge of his dark skin as a reminder of his origins. More successfully than a sociological treatise or psychological case study, it develops the theme of Zezinho's entrance into the world of "giants" with a power that frequently only art, even mediocre art, can confer on human experience. Symbolically, Zezinho overcomes the stigma of color when Belmira, a former family maid, invites him to her bed. This sexual initiation also represents the adolescent's entrance into manhood, but when his grateful partner proclaims herself his slave forever we see an inverse parallel of the incident, some years earlier, when a classmate declared Zezinho to be his slave. After this sexual awakening the narrator asserts that the boy can now consider himself a giant. Domingues probably did not intend to stress the racial aspects of his story, but he himself no doubt experienced some of Zezinho's fictional world, and his narration reflects the social and cultural mentality of a *mestiço* who is the product of a peculiarly Portuguese brand of Westernization.

Domingues's novel can help enhance appreciation of the two most important writers from São Tomé-Príncipe. For although it deals with a child's world and has only a thread, albeit a strong one, of disillusionment deriving from the alienation of the black or *mestiço* in a European culture, it also gives the perspective of the adult *filho da terra*.

Caetano da Costa Alegre may be called the first poet of São Tomé-Príncipe. Born into a creole family, Costa Alegre was a black Santomense who died in 1890 in Alcobaça, Portugal, at the age of twenty-six. His friend Artur da Cruz Magalhães collected and published in Portugal ninety-six of his poems under the title *Versos* (1916); second and third editions of the book in 1950 and 1951 offer some evidence of the poet's at least modest popularity. But judging by the theme of many of his poems, we can say that life in Portugal afforded Costa Alegre more sorrow than joy; and almost everyone who has written about him has emphasized the pain he suffered in Lisbon because his black skin caused women to spurn his love. Cruz Magalhães, wrote that fate had decreed that Costa Alegre's starry, white soul should be covered by the scorched blackness of his skin and that the torture of knowing he would always love without being loved in return overwhelmed him with bitter sorrow.[5] In a titleless poem Costa Alegre himself offers this lament:

> A minha côr é negra,
> Indica luto e pena;
>
> A tua raça é branca,
> Tu és cheia de graça.[6]

(My color is black,/It stands for mourning and sorrow;//White is your race/You are full of grace.)

And the epigraph to another poem, "Maria," reads:

Por veres meu rosto negro
Tu me chamaste *carvão* . . .
Não me admiro: fui lenha
No fogo desta paixão.
(p. 43)

(Seeing my black face/You called me *coal* . . ./I am not surprised: I was fuel/In the fire of this passion.)

Both examples offer a touch of satire that makes the sorrowful lament almost humorous. There is no mistaking the humor in "Eu e os passeantes" (The Passersby and I), a poem frequently cited as evidence of Costa Alegre's personal sorrow and disillusionment. First an English woman passes by and exclaims, "What black, my God!" (the poet's own rendition of English); next comes a Spanish woman who says, "Que alto, Dios mio!" (My God, how tall!); then a French woman's observation, "O quel beau nègre!" (Oh, what a handsome black!); and finally the Portuguese woman says with derisive intimacy, calling him by name, "O' Costa Alegre/Tens um atchim!" (p. 29) (Oh, Costa Alegre!/you are a mockery!) Like a similar English onomatopoeia, the word *atchim* refers to the sound of a sneeze, but in the poem's context its figurative meaning is insulting and possibly has some relationship to the noun *achincalhação*, which means derision, mockery, or ridicule.

The critic Lopes Rodrigues, author of *O livro de Costa Alegre* (Costa Alegre's Book, 1969), explains away specific incidents of racial prejudice involving Costa Alegre and emphasizes his patriotism and his condition of a black Portuguese who, according to official policy, is equal to his white countrymen.[7] Other commentators have pointed out that the Portuguese society of Costa Alegre's era was prejudiced against the black man because his ancestors were slaves. Portuguese society has probably demonstrated as much racism as any other society that has enslaved a people and then justified its Christian right to do so on the basis of that people's supposed inferiority. Lopes Rodrigues, in the name of official Portuguese racial tolerance, distorts the issue at one extreme, while those who go to Costa Alegre's poetry to confirm his personal sorrow as a black man exaggerate at the other extreme.

Perhaps physical aversion, on the part of certain women, did indeed have an effect on Costa Alegre, but some of his suffering was the result of his personal hypersensitivity to the realities of racism which made him overly aware of his color. It must be remembered that Costa Alegre came to Portugal at the impressionable age of ten, never to return to his native island. With regard to his physical being, Costa Alegre, in his "Eu" (Me), calls on the pale woman to recognize that which is beautiful in his appearance. His poetic self-adulation may be the desperation of one often spurned, just as his praise of the black woman, in "Negra," may be the only alternative left to a man rejected by the women of his own society. The black woman is, however, an abstract entity for Costa Alegre. He uses a coal metaphor in "Negra" to capture her essence, but he adores her by evoking whiteness: her face is *candid* and she is a *dove*.

The real point to be made here is that Costa Alegre capitalized on and exaggerated a genuine situation for artistic purposes. In other words, he assumed a pose whereby conventional poetic conceits and the traditional love complaint went beyond the accepted in his use of the black-white antithesis. Images of the diaphanous, alabaster female appear no more in Costa Alegre's poetry than they do in other European poetry of that and previous periods. Whatever the personal tragedy of Costa Alegre's life, it is difficult to believe that he did not intend some parody of the traditional love lyricism of his era. Imbued with the prejudices of his European education, Costa Alegre must have indeed looked upon his color as a badge of inferiority which, while it increased his frustration, also resulted in a subtle sarcasm and an implied satire of the society that both accepted and rejected him. One more observation on this matter will, it is hoped, help lay to rest the theory that Costa Alegre's poetry is simply autobiographical. It seems hardly plausible that the sensitive poet, given his position in society, was seen as a pariah by every upper-bourgeois woman in whom he showed an amorous interest. As Lopes Rodrigues notes, the black Brazilian poet Gonçalves Crespo, Costa Alegre's contemporary in Lisbon, married a wellborn Portuguese woman with whom he shared a prestigious position in society.

In only two or three of his published poems does Costa Alegre refer to the tropical island of his birth, and then usually in romantic childhood reminiscences or as an idealized setting for his proclamations of love. Although a Portuguese in upbringing and attitude, and more a poet *from* than *of* São Tomé, historically speaking Caetano da Costa Alegre is the first Santomense poet, and, for that matter, one of the first Afro-Portuguese poets to take artistic cognizance of his blackness.

If Costa Alegre's importance can be taken as more historical than artistic, and if his reaction to white society was based on defensiveness and disillusionment, then the poet about to be considered can be seen as an artistic revelation in Afro-Portuguese literature who reacted to the problems of African identity with the vocabulary of négritude.

Some fifty years passed between Costa Alegre's death and the appearance of another important Santomense poet. And in some respects this poet, Francisco José Tenreiro would parallel his compatriot Costa Alegre. The son of a Portuguese administrator and a "native" woman, Tenreiro, like Costa Alegre, went to Lisbon at a tender age to complete his formal education. According to several accounts Costa Alegre was very popular among his fellow university students, who accompanied his casket through the streets of Lisbon after his premature death in Alcobaça. During his short life Tenreiro gained more than popularity: he achieved success as a geographer and teacher, and he eventually became a high official in the Portuguese Overseas Ministry. The period in which Tenreiro lived differed from that of Costa Alegre; therefore while he reacted to his surroundings with a consciousness of his position as a *mestiço*, he did so with an artistic irony and a defiance born out of a cultural and racial awareness shared during that time by people of African origin in many locales. Aimé Cesaire's spiritual return to Africa and the black rebirth of American poets such as

Countee Cullen and Langston Hughes went toward influencing the attitudes and the poetry of Francisco José Tenreiro.

In 1942 Tenreiro published his first volume of poetry under the title *Ilho do nome santo* (Island of the Saintly Name). As evidence of his pan-Africanism or of his universal sense of the brotherhood of black people, he included in his collection the poem "Negro de todo o mundo" (Black Man of the World). In tones similar to those of Langston Hughes, he summons his brothers in Virginia, Cape Verde, and Brazil. With exclamatory forcefulness he calls for a vindication of the black man whose songs the white man apes on Mississippi showboats and in the cabarets of world capitals. Through the motif of music—the plaintive song, the spiritual, the Cape Verdean *morna*—he establishes a black bond of solidarity in the sorrow and melancholy of the uprooted:

> Só as canções longas
> que estás soluçando
> dizem da nossa tristeza e melancolia![8]

(Only those drawn-out songs/that you sob/can tell of our melancholy and sadness!)

In the same poem, Tenreiro considers the black man's true adventure, which is not an adventure story just because the hero is black:

> Se fosses branco
> quando jogas a vida
> por um copo de whisky
> terias o teu retrato no jornal!
> (p. 67)

(If you were white/when you wagered your life/for a glass of whisky/you would get your picture in the newspaper!)

After an invocatory isolation of the word *Negro* in a one-line stanza, the poet focuses on the Brazilian city of Salvador, Bahia, as a symbolic black Rome, an African empire reborn outside of Africa.

The same sense of commiseration and strength in a shared experience carries over into Tenreiro's posthumously published collection *Coração em África* (Heart in Africa) which is included in *Obra poética de Francisco José Tenreiro*. Some of Tenreiro's most expressive lines appear in the title poem, which deals with the culturally alienated black man's conscious, spiritual return to Africa. Not unlike the Martinican poet Césaire in his long poem "Cahier d'un retour au pays natal," Tenreiro returns to Africa through exorcisms, defiance, and an intellectualization of poetic exoticism. In some frequently quoted lines from "Coração em África" he portrays the black man and *mestiço* flaunting their color in the face of Europe with an irony that has become a hallmark of his poetry:

> De coração em África trilho estas ruas nevoentas da cidade
> de África no coração e um ritmo de be bop be nos lábios
> enquanto que à minha volta se sussurra olha o preto (que bom)
> olha um negro (óptimo) olha um mulato (tanto faz)
> olha um moreno (ridículo)
> (p. 112)

(With my heart in Africa I tread these foggy city streets/with Africa in my heart and a be bop rhythm on my lips/while all about me they whisper look at the black (how nice)/look a Negro (fine) look a mulatto (same thing)/look a *moreno* (ridiculous))

Costa Alegre made a humorous poetic study of the reaction of passersby to a black man in Europe in his "Eu e os passeantes." Tenreiro captures here the alienation of the black man or *mestiço* who defies the European city with Africa in his soul and his heart in Africa. By whistling a be bop rhythm the poet asserts his cultural and racial identity while the white city perceives him with varying degrees of curiosity, for his burden of color makes him an object to be pointed out and classified: black or Negro by those who react to the full shock, a mulatto by those who have learned to make socio-somatic distinctions, and euphemistically a *moreno* by those who are embarrassed by their own racism. Because in Portuguese the word *moreno* can mean any physical type from a white brunet to a dark mixed-blood, it is often applied to avoid the more stigmatic *preto, negro,* or *mulato.*

The full impact of Tenreiro's acceptance of his African origins comes in his "Amor de África" (Love of Africa), written in 1963, the year of his untimely death. With long discursive lines and images that convey the physical distance between him and Africa the poet broaches the question of civilization. His image in the following simile filters a nostalgic notion of Africa through a European presence: "Esparso e vago amor de África/como uma manhã outonal de nevoeiros sobre o Tejo" (p. 85) (A sparse, vague love of Africa/like an autumn morning of quiet fog over the Tagus). With his heart in Africa Tenreiro's thoughts shift to other exotic lands in a universal expression of his mental juxta-positions with Europe, a Europe that condescends to say that some black boys are very polite when they give up their seats on trolley cars to old ladies. And he mocks the ethnocentric wisdom of a Europe which contrasts a Bach fugue to a *batuque* and which concedes that with few exceptions (the Benin and Ife bronzes) Africa is, in comparison with Europe, infantile. But smiling through the woolen overcoat façade of his Europeanism, and with Africa in his heart and his heart in Africa, the poet counts the minutes until that time when humanity will be reborn. Sugges-tions in Tenreiro's poetry about Africa's role in saving humanity resemble the ideas of the Francophone négritude poets. Tenreiro never quite attained Césaire's level of antiracist racism nor did he effect what some have called the surrealism in Césaire's rework-ing of the French language. But he did introduce the first and most compelling note of négritude into Afro-Portuguese poetry.

As a poet of São Tomé, Tenreiro's African awakening led him to sing of his distant homeland with nostalgia and filial devotion: "Nasci naquela terra distante/num dia de batuque" (p. 39) (I was born in that distant land/on a day of *batuque*). There is something mysterious and incantatory, but not gratuitously exotic, in the relationship between the poet's birth and the resounding drum rhythms conjured up by the word *batuque*. This is a statement of his African identity. Having established the Africanness of his creole island, the committed son of the land offers several views of aspects of São Tomé's social and human reality in the group of poems entitled "Romanceiro" (Ballad Book). "Romance de seu Silva Costa" (The Ballad of Mr. Silva Costa) tells of the white man who arrives penniless from Portugal:

> "Seu Silva Costa
> chegou na ilha . . ."
>
> Seu Silva Costa
> chegou na ilha:
> calcinha no fiozinho
> dois moeda de ilusão
> e vontade de voltar.
>
> Seu Silva Costa
> chegou na ilha:
> fez comércio di alcool
> fez comércio di homem
> fez comércio di terra.
>
> Ui!
>   Seu Silva Costa
> virou branco grande:
> su calça não é fiozinho
> e sus moeda não tem mais ilusão! . . .
>   (p. 43)

("Mr. Silva Costa/arrived on the island . . ."//Mr. Silva Costa/ arrived on the island:/raggedy drawers/two cents worth of illusion/and a desire to return home.//Mr. Silva Costa//arrived on the island:/dealt in alcohol/dealt in human flesh/dealt in land.// Look at that!/Mr. Silva Costa/has become a big white man now:/ no more raggedy drawers/and his two cents are no illusion! . . .)

Tenreiro adds a sardonic note to his social commentary by means of a folksy, modified black Portuguese in some of the poem's expressions and vocabulary.

"Romance de Sinha Carlota" (Ballad of Miss Carlota) tells the story of an old black woman who had come to São Tomé as a girl from the lands of the south (Angola or Mozambique) in a gang of contract workers. On the plantation she had children by black men and children by white men; the black children worked at their arduous chores on the island, the *mestiço* sons had varying fates, but the fortunate ones were sent north by their white fathers where they forgot what their mother looked like. When one of Miss Carlota's former white lovers passes her, sitting serenely by the side of the road, and proffers a greeting in *forro* creole, the ancient woman replies with a distant word and continues to puff philosophically on her worm-eaten pipe.

By means of irony Tenreiro manages to give a humorous twist to the sentimentality of his implied social protest. "Canção do mestiço" (Mestiço's Song), the last few lines of which are quoted on page 15, contains an arrogant superiority whereby the mulatto has it over the white man in his ability to function in either the white or the black society. And in "Longindo o ladrão" (Longindo the Thief) arrogance becomes a case of outwitting the figure of white authority:

> Os olhos de Longindo
> saltam a noite
> como dois bichinhos luminosos.
>
> Chiu!
> Só o eco do mar!
>
> O corpo de Longindo
> segue os olhos
> como caçô atrás de homem!
>
> Chiu!
> Só o rumor do palmar!
>
> A mão de Longindo
> estendeu-se prá frente
> os olhos saltando na noite!
>
> Ui!
> Um tiro de carabina!

O coração de Longindo
começou batendo
e a navalha cantou de encontro à pele.
Hum!
Um tiro de carabina!
Longindo fechou um olho.
Depois o outro.
O branco o perdeu na escuridão! . . .
Ah!
Só o ronco-ronco do mar!

(pp. 77–78)

(Longindo's eyes/shine in the night/like two luminous bugs.//
Shush!/Just the echo of the sea!//Longindo's body//follows his
eyes/like a dog follows a man!//Shush!//Only the murmur of
the palms!//Longindo's hand/reaches out/his eyes shining in the
night!//Whew!/A carbine shot!//Longindo's heart/began to
pound/and his razor hummed against his skin.//Hum!/A carbine shot!//Longindo closed one eye./Then the other./The
white man lost him in the darkness! . . ./Ah!/Only the slosh-
slosh of the sea!)

This comic poem-parody of a minstrel joke has the petty thief
Longindo turn to his advantage the very thing that stigmatizes
him, and when he disappears into the darkness he symbolically
merges with nature, thus signifying a négritude attitude of the
African's oneness with the land.

"Ilha de nome santo," which bears the same title as Tenreiro's
first collection of poems, is a hymn to the island and to its common people. The final stanza defies and condemns the white
world and in exalting the land the poet glorifies the black man's
strength and attributes to him such virtues as loyalty and courage:

Onde apesar da pólvora que o branco trouxe num navio escuro
onde apesar da espada e duma bandeira multicor
dizerem poder dizerem força dizerem império de branco
é terra de homens cantando vida que os brancos jamais souberam

é terra do sáfu do sòcòpé da mulata
—ui! fetiche di branco!—
é terra do negro leal forte e valente que nenhum outro!

(p. 80)

(Where despite the gunpowder the white man brought in a dark ship/where despite the fact that the sword and the multicolored banner/say power say force say white man's empire/it is the land of men singing of a life that the whites have never known/it is the land of *sáfu* of *sòcòpé* of the mulatto girl/—yeah! that bewitchment of the white man!—/it is the land of the black man loyal strong and brave like no other!)

The long lines and scant punctuation impart a run-on acceleration that complements the poet's sentiments of mildly antiracist racism. The parenthetical reference to the mulatto girl's bewitching power not only interrupts the accelerated rhythm of the stanza, but it also tempers the anger, although not the defiance, by alluding to that time-honored cult of the dusky maiden.

Although not necessarily typical of Afro-Portuguese writers, Tenreiro does represent one of the better moments, artistically speaking, of a phase in the development of the literature. In this sense it seems fitting to end the main body of this study of Afro-Portuguese literature with the discussion of a man who embodies both the awareness and the ambivalence of a black, white, and *mestiço* elite whose collective voice has resounded from an empire in demise.

CONCLUSIONS

CHAPTER 18

Unity, Diversity, and Prospects for the Future

In approaching my subject from the standpoint of the modern cultural history of Portuguese Africa, I have considered the individual areas as regional entities, each with its own distinctive literary development, and I have also made references to the phenomenon of Afro-Portuguese literature; this implies, of course, that the writing of all regions, from Angola to São Tomé-Príncipe, shares something in common. Obviously, the Portuguese language is the first common denominator. At the same time, the separate histories and the cultural and social institutions of the Luso-Brazilian world account in part for the diversity of the African areas of Portuguese expression.

Cultural Unity and Diversity

Cape Verde went through its period of cultural awareness with a lesser sense of rebelliousness than Angola where regionalism combined with a growing nationalist sentiment. In the 1930s Cape Verde's intellectual elite came together in an atmosphere of pride that reflected the islands' unique situation in the so-called

391

Portuguese space. Conversely, Portuguese Guinea falls outside the concept of the integrated Portuguese space. And the small islands of São Tomé and Príncipe, partly because of their economic development as plantation colonies, had little opportunity to form an island-based intelligentsia comparable to that which appeared in Cape Verde. Still, a set of circumstances resulting from this plantation society did bring about a nascent literature produced by a small number of *filhos da terra* who, in some cases, realized their regional and African awakening in Europe. The large territory of Angola, because of its location on the African continent, the circumstances of its colonization, the dynamic history of its original inhabitants, and its assimilation process, presents the greatest possibilities for an autochthonous literature of African thematic and stylistic features. Mozambique, while in a situation similar to Angola's, entered the modern age of African literature under the onus of aggravated economic and racial distinctions.

Although in an often dialectal or stylized form, Portuguese is the literary tool of writers in all regions, but as far as a regional language is concerned Cape Verde stands out because of the attempts made to legitimize and adapt its creole speech as a literary instrument. In other regions a form of "black" Portuguese and words or phrases borrowed from local African languages often play a part in the poems and stories of committed writers. Generally speaking, an Afro-Portuguese literary language used in all regions can be identified. The word *batuque*, for example, describes African dance and drum rhythms in all Afro-Portuguese regions as well as in Brazil.

Along with a common language comes the unifying factor of Lusotropicology and its ramifications of officialized racial tolerance and romanticized miscegenation. Lusotropicology has affected the creators of the literary and cultural movements even when they have denied the whole of the mythology. Mário de Andrade put Lusotropicology into perspective in a speech originally delivered at Columbia University in 1962 and then published in French in *Présence africaine*, no. 41 (1962), p. 98:

In the Portuguese situation assimilation practically always means destruction of the black African cadres and the creation of a numerically small elite. This elite supposedly possesses the magic formula that will help lead the indigenous population out of the gloomy dark of ignorance into the bright light of knowledge. A kind of passage of the cultural non-being into the state of cultural being, to use Hegelian language.

Moreover, intellectuals of the countries under Portuguese domination are forced to formulate correctly and resolve the problem created by assimilation: a definitive rejection of the black African substratum? Dilution in the dominant culture? Acceptance of the pseudo-condition of the cultural mulatto?

The numerically small elite to which Andrade refers attempted to find answers for the three questions by seeking to incorporate an African oral tradition into their art; by struggling to gain a perspective on their own status as privileged members of a Europeanized elite; and by defining acculturation from a bilateral point of view. But Afro-Portuguese intellectuals rejected more the actual processes of Lusotropicology than the theory of acculturation. They realized that the dominant group's selective rejection and acceptance of African social and cultural values amounted to a process of deculturation and that, as the wards of assimilation, they had to reverse the process. From their favored position members of the elite had to struggle with such problems as how far to go in resuscitating their African heritage and to what extent they could talk to the masses of people. Obviously, while speaking to the people's problems they were also carrying on a dialogue among themselves and revealing or exposing social ills to the non-committed bourgeoisie. The problems that the Afro-Portuguese elite faced are not unlike those confronted by their counterparts in other areas of Africa and the Caribbean; what is different are the conditions of wardship. But the nature and durability of Lusotropicology under Portugal's colonialist policies have created a distinctive situation for the Afro-Portuguese writer and intellectual.

Unity and Diversity in Themes,
Styles, and Genres

Although several major themes related to the problem of regional identity appear with redundancy in all areas of Portuguese Africa, there are variations and subthemes that receive a greater or lesser emphasis depending on historical, social, and cultural circumstances. In Cape Verde an insular mentality and the escapism stemming from the islands' isolation and economic deprivation became important themes in the poetry and prose fiction of the aware writers. Nevertheless, all regions of Portuguese Africa, confronted with the problem of identity, cultivated variations on the themes of escapism and alienation.

Poets of Cape Verde, Mozambique, and particularly Angola have shown a preference for the romantic theme of a return to childhood as symbolic of a more creole and African past, and the nostalgic return to that past signifies more than a recapturing of innocence: it also represents an affirmation of regionalist identity and cultural authenticity in ethnic roots. Regionalist identity takes many forms in Afro-Portuguese literature, from the spiritualist transcendence of the white poetess Alda Lara to the duality and ambivalence of the *mestiço* Mário António, or from the communal solidarity of Agostinho Neto to the surrealistic metamorphosis of José Craveirinha.

Along with the quest for regionalist identity, poets and story writers have used themes that reflect an identification with their concept of Africanness, particularly in Angola, but to an extent in all regions. The neoromantic theme of invocation of the land appears in the poetry of Cape Verde, São Tomé-Príncipe, Angola, and Mozambique, often with the négritude touch and the return to a primal level of consciousness contained in the abstraction of Mother Africa. In certain cases the diversity results from a heightened sensitivity in some regions, more than in others, toward those characteristics inherent in a négritude concept.

Francisco José Tenreiro went beyond the regional and offered Afro-Portuguese literature its first négritude and pan-Africanist strains. Angolans such as Agostinho Neto and Mozambicans such as José Craveirinha have applied the techniques of négritude and cultivated an African stylistic in their poetry by adapting African drum and dance rhythms. Understandably, though, the négritude of cultural and biological mulattoes only occasionally has reached the exaltation and antiracist racism of the Francophone model.

Technically and stylistically the poetry and prose fiction of Portuguese Africa demonstrate a certain unity, befitting the period of social urgency that gave birth to these literatures. Invocational poetry—frequently incantatory in Angola and Mozambique—follows a direct line from the *engagé* poetry of the fifties to the combative verse of the sixties. Throughout, a discursive, narrative technique has alternated with the more intimist lyrical statement of those poets imbued with a communal sense. Several important poets have struggled with the problem of poetry's social function as opposed to the more individualist lyric or the universalist soliloquy on the human condition. Some, notably Mário António, have sought a kind of compromise by incorporating their intimist sentiment as displaced Africans into a Westernized form of "art" poetry. António has experimented with traditional Kimbundu poetry in a European art form. In Mozambique, as has been seen, a significant debate was waged precisely over the question of poetry as a universal aesthetic that transcends regional, ethnic, and social boundaries.

One more brief comment might be made here on surrealism in Afro-Portuguese literature, particularly on its importance in Craveirinha's poetry. We have noted above that a communal, narrative poetry alternates with intimist, lyrical verse; the latter, in many instances, demonstrates an inherent conflict in the Afro-Portuguese writer's conscious or unconscious expression of arrested action stemming from a lack of progressive events in the historical process. This perhaps accounts for the ambivalences and opaque symbolism of much of M. António's poetry and prose. On the other hand, poets such as Agostinho Neto and especially José Craveirinha have used surrealistic images as a means of seeking what might be termed a "sensual" liberation. The American critic

Fredric Jameson elucidates this concept when he writes that "it is not too much to say that for Surrealism a genuine plot, a genuine narrative, is that which can stand as the very *figure* of Desire itself: and this not only because in the Freudian sense pure physiological desire is inaccessible as such to consciousness, but also because in the socioeconomic context, genuine desire risks being dissolved and lost in the vast network of pseudosatisfactions which make up the market system. In that sense desire is the form taken by freedom in the new commercial environment, by a freedom we do not even realize we have lost unless we think in terms, not only of the stilling, but also the awakening, of Desire in general."[1] I take the liberating aspects of surrealism to apply to Craveirinha's poetry precisely because his romantic, subjective, and sensual self overruns and absorbs the external reality of a repressive urban environment and in so doing releases an African's suppressed desire manifested in the figurative destruction and actual distortion of the European language.

Protest and neorealist documentation dominate the prose fiction of Portuguese Africa, but occasionally the poetic vignettes and the infusion of an African oral substratum mitigate purely sociological concerns. António Aurélio Gonçalves has distinguished himself among several good Cape Verdean writers who delve into the psychology of social realities. And in Angola a sense of craft has occasionally taken precedence over the urgencies of social and sociological exposition. Mário António's concern with craft has resulted in stories that are too self-conscious in their poetic, esoteric presentation. But Arnaldo Santos's sense of narrative craft, coupled with his social sensitivities, has brought the chronicle into its own as an Angolan literary genre. Likewise, the Mozambican Luís Bernardo Honwana has demonstrated an artistic perceptiveness in his re-creations of the ambiguous world of the African in social and cultural transition.

Novel writing has not yet reached the quantitative and qualitative level one might expect, perhaps mainly because the committed writer has not had time to devote himself to this exacting and time-consuming task. Cape Verde is an exception in that members of an earlier generation did possess the time and serenity to channel their social concerns into a small number of significant novels. Since the early sixties, however, only António Aurélio Gonçalves, with his novellas, and Manuel Ferreira, with his linguistically and technically revolutionary *Voz de prisão*, have produced important long pieces of prose fiction. Both the Cape Verdean Luís Romano and the Angolan Manuel Lima have written their documentary and allegorical works in Brazil where the literary ambient is more conducive to the type of reflection the novel requires.

Drama has made even more infrequent and sporadic appearances than the novel in Portuguese Africa, and this probably reflects a political climate that has not encouraged the type of social immediacy inherent in the theater. The very little that has appeared—and there have been some short-lived attempts at establishing a regional theater particularly in Cape Verde and Angola—has dealt directly with the clash of cultures. The Angolan Domingos Van-Dúnem's *Auto de Natal* and the Mozambican Lindo Hlongo's *Os noivos* demonstrate to what degree an African audience can respond to a dramatization of a pressing social issue and to the codification of indigenous artistic elements.

It can safely be said that Afro-Portuguese literature offers enough quantity, quality, and regional diversity to be considered as several literatures. Yet, and despite the geographical and cultural extremes, the several literary manifestations can also be approached as a single phenomenon.

The Future of Afro-Portuguese Literature

Soon after the completion of the manuscript of this study Portuguese Guinea became the independent nation of Guinea-Bissau, Mozambique and Angola were granted independence, effective in June and November of 1975 respectively, autonomy was slated to follow for São Tomé and Príncipe in July, and Cape Verde had begun to press for changes in its political status. Before this disintegration of the Portuguese empire the future of literature in the five African territories had been fraught with pessimism and doubts. The most one could hope for was that when, in some undetermined future, the movements came out of their imposed state of suspension the basis for truly national literatures would have already been established in the efforts of those whose roles I have attempted to describe here. One could speculate that writers such as M. António, Craveirinha, Ferreira, Gonçalves, Honwana, Knopfli, Neto, and Luandino Vieira would lend their talents to a new era. That new era has arrived sooner than most expected, and although there is still room for speculation there is no longer any doubt concerning the future of a viable Afro-Portuguese literature.

One may also suppose that the cultural-literary movements will not necessarily take up at the point of apprenticeship and identity-seeking, even though independence has awakened a fervor not unlike that of the 1950s and early 1960s. Thus, in several issues of the arts and letters supplement of *A Província de Angola*, covering the months of April to November 1974, one notes the printing of poems and stories originally published in the 1950s and 1960s or previously denied publication by the official censor.[2] We find in the pages of the Angolan newspaper M. António's "O cozinheiro Vicente" (Vicente the Cook, 1952), Arnaldo Santos's poem "Puri-ficação da ilha" (Purification of the Island, 1964), an excerpt from Carlos Ervedosa's essay "Literatura angolana" (Angolan Litera-ture, 1963), and Agostinho Neto's "Certeza" (Certainty), a poem written in 1949.

Of even greater significance are those articles that celebrate writers and that reinterpret the past or prognosticate on the future of Afro-Portuguese literature. Thus we see Ernesto Lara Filho's note on Viriato da Cruz, whom he heralds as the greatest of Angolan poets and who, after his reported death in Peking in 1973, has become a hero of an independent nation and an emblem of a reborn literature. And Alfredo Margarido offers an essay in praise of Ernesto Lara Filho's *O canto do martrindinde* (The Song of the Martrindinde), which, we recall, was banned by the authorities at the time of its publication in 1963.

Along with the overdue homage paid to those pioneers of modern Angolan (and in not a few cases Mozambican, Cape Verdean, and Santomense) literature, there are declarations on the part of some eleventh-hour nationalists as well as the testimonials of those who truly suffered under the repressive regime. José Luandino Vieira who, because he survived the terror of political internment and, more importantly, because he has attained success as an authentic Angolan writer, looms larger than life on the horizon of a reborn Afro-Portuguese literature. A number of his previously suppressed stories have already been released in print and, judging by several articles in *A Província de Angola*, his name has become a rallying point for a new literary expression in the former province. The prestigious Portuguese critic Jacinto do Prado Coelho has contributed to this justifiable aggrandizement with "Na literatura também aconteceu milagre" (A Miracle Has Also Come to Pass in Literature), an essay which almost reverently places Vieira's *No antigamente na vida* (In the Long Ago of Life) on a par with the best of contemporary prose fiction. And the fact that a Portuguese critic should take such enthusiastic cognizance of an Angolan writer bodes well for the broader recognition of Afro-Portuguese literature.

The exalted literary and critical activities represented in the arts and letters supplements of *A Província de Angola* speak of a new beginning, as evidenced in such articles as "O novo Luandino Vieira" (The New Luandino Vieira) and "Um novo teatro para um país novo" (A New Theater for a New Country) by Luiz Francisco Rebelo; yet a sense of the values of the recent past comes forth in such essays as Bessa Victor's "Em torno da primeira obra de quimbundo" (Concerning the First Kimbundo Work) and M. António's "Para a história da poesia angolana" (For the History of Angolan Poetry), written in 1961 but banned from publication at that time. Thus, the past and the present hold promise for a continuity infused into the progressive development of Afro-Portuguese literature.

NOTES

Notes

Introduction

1. See the bibliography for works on Afro-Portuguese literature published in Italy, the Soviet Union, and Sweden.

2. Another English-language anthology worthy of mention is O. R. Dathorne and Willfried Feuser, *Africa in Prose* (Baltimore: Penguin Books, 1969), which includes selections by the Angolan novelist Castro Soromenho and the Mozambican short story writer Luís Bernardo Honwana. See the last section of my bibliography for Afro-Portuguese literature available in English translation.

3. In part Moser bases his contention that African literature in Portuguese was the first written on the letters from black royalty of the Congo to the Portuguese monarchs as early as the sixteenth century. See *Essays in Portuguese-African Literature* (University Park: Pennsylvania State University Studies, no. 26, 1969), p. 3.

4. Janheinz Jahn, *Neo-African Literature*, trans. Oliver Coburn and Ursula Lehrburger (New York: Grove Press, 1968), p. 22.

5. Simon Mpondo, "Provisional Notes on Literature and Criticism in Africa," *Présence africaine*, no. 78 (1971), 120.

6. Five of several studies on Anglophone and Francophone literatures are the following: Anne Tibble, *African/English Literature* (London: Peter Owen, 1965); Adrian A. Roscoe, *Mother is Gold: A Study in West African Literature* (Cambridge: At the University Press, 1971); Eustace Palmer, *An Introduction to the African Novel* (New York: Africana, 1972); Lilyan Kesteloot, *Les écrivains noirs de langue française: Naissance d'une littérature* (Brussels: Éditions de l'Institut de Sociologie, Université Libre de Bruxelles, 1971); and Claude Wauthier, *The Literature and Thought of Modern Africa*, trans. Shirley Kay (London: Pall Mall Press, 1966).

403

7. Mário de Andrade, *Literatura africana de expressão portuguesa*, vol. I: *Poesia: Antologia temática* (Algiers: published by the author, 1967), p. vi. This was a very limited edition compiled mainly for Andrade's friends. The anthology and its companion volume of prose were reissued by Kraus Reprint of Liechtenstein in 1970.

8. The Portuguese word *mestiço* is a generic term for the offspring of any racially mixed union. In this study I use the term interchangeably with the more socially charged *mulatto*, a word which specifically refers to the offspring of a union between black and white or to anyone of mixed black and white ancestry.

9. Creole refers to an indigenous, mixed African and European culture, human type, or language.

10. See James Duffy, *Portugal in Africa* (Baltimore: Penguin Books, 1962), and Ronald R. Chilcote, *Portuguese Africa* (Englewood Cliffs, N.J.: Prentice-Hall, 1967), for a discussion of the indigenous code, forced labor, and contract labor in Portuguese Africa. Also see D. M. Abshire and M. A. Samuels, eds., *Portuguese Africa: A Handbook* (London: Pall Mall Press, 1969).

For a defense of Portugal's role in Africa see Adriano Moreira, *Portugal's Stand in Africa*, trans. Willian Davis and others (New York: University Publishers, 1962), and Manuel Belchior, *Fundamentos para uma política multicultural em África* (Lisbon: Companhia Nacional Editora, 1966).

11. Kesteloot, *Les écrivains noirs de langue française*, pp. 110–111.

12. *Ibid.*, p. 111.

13. Jahn, *Neo-African Literature*, pp. 251–252.

14. See Frantz Fanon, *Black Skin, White Masks*, Eng. trans. Grove Press, 1967 (London: Paladin, 1970), pp. 87–92.

15. See Jahn's reference to Soyinka's statement in *Neo-African Literature*, p. 265.

16. Maria da Graça Freire, "Os portugueses e a negritude," *Diário de Notícias* (Lisbon) 29 September 1970, Literary Supplement, n.p. These articles, in an expanded and modified form, were published in a small volume: *Portugueses e negritude* (Lisbon: Agência-Geral do Ultramar, 1971).

17. This poem appears in its entirety in *Obra poética de Francisco José Tenreiro* (Lisbon: Livraria Editora Pax, 1967), p. 48.

18. The article in question originally appeared in the culture and arts supplement of *O Comércio do Porto* and was later reprinted in *Estrada larga* (Porto: Editora Porto, n.d.), III, 472–481.

19. Duarte's article appears in *Vértice*, no. 134 (Coimbra, 1951) and Mariano's in *Cabo Verde: Boletim de propaganda e informação*, no. 104 (Praia, 1958).

20. Andrade, *Literatura africana de expressão portuguesa*, I, x.

21. For a review of the influence of Brazilian literature on Afro-Portuguese writing see Mário António Fernandes de Oliveira, "Influências da literatura brasileira sobre as literaturas portuguesas do Atlântico tropical," *Colóquios sobre o Brasil* (Lisbon: Junta de Investigações do Ultramar, Centro de Estudos Politicos e Sociais, 1967). For a study of Brazilian *modernismo* and Northeast regionalism see Wilson Martins, *The Modernist Idea: A Critical Survey of Brazilian Writing in the Twentieth Century*, trans. Jack E. Tomlins (New York: New York University Press, 1970).

1. Social and Cultural Background of the Modern Era

1. Carlos Ervedosa, *A literatura angolana: Resenha histórica* (Lisbon: Casa dos Estudantes do Império, 1963), pp. 20–22.
2. M. António, *Luanda "ilha" crioula* (Lisbon: Agência Geral do Ultramar, 1968), p. 48.
3. *Ibid.*, p. 77.
4. *Ibid.*, p. 81.
5. Héli Chatelain, *Contos populares de Angola,* trans. M. Garcia da Silva (Lisbon: Agência Geral do Ultramar, 1964), p. 108.
6. António, *Luanda "ilha" crioula,* p. 127.

2. Colonialists, Independents, and Precursors

1. Luis Figueira, *Princesa negra* (Coimbra: Coimbra Editora, 1932), p. 7.
2. Moser, *Essays in Portuguese-African Literature,* p. 36.
3. Castro Soromenho, *Nhári: O drama da gente negra* (Luanda: Livraria Civilização, 1938), p. 39.
4. *Ibid.*, p. 84.
5. *Cultura,* no. 11 (May 1960), 7.
6. *Cultura,* no. 4 (July 1958), 5.
7. "Castro Soromenho, romancista angolano," *Estudos ultramarinos,* no. 3 (Lisbon, 1959), 129.
8. *Poesia angolana de Tomaz Vieira da Cruz* (Lisbon, n.d.), p. 50.
9. *Tatuagem* (Lisbon: Published by the author, 1941), p. 71.
10. Quoted by Eugênio Lisboa in "A poesia em Moçambique," special supplement "Moçambique" in *A Capital* (Lisbon) 14 September 1970, p. 13.
11. António, *Luanda "ilha" crioula,* p. 136.
12. Óscar Ribas, *Sunguilando* (Lisbon: Agência Geral do Ultramar, 1967), p. 184.
13. Óscar Ribas, *Uanga* (Luanda: Published by the author, 1969), p. 21.
14. Mário de Andrade, *La poésie africaine d'expression portugaise,* trans. Jean Todrani and André Joucla-Ruau (Honfleur: Pierre Jean Oswald, 1969), p. 27.
15. Geraldo Bessa Victor, *Ao som das marimbas* (Lisbon: Livraria Portugália, 1943), p. 111.
16. In Costa Alegre's poem "Maria" he employs a lump of coal as a metaphor for himself. Also see the Mozambican poet José Craveirinha's "Grito negro" on p. 204 for the same coal image.
17. Geraldo Bessa Victor, *Cubata abandonada* (Braga: Editora Pax, 1966), p. 19.
18. Geraldo Bessa Victor, *Mucanda* (Braga: Editora Pax, 1964), p. 13.
19. I am suggesting that certain social, economic, and psychological patterns, along with a verbal expressiveness of West African origin, can be identified in both Angolan slums and black American ghettos. Roger Abrahams, in his book on black American folk culture, writes about an active distrust between the sexes deriving from socioeconomic factors (i.e., the matrilocal family system), and he states that "because the Negro has identified himself so strongly with the image imposed by the whites, his rejection and conversion of the stereotype can only be seen as a first step toward achieving a sense of personal and cultural identity." *Positively Black* (Englewood Cliffs, N.J.: Prentice-Hall, 1970), pp. 73–74.

20. Geraldo Bessa Victor, *Sanzala sem batuque* (Braga: Editora Pax, 1967), p. 25.

3. *"Let's Discover Angola"*

1. Ervedosa, *A literatura angolana*, p. 33.
2. *Ibid.*, p. 34.
3. See page 293 for comments on Anahory's poem.
4. *Cultura*, no. 11 (May 1960), 12.

4. *Toward a Poetry of Angola*

1. See António Cardoso, "Poesia angolana ou poesia em Angola," *Cultura*, nos. 2 and 3 (January and March 1958), 7.
2. See excerpts from the introductory address by Agostinho Neto at a colloquium on Angolan poetry held in Lisbon, August 1959. *Cultura*, no. 11 (May 1960), p. 9.
3. "Considerações sobre poesia," *Cultura*, no. 2 (January 1958), p. 7.
4. *Etnografia do sudoeste de Angola* (Lisbon: Junta de Investigações do Ultramar, 1959?), I, 222. The Africana Publishing Company of New York announces a forthcoming English translation of Estermann's three-volume work.
5. One Imbondeiro series, published during the late 1950s and early 1960s, includes about seventy small volumes of poetry and short stories by individual authors including Angolans, Portuguese, and an occasional Brazilian. The editors of Imbondeiro also issued several anthologies under the title *Mákua*.

In the early 1970s several new series and journals have appeared in Angola: *Vector*, *Convivium*, and *Idealeda* in the city of Nova Lisboa, as well as one in Lobito, *Capricórnia*, under the direction of Orlando de Albuquerque. Several new, and some already published, writers have contributed to these series.

6. Alda Lara, *Poemas* (Sá da Bandeira: Edições Imbondeiro, 1966), p. 68.
7. Ernesto Lara Filho, *O canto do martrindinde e outros poemas feitos no Puto* (Luanda: Published by the author, 1963), p. 38. The word *Puto* in the title is a black Portuguese rendition of Portugal.
8. Alfredo Margarido, ed., *Poetas angolanos* (Lisbon: Casa dos Estudantes do Império, 1962), p. 2.
9. António Cardoso, *Poemas de circunstância* (Lisbon: Casa dos Estudantes do Império, 1961), p. 27.
10. *Poetas angolanos*, p. 39.
11. Agostinho Neto, *Poemas* (Lisbon: Casa dos Estudantes do Império, 1961), p. 21.
12. Tomás Jorge, *Areal* (Sá da Bandeira: Colecção Imbondeiro, 1961), p. 55. Jorge notes, with reference to his poem's declamatory style, that "Manga, manguinha" has been recited in Angola and Brazil by the distinguished declaimer Margarida Lopes de Almeida (p. 55).
13. M. António, *100 poemas* (Luanda: ABC, 1963), p. 157.
14. *Poetas angolanos*, p. 96.
15. *Ibid.*, p. 24.
16. António, *100 poemas*, p. 8.
17. Lara, *Poemas*, p. 50.

18. Ernesto Lara Filho, *Seripipi na gaiola* (Luanda: ABC, 1970), p. 20.
19. *Poetas angolanos*, p. 51.
20. *Ibid.*, pp. 41–42.
21. Cardoso, *Poemas de circunstância*, p. 9.
22. *Poetas angolanos*, p. 98.
23. Costa Andrade, *Terra de acácias rubras* (Lisbon: Casa dos Estudantes do Império, 1961), pp. 23–24.
24. Jorge, *Areal*, p. 57.
25. *Quatro poemas de Agostinho Neto*, in the series Cadernos de poesia organized by Augusto Ferreira (Póvoa de Varzim: Tipografia Frasco, 1957), p. 7.
26. Gerald Moser, "The Social and Regional Diversity of African Literature in the Portuguese Language," *Essays in Portuguese-African Literature*, pp. 21–22.
27. *Poetas angolanos*, p. 29.
28. Neto, *Poemas*, p. 19.
29. See Kesteloot, *Les écrivains noirs de langue française*, pp. 175–200.
30. Jahn, *Neo-African Literature*, pp. 245–248.
31. Neto, *Poemas*, pp. 9–10.
32. Richard Alan Waterman, "African Influence on the Music of the Americas," *Acculturation in the Americas*, ed. Sol Tax (Chicago: University of Chicago Press, 1952), p. 213.
33. Kesteloot, *Les écrivains noirs de langue française*, p. 192.
34. Manuel Lima, *Kissange* (Lisbon: Casa dos Estudantes do Império, n.d.), p. 31.
35. António, *100 poemas*, p. 148.
36. Virato da Cruz, *Poemas (1947–1950)* (Lisbon: Casa dos Estudantes do Império, 1961), p. 19.
37. Alexandre Dáskalos, *Poemas* (Lisbon: Casa dos Estudantes do Império, 1961), p. 55.
38. Lima, *Kissange*, pp. 17–25.
39. *Poetas angolanos*, p. 122. The Portuguese version is Andrade's own translation of the poem.
40. Arnaldo Santos, *Fuga* (Lisbon: Casa dos Estudantes do Império, 1960), p. 21.
41. Cardoso, *Poemas de circunstância*, p. 30.
42. See Douglas L. Wheeler and René Pélissier, *Angola* (New York: Praeger, 1971), for an account of forced labor practices.
43. Cardoso, *Poemas de circunstância*, p. 22.
44. Frantz Fanon, *The Wretched of the Earth*, trans. Constance Farrington, preface by Jean-Paul Sartre (New York: Grove Press, 1966), p. 179.
45. Gerald Moore and Ulli Beier, eds., *Modern Poetry from Africa* (Baltimore: Penguin Books, 1970), pp. 23–24.
46. Agostinho Neto, *Con occhi asciutti*, trans. Joyce Lussu (Milan: Il Saggiatore, Biblioteca della Silerchia, 1963), p. 108. Many of Neto's combative poems are published in this bilingual (Italian-Portuguese) edition.
47. Mário de Andrade, *Literatura africana de expressão portuguesa*, I, 277.
48. *Ibid.*, pp. 279–280.
49. *Ibid.*, p. xxiii.
50. Tomás Jorge, "Talamungongo" (unpublished collection of poetry), p. 25B.

51. Mário de Andrade, *Literatura africana de expressão portuguesa* I, 295.
52. Santos, *Fuga*, p. 15.
53. António Cardoso, "A poética de Mário António," *Cultura*, no. 12 (November 1960), 9.
54. António, *100 poemas*, p. 26.
55. M. António, *Rosto de Europa* (Braga: Editora Pax, 1968), p. 111.
56. M. António, *Coração transplantado* (Braga: Editora Pax, 1970), p. 11.

5. Prose Fiction in Angola

1. Garibaldino de Andrade, *O tesouro* (Sá da Bandeira: Coleccão Imbondeiro, 1960), p. 16.
2. Mário de Andrade, *Literatura africana de expressão portuguesa*, vol. II: *Prosa* (Algiers: Published by the author, 1968), p. 257.
3. Janheinz Jahn, *Muntu: The New African Culture*, trans. Marjorie Grene (New York: Grove Press, 1961), p. 100.
4. "Dumba e a Bangala" is included in vol. XIV of an Imbondeiro series which contains stories and poems by Benúdia, Arnaldo Santos, António Cardoso, and Luandino Vieira (Sá da Bandeira, 1961), p. 7.
5. Luandino Vieira, *Luuanda* (Belo Horizonte: Editora Eros, 1965), p. 19.
6. Luandino Vieira, *Vidas novas* (Paris: Edições Anti-Colonial, n.d.), p. 19.
7. M. António, *Farra no fim de semana* (Braga: Editora Pax, 1965), p. 12.
8. M. António, *Mahezu: Tradições angolanas* (Lisbon: Serviço de Publicações Ultramarinas, 1966), p. 71.
9. Arnaldo Santos, *Quinaxixe* (Lisbon: Casa dos Estudantes do Império, 1965), p. 47.
10. Arnaldo Santos, *Tempo de munhungo: Crônicas* (Luanda: Editorial Nós, 1968), p. 12.
11. Santos Lima, *As sementes da liberdade* (Rio de Janeiro: Civilização Brasileira, 1965), p. 89.
12. Catu, the author reveals in a final note, is a fictional name for the town of Teixeira Soares situated at the eastern terminal of the Benguela Railway, near the border of Katanga.
13. In *Contos populares de Angola* Chatelain writes: "The Vandunem [*sic*] family belongs to the native aristocracy of Luanda . . . The Vandunens say, and others have confirmed, that they are direct descendants of the kings of the Akua-Luengu or A-bidi tribe" (p. 543).
14. Domingos Van-Dúnem, "Uma história singular" (Luanda: Unpublished, 1957), p. 10.
15. In May 1971 Domingos Van-Dúnem read his play *Kioxinda* to me during a visit at his home in Luanda.
16. Domingos Van-Dúnem, *Auto de Natal* (Luanda: Published by the author in conjunction with the I.I.C.A., 1972), p. 8.

6. Portugal's East African Province

1. Abshire and Samuels, eds., *Portuguese Africa*, pp. 48–49.
2. See Allen F. Isaacman, *Mozambique: The Africanization of a European Institution 1750–1902* (Madison: University of Wisconsin Press, 1972), for a study of the *prazos*. Also see C. R. Boxer, *Race Relations in the Portuguese Colonial Empire, 1415–1825* (Oxford: Oxford University Press, 1963), especially ch. II, "Moçambique and India."

7. Mozambique's Modern Literary Climate

1. Lisboa, "A poesia em Moçambique," p. 13.
In a volume that has recently come to my attention, Lisboa offers critical essays on literature, including that of Mozambique. Of particular interest is "Algumas considerações em torno da poesia de José Craveirinha" (Some Considerations on José Craveirinha's Poetry), in *Crónica dos anos da peste* (Lourenço Marques: Livraria Académica, 1973).

2. João Dias, *Godido* (Lisbon: África Nova, Edições da Secção de Moçambique da Casa dos Estudantes do Império, 1952), p. 97.

3. Alfredo Margarido, ed., *Poetas de Moçambique* (Lisbon: Casa dos Estudantes do Império, 1962), p. 5.

4. Rui Knopfli, "Considerações sobre a crítica dos poetas de Moçambique," *A Voz de Moçambique*, 15 June 1963.

5. Eugênio Lisboa, preface to Rui Knopfli, *Mangas verdes com sal* (Lourenço Marques: Publicações Europa-América, 1969), p. 12.

6. "A poesia em Moçambique," p. 13.

7. David Caute, introduction to Jean-Paul Sartre, *What is Literature?* trans. Bernard Frechtman (London: Methuen, 1967), pp. vii–viii.

8. Northrop Frye, *The Critical Path* (Bloomington: Indiana University Press, 1971), p. 129.

8. Euro-African Writers

1. *Poetas de Moçambique*, p. 104.

2. Rui Knopfli, "Clima instável: O poeta Orlando Mendes e a crítica," *A Voz de Moçambique*, 31 May 1960, p. 10.

3. Moser, "The Social and Regional Diversity of African Literature in the Portuguese Language," p. 16.

4. Quoted by Rui Knopfli in "Uma nova teoria racista da poesia," *A Voz de Moçambique*, 14 September 1963, n.p.

5. *Poetas de Moçambique*, pp. 107–108.

6. Rui Knopfli, *Reino submarino* (Lourenço Marques: Publicaes Tribuna, 1962), p. 30.

7. Fernando Pessoa, "Autopsicografia," *Fernando Pessoa: Obra poética* (Rio de Janeiro: José Aguilar Editora, 1969), p. 164.

8. Knopfli, *Mangas verdes com sal*, p. 70.

9. Knopfli, *Reino submarino*, p. 104.

9. Poetry and Prose from a Black Perspective

1. *Présence africaine: Nouvelle somme de poésie du monde noir*, no. 57 (1966), 459–460.

2. Lisboa, preface to *Mangas verdes com sal*, p. 8.

3. *Nouvelle somme*, p. 468.

4. After many years of living in Paris, Noémia de Sousa reportedly now resides in Lisbon, but she has not published poetry for many years.

5. José Craveirinha, *Chigubo* (Lisbon: Casa dos Estudantes do Império, 1965), p. 5.

6. Moser, "The Social and Regional Diversity of African Literature in the Portuguese Language," p. 22.

7. Jahn, *Muntu*, p. 101.

8. José Craveirinha, *Paralelo 20*, no. 8 (June 1959), 15.
9. Luís Bernardo Honwana, *Nós matamos o cão tinhoso* (Lourenço Marques: Sociedade de Imprensa de Moçambique, 1964), p. 30.

10. Contemporary Trends and Prospects

1. Mário de Andrade, *Literatura africana de expressão portuguesa*, I, 285.
2. Duarte Galvão, *Poema do tempo presente* (Lourenço Marques: Published by the author, 1960), p. 65.
3. J. P. Grabato Dias and Rui Knopfli, eds., *Caliban 1* (Lourenço Marques: Published by the editors, 1971), p. 2.
4. See ch. XV, "The Negritude School" (1. Caliban and Prospero), in Jahn, *Neo-African Literature*, pp. 239–242.
5. *Caliban 3/4* (June 1972), 81.

11. Ten African Islands

1. See Jaime Cortesão, *História dos descobrimentos portugueses*, 2 vols. (Lisbon: Published by the author, n.d.); in English Abshire and Samuels, eds., *Portuguese Africa*, and Chilcote, *Portuguese Africa*.
2. Francisco José Tenreiro, "Cabo Verde e São Tomé e Príncipe: Esquema de uma evolução conjunta," *Cabo Verde: Boletim de propaganda e informação*, no. 76 (Praia, 1956), 14.
3. Gabriel Mariano, "Do funco ao sobrado ou o 'mundo' que o mulato criou," *Colóquios caboverdianos* (Lisbon: Junta de Investigações do Ultramar, 1959), p. 27.
4. Henrique Teixeira de Sousa, "A estrutura social da Ilha do Fogo em 1940," *Claridade*, no. 5 (Mindelo, 1947), 42.
5. Henrique Teixeira de Sousa, "Sobrados, lojas e funcos," *Claridade*, no. 8 (Mindelo, 1958), 2.
6. Manuel Ferreira, *A aventura crioula* (Lisbon: Editora Ulisseia, 1967), p. 220.
7. Manuel Lopes, "Tomada de vista," *Claridade*, no. 1 (Mindelo, 1936), 5.
8. Manuel Lopes, "Por uma literatura que ponha termo à especulação do 'mistério africano' e de outros lugares-comuns," *Diário de notícias* (Lisbon) 1 January 1960, p. 5. Also see Lopes's remarks in "Temas cabo-verdianos," *Estudos ultramarinos*, no. 3 (Lisbon: Instituto de Estudos Ultramarinos, 1959), 81–88.
9. Gilberto Freyre, *Aventura e rotina* (Lisbon: Livros do Brasil, 1952), p. 239.
10. *Ibid.*, p. 250.
11. Baltasar Lopes, *Cabo Verde visto por Gilberto Freyre* (Praia: Inprensa Nacional, 1956), p. 11.
12. Freyre, *Aventura e rotina*, p. 240.
13. Baltasar Lopes, "Notas para o estudo da linguagem das ilhas," *Claridade*, no. 2 (Mindelo, 1936), 10.
14. José Osório de Oliveira, "Palavras sobre Cabo Verde para serem lidas no Brasil," *Claridade*, no. 2 (Mindelo, 1936), 9.
15. Gabriel Mariano, "A mestiçagem: Seu papel na formação da sociedade coboverdiana," cultural supplement of *Cabo Verde: Boletim*, no. 109 (Praia, 1958), 13.

16. *Ibid.*
17. Mariano, "Do funco ao sobrado," p. 33.
18. *Ibid.*, pp. 39–40.
19. Mariano, "A mestiçagem," p. 19.
20. Pedro de Sousa Lobo, "A originalidade humana de Cabo Verde," *Claridade*, no. 9 (Mindelo, 1960), 56.
21. Jean-Paul Sarrautte, "O samba, a morna e o mandó," *Cabo Verde: Boletim*, no. 138 (Praia, 1961), 7–10.
22. Alfredo Margarido, "João Condé é um velho amigo de Cabo Verde," *Cabo Verde: Boletim*, no. 118 (Praia, 1959), 29.
23. Luís Romano, "Cabo Verde—Renascença de uma civilização no Atlântico médio," reprint from the journal *Ocidente* (Lisbon, 1967), p. 121.
24. Lopes, "Notas para o estudo da linguagem," p. 5.
25. Some linguists use dialect interchangeably with language, and it might be argued that certain dialects of languages such as German and Italian are not readily understood by speakers of the standard language.
26. Baltasar Lopes da Silva, *O dialecto crioulo de Cabo Verde* (Lisbon: Junta das Missões Geográficas e de Investigações do Ultramar, 1957), p. 39.
27. Jorge Morais Barbosa, *Crioulos* (Lisbon: Academia Internacional da Cultura Portuguesa, 1967), p. 39.
28. In the preface to W. A. A. Wilson, *The Crioulo of Guiné* (Johannesburg: University of Witwatersrand, 1962), p. v.
29. Wilson, *The Crioulo of Guiné*, p. 6, note. Wilson also observes that Baltasar Lopes da Silva "gives copious phonetic and etymological information, but little syntax and unfortunately no texts such as would have given more idea of the character of the language" (p. viii, note).
30. *Cabo Verde: Boletim*, no. 43 (Praia, 1953), 25.
31. Gabriel Mariano, "Em torno do crioulo," *Cabo Verde: Boletim*, no. 107 (Praia, 1958), 8.
32. There is also an 1894 edition.
33. Pedro Cardoso, *Folclore caboverdeano* (Porto, 1933), p. 18.
34. *Ibid.*, p. 86.
35. Norman Araújo, *A Study of Cape Verdean Literature* (Boston: Published by the author, 1967), p. 58.
36. Cardoso, *Folclore caboverdeano*, pp. 68–69.
37. Baltasar Lopes, *Claridade*, no. 6 (Mindelo, 1948), 37.
38. *Claridade*, no. 7 (Mindelo, 1949), 34.
39. *Ibid.*, pp. 35–37.
40. Félix Monteiro, "Ana Procópio," *Claridade*, no. 9 (Mindelo, 1960), 16.
41. Lopes, *Claridade*, no. 6 (Mindelo, 1948), 37.
42. Arnaldo França, *Notas sobre poesia e ficção caboverdiana* (Praia: Centico médio," reprint from the journal *Icidente* (Lisbon, 1967), p. 121.
43. See *Claridade*, no. 2 (Mindelo, 1936).

12. The Birth of a Literature

1. See "Carta do Padre António Vieira escripta de Cabo Verde ao padre confessor de sua alteza, indo arribado aquelle Estado," *Cabo Verde: Boletim*, no. 23 (Praia, 1958), p. 11.
2. See Mariano, "Do funco ao sobrado," pp. 43–44.

3. Juvenal Cabral, *Memórias e reflexões* (Praia: Published by the author, 1947), p. 19.

4. *Ibid.*, p. 35.

5. França, *Notas sobre poesia e ficção caboverdiana*, p. 12.

6. Brazilian intellectuals had gone through an identity phase preceding *modernismo*. The modernists were calling for more than regionalist identity; they were seeking to create a unique artistic expression through such things as the synthesis of a national language.

7. The editors of *Claridade* comment, in the eighth issue, on the long interval between appearances of the review: "because of the limitations imposed by the smallness of the milieu and by the necessity of earning a living, it is with great effort that we have been able to publish these eight issues" (p. 76). In 1969 plans were announced to publish a special commemorative issue of *Claridade* dedicated to the early creole-language poet Pedro Cardoso. As of this writing the long-awaited issue has not appeared.

8. Manuel Lopes, *Claridade*, no. 1 (Mindelo, 1936), 5.

9. M. Lopes, "Reflexões sobre a literatura cabo-verdiana," *Colóquios caboverdianos*, p. 17.

10. Fernandes de Oliveira, "Influências sobre as literaturas portuguesas do Atlântico tropical," p. 113.

11. Oswaldo Alcântara, "Poema 5," *Claridade*, no. 8 (Mindelo, 1958), 37.

12. Manuel Bandeira, *Antologia poética* (Rio de Janeiro: Editora do Autor, 1961), p. 95.

13. Virgílio Pires, *Claridade*, no. 9 (Mindelo, 1960), 10.

14. *Ibid.*, p. 8.

15. França, *Notas sobre poesia e ficção caboverdiana*, p. 20.

16. "Acerca da mulher," *Certeza*, no. 1 (São Vicente, 1944), 1.

17. *Ibid.*

18. "Seló: Página dos novíssimos," no. 1 in *Notícias de Cabo Verde*, no. 321 (São Vicente, 26 May, 1962), 4.

19. França, *Notas sobre poesia e ficção caboverdiana*, p. 15.

20. Francisco José Tenreiro and Mário Pinto de Andrade, *Caderno de poesia negra de expressão portuguesa* (Lisbon: Published by the authors, 1953), in the compiler's postscript.

21. Onésimo Silveira, *Consciencialização na literatura* (Lisbon: Casa dos Estudantes do Império, 1963), pp. 22–23.

22. Mário de Andrade, *Literatura africana de expressão portuguesa*, I, xv.

13. A New Poetry

1. In 1935 Jaime de Figueiredo put forth the original idea of a literary journal for which he chose the name *Atlanta*. He had recently returned to Praia from Portugal where he had assimilated the *Presença* spirit of modernity, and it was this spirit, rather than an exclusively regionalist one, that he envisioned for the new journal. Nonetheless, for over twenty years Figueiredo has participated in the development of modern contemporary Cape Verdean literature and culture.

2. António Pedro, *Diário* (Praia: Imprensa Nacional, 1929), p. 11.

3. Jorge Barbosa, *Arguipélago* (São Vicente: Editorial Claridade, 1935), p. 17.

4. Jorge Barbosa, *Claridade*, no. 4 (Mindelo, 1947), 39.

5. "O guardador de rebanhos," *Fernando Pessoa: Obra poética* (São Paulo: José Aguilar, 1969), p. 208.

6. "Poemas inconjuntos," *Fernando Pessoa: Obra poética*, p. 239.

7. Jorge Barbosa, *Caderno de um ilhéu* (Lisbon: Agência-Geral do Ultramar, 1956), p. 71.

8. Amílcar Cabral, "Apontamentos sobre poesia caboverdeana," *Cabo Verde: Boletim*, no. 28 (Praia, 1952), 8.

9. G. Mariano, "Inquietação e serenidade," *Estudos ultramarinos*, no. 3 (1959), 59.

10. Ovídio Martins, *Caminhada* (Lisbon: Casa dos Estudantes do Império, 1962), p. 55.

11. Terêncio Anahory, *Caminho longe* (Lisbon: Sagitário, 1962), p. 17.

12. Onésimo Silveira, *Hora grande* (Nova Lisboa, Angola: Colecção Bailundo, 1962), p. 40.

13. Aguinaldo Fonseca, *Linha do horizonte* (Lisbon: Edição da Secção de Cabo Verde da Casa dos Estudantes do Império, 1951), pp. 61–62.

14. Luís Romano, *Clima* (Natal: Published by the author, 1963), p. 33.

15. António Nunes, *Cabo Verde: Boletim*, no. 108 (Mindelo, 1958), 20.

16. Romano, *Clima*, pp. 33–34.

17. Kaoberdiano Dambara, *Noti* (Algiers: Edição do Departamento de Informação do Comité Central do Partido Africano da Independência da Guiné e de Cabo-Verde, 1965), p. 16.

18. I do not mean to suggest direct influence but rather a set of cultural patterns deriving from West African origins and from similar attitudes toward the black man vis-à-vis the dominant group. Roger D. Abrahams, in his book *Positively Black*, writes that the black American jokes that the documents "are examples of one of the ways in which Negro-white relations are handled by an aggressive and ironic approach to life" (p. 78). He also speaks of the element of "sass" in the vocabulary of "soul," particularly during the so-called black riots of the 1960s. Sass and arrogance appear also in Dambara's protest poetry, particularly in the lines quoted.

19. Mário de Andrade, *La poésie africaine d'expression portugaise*, p. 28.

20. I surveyed the literary scene in Cape Verde's capital city of Praia and in Mindelo, São Vicente, in June 1971.

14. Cape Verde in Narrative

1. In *A Study of Cape Verdean Literature* Norman Araújo translates *ao desamparinho* as simply "helpless," while Óscar Lopes describes the expression as being a lyrical Cape Verdean designation for "dusk," in "Ficção caboverdiana," *Modo de ler* (Porto: Editorial Inova, 1969), p. 140.

2. Manuel Lopes, *O galo que cantou na baía* (Lisbon: Orion, 1959), p. 125.

3. *Ibid.*, p. 191. The suffixes *-inho* and *-zinho* are Portuguese diminutives.

4. Baltasar Lopes, *Chiquinho* (Lisbon: Prelo, 1961), p. 182.

5. António Aurélio Gonçalves, "Pródiga," *Antologia da ficção caboverdiana contemporânea* (Praia: Edições Henriquenas, 1960), p. 22.

6. *Ibid.*, p. 60.

7. A. A. Gonçalves, *Virgens loucas* (Mindelo: Published by the author, 1971), pp. 20–21.

8. Conversation with A. A. Gonçalves on June 20, 1971.

9. Teobaldo Virgínio, *Vida crioula* (Lisbon: Livraria Bertrand, 1967), p. 21.

10. Nuno Miranda, *Gente da ilha* (Lisbon: Agência-Geral do Ultramar, 1961), p. 88.

11. Onésimo Silveira, *Toda a gente fala: Sim, senhor!* (Sá da Bandeira: Colecção Imbondeiro, 1960), pp. 12–13.

12. Luís Romano, *Famintos* (Natal: Editora Leitura, 1961), p. 316.

13. Fanon, *Black Skin, White Masks*, p. 19.

14. Onésimo Silveira, *Cabo Verde: Boletim*, no. 108 (Mindelo, 1958), 28.

15. Luis Romano, *Negrume (Lzimparin)* (Rio de Janeiro: Editora Leitura S/A, 1973), p. 14.

16. "Encontro com Manuel Ferreira," in "Vae Victus," young people's editorial section of *Litoral*, no. 368 (Avieiro, Portugal), 11 November 1961, p. 2.

17. Manuel Ferreira, *Voz de prisão* (Porto: Editorial Inova Limitada, 1971), p. 39.

15. The Case of Portuguese Guinea

1. The author, André Álvares de Almada, describes his book as a treatise that covers the territory from the Sanagá River to the shoals of Santa Ana and that gives an account of the coastal peoples and their customs, weapons, manner of dress, laws, and wars. See António Brásio's edition (Lisbon: Editorial L.I.A.M., 1964).

2. João Alves das Neves, *Poetas e contistas africanos* (São Paulo: Editora Brasileira, 1963), p. 25.

16. Two Plantation Islands in the Gulf of Guinea

1. See chs. II, III, and IV of Tenreiro, *A Ilha de São Tomé* (Lisbon: Memórias da Junta de Investigações do Ultramar, 1961).

2. Maria Manuela Margarido, "De Costa Alegre a Francisco José Tenreiro,"*Estudos ultramarinos*, no. 3 (1959), 96.

3. Fernando Reis, *Soiá: Literatura oral de São Tomé* (Braga: Editora Pax, 1965), p. 19.

17. Filhos Da Terra at Home and Abroad

1. Alfredo Margarido, ed., *Poetas da São Tomé e Príncipe* (Lisbon: Casa dos Estudantes do Império, 1963), p. 66.

2. *Ibid.*, p. 76.

3. See Mário de Andrade, *La poésie africaine d'expression portugaise*, p. 70.

4. Maria Manuela Margarido, "Sòcòpé," *Poetas de São Tomé e Príncipe*, p. 80.

5. See preface of *Versos* (Lisbon: Livraria Ferin, 1951), p. 10.

6. *Versos*, p. 39.

7. See ch. II in Lopes Rodrigues, *O livro de Costa Alegre* (Lisbon: Agência-Geral do Ultramar, 1969).

8. *Obra poética de Francisco José Tenreiro* (Braga: Editora Pax, 1967), p. 67.

Conclusions

1. Fredric Jameson, *Marxism and Form: Twentieth-Century Dialectical Theories of Literature* (Princeton, N.J.: Princeton University Press, 1974), pp. 100–101.

2. I am indebted to M. António for supplying me with several issues of the arts and letters supplement of *A Província de Angola*. I am also grateful to Manuel Ferreira for keeping me informed of developments in Portugal and Africa.

SELECT BIBLIOGRAPHY

Select Bibliography

This bibliography contains the major primary and secondary sources cited in this study. Also included are some items, particularly publications by representative Afro-Portuguese authors, not cited in this study.* The first five divisions of this bibliography correspond to the areas of Angola, Mozambique, Cape Verde, Portuguese Guinea, and São Tomé-Príncipe. Following are sections on Portuguese Africa in general and on other sources cited in this study; the final part consists of Afro-Portuguese literature in English translation.

Angola

Albuquerque, Orlando de. *O homem que tinha a chuva*. Lisbon: Agência-Geral do Ultramar, 1968. Novel.
Andrade (Fernando da) Costa. *Terra de acácias rubras*. Lisbon: Casa dos Estudantes do Império, 1961. Poetry.
———. "Os regressados das ilhas," *Literatura africana de expressão portuguesa*, vol. II. Algiers, 1968. Short story.
Andrade, Garibaldino de. *O tesouro*. Sá da Bandeira: Colecção Imbondeiro, 1960. Short stories.

---

*As of this writing Gerald Moser's *A Tentative Portuguese-African Bibliography* is the most complete listing of Afro-Portuguese literature. Moser, however, in collaboration with Manuel Ferreira, has scheduled for publication in 1975 a listing entitled *Bibliography of Portuguese-African Literature* to be issued by Edições 70 in conjunction with the Instituto de Alta Cultura of Lisbon.

Andrade, Garibaldino de, and Leonel Cosme. *Contos d'África: Antologia de contos angolanos.* Sá da Bandeira: Imbondeiro, 1961. Short story anthology.

———. *Novos contos d'África: Antologia de contos angolanos.* Sá da Bandeira: Imbondeiro, 1962. Short story anthology.

Andrade, Mário (Pinto) de. "Littérature et nationalisme en Angola," *Présence africaine*, no. 41 (1962). Criticism.

António (Fernandes de Oliveira), Mário. "O cozinheiro Vicente," *Mensagem*, nos. 2, 3, and 4. Luanda, October 1952. Short story.

———. *Poesias.* Lisbon: Published by the author, 1956. Poetry.

———. "Considerações sobre poesia," *Cultura*, no. 2. Luanda, January 1958. Criticism.

———. *Amor.* Lisbon: Casa dos Estudantes do Império, 1960. Poetry.

———. *Poemas e canto miúdo.* Sá da Bandeira: Colecção Imbondeiro, 1960. Poetry.

———. *Chingufo: Poemas angolanos.* Lisbon: Agência-Geral do Ultramar, 1961. Poetry.

———. *Gente para romance.* Sá da Bandeira: Colecção Imbondeiro, 1961. Short stories.

———. *A sociedade angolana no fim do século XIX e um seu escritor.* Luanda: Editorial NÓS, 1961. Historical essay.

———. *100 poemas.* Luanda: ABC, 1963. Includes most of António's previously published poems.

———. *Poesia angolana de Tomaz Vieira da Cruz.* Lisbon: Casa dos Estudantes do Império, 1963. Criticism.

———. *Crónica da cidade estranha.* Lisbon: Agência-Geral do Ultramar, 1964. Short stories.

———. *Farra no fim de semana.* Braga: Editora Pax, 1965. Short stories.

———. *Colaborações angolanas no "Almanach de lembranças," 1851-1900.* Luanda: Separata do Instituto de Investigação Científica Angolana, 1966. Historical essay.

———. *Era, tempo de poesia.* Sá da Bandeira: Imbondeiro, 1966. Poetry.

———. *Mahezu: Tradições angolanas.* Lisbon: Serviço de Publicações Ultramarinas, 1966. Folk tales.

———. *Luanda "ilha" crioula.* Lisbon: Agência-Geral do Ultramar, 1968. Essays.

———. *Nossa Senhora de Vitória.* Luanda: Published by the author, 1968. Poetry.

———. *Rosto de Europa.* Braga: Editorial Pax, 1968. Poetry.

———. *Coração transplantado.* Braga: Editora Pax, 1970. Poetry.

———. Preface to Alfredo Troni. *Nga Muturi: Cenas de Luanda.* Lisbon: Colecção Textos Breves das Edições 70, 1973. Essays.

Archer, Maria. *África selvagem: Folclore dos negros do grupo "bantu."* Lisbon: Guimarães, 1935. Colonial literature.

Assis Júnior, António. *O segredo da morta: Romance de costumes angolanos.* Luanda: A Luzitana, 1934. Novel.

Azeredo, Guilhermina de. *Feitiços.* Lisbon: A. M. Pereira, 1935. Short stories.

Cadornega, António de Oliveira. *História geral das guerras angolanas.* 3 vols. Preface and notes by Manuel Alves da Cunha. Lisbon: Agência-Geral das Colonias, 1943 (published originally in part in 1680). History.

Cardoso, António. "Poesia angolana ou poesia em Angola," *Cultura*, nos. 2 and 3. Luanda, January and March 1958. Criticism.

_____. "A poética de Mário António," *Cultura*, no. 12. Luanda, November 1960. Criticism.

_____. *Poemas de circunstância.* Lisbon: Casa dos Estudantes do Império, 1961. Poetry.

Casimiro, Augusto. *Nova largada: Romance de África.* Lisbon: Seara Nova, 1929. Colonial novel.

César (Pires Monteiro), Amândio. *Contos portugueses do Ultramar,* vol. II. Porto: Portucalense Editora, 1969. Anthology of short stories.

Chatelain, Héli. *Kimbundu Grammar.* 1888–89.

_____. *Folk-tales of Angola.* Lancaster, Pa.: American Folk-lore Society, 1894.

_____. *Contos populares de Angola.* Trans. M. Garcia da Silva. Lisbon: Agência-Geral do Ultramar, 1964. Translation of *Folk-tales of Angola.*

Cruz, Tomaz Vieira da. *Quissange—Saudade negra.* Lisbon: Published by the author, 1932. Poetry.

_____. *Tatuagem.* Lisbon: Published by the author, 1941. Poetry.

_____. *Cazumbi: Poesia de Angola.* Lisbon: Portugália, 1950. Poetry.

_____. *Quissange.* Luanda: Lello Angola, 1971. Contains the three previous collections of poetry.

Cruz, Viriato da. *Poemas (1947–1950).* Lisbon: Casa dos Estudantes do Império, 1961. Poetry.

Cultura. Monthly publication of scientific, literary, and artistic news of the Sociedade Cultural de Angola. A total of nineteen issues from April 1945 to May 1951.

Cultura. Property and edition of the Sociedade Cultural de Angola. A total of thirteen issues from November 1957 to May 1961.

Dáskalos, Alexandre. *Poemas.* Lisbon: Casa dos Estudantes do Império, 1961. Poetry.

Dias, Eduardo Mayone. "O elemento de confrontação na poesia de Angola, *Hispania*, LIV, no. 1. Amherst, March 1971.

Dionísio, Marilu. "Reencontro." Luanda, 1970. Unpublished collection of poetry.

Ervedosa, Carlos. *A literatura angolana: Resenha histórica.* Lisbon: Casa dos Estudantes do Império, 1963. Historical-critical essay.

Estermann, Carlos. *Etnografia do sudoeste de Angola,* vol. I. Lisbon: Junta de Investigações do Ultramar, 1959? Ethnography.

Figueira, Luís. *Princesa negra: O preço da civilização em África.* Coimbra: Coimbra Editora, 1932. Colonial novel.

Galvão, Henrique. *O velo d'oiro.* Lisbon: Livraria Popular, 1930. Colonial novel.

_____. *O sol dos trópicos.* Lisbon: Published by the author, 1936. Colonial novel.

_____. *Kurika: Romance dos bichos do mato.* Lisbon: Livraria Popular, 1944. Novel.

_____. *Impala: Romance dos bichos do mato.* Lisbon: Livraria Popular, 1946. Novel.

_____. *Vagô.* Lisbon? 1953. Novel.

_____. *Pele.* Lisbon, 1958. Novel.

Guerra, Mário (Benúdia). "Dumba e a bangela," Imbondeiro series no. 14. Sá da Bandeira: Imbondeiro, 1961. Short story.

Jacinto, António. *Poemas*. Lisbon: Casa dos Estudantes do Império, 1961. Poetry.

Jorge, Tomás (Tomás Jorge Vieira da Cruz). *Areal*. Sá da Bandeira: Imbondeiro, 1961. Poetry.

―――. "Talamungongo." Unpublished collection of poetry.

Lara, Alda. *Poemas*. Sá da Bandeira: Colecção Imbondeiro, 1966. Poetry.

Lara Filho, Ernesto. *O canto do martrindinde e outros poemas feitos no Puto*. Luanda: Published by the author, 1963. Poetry.

―――. *Seripipi na gaiola*. Luanda: ABC, 1970. Poetry.

Lima, Santos (Manuel Lima). *Kissange*. Lisbon: Casa dos Estudantes do Império, n.d. Poetry.

―――. *As sementes da liberdade*. Rio de Janeiro: Civilização Brasileira, 1965. Novel.

―――. "O sapo e o mocho," *Literatura africana de expressão portuguesa*, vol. II. Algiers, 1968. Short story.

Lopo, Júlio de Castro. *Jornalismo de Angola: Subsídios para a sua história*. Luanda: Centro de Informações e Turismo de Angola, 1964. Essay.

Macedo, Jorge. *1° Tetemba*. Luanda: Published by the author, 1965. Poetry.

―――. *As mulheres*. Luanda: Published by the author, 1970. Poetry.

―――. *Pai Ramos*. Luanda: Published by the author, 1971. Poetry.

Machado, Pedro. *Scenas d'África* (romance íntimo). 2nd ed. Lisbon: Ferin, 1892. Novel.

Maciel, Artur. *Angola heróica: 120 dias com os nossos soldados*. Lisbon: Livraria Bertrand, 1964. Nonfiction.

Margarido, Alfredo. "Castro Soromenho, romancista angolano," *Estudos ultramarinos*, no. 3. Lisbon, 1959. Critical essay.

―――. "A osga," *Novos contos d'África*. Sá da Bandeira: Colecção Imbondeiro, 1962. Short story.

Matta, Joaquim Dias Cordeiro da. *Delírios*. Lisbon: Published by the author, 1887. Poetry.

―――. *Philosphia popular em provérbios angolenses*. Lisbon: Typographia e Stereotypia Moderna, 1891. Folklore.

Mensagem: Revista trimestral de arte e cultura. Luanda. Two issues, the second including numbers 2, 3, and 4, 1951 and 1952. From 1949 until 1964 another *Mensagem* served as a circular and then as a sporadically published official organ, along with the *Boletim da CEI*, of the Lisbon-based Casa dos Estudantes do Império.

Neto, Agostinho. *Quatro poemas de Agostinho Neto*. Published in the series Cadernos de poesia organized by Augusto Ferreira. Pôvoa de Varzim: Tipografia Frasco, 1957. Poetry.

―――. *Poemas*. Lisbon: Casa dos Estudantes do Império, 1961. Poetry.

―――. *Con occhi ascuitti*. Trans. Joyce Lussu. Milan: Il Saggiatore, Biblioteca della Silerchia, 1963. Bilingual, Portuguese-Italian poetry.

Organissia, Y. S. ed. *Doróga (O caminho: Contos e narrativas dos escritores angolanos)*. Trans. L. V. Nekrassova. Moscow: Khudozhestvennaya Literatura, 1964. Angolan stories in Russian translation.

Paiva, António de Aragão. *Terras do nu e do batuque*. Lisbon: Informação Colonial, 1933. Colonial literature.

Poetas angolanos, preface by Alfredo Margarido. Lisbon: Casa dos Estudantes do Império, 1962. Poetry.

Riausova, Elena A. "A ficção de Angola: As tendências nacionalistas libertadoras," *Folclore e literatura de África*. Moscow, 1969. Critical essay.

Ribas, Óscar (Bento). *Nuvens que passam*. Luanda: Published by the author, 1927. Novella.

———. *O resgate de uma falta*. Luanda: Published by the author, 1929. Novella.

———. *Uanga: Romance folclórico angolano*. Luanda: Lello, 1951. Folklore.

———. *Ecos da minha terra: Dramas angolanos*. Luanda: Lello, 1952. Stories.

———. *Missosso: Literatura tradicional angolana*, vol. I (1961), vol. II (1962), vol. III (1964). Luanda: Lello. Folklore.

———. *Izomba: Associativismo e recreio*. Luanda: Lello, 1965. Popular customs.

———. *Sunguilando*. Lisbon: Agência-Geral do Ultramar, 1967. Folklore.

Santos, Arnaldo. *Fuga*. Lisbon: Casa dos Estudantes do Império, 1960. Poetry.

———. *Uíge*. Sá da Bandeira: Colecção Imbondeiro, 1961. Poetry.

———. *Quinaxixe*. Lisbon: Casa dos Estudantes do Império, 1965. Short stories.

———. *Tempo de munhungo: Crônicas*. Luanda: Editorial Nós, 1968. Short stories.

Silva Afonso, Maria Perpétua Candeia da. "O homem enfeitiçado," Imbondeiro series. Sá da Bandeira: Colecção Imbondeiro, 1961. Short story.

———. *Navionga, filha de branco*. Colecção Unidade Ficção. Lisbon: Agência-Geral do Ultramar, 1967. Novel.

Soromenho, (Fernando Monteiro de) Castro. *Nhári: Drama da gente negra*. Luanda: Livraria Civilização, 1938. Stories.

———. *Homens sem caminho*. Lisbon: Portugália, 1942. Stories.

———. *Rajada e outras histórias*. Lisbon: Portugália, 1943. Stories.

———. *Terras mortas*. Colecção Gavista. Rio de Janeiro: Casa do Estudante do Brasil, 1949. Novel.

———. *Viragem*. Colecção Atlântida. Lisbon: Ulisséia, 1957. Novel.

———. *Histórias da terra negra: Contos e novelas e uma narrativa*. Lisbon: Gleba, 1960. Two-volume collection of stories published earlier.

Van-Dúnem, Domingos. "Uma história singular." Luanda, 1957. Unpublished short story.

———. "Kioxinda." Luanda, 1967. Unpublished three-act play.

———. "Oh! o Sporting destruiu tudo," *Noite e dia*, no. 195 (22 April 1971). Short story.

———. *Auto de Natal*. Luanda: Published by the author, 1972. Play.

Ventura, (Manuel Joaquim) Reis. "O drama do velho Cafaia," *Novos contos d'África*. Sá da Bandeira: Colecção Imbondeiro, 1962. Short story.

———. *Soldado que vais à guerra: auto em louvor dos soldados que acudiram em defesa de Angola*. Braga: Cruz, 1964. Poetry.

Victor, Geraldo Bessa. *Ecos dispersos*. Lisbon: Imprensa Portugal-Brasil, 1941. Poetry.

———. *Ao som das marimbas*. Lisbon: Livraria Portugália, 1943. Poetry.

———. *Mucanda*. Braga: Editora Pax, 1964. Poetry.

———. *Cubata abandonada*. Braga: Editora Pax, 1966. Poetry.

———. *Sanzala sem batuque*. Braga: Editora Pax, 1967. Short stories.

———. *Quinjango no folclore angolense*. Braga: Editora Pax, 1970. Folklore and history.

———. *Monandengue*. Lisbon: Livraria Portugal, 1973. Poetry.

Vieira, Luandino (José Vieira Mateus de Graça). *A cidade e a infância*. Lisbon: Casa dos Estudantes do Império, 1960. Short stories.

———. *Duas histórias de pequenos burgueses*. Sá da Bandeira: Imbondeiro, 1961. Short stories.

———. *Luuanda*. Belo Horizonte: Editora Eros, 1965. The three long short stories of *Luuanda* were originally published under that title in Luanda: ABC, 1963.

———. *A vida verdadeira de Domingos Xavier*. Lisbon: Edições 70, 1974. Novel.

———. *No antigamente na vida*. Lisbon: Edições 70, 1974. Short stories.

———. *Velhas estórias*. Lisbon: Plátano Editora, 1974. Short stories.

———. *Vidas novas*. Paris: Edições anti-colonial, n.d. Short stories.

Wheeler, Douglas L., and René Pélissier. *Angola*. New York: Praeger, 1971. Cultural and political history.

Mozambique

Craveirinha, José. *Chigubo*. Lisbon: Casa dos Estudantes do Império, 1965. Poetry.

———. *Karingana ua karingana*. Lourenço Marques: Edição da Académica, 1974. Poetry.

Dias, João. *Godido*. Lisbon: África Nova, Edição da Secção de Moçambique da Casa dos Estudantes do Império, 1952. Short stories.

Dias, J. P. Grabato, and Rui Knopfli, eds. *Caliban 1*. Lourenço Marques, 1971. Poetry magazine. *Caliban 2* appeared November 1971 and *Caliban 3/4* June 1972.

Galvão, Duarte. *Poema do tempo presente*. Lourenço Marques: Published by the author, 1960. Poetry.

Hlongo, Lindo. "Os noivos ou conferência dramática sobre o lobolo." Unpublished play except for an excerpt in *Caliban 3/4*.

Honwana, Luís Bernardo. *Nós matamos o cão tinhoso*. Lourenço Marques: Sociedade de Imprensa de Moçambique, 1964. Short stories.

Isaacman, Allen F. *Mozambique: The Africanization of a European Institution 1750–1902*. Madison: University of Wisconsin Press, 1972. Social and economic history.

Knopfli, Rui. *O país dos outros*. Lourenço Marques: Published by the author, 1959. Poetry.

———. "Clima instável: O poeta Orlando Mendes e a crítica," *A Voz de Moçambique*. Lourenço Marques, 31 May 1960. Criticism.

———. *Reino submarino*. Lourenço Marques: Publicações Tribuna, 1962. Poetry.

———. "Considerações sobre a crítica dos poetas de Moçambique," *A Voz de Moçambique*. Lourenço Marques, 15, 22, and 29 June 1963. Criticism.

———. "Uma nova teoria racista da poesia: Poetas em escala menor," *A Voz de Moçambique*. Lourenço Marques, 14 September 1963. Criticism.

———. "Ainda o diletante Alfredo Margarido," *A Tribuna*. 1963? Criticism.

———. *Máquina de areia*. Beira: Edição do *Notícias da Beira*, 1964. Poetry.

———. *Mangas verdes com sal*. Lourenço Marques: Publicações Europa-América, 1969. Poetry.

———. *A Ilha de Próspero*. Lourenço Marques: Editora Minerva, 1972. Photographs and text.

Lacerda, Alberto de. *Exílio*. Lisbon: Livraria Portugália, 1966. Poetry.

Lisboa, Eugénio. Preface to Rui Knopfli's *Mangas verdes com sal*. Critical essay—see listing under Knopfli.

———. "A poesia em Moçambique," special supplement "Moçambique," *A Capital*. Lisbon, 14 September 1970. Criticism.

———. *Crónica dos anos da peste—I*. Lourenço Marques: Livraria Académica, 1973. Includes the following essays on Mozambican literature: "Algumas considerações em torno da poesia de José Craveirinha," "A literatura moçambicana à vol d'oiseau," "*Mangas verdes com sal*—um novo livro de Rui Knopfli."

Margarido, Alfredo. "A poesia moçambicana e os críticos de óculos," *Mensagem*. Lisbon: Casa dos Estudantes do Império, April 1963. Criticism.

———. "Do poeta Knopfli à cultura moçambicana," *Mensagem*. Lisbon: Casa dos Estudantes do Império, June 1963. Criticism.

———. "Outra vez o poeta," *A Voz de Moçambique*, no. 88. Lourenço Marques, 3 August 1963. Criticism.

Mendes, Orlando, *Clima*. Coimbra: Published by the author, 1959. Poetry.

———. *Portagem*. Beira: Edicão do *Notícias da Beira*, 1965. Novel.

Msaho: Folha de poesia em fascículos. Lourenço Marques: Empresa Moderna, 25 October 1952. Poetry anthology.

Nekrassova, L. V., ed. and trans. "Quando as lutas são o sentido da vida," *Inostrannaya literatura*, no. 5. Moscow, 1968. Anthology of poems from Mozambique in Russian translation.

Paralelo 20. Beira, August 1957 to February 1961. Monthly cultural and literary review.

Poetas de Moçambique. Intro. Alfredo Margarido. Lisbon: Casa dos Estudantes do Império, 1962. Poetry.

Simões, Eduardo Vieira. *Vagabundo na cidade: Crónicas e histórias quase verdadeiras*. Coimbra: Atlântida, 1959. Short stories.

———. *Cidade dos confins*. Beira: Notícias da Beira, 1963. Short stories.

Cape Verde

Alcântara, Oswaldo (Baltasar Lopes da Silva). "Poema 5," *Claridade*, no. 8. Mindelo, 1958. Poetry.

Almanach luso-africano, for 1898 (vol. I) and for 1899 (vol. II). Organized by António Manuel da Costa Teixeira. Paris: Aillard Guillard. Folklore and popular literature.

Anahory, Terêncio. *Caminho largo*. Lisbon: Sagitário, 1962. Poetry.

Antologia da ficção cabo-verdiana contemporânea. Intro. Manuel Ferreira. Selection and notes by Baltasar Lopes. Commentary by A. A. Gonçalves. Praia: Edições Henriquinas do Achamento de Cabo Verde, 1960. Stories and prose fiction excerpts.

Araújo, Norman. *A Study of Cape Verdean Literature*. Boston: Published by the author, 1966. Critical study.

Barbosa, Jorge. *Arquipélago*. Mindelo: Editorial Claridade, 1935. Poetry.

———. *Ambiente*. Praia: Minerva de C. Verde, 1941. Poetry.

———. *Caderno de um ilhéu*. Lisbon: Agência-Geral do Ultramar, 1956. Poetry.

Boletim dos alunos do Liceu Gil Eanes. One issue. Mindelo, 1959. Literary and cultural bulletin.

Cabo Verde: Boletim de propaganda e informação. October 1952 to June 1964.

Cabral, Amílcar. "Apontamentos sobre poesia caboverdeana," *Cabo Verde: Boletim de propaganda e informação,* no. 28. Praia, January 1952. Critical essay.

Cabral, Juvenal. *Memórias e reflexões.* Praia: Published by the author, 1947. Memoirs.

Cardoso, Pedro. *Folclore caboverdiano.* Porto: Edições Maranus, 1933. Folklore.

Certeza: Folha da Academia. Two issues. Mindelo, 1944. Literary and cultural journal.

Claridade: Revista de arte e letras. Nine issues: March 1936, August 1936, March 1937, January 1947, September 1947, July 1948, December 1949, May 1958, December 1960. Mindelo. Culture, art, and literary journal.

Colóquios cabo-verdianos. Preface by Jorge Dias. Lisbon: Junta de Investigações do Ultramar, 1959. Articles on Cape Verdean culture and literature.

Costa, José Maria da. "Devemos evitar o crioulo: O crioulo é uma inferioridade," *Cabo Verde: Boletim,* no. 43. Praia, April 1953. Article.

Dambara, Kaoberdiano. *Noti: Edição do Comité Central do Partido da Independência da Guiné e de Cabo Verde.* This edition of creole poems was published by the PAIGC—African Party for the Independence of Guinea and Cape Verde; place and date of publication are uncertain, but perhaps Algiers, 1968.

Duarte, Manuel. "Caboverdianidade e africanidade," *Vértice,* no. 134. Coimbra, 1951. Essay.

Ferreira, Manuel. *Morna: Contos de Cabo Verde.* 1948. 2nd ed., "rewritten," Lisbon: Início, 1967. 3rd ed. included in *Terra trazida.* Short stories.

———. *Morabeza.* 1958. 2nd ed. amended and augmented, Lisbon: Editora Ulisseia Limitada, 1965. 3rd ed. included in *Terra trazida.* Short stories.

———. "Encontro com M. Ferreira," "Vae Victus," young people's editorial section of *Litoral,* no. 368. Avieiro, 11 November 1961. Interview.

———. *Grande fabulário de Portugal e Brasil: Fabulário do Ultramar Português.* 2 vols. ed. Vieira de Almeida and Câmara Cascudo. Lisbon: Fólio, 1962. Folk tales.

———. *Hora di bai.* 1963. 3rd ed. Lisbon: Plátano, 1973. Novel.

———. *A aventura crioula.* Lisbon: Editora Ulisseia, 1967. 2nd ed. rev. Lisbon: Plátano, 1973. Cultural study.

———. *Voz de prisão.* Porto: Editorial Inova, 1971. Novel.

———. *Terra trazida.* Lisbon: Plátano, 1972. Short stories; most published previously, some revised, in *Morna* and *Morabeza.*

Fonseca, Aguinaldo. *Linha do horizonte.* Lisbon: Edição da Secção de Cabo Verde da Casa dos Estudantes do Império, 1951. Poetry.

França, Arnaldo. *Notas sobre poesia e ficção caboverdiana.* Praia: Centro de Informação e Turismo, 1962. Critical essay.

Gonçalves, António Aurélio. "Recaída," pt. I in *Claridade,* no. 5, Mindelo, 1947; pt. II in *Claridade,* no. 6, Mindelo, 1948. Short story.

———. *O enterro de Nhâ Candinha Sena.* Praia: Divisão de Propaganda e Informação, 1957. Long short story.

———. "Pródiga," *Antologia da ficção caboverdiana contemporanea.* Also published with "O enterro de Nhâ Candinha Sena," Imbondeiro series. Sá da Bandeira: Colecção Imbondeiro, 1962. Short story.

———. *Noite de vento*. Praia: Centro de Informação e Turismo, 1970. Novella.

———. *Virgens loucas*. Mindelo: Published by the author, 1971. Novella.

Lobo, Pedro de Sousa. "A originalidade humana de Cabo Verde," *Claridade*, no. 9, Mindelo, 1960. Essay.

Lopes, Manuel. *Chuva braba*. Lisbon: Instituto de Cultura e Formento de Cabo Verde, 1956. Novel.

———. *O galo que cantou na baía*. Lisbon: Orion, 1959. Short stories.

———. *Os flagelados do vento leste*. Lisbon: Ulisseia Editora, 1959. Novel.

———. "Reflexões sobre a literatura cabo-verdiana," *Colóquios cabo-verdianos*. Lisbon: Junta de Investigações do Ultramar, 1959. Essay.

———. "Temas cabo-verdianos," *Estudos ultramarinos*, no. 3. Lisbon: Instituto de Estudos Ultramarinos, 1959. Essay.

———. "Por uma literatura que ponha termo à especulação do 'mistério africano' e de outros lugares comuns," *Diário de Notícias*. Lisbon, 1 June 1960. Article.

———. *Crioulo e outros poemas*. Lisbon: Gráfica Eme Silva, 1964. Poetry.

Lopes, Óscar. "Ficção caboverdiana," *Modo de ler*. Porto: Editorial Inova, 1969.

Lyall, Archibald. *Black and White Make Brown*. London: Published by the author, 1928. Popular anthropology.

Margarido, Alfredo. "João Condé é um velho amigo de Cabo Verde," *Cabo Verde: Boletim*, no. 118. Praia, 1959. Essay.

Mariano, Gabriel. "O rapaz doente," *Cabo Verde: Boletim*, no. 94. Praia, 1957. Short story.

———. "Negritude e caboverdianidade," *Cabo Verde: Boletim*, no. 104. Praia, 1958. Essay.

———. "Em torno do crioulo," *Cabo Verde: Boletim*, no. 107. Praia, 1958. Essay.

———. "A mestiçagem: Seu papel na formação da sociedade caboverdiana," cultural supplement of *Cabo Verde: Boletim*, no. 109. Praia, 1958. Essay.

———. "Do funco ao sobrado ou o 'mundo' que o mulato criou," *Colóquios caboverdianos*. Lisbon: Junta de Investigações do Ultramar, 1959. Essay.

———. "Inquietação e serenidade," *Estudos ultramarinos*, no. 3. Lisbon: Instituto Superior de Estudos Ultramarinos, 1959. Essay.

Martins, Ovídio. *Caminhada*. Lisbon: Casa dos Estudantes do Império, 1962. Poetry.

———. *Tutchinha (Tchutchinha)*. Imbondeiro series, no. 30. Sá da Bandeira: Colecção Imbondeiro, 1962. Short story and poetry.

Melo, Virgínio Nobre de (Teobaldo Virgínio). "Beira do cais," *Claridade*, no. 9. Mindelo, 1960. Also published in *Na beira do cais*, Imbondeiro series, no. 44. Sá da Bandeira: Colecção Imbondeiro, 1963. Short story.

Miranda, Nuno. *Cais de ver partir*. Lisbon: Orion, 1960. Poetry.

———. *Gente da ilha*. Lisbon: Agência-Geral do Ultramar, 1961. Short stories.

Modernos poetas cabo-verdianos, ed. Jaime de Figueiredo. Praia: Edições Henriquenas do Achamento de Cabo Verde, 1961.

Monteiro, Félix. "Tabanca," pt. I in *Claridade*, no. 6, July 1948; pt. II in *Claridade*, no. 7, December 1949. Mindelo. Ethnographic essay.

———. "Ana Procópio," *Claridade*, no. 9. Mindelo, 1960. Essay.

Morais-Barbosa, Jorge. *Crioulos*. Lisbon: Academia Internacional da Cultura Portuguesa, 1967. Book-length study of Portuguese creoles.

Oliveira, José Osório de. "Palavras sobre Cabo Verde para serem lidas no Brasil," *Claridade*, no. 2. Mindelo, 1936. Essay.

Parsons, Elsie Clews. *Folk-lore from the Cape Verde Islands*. 2 vols. Cambridge, Mass., and New York: American Folk-lore Society, 1923. Folktales.

Pedro, António. *Diário*. Praia: Imprensa Nacional, 1929. Poetry.

Pires, Virgílio. "Titina," *Claridade*, no. 9. Mindelo, 1960. Short story.

Romano, Luís (Madeira de Melo). *Famintos*. Natal: Editora Leitura, 1961. Novel.

————. "Cabo Verde—Renascença de uma civilização no Atlântico médio," *Ocidente*. Lisbon, 1962. Essay.

————. *Clima*. Recife: Imprensa Oficial, 1963. Poetry.

————. *Negrume (Lzimparin)*. Rio de Janeiro: Editora Leitura, 1973. Bilingual, Portuguese-creole story.

Saurrautte, Jean-Paul. "O samba, a morna e o mandó," *Cabo Verde: Boletim*, no. 138. Praia, 1961. Essay.

Seló: Página dos novíssimos, no. 1, in *Notícias de Cabo Verde*, no. 321. Mindelo, 26 May 1962. Literary page.

Silva, Baltasar Lopes da (Baltasar Lopes). "Notas para o estudo da linguagem das ilhas," *Claridade*, no. 2. Mindelo, 1936. Essay.

————. "Uma experiência românica nos trópicos," *Claridade*, no. 4. Mindelo, 1947. Essay.

————. "O folklore poético da Ilha de Santiago," *Claridade*, no. 7. Mindelo, 1949. Essay.

————. *Cabo Verde visto por Gilberto Freyre*. Praia: Imprensa Nacional, 1956. Essay.

————. *O dialecto crioulo de Cabo Verde*. Lisbon: Junta das Missões Geográficas e de Investigações do Ultramar, 1957. Book-length study of Cape Verdean creole.

————. *Chiquinho*. Lisbon: Prelo, 1961. Novel.

Silveira, Onésimo. "Destino de Bia de Rosa," *Cabo Verde: Boletim*, no. 108. Praia, 1958. Short story.

————. *Toda a gente fala: Sim, senhor*. Sá da Bandeira: Colecção Imbondeiro, 1960. Short story.

————. *Hora grande*. Nova Lisboa: Colecção Bailundo, 1962. Poetry.

————. *Consciencialização na literatura*. Lisbon: Casa dos Estudantes do Império, 1963. Essay.

Sousa, Henrique Teixeira de. "A estrutura social da Ilha do Fogo em 1940," *Claridade*, no. 5. Mindelo, 1947. Essay.

————. "Sobrados, lojas e funcos," *Claridade*, no. 8. Mindelo, 1958. Essay.

————. "Dragão e eu," *Antologia da ficção cabo-verdiana contemporânea*. Praia: Edições Henriquinas do Achamento de Cabo Verde, 1960. Short story.

————. "Na corte d'El Rei D. Pedro," *Livro de Natal* (annual promotional volume of the pharmaceutical firm Lusofármaco). Lisbon: Lusofármãco, 1970. Short story.

"Suplemento cultural de Cabo Verde," cultural-literary supplement of *Cabo Verde: Boletim*. Praia, 1958.

Tavares, Eugênio. *Morna*. Lisbon: J. Rodrigues, 1932. Poetry and folklore.

Tenreiro, Francisco José. "Cabo-Verde e São Tomé-Príncipe: Esquema de uma evolução conjunta," *Cabo Verde: Boletim*, no. 76. Praia, 1956. (Essay).

Virgínio, Teobaldo (Virgínio Nobre de Melo). *Vida crioula*. Lisbon: Livraria Bertrand, 1967. Novella.

Wilson, W. A. A. *The Crioulo of Guiné*. Johannesburg: University of Witwatersrand, 1962. Monograph on Cape Verdean creole in Portuguese Guinea.

Portuguese Guinea

Almada, André Álvares de. *Tratado breve dos rios de Guiné e Cabo Verde*. Intro. and notes by António Brásio C.S.Sp. Lisbon: Editorial L.I.A.M., 1964. Ethnology.

Barbosa, Alexandre. *Guinéus: Contos, narrativas, crónicas*. Lisbon: Agência-Geral do Ultramar, 1962. Stories.

Belchior, Manuel. *Grandeza africana: Lendas da Guiné Portuguesa*. Lisbon: Edições Ultramar, 1963. Folklore.

————. *Contos mandingas*. Porto: Portucalense Editora, 1968. Stories and legends.

Boletim cultural da Guiné Portuguesa. Bissau. Culture and folklore.

Castro, Fernanda de. *África raiz*. Lisbon: Published by the author, 1966. Poetry.

Conduto, João Eleutério. *Contos bijagós*. *Boletim cultural da Guiné Portuguesa*, vol. X., no. 39. Bissau, 1955. Stories and essays.

Duarte, Fausto. *Auá: Novela negra*. Lisbon: Livraria Clássica, 1934. Novel.

————. *O negro sem alma*. Lisbon: Livraria Clássica, 1935. Novel.

————. *Rumo ao degredo*. Lisbon: Guimarães, 1936. Novel.

————. *A revolta*. Porto: Livraria Latina, 1942. Novel.

————. *Foram estes os vencidos*. Lisbon: Editorial Inquérito, 1945. Novel.

Ferreira, António Baticã. "Infância," in João Alves das Neves, ed. *Poetas e contistas africanos*. São Paulo: Editora Brasileira, 1963. Poetry.

Zurara, Gomes Eanes da. *Feitos da Guiné*. Intro., notes, and glossary by José de Bragança. Porto: Livraria Civilização Editora, 1937. Historiography.

São Tomé and Príncipe

Alegre (Caetano) da Costa. *Versos*. Lisbon: Livraria Ferin, 1951. Poetry.

Almeida (José Maria de Fonseca de) Viana de. *Maiá póçon: Contos africanos*. Lisbon: Momento, 1937. Stories.

Domingues, Mário. *O menino entre gigantes*. Lisbon: Prelo, 1960. Novel.

Margarido, Maria Manuela. "De Costa Alegre a Francisco José Tenreiro," *Estudos ultramarinos*, no. 3. Lisbon: Instituo Superior de Estudos Ultramarinos, 1959. Essay.

Poetas de São Tomé e Príncipe. Preface by Alfredo Margarido. Lisbon: Casa dos Estudantes do Império, 1963. Poetry anthology.

Reis, Fernando. *Roça*. Lisbon: Ad Astra, 1960. Novel.

————. *Soiá: Literatura oral de São Tomé*. Braga: Editora Pax, 1965. Folktales.

————. *Histórias da roça*. Lisbon: Published by the author? 1970. Stories.

Rodriques, Lopes. *O livro de Costa Alegre*. Lisbon: Agência-Geral do Ultramar, 1969. Critical study.

430   Voices from an Empire

Tenreiro, Francisco José. *A Ilha de São Tomé*. Lisbon: Memórias da Junta de Investigações do Ultramar, 1961. History, geography, ethnology.
———. *Obra poética de Francisco José Tenreiro*. Braga: Editora Pax, 1967. Poetry.

Portuguese Africa

Abshire, D. M., and M. A. Samuels, eds. *Portuguese Africa: A Handbook*. London: Pall Mall Press, 1969.
Andrade, Mário de. *Antologia da poesia negra de espressão portuguesa*. Paris: Pierre Jean Oswald, 1958.
———. *Literatura africana de expressão portuguesa*, vol. I: *Poesia: Antologia temática*. Algiers, 1967; vol. II: *Prosa*. Algiers, 1968. Both reprinted, Liechtenstein: Kraus Reprint, 1970.
———. *La poésie africaine d'expression portugaise*. Trans. Jean Todrani and André Joucla-Ruau. Honfleur: Pierre Jean Oswald, 1969.
Belchior, Manuel. *Fundamentos para uma política multicultural em África*. Lisbon: Companhia Nacional Editora, 1966.
Boxer, C. R. *Race Relations in the Portuguese Colonial Empire, 1450–1825*. Oxford: Oxford University Press, 1963.
Brambilla, Cristina. *Poesia africana*, Collection Quaderni Nigrizia, 3. Bologna: Editrice Nigrizia, 1964.
César, Amándio. *Parágrafos de literatura ultramarina*. Braga: Editora Pax, 1967. Anthologized prose selections.
———. *Contos portugueses do Ultramar*, vol. I: *Cape Verde, Guinea, São Tomé-Príncipe*. Porto: Portucalense Editora, 1969. First volume of proposed anthology of Afro-Portuguese short stories.
———, and Mário António. *Elementos para uma bibliografia da literatura e cultura portuguesa ultramarina contemporánea*. Lisbon: Agência-Geral do Ultramar, 1968. Afro-Portuguese bibliography.
Chilcote, Ronald R. *Portuguese Africa*. Englewood Cliffs, N.J.: Prentice-Hall, 1967.
Cortesão, Jaime. *História dos descobrimentos*. 2 vols. Lisbon: Published by the author? n.d. Historical account of Portuguese overseas exploration.
Dathorne, O. R. *The Black Mind: A History of African Literature*. Minneapolis: University of Minnesota Press, 1974. Contains a section on African literature of Portuguese expression.
Duffy, James. *Portugal in Africa*. Baltimore: Penguin Books, 1962.
Estudos ultramarinos, no. 3: *Literatura e arte*. Lisbon: Instituto Superior de Estudos Ultramarinos, 1959. Special edition of essays on Afro-Portuguese culture and literature.
Freire, Maria da Graça. "Os portugueses e a negritude," literary supplement of *Diário de Notícias*. Lisbon, 29 September 1970. Newspaper essay on négritude.
———. *Portugueses e negritude*. Lisbon: Agência-Geral do Ultramar, 1971. Expanded and revised version of essay cited above.
Freyre, Gilberto. *Um brasileiro em terras portuguesas*. Lisbon: Livros do Brasil, n.d. Account of an itinerary.
———. *Adventura e rotina*. Lisbon: Livros do Brasil, 1952. Account of a voyage.
Galpérina, E. L., and L. V. Nokrássova. *Stikhi poetov Afriki*. Moscow: Ed.

Votochaya Literatura (N.A.U.K. USSR, Institute of Oriental Studies), 1958. Russian translation of Afro-Portuguese poetry.

Kovadloff, Santiago. "Poesia afro-portuguesa del Siglo XX," *Latinoamericana*, no. 3. Buenos Aires, April 1974. Article.

Mákua, antologia poética, ed. Garibaldino de Andrade and Leonel Cosme. Five issues. Sá da Bandeira, 1962–64.

Mensagem. A cultural circular of the Casa dos Estudantes do Império. Published irregularly in Lisbon as an organ of the Student Empire House from January 1949 to June 1963.

Moreira, Adriano. *Portugal's Stand in Africa*. Trans. William Davis et al. New York University Publishers, 1962.

Moser, Gerald. "African Literature in the Portuguese Language," *Journal of General Education*, vol. XIII, no. 4. University Park, Pa., January 1962.

————. "African Literature in Portuguese: The First Written, the Last Discovered," *African Forum*, vol. II, no. 4. New York, Spring 1967.

————. *Essays on Portuguese-African Literature*. University Park, Pa.: Pennsylvania State University Studies, no. 26, 1969.

————. *A Tentative Portuguese-African Bibliography: Portuguese Literature in Africa and African Literature in the Portuguese Language*. University Park, Pa.: Pennsylvania State University Libraries, 1970.

Nekrássova, L. V., ed. and trans. *Sdies i travá roditsia krassoi*. Moscow: Ed. "Progresso," 1962. Poems from Angola, Mozambique, Cape Verde, São Tomé, and Príncipe translated into Russian.

Neves, João Alves das. *Poetas e contistas africanos*. São Paulo: Editora Brasileira, 1963. Anthology of Afro-Portuguese poetry and prose.

"Nouvelle somme de poesie du monde noir," *Présence africaine*, no. 57. Paris, 1966. Representative Afro-Portuguese poems published in the original.

Oliveira, Mário António Fernandes de (Mário António). "Influência da literatura brasileira sobre as poesias portuguesas do Atlântico tropical," *Colóquios sobre o Brasil*. Lisbon: Junta de Investigações do Ultramar—Centro de Estudos Políticos e Sociais, 1967. Essay.

Preto-Rodas, Richard A. "The Development of Negritude in the Poetry of the Portuguese-Speaking World," *Artists and Writers in the Evolution of Latin America*, ed. Edward Davis Terry. University: University of Alabama Press, 1969.

————. *Negritude as a Theme in the Poetry of the Portuguese-Speaking World*. University of Florida Humanities Monograph, no. 31. Gainesville: University of Florida Press, 1970.

Riáusova, Elena A. "Aprender a escutar o povo: Algumas tendências de desenvolvimento da poesia africana de expressão portuguesa," *Problemas de literatura*, no. 8. Moscow, 1969. Essay and poetry selections.

————. "O papel das tradições estrangeiras na formação das literaturas africanas de expressão portuguesa," *Problemas actuais do estudo das literaturas da África*. Moscow, 1969. Essay.

————. *Formação das literaturas africanas de expressão portuguesa*. Moscow: Ed. Nauka (N.A.U.K.A. USSR, Institute of World Literature M. Gorki), 1970. Essay.

————. "As fontes da literatura d'África de lingua portuguesa," *Os povos da Ásia e da África*, no. 3. Moscow, 1970. Essay.

————. *Portugaloiasitchniie literaturi Afriki*. Moscow: Ed. Nauka, 1972. Critical study.

————, ed. and trans. *A noite era escura*. Moscow, 1962. Anthology that includes Castro Soromenho's "Samba."

Tavani, Giuseppe, and Maria Vargas, trans. *Poesia africana di rivolta*, Collection Tempi Nuovi, 31. Bari: Giuseppe Laterza & Figli, 1969. Bilingual Italian-Portuguese edition of Afro-Portuguese poetry.

Tenreiro, Francisco José, and Mário Pinto de Andrade. *Caderno de poesia negra de expressão portuguesa*. Lisbon: Published by the author, 1953. Poetry anthology.

————. "Acerca da literatura negra," *Estrada larga*. Porto: Editora Porto, n.d. Essay.

Tultchinskaya, N. Y., ed. *Vegliadom serdza: Stikhi poetov Angola, Mozambika, Ostrovov Eicloenogo Missa, Ostrova San-Tomé*. Moscow: Izdutelstvó Vostocknoi Literaturi, 1961. Translations into Russian by L. V. Nekrássova of Afro-Portuguese poetry.

Wästberg, Per. *Afrikansk Lyrik*. Stockholm: Svalaus Lyrikklub, Albert Bonniers Förlag, 1970. Includes poems in Swedish translation from Angola, Mozambique, and São Tomé.

General Sources

Abrahams, Roger. *Positively Black*. Englewood Cliffs, N.J.: Prentice-Hall, 1970.

Caute, David. Introduction to Jean-Paul Sartre, *What is Literature?* Trans. Bernard Frechtman. London: Methuen, 1967.

Fanon, Frantz. *The Wretched of the Earth*. Trans. Constance Farrington. New York: Grove Press, 1966.

————. *Black Skins, White Masks*. Trans. Grove Press, 1967. London: Paladin, 1970.

Frye, Northrop. *The Critical Path*. Bloomington: Indiana University Press, 1971.

Jahn, Janheinz. *Muntu: The New African Culture*. Trans. Marjorie Grene. New York: Grove Press, 1961.

————. *A Bibliography of Neo-African Literature from Africa, America, and the Caribbean*. London: André Deutsch, 1965.

————. *Neo-African Literature*. Trans. Oliver Coburn and Ursula Lehrburger. New York: Grove Press, 1968.

————, and Claus Peter Dressler. *Bibliography of Creative African Writing*. Liechtenstein: Kraus Reprints, 1971.

Jahn, Janheinz, Ulla Schild, and Almut Nordmann. *Who's Who in African Literature: Biographies, Works, Commentaries*. Tübingen. Horst Erdmann Verlag, 1972. Includes photos of Agostinho Neto, Mário António, Óscar Ribas, and Castro Soromenho; also references on forty Portuguese-language and one creole-language Afro-Portuguese writers.

Jameson, Fredric. *Marxism and Form: Twentieth-Century Dialectical Theories of Literature*. Princeton, N.J.: Princeton University Press, 1974.

Kesteloot, Lilyan. *Les écrivains noirs de langue française: Naissance d'une littérature*. Brussels: Èdition de l'Institut de Sociologie, Université Libre de Bruxelles, 1971.

Martins, Wilson. *The Modernist Idea: A Critical Survey of Brazilian Writing in the Twentieth Century*. Trans. Jack E. Tomlins. New York: New York University Press, 1970.

Mpondo, Simon. "Provisional Notes on Literature and Criticism in Africa," *Présence africaine*, no. 78. Paris, 1971.

Palmer, Eustace. *An Introduction to the African Novel*. New York: Africana, 1972.

Paz, Octavio. *El arco y la lira: La revelación poética*. Mexico City: Fondo de Cultura Economica, 1956.

Pessoa, Fernando. "Autopsicografia," *Fernando Pessoa: Obra poética*. Rio de Janeiro: José Aguilar Editora, 1969.

Roscoe, Adrian A. *Mother Is Gold: A Study in West African Literature*. Cambridge: At the University Press, 1971.

Tibble, Ann. *African/English Literature*. London: Peter Owen, 1965.

Waterman, Richard Alan. "African Influence on the Music of the Americas," *Acculturation in the Americas*, ed. Sol Tax. Chicago: University of Chicago Press, 1952.

Wauthier, Claude. *The Literature and Thought of Modern Africa*. Trans. Shirley Kay. London: Pall Mall Press, 1966.

Afro-Portuguese Literature in English Translation

Black Orpheus: A Journal of African and Afro-American Literature, ed. E. Mphahlele, W. Soyinka, and U. Beier. Ibadan. No. 10 (1960?) contains two poems by Valente Malangatana (Mozambique). No. 15 (August 1964) contains three poems by Agostinho Neto (Angola).

Dathorne, O. R., and Willfried Feuser, eds. *Africa in Prose*. Baltimore: Penguin Books, 1969. One selection by Castro Soromenho (Angola); one by Luís Bernardo Honwana (Mozambique).

Honwana, Luís Bernardo. *We Killed Mangy-Dog and Other Mozambique Stories*. Trans. Dorothy Guedes. London: African Writers Series, Heinemann Educational Books, 1969. Seven short stories by Honwana (Mozambique).

Kgositsile, Keoropetse, ed. *The Word Is Here: Poetry from Modern Africa*. Garden City, N.Y.: Anchor Books, Doubleday, 1973. Three poems by Agostinho Neto (Angola).

Mphahlele, Ezequiel, ed. *African Writing Today*. Baltimore: Penguin Books, 1967. Two poems by José Craveirinha (Mozambique); one short story by Luís Bernardo Honwana (Mozambique); one poem by Kalungano (Mozambique); one poem by Rui Nogar (Mozambique).

Moore, Gerald, and Ulli Beier, eds. *Modern Poetry from Africa*. Baltimore: Penguin Books, 1968. One poem by Aguinaldo Fonseca (Cape Verde); two by Alda do Espírito Santo (São Tomé); three by Agostinho Neto (Angola); one by António Jacinto (Angola); two by José Craveirinha (Mozambique); one by Noémia de Sousa (Mozambique); two by Valente Malangatana (Mozambique).

Whiteley, W. H., ed. *A Selection of African Prose*, vol. II: *Written Prose*. Oxford: Clarendon Press, 1964. One prose selection by Óscar Ribas (Angola).

INDEX

Index

437